# The Magdalen Manuscript

## The Alchemies of Horus &
## The Sex Magic of Isis

by Tom Kenyon
and Judi Sion

Published by
ORB Communications
P.O. Box 98, Orcas, WA 98280

By Tom Kenyon and Judi Sion
Cover and text design by Rebecca A. Cook
Cover photo by Judi Sion
Illustration by Jennifer Koteen

Disclaimer
This book is designed to provide information
in regard to the subject matter covered. The purpose
of this book is to educate. The authors, editors, and
publisher shall have neither liability nor responsibility
to any person or entity with respect to any perceived
loss or damage caused, directly or indirectly,
by the information contained in this book.

ISBN 1-931032-05-X
Library of Congress
Catalog Card Number: 2002112016

# TABLE OF CONTENTS

## The Magdalen Manuscript

## Internal Alchemy

## One Woman's Story

# The Magdalen
# Manuscript

# Invocation
# of the
# Cosmic Mother

*Oh, Great Mother, divine feminine, birther of the cosmos, lover unto Spirit, Creatrix of all matter and queen of all worlds within worlds and those without, we call you to us in this hour.*

*We are your children; hear our call.*

*We are the daughters and sons of your divine union, the flesh of your passion for life. You, who lay with Spirit, our Father, in the beginning of time, and brought us forth from the blessed union of Spirit and Matter, we are your children, the sons and daughters of your flesh and your heart, and we remember your touch and the fragrance of your essence, and we long for you.*

*Come to our hearts and gift us the remembering. Come to our minds and open our genius.*

*Enlighten us with your presence.*

*Draw back the veils that we might see, and harken the doors to open, that beauty and ecstasy may live in our homes and hearts more fully.*

*This is our hour of greatest need. We call you through fire and water, through earth and wind, through all that bears your name. We call all your lineages and all your names. Come unto us. Come into us. So be it.*

—Judi Sion

# Tom's Introduction to
# The Magdalen Manuscript

Personally, I have tremendous challenges with this manuscript. For one, it is channeled, and I thought that I had left that kind of writing behind me after I finished the Hathor Material (SEE Publishing).

For me, channeling is a questionable activity. It reminds me of the seine nets people cast in the waterways of the Carmargue in southern France, an area believed by many to be where Magdalen came ashore. Along the banks, large nets sit in the river. Occasionally someone cranks a hoist and pulls the net out of the water to see what got caught. I think channeling is a lot like this.

There are currents within our psyches. They carry a hodgepodge of things, some of them interesting, some of them worthless, and some of them downright strange. Sometimes the channeling net catches something of unquestionable value, but often it is mixed in with a bunch of junk.

My first experience with channeling was in the late seventies. A friend of mine happened to be a medical researcher at Duke University, and we conducted a series of informal experiments on the phenomenon. Since I worked with hypnosis in my psychotherapy practice, we decided to see what might emerge from hypnotic states in relation to channeled material.

The very first evening we made "contact" with an immense intelligence that we euphemistically called "Big Dude." I have quite an irreverent streak, and anyone who knows me will attest to this.

Big Dude spoke in a characteristically grand style typical of channeled entities or intelligences. It spoke about possible earth changes, and it spoke about the interconnectedness of the universe. While the transcripts of the talks were intriguing, both my friend and I agreed that there was nothing of real substance, and after three months of meeting once every two weeks or so, we dropped the experiment.

As a psychotherapist working in the area of Transpersonal Psychology for many years, I have seen a lot of clients who channeled. Some of them were quite comfortable with it. Some were quite disturbed by it— like the woman in her late forties who was awakened at three every morning for the last year. She would sit, pen in hand, and scribble out messages from the other side. The other side of what is the question. Her transcriptions talked about the power of love to heal; sometimes they offered some decent solutions to problems; sometimes, quite frankly, they said some very strange things.

Strange is, of course, a relative term. What is strange to one person may seem quite reasonable to another. The cultural filters we use to sieve our experiences are often arbitrary and based on inherited nonsense.

My task as a psychotherapist was to help my channeling clients make sense out of their transpersonal babble. I use these words on purpose. The collective unconscious is filled with all sorts of things. The psychological entities that reside there are varied, like the characters in real life. Some of these denizens from the collective are brilliant and well-intentioned. Some of them are idiots masquerading as spiritual beings.

There is a tremendous increase in channeling among both laypersons and professionals alike. I think it is just a sign that as a collective, we are beginning to gain access to our psychological and spiritual depths. Many people are having spiritual emergencies in which their views of the world are quickly and radically altered by peak spiritual experiences. I believe that we will be seeing even more of these psycho-spiritual crises over the next several decades as the new mythos within our collective mind begins to surface.

Channeling, within this context, is nothing more than a message from the deep. But like the summer fishing holes of my youth, some of the things down there are not worth fishing for. But still they come to the surface of the mind, like an old shoe or a rusted beer can.

One of the tasks for anyone faced with channeling is to separate the valuable from the inane, the uplifting from the dangerous. Just because the information is coming from the other side should not imbue it with any more authority than the words from someone down the street.

In fact, when someone hands me something and tells me that it has been channeled, my guard goes up. And when a being from the other world shows up on my doorstep, so to speak, I look for logical inconsistencies. I lay traps. If they pass these tests, I am more likely to consider what they are telling me. But I am the final judge. If what they say does not make sense to me, I dismiss it.

And so, in the midst of my immense resistance to the channeling phenomena, Magdalen showed up one night in Zurich, Switzerland. My partner, Judi, had asked me to see if I could get anything about the Magdalen since we were shortly going to be in Sainte Maries de la Mer, the site where Magdalen supposedly landed after the crucifixion.

I closed my eyes and entered a light hypnotic trance. Immediately, a being appeared in my mind's eye, and announced that she was the Magdalen herself. She began to dictate the manuscript you now hold in your hands. Over many sessions she spoke with an undeniable clarity and urgency. Every word was precise, and the feeling in the room during these sessions was electric.

Now, several months later, as I look at the manuscript with a critical eye, I am struck by several things. The first is a personal dread at adding to the glut of channeled books. That's the last thing any of us need, I tell myself.

But the material is like nothing I have ever seen. As a student of internal alchemies for over three decades, I have been fascinated by the similarities as well as the differences between the world's alchemical traditions. And I have made it one of my personal quests to experience a vast array of alchemical methods for transforming and elevating consciousness. From this perspective, the techniques offered by the Magdalen are quite extraordinary. As a spiritual pragmatist I have always tried everything myself. If it works, I keep it. If it doesn't, I toss it out. I have personally used the techniques Magdalen describes, and they work. They work extraordinarily well. In fact, I can honestly say that practicing them has enhanced all of my other alchemical practices, regardless of the lineage from which they come.

All of this led me to one final logical conclusion. For those fellow students of alchemy, for those seeking deeper experiences of spiritual transformation, and for those who desire Sacred Relationship, this material may well prove invaluable. For this reason, I have decided to release the manuscript.

There are still some problems for me. I am a stickler for accuracy. And there is no way to verify if the story is true or not. There are so many versions of the Magdalen legend and it happened so long ago, I suspect we will never know for sure, at least from an objective point of view.

I found the story Magdalen painted during the sessions extremely evocative; parts of it I still do. However, the bulk of the story is, to me, just another story—could be true, could be false.

As a person firmly anchored (some would say marooned) on the shores of logic, I can't say whether the story is true or not. And this disturbs me. But I can say that the methods she shares and the insights she offers are extraordinary. And so, for me, as I sorted through the manuscript, I put the story back in the river and kept the methods. I ask you to do the same.

Read this with your own heart and mind. Keep what is of value for you, and leave the rest.

I realize that this book may very well be controversial in many circles. Still, I think it right to release this manuscript into the world. If it does nothing more than get us to question the various issues it brings up, then I think the book's existence will be justified. It is, after all, a time for all of Christendom to question its misappropriation of the feminine.

For those seeking a deeper understanding of internal alchemy as a means to transform consciousness, I believe the material unquestionably stands on its own.

During my re-reading of the manuscript, a funny thing happened. So get this: here I was looking at the material with a rational and critical mind. As I considered whether to publish it or not, Isis appears to me—yes, Isis. She asked me to finish the book as soon as possible.

What's a guy to do?

The Island of Paros,
The Cyclades, Greece

# Judi's Introduction to
# The Magdalen Manuscript

It was a chilly night, hung with heavy fog in Zurich, Switzerland. We'd had a splendid dinner at our favorite Thai Restaurant, next door to the Alstadt Hotel, and we had time on our hands. It was a rare window in our lives. It was Thursday, November 30, 2000.

I've had a growing passion for the Magdalen, both as an archetype and Magdalen the Being. Who was she really? So much we live with everyday in this civilization is based upon the church's branding of her and ergo, all of the feminine as whore, as shameful. Because of this branding—no less than holding down divinity and burning a hot iron into her flesh—the feminine has carried shame and been held as "less than" for over 2000 years.

There is absolutely no basis for the Church labeling her as whore; not one word from the original texts supports such accusations. It was, in fact, the Council of Nicea, under orders from Emperor Constantine that chose the prostitute "spin" to support the patriarchy, depose the authority of the feminine, shame all that is feminine, and unite the many diverse religions and the popular upstart religion called Christianity—all for the sake of Rome, for the sake of government.

Their grounds for branding Mary Magdalen a whore? Jealousy and fear of the power of the feminine, especially the kind of power that Magdalen had.

I have never believed that we were born in sin, and I have never believed that Mary Magdalen, hence all women in her stead, were whores. And I have never bought the image of Jesus Christ as a pious, celibate, holier-than-thou, fanatic evangelical.

I had followed the trail of the Magdalen through Southern France years before, and I wanted to take Tom on the same route my heart had found, to retrace my steps with my Beloved.

But I was afraid to trust my own heart and I desperately wanted more background. I wanted the story. I wanted more than the story. I wanted the truth. I remember telling Tom that I would only consider validity in the story he brought through, because I so value his integrity and his ability to contact true source. And so I asked him if he'd ever consider contacting her.

Now, I need to tell you that Tom Kenyon does not like to channel! The scientist and the mystic do frequent battle internally. And I love them both, equally. So I usually stand back and watch the scientist ultimately yield to the sweet light of truth that the mystic can evoke. And in the dance that prevails, in the end, the world is presented great teachings, cloaked in the veil of science the ignorant of this time demand. So be it.

But this night, for whatever reason, grace was standing by, and she was on my side. I asked if he would consider trying to contact Mary Magdalen.

And he said, "Yes."

"When?" I held my breath.

"How about now?"

He lay back on the bed and I grabbed the laptop. He quickly moved aside and the Hathors came to assist by adjusting his neurology, which they frequently do to quiet the scientist who protests too much.

And she entered. The room swelled with power and an intensity of electricity that I felt in my fingertips. My fingers trembled on the keys when she began to speak. It was as if all of eternity reached out and closed the gap of time. She was there. We were there. The hourglass cracked and time suspended.

I hope I never forget hearing her words. I swear I will

never forget to be grateful for her truth, for Tom's open heart, for Yeshua's honor, and for the trust that she extended to me, in telling me her story.

She continued over a period of weeks as we traveled through Switzerland, the Italian Alps, and down across Tuscany. She came through on a boat from Genoa, Italia to Palermo, Sicilia. And when Sicilia turned out not to be where we were meant to winter, she visited us on the boat from Livorno to Malta. She continued on Oudish (Gozo), the smaller island of Malta, oddly enough, within sight of where she landed to re-provision on her trip from Egypt to France. She uttered the words, "We are complete," just before Christmas, 2000.

Every night before she began, she made me read back what I had taken down from the previous visit. She corrected any word I hadn't gotten correctly and altered an occasional word, clarifying here and there. And before she left us each night, she asked me to read back what she'd given that night.

Many nights she waited, at a particularly poignant juncture in her story, while Tom emotionally experienced her story as she told it, emitting moans and little whimpers.

She would say to me, "This channel is feeling the emotion of what I am telling you."

My heart goes out to Tom that he felt, even for a moment, what it must have been like for her to love a man as she loved Yeshua and to lose him to death, for the sake of all humankind. And my heart goes out to Yeshua, only now after hearing and knowing her story is the truth. He loved her so, he almost didn't do what he came to do.

When we left Malta in the spring, the computers were safely packed and shipped home. I hand carried a disc with the manuscript on it with me everywhere, along with a hard copy. Thus Magdalen went with us into Russia, the Ukraine, back to Germany and Switzerland and Venezia, and then it landed, so to speak, back in St. Maries de la Mer, where she landed in Southern France. The disc and hard copy waited patiently in my suitcase while we toured Rennes le Chateau and imagined how the Pyrenees must have looked when she dared to brave the wilds of those majestic peaks.

And finally, at our tiny apartment overlooking the Mediterranean on the island of Paros in the Cyclades, she came back once more, to answer some questions about specific words in the manuscript. Until we received her permission, we did not change one single word, not even a simple and obvious change in tense, and she thanked us for our impeccability.

I figured if the ignorance we've had to live with for 2000 years was a result of someone editing Yeshua's words badly, I wanted to do my best to see that no one could possibly misunderstand what she was saying now, in setting the story straight.

I asked her several personal questions that I knew someone would ask us, when we presented this manu-script. I know the questions some of you hold in your hearts, and I asked her what to say to you when you asked us those questions.

Frequently she said, "Tell them Mary Magdalen has no comment."

The questions she did answer are in the last section at the back of the book.

We approached her one more time on Orcas Island. She spoke about the critical importance of this manuscript and its significance in the return of the Cosmic Mother. She said, "for the whole of the Earth, for the Galaxy, for the Universe and those contiguous." She said she would call people to this truth from all over the world and those who were ready would find the manuscript, one way or another.

She congratulates you for hearing the call and she thanks you, from the bottom of her heart, on her behalf and on behalf of the Cosmic Mother for being here. She says nothing will ever be the same.

Orcas Island

One

I was raised in the understanding of magic. My father was from Mesopotamia and my mother from Egypt. Before I was born she prayed to Isis to bless her with a child. I am that child. And I was known as Mary Magdalen.

When I was 12 years old I was sent to study with a secret sisterhood of Initiates, under the wings of Isis. I was trained in the secrets of Egypt, the Alchemies of Horus, and the Sexual Magic of the Isis Cult. When I met who you call Yeshua, I had passed all my Initiations. I had prepared for the meeting with him by the well.

The Gospels recount me as a prostitute, for all Initiates of my order wore a gold arm bracelet that was a serpent; and it was understood that we practiced sexual magic; and in the eyes of the Hebrews, we were whores.

When I saw Yeshua and our eyes met, I understood that we had been destined for each other.

What I am about to tell you has not been known, except by those who were with me. Many legends abound as to what happened. But for me it is a story of deepest love. That

Yeshua had a vision of the world does not touch me. My story is a love story.

Many people followed Yeshua. And the opportunities for us to be alone together were very few.

It is not written in the Gospels for no one knew, only the closest to us. Before Yeshua went to the Garden of Gethsemane, we conceived a child, and her name was to be Sar'h.

*Two*

The story I am about to tell sounds fantastical.

I remember the reeds of Maries de la Mer, although then, of course, it was not called that. It is a place where our boat came ashore. Sar'h was quite young. Not quite one year old. I was torn by grief and amazement.

I was there when Yeshua was crucified. I saw him in the tomb and wrapped him with his mother beside me. I will forever remember the smell of myrrh. That was one of the ointments we used.

Yeshua appeared to me in his luminous light. I could not believe my eyes, and so I touched his wounds. The disciples were jealous that he had come to me first.

It was strange to have my beloved transported to another realm, another world, while I and our daughter crossed the Mediterranean alone. We were no longer safe and had to leave Egypt, for that is where we had gone.

When we crossed onto the shores of what was to become France, it was all wilderness. We were met by priestesses of the Isis Cult, and we headed north to the protection of the Druids, for Isis had spoken to them, and they had heard the call to protect her daughter, Sar'h. And so we headed North to another great body of water and crossed over into what was to become England.

And there we were secreted up into the most sacred heart of the Druids, to the Tor and the Glastonbury. Although we were safer than we had been in Israel or Egypt, the Roman influence extended up into England as well, and we were hidden.

We lived in this area for many years, and Sar'h wedded a man whose heirs would become the Templar Knights, and I went north into Wales and lived by the sea for the rest of my days.

I will say this, that in those years when I lived alone by the sea, Yeshua would often visit. Of course, it was not like before, for his body was more energy than flesh, more light; but still it was extraordinary to be with him again.

When I died he was there and took me into what some call heaven, but is just a place in the soul.

*Three*

I begin my story at the well, for in many ways that is when my life truly began. All the years previous were preparation for this meeting.

That morning I knew something was stirring, a kind of excitement—a trembling in the arms and legs—before I even met him. I was already at the well when he arrived. I had already sunk my jar into the shaft, and he helped me raise it. Some of the apostles saw my gold serpent bracelet and assuming me to be a whore, were aghast that the Master would help such a one.

But this did not touch me. I was in another world, transported by the eyes of Yeshua. When our eyes met it was as if I was looking into all of eternity, and I knew that he was the one that I had been prepared for—and so did he.

I continued at the fringes of those who followed him, and in the evenings we would go off together; not every evening for he was constantly sought after.

I, who was trained in the Alchemies of Horus and the Sex Magic of Isis, was considered to be highly advanced by my teachers, yet the first time in Yeshua's arms, I was a trembling woman, and I had to fight to find that central pathway through my desire to the highest throne, for that was my training.

Yeshua and I, using the techniques that I had been trained in, as well as the methods he had learned in Egypt, were able to charge his Ka, his energy body, with greater light and greater force, so that he could more easily work with those who came to him. And so it was.

And I still find it ironic that the Gospels report that I was at the well when Yeshua arrived; but those many nights when Yeshua and I were alone, he came to my well, to draw from me the powers of Isis, to build and strengthen himself.

*Four*

I stand in time now, looking at all of this as if it were a dream and yet so—still, vividly clear. My heart trembles as I recount the story as if it were yesterday. That first night with Yeshua is sketched within my mind as clear as the skies over Jerusalem.

After I had been able to pass through the desires of myself as woman and ascend the path into spiritual alchemy in which I was trained, I could see Yeshua's spirit form— already luminous, already brilliant with light.

A dove was above his head, golden rays of light poured forth from it. The seals of Solomon, of Hator, of Isis, of Anubis, and Osiris were in his spirit form. They were signs that he had passed through these Initiations. There were other symbols I did not understand; for they were from cultures I had no knowledge of

or training in; but of the Egyptian seals of
which I knew he was on the path of the High
God Horus.

But he had not yet passed through his
death Initiation, and I knew in my trembling
heart that that is why I had been drawn to
him at this time—to fortify his soul with the
powers of Isis and the Cosmic Mother, so that
he could pass through the dark portal and
attain the Horus.

That night, after we had made love and
wielded and blended our spirit bodies together,
the action of alchemy having begun between
us, Yeshua drifted off to sleep. As I held him in
my arms, I felt a turning within me, a desire to
protect him, a desire to be always with him,
and the knowledge, like the edge of a cold
knife, that we would be parted by forces
greater than my desire.

*Five*

The Church would have you believe I was a
whore, but I tell you now that the Church is the
whore, for she would have you believe that
woman is tainted and that the sexual passions
between a man and a woman are evil. Yet it is
here, in the magnetics of passion, that the
womb of ascension is created.

This secret of secrets was known by all
Initiates of Isis, and yet I had never imagined

that I would be the one to bring it into fullest expression in union with such a one as Yeshua.

For me, this journey is of my spirit and heart.

But for those who wish to know the physical journey...after Yeshua's crucifixion, I, and his mother, Mary, Joseph of Arimathea, his twelve-year-old son, named Aaron, and two other young women set off from Northern Egypt.

Our course took us ironically east before we could turn westward, and we had to stop for provisions along the way, as our boat was very small. Our path took us to Malta and the tiny island of Oudish, from there to Sardenia and to the tip of what is now the Cinque Terra, finally landing at Saintes-Maries-de-la-Mer and making our trek Northward through Rennes-le-Chateau into Northern France, and across the channel into what is now England. We settled in Glastonbury for several years, until Sar'h was twelve.

Upon her twelfth birthday, we set off for the place among the reeds where we had landed. There, as close to Egypt as was safe for us to go, I initiated my daughter into the Cult of Isis and bathed her in the waters of the Mediterranean in accordance with the teachings I had been given.

We then returned to Glastonbury, until Yeshua's and my daughter, Sar'h, wedded at age sixteen. She married into a well-known family whose heirs became the Templars, although at that time the Templar Knights did not exist.

This family bloodline, through Sar'h, would be carried into the Templars themselves. When Sar'h was married and secure in her new life, I headed North for Wales and lived in a small stone cottage by the sea for the rest of my days.

Behind my cottage there was a stream that came out of the hill, and I would sit there many days. For there was a time when this stream split in two, and the two streams followed each other, and then one veered off to the left and one to the right. And I would sit there, in-between them, thinking about the stream of my life and the stream of Yeshua's— how, for a while, our lives flowed together and then parted.

*Six*

I will forever remember the first time Yeshua came to me after his resurrection.

It was a new moon and the sky was clear. A light fog hung over the heather and everything was silver from the light of the moon and stars. I saw a figure approaching me on the windy trail that led to my cottage.

Ironically, I had just gone outside to draw water from the well and there he was. He looked the same, yet with a radiance—unmistakable! My eyes filled with tears; my heart trembled.

I ran to him and stopping short, I remembered his words to me right after the resurrection.

"Do not touch me yet," he had said then, "for I am not ascended to the Father."

Oh, how I, an Initiate of Isis, have yearned all these years to set the record straight!

What did he mean by these words? For the Christians have inherited only a part of the truth. The greater part of the truth is hidden within the mysteries of the Great Mother; and because the Church sought to disenfranchise women and all that is feminine, it sealed away this truth.

And the truth has to do with the Ka body itself—what we learned as Initiates to call the Etheric Double or Spiritual Twin—for the Ka body, when charged with enough energy and vitality, looks like the physical body. But unlike the physical body, the Ka body is not made of flesh, but of energy itself—energy and light.

And so when Yeshua came to me after his resurrection, he was in his Ka, but it had not been stabilized yet, for he had not gone to the Father—meaning into the Great Spirit of his own soul. So before he could do this, he had to pass through the portal of death and travel through the underworld of his own being.

He did this for two reasons, as I understand it. The first was, as a master soul, to do such a thing brings great power to the Ka. And the second reason was to cut a passage through death itself, so that others could follow and pass through the dark world more easily by following the trail of his light.

And so that first night when we were rejoined—I feel it now, still vividly clear and strong—my heart filled with joy at being with him again. He came to me that night just before midnight and left just before dawn. In those hours we lay together, our Ka bodies interconnecting yet again, no need for talk. Our communication was telepathic. And without the physical act of sex, the Serpent Power within him joined the serpent power within me and climbed upward along the sacred paths in our spines, to the throne of the crowns of our heads, sending me into sheer ecstasy and bliss. And this was how it was for many years. He would come to me this way several times each year. Sometimes we would speak. Most of the time was in union.

I asked him where he went in these times when we were not together. He said that he had gone to many sacred places throughout the earth—that he had met with many different peoples. He said that he was laying a path of light.

During one of his visits I asked him to explain to me this rather strange concept.

He drew a circle onto the dirt floor of my cottage and then what I recognized as the two triangles intersecting, to make the Seal of Solomon, becoming the Star of David. He said that there were many lands that we, in this part of the world, did not have knowledge of. Many of these lands had points corresponding to the points of the Seal of Solomon. By going to these areas, he was ensuring that his work would take a deeper rooting into the soil of this world.

## Seven

Of all the times that he visited, the time that stands out the strongest is the time he came when Sar'h had come to visit.

She had just become pregnant and wished to see me for my blessing, and so I was thrilled to see her and her traveling companions. She had sent word of her coming through the Druids, but their word got to me only one day before her arrival. She stayed with me for three days, and on the second night, Yeshua appeared.

I don't know if you can appreciate how odd it was. For Sar'h had never met her Father, nor Yeshua, his daughter. And yet here they met for the first time! And her father's body had returned to the elements in a flash of light in his resurrection, so now he was in his Ka body, which emitted a kind of unmistakable light.

Both of them were moved, Sar'h to tears and Yeshua to great pathos. They spent an hour together, just themselves, walking outside. I do not know what they talked about. But from the time they began, until the time that they ended, the sky was filled with falling stars.

Before Yeshua had left that evening, just before dawn, as was his way, he placed his hands over Sar'h's stomach and blessed the child. Sar'h left me the next day, filled with an unmistakable sense of peace.

And so I have told you what I wish to say about my life as a mother, and now I will turn my story to me as an Initiate, to the Alchemies of Horus, unto the secrets of Isis.

I turn now to my beloved sister, my sister in spirit, the Mother of Yeshua, also known as Mary.

Mary was a high Initiate in the Cult of Isis, having received her training in Egypt. That is why, when she and Joseph fled the king's wrath in Israel, they took flight into Egypt, for she had safety there, among the Priestesses and Priests of Isis.

Her training was different than mine, yet we served the same. In order for me to explain my understanding of Mary I must explain one of the deepest secrets of the Isis

Cult. For it was believed, and I hold this to be true, that under certain conditions the Goddess herself would Incarnate, either at birth or through spiritual Initiation.

Mary, the Mother of Yeshua, when she was quite young, was recognized for her purity of spirit by the great Priestesses of the Isis Temples. She was trained as an Initiate and reached the highest levels. But rather than becoming a Priestess, she was trained to become what is called an Incarnate.

To be an Incarnate is to be a very highly advanced soul and requires undergoing tremendous spiritual training and discipline. In a final Initiation, Mary became the holder of an energy stream directly from Isis herself. In this regard, she was an embodiment of the Cosmic Mother. It is as if there were two— Mary the human, pure of spirit and heart, holding within her a direct portal into the Great Mother, the Creatrix of all matter, of all time and space.

Thus the table was set, so to speak, for the conception of a being of remarkable qualities who would become her son, Yeshua.

When Mary underwent what the Church refers to as the Immaculate Conception, she was a witness to a Celestial and galactic insemination process, by which the Father Principle, or Spirit as we understood this in the Isis Cult, transferred his essence into Isis, the

Mother that receives the seed of the Father—
Matter receiving the impulse of Spirit. And this
highly refined and potent spiritual energy took
root in Mary's womb and gave birth to Yeshua.

*Nine*

Mary was with the apostles when they came
upon me at the well. She immediately recognized me as a fellow Initiate by the gold serpent
bracelet I wore on my arm and by the Seal of
Isis which glowed within my Ka body, for Mary
was quite clairvoyant and psychic.

The first person whose eyes I met were those
of Yeshua, and as I said, I felt transported into
other worlds in his immense presence. The second person whose eyes I met were those of his
mother. In her eyes was recognition and acknowledgement of my status as a fellow Initiate within
the Isis Cult, and although her training had not
been in Sex Magic, as mine had been, she understood that I had been prepared for Yeshua.

Between them, I felt lifted up on wings of
transcendent love. I felt my spirit soar.

Ironic then that the next eyes I would see
were those of Yeshua's disciples, who judged
me to be a whore, and countless generations
have held me this way.

But I say to you that in Yeshua's eyes and
those of his mother, I was not a whore, but a

clear vessel for the healing and nurturing powers of Isis herself.

There comes a time, in a man's life, whether human or divine, when his mother cannot give him the essence of what he needs. Her love continues, but what is required is sustenance from another woman. I was that woman.

Mary recognized me and my status, and passed her son to me in that moment by the well.

Mary and I spent much time together, time in which we discussed Yeshua's work, his needs and my place in his life. It was understood that I was a servant to a greater power. I had been trained for this, but I must tell you that the power of the recognition still shakes me. I still tremble at his recognition.

In those many nights and days together, Mary and I attended to the needs of Yeshua and his disciples, and in that period Mary and I became very close, for I loved her, and I love her still—for her physical beauty, the purity of her heart and spirit and the gentleness with which she dealt the world.

I can say, from my own clarity that Mary, having served as the vessel for Isis as an Incarnate, was a highly developed Master, but now having served in these ways, her mastery and perfection—her spiritual perfection— is staggering.

*Ten*

She exists within the heavenly realms, her compassion and love continually flowing to all humans. She is available to all, regardless of their beliefs. When someone calls upon her, know that they are heard.

I wish now to clarify my understandings. I wish to speak about the Sex Magic of the Isis Cult and The Alchemies of Horus. I wish to reveal secrets that an Initiate would never have revealed, even under threat of death. But the times are different now.

Time as you know it, is running out, and I have received permission from the Goddess herself—indeed, I have been asked by the Goddess herself—to reveal to you some of the most closely guarded secrets of all times. These are revealed to you in hopes that you will elevate yourselves in time.

*Eleven*

The Alchemies of Horus refer to a body of knowledge and methods for the alteration of the Ka body. In this understanding, as the Ka embodies, or acquires greater energy and light, there is an increase in one's magnetic field, and that which the Initiate desires becomes more quickly manifest.

However, in surrender to one's own Celestial Soul, or the Ba, the pursuit of personal desires, although not abandoned, is no longer the focus of one's entire existence. Instead, one looks upward, so to speak, to the higher capabilities of one's self, as perceived through the Ba, or the Celestial Soul.

The Celestial Soul, or Ba, exists within a much higher level of vibration than the physical body (the Khat) or the Ka (the spiritual or etheric twin to the physical form). Within the Ka body there are pathways that can be stimulated and opened. The activation of these secret passages within the Ka brings it much greater power. The Alchemies of Horus are designed to strengthen these, to activate the latent powers and abilities of the Initiate through what is called the Djed, or the ascending seven seals, what the yogis and yoginis of India call the chakras.

*Twelve*    Within the School in which I was trained we learned how to activate the Serpent Power, moving it in specific paths in the spinal column, and opening up circuits within the brain. This created what is called the Uraeus.

The Uraeus is often a blue fire that extends up the spine both laterally and horizontally and into the brain, and it undulates with the changes in energy within these pathways. The activation of the Uraeus increases the brain's potential for intelligence, creativity, and most importantly—receptivity, for the task of the

Initiate is to change the quality of one's being, so that the attunement to the Ba or Celestial Soul is clear and unobstructed.

*Thirteen*     When I met Yeshua by the well for the first time, the mere proximity of his presence activated my internal Alchemies. A Serpent Power moved up my spine as if I had practiced the disciplines I had learned.

That first night when we were together alone, arm in arm, lying next to each other, we practiced the Sexual Magic of Isis. This specific form of magic charges the Ka body with tremendous magnetic force through the power of physical orgasm, for when one has a sexual orgasm there is a tremendous release of magnetic energy within the cells. As this energy spreads it releases a magnetic potential that can be used.

I wish to share the specifics of this, but in order to do so I must explain more of the basic understanding of sex and spiritual realization, for this secret was stolen by the Church.

*Fourteen*     When I, an Initiate of Isis, joined together with Yeshua, there were specific pathways I had to open within myself. I was stunned, however, to discover that many of these pathways were spontaneously opening in his presence. I mentioned at the beginning of this story how I trembled as a woman, having to struggle with my own passions and desires; for the path of the Initiate is to use the energy of passion in a highly specific way, and not to simply be carried off by it; for alchemy requires that energy be contained so that it can be transformed.

Very quickly Yeshua and I achieved the *state*—what is known as the Four Serpents. This occurs when both have mastered the internal Alchemies of Horus to the extent that they can activate both the Solar and the Lunar Serpents within their spines.

Clairvoyantly there is a central channel that runs up through the spine, and to the left there is a Lunar Circuit and to the right a Solar Circuit, called the Ida and Pingala by the yogis and yoginis.

In the Alchemies of Horus one causes these two circuits to be activated by magnetic fields that are snakelike.

The Lunar Snake on the left side is pitch black, the color of the Void; so indeed, it is the embodiment of the Void itself and holds the potential as the Creatrix for all things.

The Solar Serpent is gold.

An Initiate causes these Two Serpents to rise upward. As they rise upward they pierce the chakras and cross over each other. In the Alchemy of Horus these Two Serpents cross each other through the fifth seal, or throat, and all seals beneath.

They then face each other, at an area approximately where the pineal gland is, or the center of the head. Here a chalice is envisioned with the pineal gland at the very bottom of the chalice itself.

These Two Serpents are living—in that they are not static but vibrate and scintillate and ripple with energy—and the writhing of their bodies within the Ka activates an increase of magnetic potential.

There are specific practices, which I will share at a later time, but what I wish to address in this moment is the practice of the Four Serpents.

*Fifteen*

When Yeshua and I made love, as you call it, we caused our Serpents to rise up our spines, up our Djed. We did this simultaneously, and at the moment of mutual orgasm the charge released from the first seals in the pelvic areas of our bodies was sent upward, into the Throne, which is in the upper part of the head—stimulating the higher brain centers.

At the same time during this moment of sexual ecstasy we placed our awareness fully within our Ka bodies, for the Ka is strengthened by ecstasy. Ecstatic states are nourishing and strengthening to the Ka body, and as I said earlier, with each strengthening of the Ka it becomes more magnetic, drawing to the Initiate that which he or she desires.

The Sexual Magic of Isis has to do with the innate ability of the feminine being to utilize magnetic energies to open deeper levels of consciousness through the act of surrendering to the sexual energies and pathways that are opened.

When a woman is deeply loved and appreciated, as was I by Yeshua, something lets go at the deepest levels of herself, and at the moment of orgasm there is an uncontrollable shuddering that takes place. If she feels safe and allows this shaking, this quivering, to overtake her, there is a tremendous magnetic vortex that opens, the center of which is in her womb.

Two Initiates engaged in the Sexual Magic of Isis can strengthen themselves and rapidly expand their consciousness through the power of this magnetic field.

In the advanced practices of the Sexual Magic of Isis the male Initiate causes both of his Serpents to rise through the Ka body of the female and the female causes her Two Serpents to rise through the Ka body of the male. The explosive power of this practice is like the energy released by an atomic bomb. The massive tidal waves of magnetics can strengthen the Ka beyond imagination—or destroy it, if not handled properly.

It was this advanced practice of the Ka that Yeshua engaged that night before the Garden of Gethsemane. For him this tremendous increase of magnetic potential within his Ka strengthened him for his hardships and for the task that faced him in his final Initiation through the portal of death; so that when his physical body dissolved into it's constitute elements it was done so in a flash of light and heat—that the church calls the Resurrection. But this was simply an effect of something that was occurring much deeper within him. It was caused by the magnetics of his Ka body, for it was through his potentized Ka that he journeyed through his underworld, through death itself.

As Yeshua and I engaged the Sexual Practices of Isis in our relationship we both understood that this was the purpose.

For him each union with me was a means to strengthen his Ka. This is why I said earlier that he came to my well, for the well that the woman Initiate offers to the male is an endless well of magnetic potential. But it is only opened when the female feels safe and loved. Only then will the practices work. For the practices without the nurturance of love become just techniques and will not give the result required or desired.

For me, I was both woman and Initiate. I had been trained for years and knew what to do with the pathways, but I was surprised to find myself swept away as a woman.

I found myself waiting in deepest anticipation for a look or a touch by Yeshua, and our times together alone were the most precious times I had ever experienced. Something about his touch and his eyes—the feel of him—caused something within me to open, and I found myself sometimes almost laughing at myself.

I, who had been trained in the most secret practices of the Sex Magic of Isis and had been judged by my Priestesses to be very advanced— this Initiate—found herself, a mere beginner in the presence of the woman.

For I tell you now that within the heart and the mind and the body wisdom of the feminine lie some of the greatest secrets and greatest powers—and they await to be revealed.

And all of it is laid open by the touch of another!

And so whenever I speak of Yeshua I am overcome by my love and the feelings that I hold for him throughout all time.

*Sixteen*     The Sex Magic of Isis is based upon the realization that the feminine principal holds within her
nature, specifically her sexual nature, an alchemical key. This alchemical key is revealed in the act
of what you call love—sexual love. When this is
activated strongly enough, the Alchemies of
Horus spontaneously present themselves.

Within my training it was understood that
there were two paths, alchemically speaking, to
the same goal.

The Alchemies of Horus were the foundation
of both alchemies, or practices, since the same
fundamental pathways were used. For those
who did not wish to engage in partnership, the
Alchemies of Horus would provide a means to
strengthen and activate the Ka body to the
levels of High Initiateship.

For those in partnership, the Sexual Magic
of Isis would provide the wings by which they
would ascend the Djed and enter the Throne of
Highest Consciousness.

From my vantage point I see a great
tragedy in that the secrets and the holiness of
our sexual natures was made evil by the
Church—by the Church Fathers. And for nearly two thousand years now the most dynamic
and one of the most rapid ways to God
Realization has been made wrong.

And I find it indeed ironic that the Church

has made it a sin—and therefore terrified those who might have stumbled upon it.

## Seventeen

While the miracles of Yeshua are considered extraordinary by many, they are from the standpoint of the Initiate, simply the expressions—the natural expressions—of the potential of consciousness. They are a sign. There are reasons for miracles, and I wish to discuss these from the standpoint of the Initiatory knowledge that Yeshua and I possessed.

By the time I met Yeshua, he was already demonstrating the signs. His level of creation was very high.

My task was to assist him to strengthen his Ka body for his final Initiation through the death portal to the High God Horus. This was accomplished, as I have said, through the Sex Magic of Isis and the Alchemies of Horus.

Of all the miracles that I witnessed Yeshua perform, the one that is most dear to me is that of the loaves and the fishes.

It was a very long hot day. The disciples, Mary and myself were following the Master as usual. A very large crowd formed, listening intently upon every word from Yeshua's mouth. We were all enraptured by his vision and his means of expressing.

It was as if, for several hours, we were transported into heaven itself, and I noticed that Yeshua's Ka had expanded to include everyone—another sign.

When he had completed his speaking it was late in the afternoon and filled with compassion for them, realizing that their walk home would take some of them several days, he called upon food to be gathered and shared.

So the disciples, Mary and I, and a few others who joined us from the crowd began to collect food.

But when it was all gathered, there were only a few fishes and a few small loaves of bread. Hardly enough.

It was then that I witnessed a most remarkable event.

Yeshua went inside and closed his eyes. I could feel the intent of his prayer, although I did not hear the words. Running the full course of his Djed from the base of his spine to the top of his head, I clairvoyantly saw a burst of light flowing upwards through his crown, into his Ba, his Celestial Soul. And then an energy descended, as if in answer to his request; and he placed his hands over the two small baskets and began to hand out the loaves and fishes, breaking them into pieces and handing one to each person himself.

It was most remarkable; over a thousand people were fed and the loaves and fishes never exhausted themselves. After the crowd had been fed, Yeshua gave pieces to his Disciples and to Mary and myself, and the bread had the most sweet taste and the fish a wonderful flavor I have never experienced again.

Such miracles are natural to a Master of Yeshua's caliber, and from the Initiatory standpoint, such miracles are the potential of anyone if they practice what is required.

*Eighteen*    Yeshua often used the phrase, "I and the Father are One." This has led to great misinterpretation. For from the Initiatory standpoint, it is simply another word for Spirit. And in these words Yeshua was indicating that he merged with his Spirit, and that is how the miracles were accomplished.

And so he would go back and forth between two ideas, which the gospels report in their own limited way.

On the one hand, Yeshua would sometimes say, "I and the Father are One." At other times he would say, "Without my Father, I can do nothing." This is the oscillation that occurs with the Initiatory process in which the Initiate oscillates between the strength and conviction of his/her connection to the Spirit Source and then to the other state of mind, in which they realize that they are nothing and can do nothing without Spirit.

So the one state of mind has a feeling of omnipotence. And the other state of mind has the feeling of impotence. And the Initiate must pass between these two. That Yeshua used these phrases several times indicated to me, as a fellow Initiate, that he was in the middle of this paradox.

And he lived with this paradox in consciousness until the Garden of Gethsemane. For it was before his time in the Garden, as reported by his Disciples, that he came to me and we practiced the Four Serpents for the last time. There was an intensity in our time together, for we both knew that the time was near at hand.

With the explosive force released with the practice, Yeshua's Ka body scintillated with power and conviction, which he took with him into the final hours of his life, fortifying him for his journey through death. But the times before were often spent—I search for the right words—in a kind of self-questioning.

Those who followed Yeshua, who call themselves Christians, like to think that he was surefooted and always clear about his purpose and mission and that he never wavered. But I, who spent the nights with him, tell you otherwise.

Just because a being has attained a level of mastery does not mean that they are able to pass through uncertainty—untouched.

Yeshua felt the pressure of his Celestial Soul, but it is an odd thing being an Initiate. For one is human with all that goes with it— and one is increasingly connected to, and a part of, one's Celestial Soul.

It is the Ba, the Celestial Soul, that is the voice of God speaking. The high Initiate acts like a reflex from the mouth of God, but just because the Celestial Soul is clear does not mean that the human is necessarily so.

Yeshua saw in others the potential for God-Realization, and he spoke to this several times. One of these was mentioned in the Gospels when he said, "you shall do greater things than me." For he understood that miracles are a natural expression of con-sciousness, and that as the consciousness of mankind expanded, miracles would be commonplace.

And yet at the same time he was very aware of the limitations of those around him— of their addiction to hatred, ignorance and bigotry—and this troubled him deeply. We spent many evenings talking about this. And until a few days before Gethsemane, he was not sure if he could attain what was required to pass through the final Initiation.

I do not know the reason for the change in him, but a few days before the Garden and our final Initiatory act together through the Four Serpents, a deep sense of peace came over him, and he was sure in a way I had never seen him.

*Nineteen* I stand in time nearly two thousand years after Yeshua's crucifixion, and still I shake at the thought of that. It was very strange to be both the Initiate and the Woman.

As the Initiate, I stood by Yeshua through the crucifixion holding my Ka in fervent prayer—which is another way of saying I held steadfast in my intention to be there for him as he passed into death. This was an Initiatory action on my part that required detachment.

As a trained Initiate such a task was easy, but as the Woman in love with Yeshua, the Man, my heart was ripped apart. And so I stood at Golgotha, wavering in my strength as an Initiate, and my grief as the Woman in love whose beloved was suffering.

In that moment I did not care for the Initiation. I did not care that Yeshua was laying a trail of light through the death realms for all those who would follow him.

I even yelled at Isis.

"How dare you," I said!

In the greatest moment of my torment, Mary reached out and touched my hand. I had been alone in my grief and had not noticed hers. Our eyes met, filled with tears, and we sobbed in each other's arms. She for her son, and I for my beloved.

The Gospels report that an earthquake struck right after Yeshua's passing, and I say to you that this is true. It was as if all of nature went into travail, and the earth shook with anger and rage, that such a Master, such a being, could suffer at the hands of his fellow men.

But such is the paradox of life on earth.

A great storm came across the city as well—winds like I had not seen. The sky filled with dark clouds and bolts of lightning—the sound of thunder shaking everything. This horrific display lasted it seemed, forever, but I suspect it was only for an hour or so.

At the tomb, Mary and I washed his body in accordance with Jewish ritual and tradition, wrapped him and left the tomb. We did this in silence. The only sound the sound of our muffled tears.

I thought it odd that he had been able to raise Lazurus from the dead, but had not been able to help himself.

I did not understand what he was doing.

But after his resurrection, and I saw him in his Ka, radiant and beautiful as ever, I understood.

From the Initiatory standpoint, to become the High God Horus means that one has activated the highest potentials of consciousness within the human form. But this was traditionally done for one's self only. But Yeshua had done it on behalf of all mankind. This is his legacy.

But I say to you it has nothing to do with religion! It has to do with physics and alchemy.

The simple teaching of Yeshua was that we are all Gods—that we all have within us the power to love and to heal—and he demonstrated this as best he could.

In the early days of the Church—meaning the community of those who formed around Yeshua's teachings—a most beautiful ritual emerged.

Those who wished to continue to be in his energy or presence would share bread and wine. Sometimes the men would share the ritual and sometimes the women. This simple act of sharing among each other was in keeping with Yeshua's intent, and yet as the years progressed the simplicity of this got lost, and only those ordained by the Church could give Communion, something which Yeshua would find most distasteful. (Having known him as well as I did, I can tell you this.)

The truth and power of Yeshua's teaching has been perverted by the Church.

And the secrets of the elevation of consciousness through Sacred Sex, as was practiced by I and Yeshua, has been stolen by the Church.

I realize in the sharing of my story that only a handful will understand—but that is enough.

*Twenty*    I wish now to reveal some of the secrets of the Sex Magic of Isis.

As I said earlier, it is possible to scale the heights of consciousness alone, without partnership; and in this, the Alchemies of Horus were designed to assist the Initiate.

However, for those in partnership—Sacred Relationship—the Sex Magic of Isis was revealed. There are several aspects to this I wish to discuss.

The first of these is the understanding that at the moment of orgasm, magnetic fields are generated. In truth, these fields are created through what you would call foreplay—the stimulation of the senses through touch. This sensory stimulation begins the process of building the magnetic fields and is crucial to the alchemical practice of Sex Magic.

There are several methods available to Initiates, and I will discuss some of these—but essential to the practice is the understanding of the nature of the interaction of the two alchemical elements within the man and the woman.

On a mundane level the semen of the man carries the information of his genetic lineage, which is passed on to the child. When the sperm within his semen joins with the egg of the woman life is created, and life is a complex interconnecting of magnetic fields. The growing child within the womb develops organs and systems, but at the magnetic level these can be viewed as interconnecting, complex vibrational and magnetic fields. And so at the mundane level, the act of sex creates new patterns of magnetics.

Initiates trained in alchemy use the sexual energy to also create complex magnetic fields—but these fields do not become a new being, a child; they become incorporated into the Ka bodies of the two Initiates themselves, strengthening and elevating their Ka bodies. This is the first essential point to understand. Everything revolves around this.

The task of the Initiate within this system that Yeshua and I were trained in is to strengthen the Ka body beyond the confines of the physical form, or Khat.

The next level to understand has to do with the emotional tuning of the female Initiate—for the female Initiate's receptivity is dependent upon her emotional state. This is part of her nature and cannot be sidestepped if these techniques are to work.

Essential to the female Initiate is the authentic feeling of safety and love, or appreciation at the very least. When these are in place, something within her being lets go and allows the alchemy to occur.

The alchemy is created by the joining of the male Initiate's Ka and the female Initiate's Ka. As they make love, the Ka bodies interconnect, and this causes the female to open her *Magnetic Floor*. This is a strange term. It comes from the language used in the Temples of Isis.

The floor Is the foundation upon which one stands. When we set something to be secure, we place it on the floor. So the floor was used as a type of slang within the Temples, referring to the very basic piece that is required. So when I say "the female's Magnetic Floor," I am saying that this is the fundamental piece that has to occur.

As the two Initiates continue in their lovemaking, and as the passion of their connecting increases, powerful chemicals are released in the brain and in the body. These transport the Initiates into another space than their normal ways of being. This further opens the magnetic fields and generates an increase in magnetics.

There are two options to the male Initiate at the moment of orgasm. He can ejaculate, or hold his seed. If he ejaculates, and the previous conditions have been met, there is an instantaneous reaction that occurs within the womb of the female. As the energetic essence of his sperm strikes the walls of her inner sanctum there is an explosion of magnetic energy—worlds within worlds, spinning. And to the extent that the male Initiate has attained a high status as well as the female, the magnetics released from such contact between such sexual fluids can be enormous. So it is important to understand that this creates complex magnetics that both the male and female can draw into their bodies.

A second phenomenon occurs in which the female Initiate may begin to shake uncontrollably. As she shakes, the center of it is usually the womb itself, which sets off a cascade, a rocking effect in the pelvis. This action also creates very complex magnetic fields, again, which the male and female Initiates can draw into their Ka bodies. This is the fundamental or basic understanding.

As Initiates, it is possible to also cause the Serpent Powers to rise within the spine during the sex act and wherever the Two Serpents meet, will tend to magnetize that chakra and its attendant abilities or powers.

More than this I am not permitted to say, since the attainment of this practice can lead to a significant increase in one's powers. I leave it to those who read this to see between the lines. If you are ready for this practice, you will know how it is done.

*Twenty-One*

In the training of both the Sex Magic of Isis and the Alchemies of Horus, Initiates would be trained in the basic exercises of the Two Serpents.

In this practice, the Initiate alone generates energy through the power of RA, or the internal fire, to create an elevation in awareness—to create complex magnetic fields within his or her own body—and then to bring these into the Ka.

I wish to share this method. It is the core practice for both those who wish to do this work alone, and for those who wish to do this work in partnership.

The fundamental practice requires that the Initiate sit upright, breathing in a rhythmic, calm manner.

Then the Initiate becomes aware of the base of the spine, and on the breaths draws the Black Serpent rising from the left and the Gold Serpent rising from the right, up the spine.

As the Two Serpents enter each chakra, they cross over, making their way up to the crown. But in this practice, the Two Serpents are brought up to the center of the head, to the vicinity of the pineal gland.

The Initiate then, using the power of the breath, sends the energy of the inhales into the Serpents and then with the exhales sends the energy of the breath deeper into the serpentine bodies, causing them to become "alive," so to speak.

Eventually they will writhe, or move, from the power of the breath and the intention of the Initiate.

At this point, a Chalice is imagined inside the head with the Two Serpents facing off each other at the lip, the pineal gland resting at the bottom of the Chalice.

The next phase draws the energy of RA upward. The Initiate images a living ball of fire, like the sun, at the solar plexus, and with each exhale the Initiate silently repeats or intones the sound RA. This causes the light, the fire of the internal RA, to be activated, and it spontaneously begins to move up.

As this light and heat moves upward it passes through the center of the Chalice between the Two Serpents, up to the crown of the head. From here, a most remarkable phenomenon occurs.

From the left side of the crown an energy descends that is liquid-like in its nature. This liquid is called the Red Serpentine Drops. From the right side of the crown another liquid-like energy moves down into the Chalice, called the White Serpentine Drops. It is the heat and light of the internal RA that causes the crown to secrete these substances.

The Red Serpentine Drops are related to the biological mother of the Initiate. The White Serpentine Drops are related to the father of the Initiate. As the two mix together several things can occur. There can be the sensation of a sweet taste in the back of the throat— what the yogis and yoginis call Amrita—but which we in the Isis Cult refer to as the Spring Waters, for they seem to come from the spring within the head.

Sometimes this is the first presentation; and if an Initiate focuses upon the sensation of the Spring Waters, a kind of ecstasy arises. Sometimes the Initiate senses light in their head. Again, if they focus upon this light, a kind of ecstasy arises.

Sometimes as the Red and White Serpentine Drops mix, there is a spontaneous arising of ecstasy. This ecstasy, no matter what caused it, is crucial to this alchemy. For ecstasy is food and nourishment to the Ka body.

There is a tendency for this ecstasy to remain in the higher centers, since this is where they were birthed in this practice. But in this method, upon the first arising of ecstasy, the Initiate must shift his or her awareness to the entire Ka body itself. This causes the ecstasy to spread throughout the entire physical body, Khat, and is then absorbed by the Ka, strengthening and revitalizing it.

This is the basic, fundamental practice.

For those in partnership practicing the Sex Magic of Isis, the ecstatic states naturally arise. For those in the solitary practice, the ecstasy must be self-generated.

Both practices, however, require that the Initiate become aware of the Ka during moments of ecstasy, so that the Ka body can partake of the rich, magnetic fields created by such bliss.

*Twenty-Two*  In a very real sense, the male Initiate faces the greatest challenges in the practice of the Sex Magic of Isis, for it requires that he seemingly go against his own nature. By nature the male is electric from an alchemical standpoint, while the female is magnetic.

It is the nature of electricity to move and to act, while it is the nature of magnetics to nest—enfold.

In the practice, the focus becomes the strengthening of the Ka body through the incorporation of magnetic fields released by the sex

act. Right after orgasm, the magnetic fields generated by the female Initiate continue to unspiral
and circulate. This is a time to rest and be with
the magnetics, but by nature males tend to
either get up and do something, or go to sleep.

So the male Initiate must train himself to
nest, to allow the magnetics that have been
created to spiral into his Ka and his body.

This is different from what occurs normally, for in the male, orgasm is confined to the
pelvic area, and in some cases it spreads.
But for the female Initiate, especially one who
has been able to relax into the experience,
the orgasm spreads through the entire body
and can continue in various levels of intensity
for several hours.

Some male Initiates might be concerned
that by changing themselves, by nesting,
they will become less masculine—but I can
assure you that nothing could be further from
the truth.

For the truth is, that as the male Initiate
nests in the magnetics, his Ka body becomes
stronger, and his sexual energy becomes more
potent. One of the tasks for the male Initiate is
to sensitize himself to new levels of feeling, so
that he can incorporate the magnetic fields
released through sex into his own body and Ka.

To clarify the term nesting, it does not mean
that the male's member remains inside the

female, necessarily. It does mean that the male remains close to the female—touching, stroking, being with the physical sensations and the emotions after orgasm. It is through the portal of nesting that the male Initiate is able to enter the feminine mysteries of creation.

Another aspect that the male Initiate needs to be aware of is what is called Adoration of the Beloved.

As the alchemy of the Sex Magic becomes stronger there are certain signs that occur. One of these is that the Beloved becomes adored or cherished.

This happens both for the male and female Initiate. When Adoration of the Beloved occurs from both partners, the alchemy and Sex Magic greatly intensifies, for the harmonics and magnetics created by such emotion are very beneficial to the magic.

*Twenty-Three*   I would like to speak to the term magic at this time.

The reason the term magic is used refers to the transformation of the individual human into a God. This is indeed magic. It is symbolized by the God Horus, part man, part hawk, and through the practices of alchemy, is raised to the status of the High God Horus, meaning that one has attained the most elevated states of consciousness.

So the Sex Magic of Isis is precisely a method for the elevation of consciousness, which is, in itself, magic—and this is done through the energies and ecstasy created through sex.

The other reason the term magic is used is that there are methods, once the Ka body is potentized, that one can use to affect one's reality in very direct ways in methods that seem magical. Take, for instance, the basic core practices of the Alchemies of Horus—the raising of the Black and Gold Serpents up the spine, the creation of the Chalice, the activation of the internal fire of RA, and the meeting of the Red and White Serpentine Drops— are all acts of magic, acts of intent and both personal and spiritual will. This is why it is referred to as magic.

Returning to the paradox facing the male Initiate, we find that his nature works against him to a certain extent in these practices, specifically the Sex Magic. For once a male Initiate's Ka is charged, he, by nature, wants to act, to do something. Yet if he can discipline himself, train himself to continue lying with his Beloved, he can nest himself in the rich magnetics created through their love, their sex, and strengthen the Ka to a greater extent.

*Twenty-
Four*

There is another aspect facing the male Initiate in this process, and it has to do with what we in the temples refer to as Obstacles To Flight, but which in your language is best stated as "psychological issues." The term Obstacles To Flight refers to hindrances to the unfolding of one's Horus nature, the aspect specifically that can fly upward into elevated states of consciousness.

There are attitudes, beliefs and emotional habits that are counter-productive to flight, or the elevation to consciousness, which is what we refer to when we say Obstacles To Flight. It is here for the male Initiate that one of the most intricate passages, requiring great skill, occurs.

As a child, the male was carried by his mother in her womb and protected and nurtured by his mother in his infancy, until a point where he had autonomy and could act for himself. At this point the male child pushes the mother away, so to speak, in order to face the world.

It is at this juncture in his development that he may feel confined or limited by his mother, and a battle of wills can ensue. As a man, as a male Initiate, he may still carry these emotional habits within him. If this is the case, he will find it difficult to relax into the nesting of the magnetic fields, since at a psychological level, it is experienced as surrendering to the feminine.

If the male Initiate has issues with his mother of childhood, he may engage these consciously or unconsciously with his partner.

*Twenty-Five*

It is important for both Initiates undertaking the Sex Magic of Isis to realize that they are embarking on a long journey and that the process is essentially one of alchemy. The purpose of alchemy is to transform one substance into another. It does this by burning off the dross, or the negativity of a substance, so that the pure substance remains or is created.

In the process of the Sex Magic of Isis the substances transformed are literally the sexual fluids, hormones, neurotransmitters and other substances not yet discovered by your science. But it also involves a transformation of one's psychology.

By nature, the Sex Magic of Isis steps up the alchemical process. The heat gets turned up, so to speak, the dross becomes clear, that which needs to be purified comes painfully into focus.

If one does not understand that this is one of the byproducts of alchemy, one might be disturbed by the arising of difficult psychological material. But actually this is one of the results, for the internal pressure created through the intense alchemy generated through the Sex Magic of Isis causes the Ka body to extrude, or press out of itself all impurities and to clear itself of all Obstacles To Flight.

In those practicing alone, without a partner, the Alchemies of Horus also create internal pressure, extruding impurities, but the task is more difficult in that the energy required comes from one's own personal efforts, and there is not the benefit of reflection from another. However, it can be done.

*Twenty-Six*

This is the basic understanding required for the practice of the Sex Magic of Isis. In the previous pages I have revealed to you the secrets of the ages, one of the most closely guarded secrets of the Temples of Isis.

Understanding of these practices was reserved for the most advanced students.

Whether one practices the solitary path through the Alchemies of Horus or the path of Sacred Relationship through the Sex Magic of Isis, one is stepping upon the road to Godhood.

The central key in this journey is the strengthening of the Ka through ecstatic states of consciousness. Whether self-generated or created through the ecstasy of sex does not inherently matter; the Ka is nurtured and potentized by ecstatic states, regardless of their source.

On the contrary, shame is a poison to the Ka body, a toxic element that decreases its vitality and potency.

I, an Initiate of Isis, find it tragic that the Church has shamed women and men around their sexual natures and closed a door on one of the most direct paths to God-Realization. Whatever you do along this path, my advice is to free yourself of all shame.

Search out the catacombs of your own mind and heart, seek out the dark places in yourself where shame resides and remove it.

Find every opportunity to create ecstasy, for it strengthens you and potentizes the Ka.

May the obstacles to your flight be few and the blessings along your journey be many.

Twenty-Seven

I wish to turn my attention now to some loose threads concerning the practice of Alchemy and the Sex Magic of Isis.

For the male Initiate, it is essential to understand that it is the magnetic fields created first by the touching and stroking of the female Initiate, his beloved, that starts the cascade of magnetic fields, building an intensity to the point of orgasm.

It is important that the male Initiate train himself to be able to nest in the magnetic fields.

It is extremely important to both Initiates to

place their attention on the Ka body during the ecstatic states of consciousness that are generated by their lovemaking, for this strengthens and potentizes the Ka body, and this is essential for this type of alchemy as was practiced by I and Yeshua.

At the moment of physical orgasm, there is a tendency for the magnetic surge to move either up through the top of the head or down through the feet—but in either case, this magnetic field exits the body and dissipates. It is important during the moment of orgasm to contain the magnetic field or surge. Ideally the Initiate would place his awareness in the upper Throne or the upper brain centers. This would cause the surge of orgasm to rise up into the head, sending its energy into the brain itself and into the Ka body.

 *Twenty-Eight*

There are times when the male Initiate may wish to hold back his seed. Within the Sex Magic of Isis male Initiates were taught a specific practice called Stopping the Lower Nile.

From the Initiatory knowledge of ancient Egypt, the Nile existed both externally and internally, the external Nile being the physical river and the internal Nile being the Djed and its flow through the seven seals or chakras. At the moment of physical orgasm, when a man ejaculates, the creative powers that have descended from the upper Nile into the lower Nile are released.

This semen carries great potential for creating magnetic fields in the form of new life or an alchemical reaction in the womb of the female Initiate, as we discussed earlier.

At times, however, a male Initiate may wish to hold his seed, primarily because, depending upon his vitality, ejaculation may actually decrease his energy, and it was for these times that the technique for Stopping the Lower Nile was developed.

The male places a finger over the prostate, just in front, so that at the moment of ejaculation the semen goes back instead of forward, and the magnetic fields of his sexual essence re-circulate through his body and his Ka. But even in these moments there are magnetic fields generated by his Ka which interact with those of the female Initiate and they can both nest within these interactions.

*Twenty-Nine* And now I wish to address a relatively rare form of partnership but which sometimes occurred within the Initiates of Isis. You would call this same sex partners.

While the building of magnetic fields and the nesting in these fields and the arising of ecstatic

states can be created through same sex partners, the interaction of semen and the womb
does not occur, and so this aspect of the alchemy is not present.

However all other aspects of the Alchemy
and the Sex Magic are relevant.

*Thirty*   Finally, I wish to turn my attention to the
term Initiate, for I have used this term exten-
sively throughout this material. The term
Initiate refers to one who has decided to live
upward in consciousness, one who has decided
to leave behind the mundane life and to enter
into an adventure of consciousness.

Generally speaking, the crossing of the
threshold from mundane to sacred life is marked
by a ritual of Initiation. In the ancient practices a
candidate would be Initiated by a Priest or
Priestess, and this Priest or Priestess would have
the power to confer upon that individual the relative power of the lineage to which they belong.

In certain types of transitions an external
Initiator is needed or required.

However for the beginning phases it is
possible for a person to Initiate themselves,
for the true essence of Initiation means to
mark a threshold, the crossing from mundane
life into sacred life.

For those who feel drawn to practice the Alchemies of Horus and who wish to mark their commitment to living the sacred life, I offer this simple ritual. I give this instruction because there is such a scarcity of qualified persons to conduct Initiations into the ancient lineages of Egypt.

For this ritual one would need a candle and two glasses or cups.

One cup is filled with water and the other is empty. If you wish, you could add flowers and incense, making the ritual as aesthetically pleasing as you desire, but fundamentally Self-Initiation is an act of intention and personal and spiritual will.

The ritual is simply an external reflection of something that is occurring deep within oneself. And indeed, this internal choice can be made without the need for an external ritual at all, for the ritual without internal choice is worthless.

For this ritual you would light the candle and then speak these words...

*"Spirit of all life, be my witness here. For the sake of my own elevation and the elevation of all life, I shall strive to be harmless to myself and all others."*

Then holding the glass or container of water in the right hand, you would pour the water into the container or glass In the left hand, and by these words you would seal this action...

*"By the pouring of this water, I signify the transfer of my sacred waters of life*
*From the mundane to the sacred. Spirit of all life, by my witness here.*
*Amen. Amen. Amen."*

## Thirty-One

I wish to end my story with thoughts about my beloved, Yeshua. As an Initiate of Isis, I had been trained for the moment when I met him. And from the moment our eyes met, I was transported into other worlds.

I understood the teachings that had been obscure. I understood the deepest secrets of Isis, as she revealed them to me not through the sacred writings, but through the living presence of my love for Yeshua.

As the Alchemy between us intensified, I came to adore him and he me. It was a great difficulty for him to part from me.

There were stirrings within him that longed to be with me rather than to face the death Initiation of Horus; yet as a master soul he had come to lay a trail of light through the dark realms of death. He did this for his own sake and for the sake of all mankind.

There are many who misunderstand what he did and why he did it.

There are those who believe that all they need to do is believe in him and no effort on their part is required. This was never Yeshua's belief or understanding. He came as a *shower of light*, a beacon of love at a time when the world was still in the shadow of a jealous god. Yeshua, as a master soul, demonstrated immense courage and strength, to teach love at such a time.

It was odd for me, being both the Initiate and the woman in love, for I understood that my task was to assist him to build his Ka, in order that he could face the realms of death with greater power.

As an Initiate, I understood my task; and to some extent I understood what Yeshua's vision was. But as the woman in love, I was swept away by my feelings for my Beloved.

And so I stand in time, looking back, as it were, upon our life together; and it is a bitter-sweet taste.

The sweetness of Yeshua's presence will, for always, fill and sustain me, yet the bitterness of our parting will always be there as well.

In my last days upon this earth, Yeshua came to me again in his Ka body, as he had done for so many years. He was with me as I took my last breath and took my Ka through the realms of death, through the trail of light that he had laid through the power of his intention, and took me into what you would call heaven, but is a place in the soul.

I rest in this place with his presence through all time and space.

## Thirty-Two

I was content to remain here with his essence that I carry in my heart and mind, but Isis, herself, came to me and said that now I must tell my story...that the lies of the last two thousand years must come to an end...that the feminine is returning in balance to the male...that the Cosmic Mother is revealing herself at the beginning of the ending of time.

And so it is that I reveal one of the lost secrets of the ages—that Spirit, the male principle, in order to return to itself through it's journey into Matter, requires the assistance of the feminine principle, the Intelligence of Matter itself.

But from the solar light-filled perspective of the masculine principle, the feminine principle carries within her a dark, moist and dangerous abyss. The solar principle feels threatened by the darkness of the lunar aspect. But it is in the joining of the Sun and the Moon, the joining of the masculine and feminine principles, in equilibrium, in energetic balance, that true illumination is attained.

When Yeshua prepared himself with me for his ordeal before the Garden at Gethsemane, I was the embodiment of Isis. I was she. There was no difference between her and myself. I had been trained in the practices that would ensure this. And so, Yeshua as the Sun, the solar principle manifest in the realms of matter, joined with me, the Moon; and he was joined with Isis herself and his elevation could not have occurred without her. She is the Cosmic Mother. Other cultures call her by other names, but she is the same.

To the extent that the male Initiate is able to nest into the magnetic fields with his Beloved and draw into himself the vibrational energies of these magnetics—to this extent he is making contact with Isis herself, the Cosmic Mother, the Creatrix of all time and space.

To the extent that the female Initiate is able to surrender to the magnetics and the letting go into her own nature, she becomes Isis herself. When these two events occur at the cosmological level, the male Initiate becomes energetically attuned to Osiris and the female Initiate becomes attuned to Isis, and out of the co-mingling of their magnetic fields, Horus is born—except that Horus in this case does not take form as a child. Horus takes form and Horus takes flight within the Ka bodies of the Initiates themselves. They are raised up in a very real manner. They can take flight within the celestial realms of their own being.

The truth is that Osiris cannot rise without Isis, nor Isis without Osiris. The High God Horus is birthed from the magnetics of their joining.

The male Initiate, being electric by nature, thinks that he can make it happen by himself, but he cannot.

Isis waits for him to recognize this, but he does not.

For centuries she has waited, and now we are at the beginning of the ending of time, and the pressure is strong. This is one of the reasons I have come forward.

To those male Initiates able to find the pathways in themselves to surrender to the Isis powers carried within the natures of their Beloved, or carried within their own natures if practicing the solitary path, know that you do this not just for yourselves, but for all mankind.

When one undertakes the Sex Magic of Isis, it is not possible to do this just for oneself, for the practices quickly elevate the Initiate into the level of the living myth, for in its highest expressions, as we have indicated before, the male Initiate becomes Osiris himself, and the female Initiate becomes Isis...and the Horus is birthed out of their magnetics.

For those engaged in the solitary practice of alchemy, this is accomplished through the magnetics of the Lunar and Solar Circuits. As the basic practice shared earlier is mastered, the Black Serpent of the Moon, holding the essence of the Void, quivers and shakes within the Ka body of the Initiate, much like the female Initiate quivers and shakes within the arms of the male when practicing the Sex Magic.

Within the Initiate practicing the solitary way the Gold Serpent of the Sun meets the Black Serpent of the Moon in the center of the head, and the magnetic fields created by their co-mingling and the energetic reactions created by their intersections through the chakras or seals, creates the Horus.

So whether it is done alone or with another does not intrinsically matter, but what must occur in both is the same. The Sun and the Moon must be in balance, and then the Illumination, what we call Horus, occurs.

Thirty-Three

I have offered you my story and the teachings I have been given in deepest hopes that you will find a passage into your own greatness, for that is what this world needs now more than ever.

It is my hope that you will be uplifted by my insights, and that you will be inspired, as was I, by the magnificent being you call Yeshua, but that I call my Beloved.

To those who have the courage to practice the Alchemies of Horus, and for those who choose to live in Sacred Relationship with themselves or with another, I give my blessing.

May the blessings of the Cosmic Mother follow you upon your journey to yourself. May the path between the Sun and the Moon be revealed.

Spirit of all life, bear witness. Amen.

*~Mary Magdalen*

# Training Protocols
# in the
# Alchemies of Horus

This section is for those who wish to explore a basic practice within the Alchemies of Horus. Magdalen gave an advanced form of the individual practice in the *Manuscript*, but this may be too complex for many readers. I therefore asked her if she might offer a simpler form of preparatory exercise, and this is the result.

The *Manuscript* was not meant as a teaching manual, but to convey a message. And so the protocols below serve as the teaching function. They will give you the basic experience needed to enter into the advanced *Practice of the Two Serpents,* mentioned in the *Manuscript.*

According to the Magdalen, the Alchemies of Horus were the foundation for both those on the solitary path and for those in partnership. The main difference between these two paths is that the person on the solitary path must generate the extra energy and ecstasies from his or her own efforts. Those in sacred Tantric relationship acquire the needed energy and ecstasies spontaneously from the sex act.

The *djed* or sacred pathway of the chakras begins at the base of the spine and goes up through the spine and into the head. There is a secondary *djed* pathway that moves from the perineum directly up to the crown called the *Central Column* or *Central Pillar.* In some esoteric schools it is referred to as the *pranic tube.* The training exercises, below, use both of these pathways.

The fundamental alchemical task in relation to the *djed* is to accumulate enough energy so that it can be sent up through the pathway and into the head centers.

The training exercises below generate the needed energy from the power of the breath. Their purpose is to familiarize you with the feeling, the physical sensation, if you will, of subtle energy moving up the *djed*.

The first section of the training protocol consists of three different exercises. The first one deals with the secondary *djed* (*the Central Column or Pillar*) that runs directly from the perineum up to the crown. The second exercise deals with the primary *djed* that runs up the spine. And the third exercise works with the energy after it is brought up into the head.

The second section of the training protocol familiarizes you with how to transform the energy moving through the *djed* into a serpent-like form. And finally, the last exercise familiarizes you with activating the pathway of the *Two Serpents* by experiencing energy moving simultaneously through both the lunar and solar pathways.

## Cautions to the Reader:

Due to the fact that these exercises bring energy into the brain and upper head centers, they are contraindicated for some individuals. If you have suffered a head injury or experienced a stroke, speak with your physician before proceeding. Those who suffer from seizures such as epilepsy should also seek the advice of their physicians before undertaking these training meditations. Finally, for those who are manic-depressive, these exercises are contraindicated, especially during manic phases. For all other persons, the meditations are quite harmless and very beneficial. If you experience headaches at any time during the meditations, stop and rest.

# First Section

## The First Exercise

Sit comfortably and close your eyes. Place the focus of your attention, in other words, the *alchemical container of your awareness*, on your pelvic floor. This is the area of your body at the lowest part of your abdomen in the cradle of your pelvis. Find a rhythm that is pleasurable for you and breathe deeply (yet comfortably) drawing the breath into your belly. As you inhale, let the lower abdomen expand, and as you exhale pull in the lower abdomen. This form of breathing is called abdominal breathing and may feel odd to you at first. After awhile, however, it will feel natural and comfortable. Throughout all of these exercises it is very important that all breaths be gentle and comfortable. Nothing should ever be forced in these practices.

As you inhale, imagine the energy of your breath reaching down into every nook and cranny of your pelvis. The reason for this is that you are causing *sekhem* to stir, and *sekhem*, or your life-force, is cradled in the pelvic area. As you exhale, keep your focus in the pelvis. This will cause the energy of sekhem to build or intensify in the pelvic area. Continue this for a couple of minutes or so.

Then imagine a subtle energy pathway or channel that runs from your perineum up to the top of your head (the crown). The perineum is located at the lowest point of your torso, midway between your genitals and the anus. Next, there is a slight but significant shifting of your attention.

As you inhale keep your focus in the pelvis as before. But when you exhale, shift your attention, *the alchemical container of your awareness*, into the channel. This will cause the energy of *sekhem* to enter the channel and begin to move upward. As you continue to exhale, move your attention all the way up the channel and into your head. Then repeat the breathing pattern all over again. In other words, each time you inhale, shift your attention to the pelvis, and hold it there throughout the entire inhale. As you exhale, shift your attention to the channel, and begin to move your focus up the channel towards the head. Repeat as many times as needed to clearly sense a movement of energy up the secondary *djed* and into the head.

These exercises are built upon each other so it is important to master each one before proceeding to the next. Make sure that you feel a definite movement of subtle energy up the secondary *djed* and into the head. If you don't have a clear sense of this, repeat the exercise over and over again until you do.

## A note about uncomfortable physical sensations:

Occasionally a person might experience tension or headache from these exercises. This may occur if there is habitual tension in the muscles of the jaw, face and/or neck since this type of muscle tension tends to constrict the movement of *sekhem* or life-force as it moves up into the head. If you experience discomfort at any time during these exercises, you should stop, put them aside and return to them later.

If you find that this type of tension arises whenever you do the exercises you might try yawning since yawning helps to lessen muscle tension in the face, jaws and shoulders. Simply yawn as you inhale and exhale. It can be quite effective and besides that, it's fun.

If tension persists, I suggest you shift your attention to the area of tension and imagine that the tension dissolves and leaves with each exhale. Try it for a few minutes. It often dissolves this type of muscular tension quite nicely.

## The Second Exercise

In this exercise you basically do the same thing you did in the first, except that the movement of *sekhem* is up the spine (or *the primary djed*).

Sit comfortably and close your eyes. Place the focus of your attention, in other words, the *alchemical container of your awareness*, on your pelvic floor. Find a rhythm that is pleasurable for you and breathe deeply (though comfortably) drawing the breath into your belly. As you inhale, let the lower abdomen expand, and as you exhale pull in the lower abdomen.

As you inhale, imagine the energy of your breath reaching down into every nook and cranny of your pelvis. The reason for this is that you are, as in the first exercise, causing *sekhem* to stir and *sekhem*, or your life-force, is cradled in the pelvic area. As you exhale, keep your focus in the pelvis. This will cause the energy of *sekhem* to build or intensify in the pelvic area. Continue this for a couple of minutes or so.

Then your attention changes somewhat. On the inhales, attention is still in the pelvis, but on the exhales shift your attention into the spine (the djed), and move your attention up the spine from the base to the top of your head with each exhale.

Continue this for a few minutes until you sense a clear sensation of energy moving up the spine and to the top of the head.

After you clearly sense this flow of subtle energy, proceed on to the next exercise. If you do not sense this flow of energy then repeat the exercise until you do.

## The Third Exercise

In this exercise, you follow the same procedure as you did in exercise number two with one difference. When you exhale and the energy of sekhem or life-force moves up the spine, you bring it into the center of the head instead of to the top. As the energy is brought into the center of the head you allow it to circulate through the brain sensing the movement of energy.

Sit comfortably and close your eyes. Place the focus of your attention, in other words, the *alchemical container of your awareness*, on your pelvic floor. Find a rhythm that is pleasurable for you and breathe deeply (though comfortably) drawing the breath into your belly. As you inhale, let the lower abdomen expand, and as you exhale pull in the lower abdomen.

As you inhale, imagine the energy of your breath reaching down into every nook and cranny of your pelvis. The reason for this is that you are, as in the first exercise, causing sekhem to stir, and sekhem, or your life-force, is cradled in the pelvic area. As you exhale, keep your focus in the pelvis. This will cause the energy of sekhem to build or intensify in the pelvic area. Continue this for a couple of minutes or so.

After a few minutes of building the energy in the pelvis, you are ready for the next phase. On the inhales, attention is still in the pelvis, but on the exhales shift your attention into the spine *(the djed)*, and move your attention up the spine from the base to the center of your head with each exhale. The energy of sekhem will follow the circuit of your attention and flow upwards into the central area of the brain. Then pause for a moment and sense the flow of energy as it moves on its own through different areas of the brain.

Continue this for a few minutes until you sense a clear sensation of energy moving up the spine and into the center of the brain.

# Second Section

## First Exercise: Rising of the Single Serpent

In this exercise, you repeat what you did in the last exercise of the previous section. However, instead of taking the energy into the center of your head, you bring the energy up and over the two hemispheres just under the top of the skull. This movement of the energy is cobra-like, in that the tail of the serpent extends down the full length of the spine to the base while the hood of the cobra is extended over the two hemispheres of the brain. Holding the energy in the image of a cobra in this way causes a distinct type of brain stimulation and is a precursor for the *uraeus*.

Sit comfortably and close your eyes. Place the focus of your attention, in other words, the *alchemical container of your awareness*, on your pelvic floor. Find a rhythm that is pleasurable for you and breathe deeply (though comfortably) drawing the breath into your belly. As you inhale, let the lower abdomen expand, and as you exhale pull in the lower abdomen.

As you inhale, imagine the energy of your breath reaching down into every nook and cranny of your pelvis. The reason for this is that you are causing *sekhem* to stir and *sekhem*, or your life-force, is cradled in the pelvic area. As you exhale, keep your focus in the pelvis. This will cause the energy of *sekhem* to build or intensify in the pelvic area. Continue this for a couple of minutes or so.

After a few minutes of building the energy in the pelvis, you are ready for the next phase. On the inhales attention is still in the pelvis, but on the exhales shift your attention into the spine (*the djed*), and move your attention up the spine from the base to a space above the two hemispheres of the brain and directly under the top of the skull.

As you sense this space above the brain, allow yourself to feel the movement of the energy. Imagine the form of this energy as a cobra with its hood extended over the brain itself. Then repeat the procedure until you have a clear sense of the serpent-like form of this energy over the brain.

## The Second Exercise: The Two Serpents

In this exercise, it is assumed that you have successfully experienced the single serpent in the previous exercise. If you haven't clearly experienced the single serpent, return to the previous exercises before continuing.

In the *Manuscript,* you will find a description of the Black and Gold Serpents. The Black Serpent rises through the lunar pathway on the left side of the *djed* and is connected with the Darkness of the Void or the creatrix of all creation. The Gold Serpent rises through the solar pathway on the right side of the *djed* and is connected with light. In a sense the Two Serpents are alchemically opposites and when you bring two opposites together within an alchemical container there is the possibility of immense energy.

In this preliminary training you will be causing the energy of sekhem to split into two different streams of energy. As the life-force rises up the *djed* it takes two different yet parallel paths. The Black Serpent rises from the left side at the base of the *djed* while the Gold Serpent rises from the right side of the *djed,* also from the base. However, as they continue to rise up the *djed* toward the head, they cross over each other as they enter the chakras.

Thus the Gold Serpent crosses over to the left side of the djed as it enters the sexual chakra and the Black crosses over to the right. As they climb further up the djed, the Gold Serpent crosses back over to the right side as it enters the solar plexus and the Black Serpent crosses back over to the left.

Next, the Gold Serpent crosses to the left side as it enters the heart and the Black crosses over to the right side. As they enter the throat chakra, the Gold Serpent returns to the right side of the *djed* and the Black Serpent returns to the left side.

Finally, they meet at the center of the head with the Gold Serpent hovering on the right side while the Black Serpent hovers on the left side. Both of them face each other with the pineal gland sitting between them.

The *Manuscript* gives further instruction on how to do the practice. The purpose of this exercise, however, is just to familiarize you with the phenomenon of raising both serpents up the *djed* and into the head.

To do the exercise, sit comfortably and close your eyes. Place the focus of your attention, in other words, the *alchemical container of your awareness*, on your pelvic floor. Find a rhythm that is pleasurable for you and breathe deeply (though comfortably) drawing the breath into your belly. As you inhale, let the lower abdomen expand, and as you exhale pull in the lower abdomen.

As you inhale, imagine the energy of your breath reaching down into every nook and cranny of your pelvis. The reason for this is that you are causing sekhem to stir, and sekhem, or your life-force, is cradled in the pelvic area. As you exhale, keep your focus in the pelvis. This will cause the energy of sekhem to build or intensify in the pelvic area. Continue this for a couple of minutes or so.

After a few minutes of building the energy in the pelvis, you are ready for the next phase. On the inhales, attention is still in the pelvis but on the exhales shift your attention into the base of the djed. Through the power of intention (will) imagine the Two Serpents being charged with the energy of the breath. As you continue to exhale, send the energy up through the two pathways of the ser-pents. Imagine them as clearly in your mind as possible sensing them crossing each other at each of the chakras and finally ending in the center of the head.

Continue the practice until you have a clear sense of the two serpent-like energies running up the spine and into the head. Allow yourself to sense the movement of life-force up these two pathways as the serpents "writhe" in response to your breath. Sense the subtle energies that are generated within the brain as a result of this practice.

# The Pathway of the Two Serpents

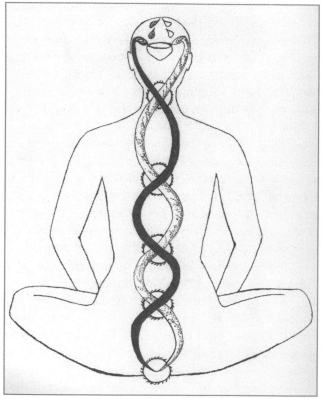

Left Side:
Black Lunar Serpent
Red Serpentine Drops

Right Side:
Gold Solar Serpent
White Serpentine Drops

# Internal
# Alchemy

## Tom Kenyon

# Introduction
# to the Fundamentals of
# Internal Alchemy

*Without an understanding of the alchemical terms*
*used in the* Manuscript, *it will be rather difficult to under-*
*stand its essential concepts. In addition, some of the cen-*
*tral ideas at the heart of internal alchemy may not be*
*familiar to many readers. For this reason, I have included*
*a brief overview of internal alchemy in general and a*
*larger overview of Egyptian alchemy in particular. It is*
*my hope that these introductory sections will provide the*
*reader with a deeper understanding and appreciation of*
*the* Manuscript.

—A Personal Note from Tom

I decided to make tea this morning. Rumbling through
the cupboard, half-awake, I found a small kettle hiding
in the corner. I poured some water in and sat it on the
stove. Lighting the burner, I went off to do other things,
like cleaning the counter from last night's dinner.

Soon I heard the familiar rumbling of boiling water.
Sure enough, small clouds of hot mist were hovering over
the stove. I turned off the gas and poured the hot water
into an empty cup. The water hissed as it slid over the hot
metal surface of the pot into the waiting container. I
plopped in a tea bag and finished cleaning the counter.
While attending to the task at hand, invisibly, imperceptibly, the hot water found its way into the tea leaves. What
had been just a cup of hot water was now a cup of tea.

What, you may ask, does making tea have to do with alchemy? Plenty.

The art of alchemy is simply changing one form into another. Most people think of alchemy as a medieval obsession for changing lead into gold. And while this is one form of alchemy, anything that causes a change in form is alchemy as well. Turning water into steam is alchemy. Changing a dry tea bag into tea is also alchemy.

While external alchemy, like changing lead into gold, is a fascinating enterprise, I am more intrigued by internal alchemy, like the type discussed by Magdalen in the *Manuscript*. But whether one is attempting to create enhanced abilities in oneself or to brew a cup of tea, some of the principles are the same.

All successful alchemies must have three elements: 1) a substance to be transformed; 2) a container to hold the alchemical reaction; and 3) energy. Had I, for instance, stumbled into the kitchen this morning and poured water onto the burner instead of into a kettle, I would not have created alchemy. I would have created a mess.

In external alchemies, like making tea or nuclear fission (yes, atomic power is alchemy as well), the containers are pretty obvious. Different containers are required for different tasks. A teacup, for instance, will do quite well for making tea, but is a very poor container for a nuclear reactor. For that you will need massive amounts of concrete, lead, and a tremendous quantity of water.

With internal alchemies, the containers are more abstract, as are the goals. The purpose of internal alchemy is to change consciousness, to accelerate one's own personal evolution. I do not, by the way, mean evolution in the usual sense. I doubt that anyone will physically sprout wings and fly as a result of practicing internal alchemy. However, the changes wrought by such practice can be so profound that one feels as if one is flying above life and viewing it from a greatly expanded perspective. This is why many of the alchemical symbols from around the world involve flying beings—like the garudas of Balinese Hinduism, the dragons of Taoism, or Horus, the hawk-headed god of Egyptian alchemy, to name a few.

In all systems of internal alchemy, the container for the alchemical reaction is awareness itself—in other words, mental focus. As you read these words, you are holding them in *the container of your awareness,* and they are, hopefully, making sense to you. But if your awareness were to wander, say to a conversation in the next room, the container would shift and my words would not register. Even though you might be going through the motion of reading, the words would not be impacting you because they were *outside* the container of your awareness.

There is a basic concept in all forms of internal alchemy which can be stated quite simply: *energy follows awareness.* In the reading example above, for instance, the energy of your attention follows where you put your awareness. If you pay attention to what you are reading, the words will make an impression in your mind. If, however, you pay attention to that conversation we were talking about, the words of this book won't impress your mind, but the words in the conversation will.

*The alchemical container of inner alchemy is awareness itself.*

The substances transformed through the processes of inner alchemy vary according to the stream or lineage. Some of these substances include such things as physical neurotransmitters, hormones, saliva and sexual fluids. There are also, however, whole classes of *subtle substances* that include such ephemeral things as *chi* in the Taoist stream, *prana* in the Yogic stream, the *winds* (lhung) in the Tibetan stream, and *neters* in the Egyptian.

It is this class of *subtle substances* that inner alchemy is most concerned with. And for the average person this is one of the most difficult concepts to understand. The reason, I think, has to do with our conditioning to the Newtonian world of everyday reality. We are not trained, generally speaking, to attend to the subtle energies behind the shadow play of physical reality. Let me give you an example of what I am talking about.

Remember that cup of tea I made this morning? Well, I never finished it, and it now sits cold on the counter. I got caught up in other things and forgot about it. For some reason, I didn't rinse out the old cup, but instead got a clean one from the cabinet. I put it next to the old one, filled it with hot water and plopped in another tea bag. There were small billows of steam rising from the new cup of tea, but nothing was rising from the old cup except the smell of cold tea. How odd, I thought. I picked up both cups of tea, one cold and one hot. I felt like Goldilocks and the three bears. This one's too cold. This one's too hot. I put down the hot one to let it cool off so that it might get to be "just right."

I was in the two side-by-side worlds of Newtonian and quantum reality. I could hold the tea cups in my hands. One was cold and one was hot. But the reason for this difference was from a realm much subtler than the two teacups or the watery tea they contained. It had to do with the individual molecules of water. Although I could not see it, the molecules in the hot water were running about helter-skelter like a mob at a shopping mall, bumping into each other and in the process heating up things. In fact, when I had brought the water to a boil on the stove, they were at their most riotous, a molecular Mardi Gras of extreme proportions.

The cold cup of tea, on the other hand, held a group of lethargic molecules. The energy that had heated them up had long ago passed out of the cup in the form of radiant heat, and the once riotous molecules were now slow like dowagers in a nursing home. The only difference between the party animals in the hot cup of tea and the sleepy ones in the cold cup was energy.

I could not, with my physical senses, see the difference between the molecules of water, since they were too small for me to see. All I could sense was the after-effects of their energy or lack of it, namely heat or cold. In point of fact, that is all any of us experience in the physical world: the after-effects of something happening in the subtle or quantum world. The task of the alchemist is to become aware of and sensitive to the subtle realms that escape most people. The reason for this is that the subtle realm or quantum world holds the best types of substances for alchemical transformation. For the most part, the sub-stances in the Newtonian or dense physical world are too gross, too dense to be transformed through the power of alchemical attention. But the subtle realm, the quantum world, is very receptive to the focus of such attention.

In my example of the two teacups, the common ele-ment was energy or lack of it. In this case, the energy was applied from an external source. In most internal alchemies, however, the source of energy is usually the energy of consciousness itself. What do I mean by this?

Become aware of one of your hands for a moment. Just shift your attention to it. Be aware of its position, its weight, and the physical sensations in the hand. After a moment of this become aware of your other hand. Which hand has more sensation in it? In other words, which one has more *energy?*

For most people, the hand that has been focused on will have more sensation. This is because energy follows awareness. The alchemical container of awareness was focused on a particular hand and this resulted in an increase of perceived energy in the hand. The neurologi-cal reasons for this are quite complex, but the practice of holding attention is quite simple. We do it everyday.

Sometimes the energy of the breath is used to power an alchemical reaction. At times, an external energy source might be used, such as the sun or a ceremonial fire. In some rare forms of alchemy, other elements such as water or air are used.

In the use of external energies to *drive* an alchemical reaction, the alchemist might focus on a flame while holding (within the container of awareness) the substance to be transformed. Or the energy of the sun might be used to power an internal alchemical reaction in the same way.

To give you an example, I am writing this part of the book in the month of August on the island of Paros in the Cyclades of Greece. Every afternoon around six, when the sun is not blazing hot, I sit on the deck for about an hour and do an alchemical practice within the ancient Egyptian stream.

To explain how I do this practice, I need to define a term from Egyptian alchemy: the *Ka*. The Ka body is sometimes called the *etheric double* or *spiritual twin*. It is the same shape and size as the physical body (the *khat*), but it is made of energy and has very little mass (or density). As I hold this subtle body in the *container of my awareness,* I sense the sun. And I draw the subtle energies available to me through the sunlight into my *Ka*. Some of these energies from the sun have been scientifically documented such as ultraviolet radiation and the primary colors of full-spectrum light. Studies have shown that full-spectrum light has a very positive effect on health. But there are whole classes of more subtle energies that science has not yet verified. These extremely subtle energies are presumably too subtle for our current methods of measurement.

Taoists might refer to this type of subtle energy as *solarized yang chi*. A yogi might refer to it as the *prana of sureya* (the sun). And an alchemist within the Egyptian stream might simply say that it is the *neter of RA* (the power of the sun god).

But whatever you call it, there is another type of subtle energy in sunlight. In my practice of this technique, I have discovered what I call the *armchair method*. I used to use an elaborate system of standing movements to draw the sun's energy into my Ka. I still sometimes do this when I am feeling particularly energetic. But I have also found that the method works just as well if I am sitting on my butt.

In this case, at around six in the afternoon I sit in a canvas lounge chair provided by our benevolent landlord, Stephanos. I take off my shirt and lean back. Holding my Ka body in the container of my awareness... I simply become aware of my Ka, or you might say I imagine it, as a body of luminous light. Then I breathe in a relaxed manner and on the inhales I draw the subtle energy of the sun into my Ka.

Sometimes I draw the energy in through my navel and circulate it through the Ka. At other times I draw the energy of the sun into my solar plexus, which is, from the viewpoint of Egyptian alchemy, an aspect of RA. As I charge this miniature sun within my Ka, the excess energy spontaneously flows outward into my body. Sometimes I prefer to imagine my Ka as some kind of magnet (which it is), and draw the energies from the sun directly into the entire Ka at once.

While this method may seem odd or lackadaisical, it has all three elements of substance, container, and awareness, and so it is, in fact, a form of alchemy. As I focus on my Ka, I am holding it in the *alchemical container of my awareness*. The substance to be transformed is the Ka itself. In this case I am engaging something called an *energy building practice*. Why I would do such a thing will become clear in the next section when I talk about Egyptian Alchemy.

So there we have it, two of the essential elements: a substance to be transformed (my Ka) and a container to hold the alchemical reaction (my own awareness). The third element, energy, is of course provided by the sun itself (RA). When I do this practice correctly (i.e., hold all three elements together), there is a tremendous increase of energy and vibration within my Ka body. At times, however, my mind will wander into thoughts or fantasies, and at these moments the building of energy in the Ka decreases. If I don't bring my mind back to an awareness of the Ka, the building of energy will completely stop. This is, of course, because I have lost the container for the reaction when my mind wanders. To use our tea analogy, whenever my mind wanders, it's like taking the kettle off the stove.

The art, if you will, of internal alchemy is to hold all three elements of substance, energy, and container together long enough for an alchemical reaction to occur. And the discipline required of an alchemist to accomplish such a feat can be considerable.

All alchemists, regardless of their lineage, must attend to these three elements: container, substance, and energy. Each stream offers its own particular ways to strengthen the alchemical container. And by practicing the methods for strengthening the container of awareness, the alchemist can hold together ever-increasingly intense alchemical reactions.

The alchemical practitioner must also become keenly sensitive to the subtleties of substance. As awareness becomes refined, the alchemist is able to distinguish the most subtle characteristics of energetic substances. And a sense begins to unfold of how best to use these substances in an alchemical reaction and to what end. These substances range from actual physical materials such as saliva, sexual fluids, etc., to very subtle substances that are purely in the quantum realm of existence. As I mentioned earlier, it is these quantum substances that are most easily transmuted during the process of inner alchemy.

Finally, the alchemist must collect energy, since it is needed to drive alchemical reactions. There is a virtually unlimited field of possible energy sources for such inner work, and each alchemical tradition or stream offers its own suggestions on how to collect these types of energy. Indeed, the various streams of internal alchemy throughout the world offer a wide variety of clever, ingenious and, sometimes remarkable methods for the cultivation of energy.

In the *Manuscript*, Magdalen states that her task, as an Initiate, was to assist Yeshua in the building of his subtle body (the Ka) through specific *energy-building practices*. This was accomplished, according to the Magdalen, through the masterful use of sexual energy. As an Initiate of Isis, she was using methods from one of the oldest alchemical streams on the planet, and it is to this that we now turn our attention.

# Egyptian Alchemy

According to the alchemists of ancient Egypt, we posses two bodies. The first, called the *khat,* is our physical body of flesh and blood. It is the body we normally identify with, the body we eat and drink with. The body that lives and dies.

The second body is called the *Ka,* and is sometimes referred to as the *etheric double* or *spiritual twin.* It is a duplicate of the physical body (khat) but is made of pure energy, not flesh and blood. This Ka body interpenetrates the khat (physical body) and there is no part of the khat or physical body that is not enclosed by the Ka.

Transformation of the Ka body is a fundamental focus of Egyptian alchemy. But before we discuss how this is done, I think it would be good to take a look at these two bodies (the Ka and the khat) from the standpoint of physics. I believe this modern context will give us a foundation to better understand the strange world of the Ka body and its non-ordinary potentials.

## Quantum Physics

We can describe the khat (the dense physical body) quite well in terms of Newtonian physics. It obeys, for instance, the laws of gravity. And you can predict with a good deal of certainty where it will be physically, if you know the direction it is heading and the speed at which it is moving.

Not so with the Ka. The Ka body is outside the realms of Newtonian physics, and is best described using the laws of quantum physics. And what, you might ask, determines if something is bound by Newtonian laws or the laws of quantum mechanics? Size.

Objects larger than one thousandth of an inch obey the laws of Newtonian mechanics. This is because they have enough mass (i.e., density or weight) to have gravitational fields.

However, objects less than one thousandth of an inch follow a different drummer. This is because their density or mass is too small to create a gravitational field of any consequence. The Ka *body* exists within this realm (the quantum world) since the Ka is primarily light/energy and has very little mass.

The quantum world that the Ka body dwells in is very strange indeed. So is the fact that you and I live in both the Newtonian and quantum universes simultaneously. Our bodies are squarely in the Newtonian world. If we jump off a cliff, for instance, we will fall until we hit the ground, victims of gravity. (Unless of course, we are bungee jumping, in which case, an equal and opposite force pulls us back.)

But if we enter the atomic and subatomic levels of our bodies, we are in a different world altogether. The minuscule particles that comprise our bodies are not bound by the laws of Newtonian physics. They are, instead, bound by quantum mechanics.

The quantum world is very bizarre by our standards. Perhaps one way to describe this is to discuss experiments with light. Now, light can take two very different forms, with very different properties. It can, for instance, take the form of particles (photons), or it can take the form of waves.

As absurd as it sounds, if a researcher is looking for light in the form of waves, that is how light will present itself in the experiment. If, however, the researcher is looking for light in the form of particles, that is what he or she will see. This early discovery in quantum physics eventually became formalized as Bell's Theorem which states that at the quantum level, there is no objective observer, since the intention of the experimenter affects the outcome.

Somehow the *intention* of the researcher mysteriously affects the behavior of subatomic particles. How this happens has not yet been explained by science, but it is generally accepted that Bell's Theorem is true.

Physicists are reluctant to ascribe Bell's Theorem to phenomena outside the minuscule world of subatomic particles. The reason for this is, of course, because everyday objects, like billiard balls and rockets, are too large to be affected by intention. Intention is known to have an effect at the quantum level, but not so much in the Newtonian world.

But there is a weird place where the quantum world and the Newtonian world meet, and it is, of all places, inside our minds.

Tucked away inside our brains are teeny tiny gaps between nerve cells. These spaces between neurons are called synapses, and the average distance of these gaps: you may have already guessed it, is approximately one thousandth of an inch, the entry point into the strange world of quantum events.

A nerve impulse has to travel the length of a neuron and jump across the tiny synaptic gap if it is to get to the next neuron. Nerve impulses are much like relay races in which they run the length of a neuron and jump a hurdle. What actually jumps the hurdle is a little molecule called a neurotransmitter.

At any one moment, there are thousands upon thousands of these neurotransmitters jumping hurdles. And each moment is a *quantum event* since these molecules are approximately less than one thousandth of an inch. This is one reason why our thoughts can be so novel and unpredictable. Some of the neurotransmitters jumping the synaptic hurdle "make it" while others do not. Those that make the leap create a response within the next nerve cell. If these hurdles take place in the thinking part of the brain (neocortex) then we will have the experience of thought.

The concept of *intention* is crucial to both quantum physics and internal alchemy. Indeed, we will find that it is through the agency of both mental attention and personal will (*intention*) that the alchemist is able to affect specific quantum events within his or her body/mind.

We will see this very clearly later on. But for the moment, let me just say that internal alchemies, such as the Egyptian system, are primarily methods to alter certain aspects of the quantum universe. The Ka body is, itself, in the quantum realm and as such is easily affected by the *intentionality* of the alchemist.

There are other oddities in the quantum world. You can't, for instance, predict things. In the Newtonian world, if you throw something, you can predict where it will land, but not so in the quantum. Here there are only probabilities, possibilities. Objects flying around in the quantum world might land where you'd expect them to, or they might just spin around in circles or dissolve into light. The possibilities are virtually endless.

There are other strangenesses tucked away in the quantum realm. A very bizarre phenomenon develops when two particles meet in the quantum world. Now get this: after their chance meeting, the two particles spin off into space, each of them going along its merry way. But if one of them changes the direction of its spin, the other one instantaneously changes the direction of its spin as well. There is simply no current plausible explanation for this weird behavior. And although we need not concern ourselves with such shenanigans in the Newtonian world, they are part and parcel of the quantum.

I already mentioned how our thoughts exist within the weird twilight zone of quantum reality. What I mean by this is that the neurological events responsible for thought (i.e., the jumping of neurotransmitters across the synaptic gap) are clearly in the quantum world. And it is this strange quirk in our neurology that affords us the possibility of affecting quantum events within our own bodies and minds.

So what do I mean by this statement? Am I implying that you and I can have an effect on our own physiology through mere mental attention? Yes, I am, and this is one of the reasons internal alchemies are so effective.

Our bodies and minds are intimately connected. They are, in a very real way, two sides of the same coin, and research verifying the interconnectedness of body and mind is flooding scientific journals all over the world.

A relatively new field in medicine is an area called psychoneuroimmunology. It's a big word, but it basically means how our thoughts and emotions affect our physiology and specifically our immune systems.

I could quote numerous studies in this regard, but I think a story might serve our purposes more effectively. Although the situation involved pain management and not internal alchemy, some of the principles are the same.

Several years ago, a client was referred to me for the treatment of immense physical pain. She was in the advanced stages of cancer, and it had metastasized into her spine. She was, in her own words, in constant and unrelenting pain.

As Joan (I have changed her name) described her situation, I asked her to rate her current level of pain and discomfort, ten being the worst she had experienced and zero being the least. She self-assessed her pain level at around eight.

I then asked her to describe the most relaxing and refreshing experience she had ever had. She went into a long detailed account of her visit to Sedona, Arizona, and how she loved the red rocks and canyons of the area.

Reaching over to a stereo that I had in my office, I played some music that had been specifically written to lower brain wave activity into the more relaxed states of increased alpha activity. I then asked her to imagine being in Sedona again. I asked her to make it as vividly real as possible, seeing it, hearing the sounds, sensing the physical sensations, perhaps even smelling the aromas.

- 102 -

Her face muscles, which had been quite taut, relaxed a bit as she recalled the scene. I then suggested she find a place that she found particularly beautiful and soothing. She chose a large boulder overlooking a canyon. I then suggested that this boulder had powerful healing energies and that with each breath she was effortlessly drawing these healing energies into her body.

After a few minutes of this, Joan opened her eyes suddenly and reached for her purse. Opening it, she pulled out a tissue and deftly patted the area around her eyes.

"What happened?" I asked.

"It's gone," she said.

"What's gone?" I asked.

"The pain," she said. "The pain is gone!"

The release from pain had been quite emotional. And after giving her a moment to compose herself, I asked her to rate her level of pain for me. Zero.

Over several sessions, I showed Joan how to control her own pain through both mental attention and intention. She reported that although the cancer was still spreading, she was able to greatly reduce her pain without the need for medication.

The neurological events responsible for ending Joan's pain were quite complex and they were birthed— spawned if you will, from the quantum world.

Had someone stumbled into my office, they would have seen a woman with her eyes closed, sitting in a chair listening to some music. But this was the Newtonian realm, the world of objects and people.

The quantum realm would have remained unseen, but it was this world that was responsible for the change in Joan's condition. It was in this realm, tucked between the synaptic gaps within her brain, that neurotransmitters battled for supremacy. Some of these neurological messengers carried messages of pain. The dying cells in her spine were, after all, sending their constant death cries to her brain. But at the same time, other messengers were carrying feelings of peace, relaxation, and comfort. For a moment, the messengers of comfort won out over the messengers of pain and death. And, if I may be so poetic, all this took place in the froth and foam of the quantum sea.

This ocean, though hidden from our eyes, is the birthplace of everything that exists both inside and outside our minds. It is the *mother-spring* of all creation and it is this that is ultimately the focus of all internal alchemies, regardless of their methods.

The means to alter quantum events within the body and mind of an alchemist is similar in many regards to what happened with Joan. The primary difference is that the alchemist is not seeking to alter pain, but rather to alter consciousness itself.

The agency responsible for this momentous alteration is nothing less than *thought joined with awareness.* Thought and awareness are ephemeral *things,* as anyone who has tried to hold either for a long period of time knows.

It is also in thought that we can experience things we could never do in *the real* world. By the real world I mean the Newtonian reality of everyday life. We are used to the force of gravity, for instance. We expect things to fall if we drop them. We do not expect things to float in air, perhaps in our dreams but not in *reality.*

What I would like to propose to the reader is the idea that we live in two realities simultaneously. One of these realities we are quite familiar with. It is our everyday world, the world where things fall if you drop them.

There is another reality, however, just as real as this one. It is the reality of the quantum world, and although you are not aware of the zillions of neurotransmitters leaping across space to create your experience of thought at this moment, it is happening nonetheless. And this reality is not Newtonian; it is quantum, with all of its attendant unpredictability and paradox.

The closest most of us come to an experience like the quantum world is when we dream. Things have a weird logic here. In the Newtonian world, the alarm clock you set on your bed stand will stay there the whole night. It will not budge, a captive of gravity and entropy. Unless someone or something knocks it off, it isn't going to move. But in one of your dreams, the clock could very well float in the air, and its hands might move backwards propelling you into your past, or the hands might move forward and rocket you into some distant version of your future. Our *quantum-like dreams* are not inhibited by the logic of the Newtonian world. These phantoms from the subconscious realms are anarchists when it comes to logic and predictability.

Now in the Western consensus view of reality (Newtonian that is) such things as dream experiences are viewed as imaginary and summarily dismissed. What I wish to suggest to you is that not all of them are imaginary—certainly not any more imaginary than your current view of yourself.

I suggest you think of some of these weird dream-like events as alternate perceived realities, not more or less real than your Newtonian version of reality, just different. After all, scientific studies have demonstrated beyond a shadow of a doubt that you and I do not experience *reality* (whatever that is) directly. Our perceptions of reality are filtered through the limitations of our physical senses as well as our beliefs and expectations.

You are, for instance, inverting the pages of this book inside your brain. Your retina actually receives the image of these pages upside down. But your brain creatively turns them right side up! Your brain also tends to perceive what it thinks should be there, even when it isn't! And anyone who has tried to proofread a document knows what I am talking about. The brain tends to see what it expects to see. A misplaced comma often slides past the attention of a copy editor just because the brain doesn't expect one to be there.

All of this mumbo-jumbo is just to point out that we do not directly experience reality, our perception of it being a co-creation of both our body and our mind.

Dreams, in this context, are just another form of created perceptual reality.

I do not, by the way, believe that all dreams are alternate realities bearing significance, only some of them. Most dreams are just the brain unraveling stress and some, quite frankly, are the result of bad food combining at dinner. But some dreams are deeply significant from a psychological standpoint and can even be portentous. These types of dreams, I believe, are of a different order than the others, and anyone who has had such a dream knows what I am talking about.

Indeed, in the actual practice of internal alchemy, the alchemist enters a state of mind that is quite dream-like. This is, I believe, a result of specific brain changes that are created through alchemical meditations. Many internal alchemical practices increase alpha and/or theta wave activity in the neocortex. And the deeper states of theta are experienced very much like dream states. These waking-dreams allow the practitioner to enter worlds of experience that are not possible in normal waking states.

As I said earlier, the methods of internal alchemy can be viewed as a means to directly affect certain aspects of the quantum universe. We will also find that manipulations of quantum reality (through the actions of internal alchemy) take place, most effectively, in dream-like states of mind. And every alchemical tradition has developed its own methods for generating dream-like states of awareness.

## Operational Reality

*It is really simply a matter of what world you are identifying with and what behaviors best operate in that world.*
You have learned, no doubt, how to operate in the everyday world of Newtonian reality. You know that if you drop something, it will continue to the floor. You know how to pick up this book and turn the pages. When you are

done, you know how to put the book down again. These are learned neuromuscular behaviors. You did not know how to do this when you were six months old, but now you do. You have learned this skill over the course of interacting with the everyday world of Newtonian-bound things.

I suggest you think of internal alchemies (including the Egyptian system) as simply a means to operate in another reality, namely the quantum. Just as you learned how to pick up a book and put it down, you can learn how to do things in the quantum world as well. You just need a reliable "teaching method." And internal alchemical systems are just that: teaching methods.

Alchemical mastery brings with it an amazing array of non-ordinary abilities or powers of consciousness which are called *siddhis* in yoga. These abilities may seem very strange to Western minds, as weird as the quantum world from which they are derived. But they are simply the natural expression of an evolving consciousness.

## Siddhis and the Powers of Consciousness

The siddhis or powers of consciousness naturally unfold as one progresses along the path of spiritual development. There are many well-documented cases of Buddhist, Christian, Islamic, Jewish, and Taoists saints and mystics who have attained these states. In addition, it is well known among indigenous cultures that shamans often exhibit such powers as well.

I have personally made a study of siddhis for the last few decades. To the Western materialistic consciousness some of these powers seem outlandish, but they have been well documented in numerous cultures. Several years ago, I had an experience with the *siddhis* of a mystic in one of the most unlikely places on earth—Kodiak, Alaska.

I had been invited to teach a workshop in Anchorage, and the following weekend I taught a workshop on Kodiak Island. After the final session on the island, I had a few days off. My organizer gave me a few options, and I chose the boat ride to a small island inhabited by Russian Orthodox monks where an Orthodox saint had lived. I was told that visitors more often than not had to turn back due to rough seas. In fact, I was told, the prelates of the Church in charge of the monastery had never been able to see it, as every time they went for a visit, high seas forced them back.

This was a source of immense humor among the native peoples.

We took a small airplane ride to a nearby island and landed on a spit of land that ended abruptly into turbulent and frigid waters. We were greeted by a local fisherman's wife driving a pickup truck, and I hopped in the back. My organizer got in the front.

It was summer, but there was a light snowfall as we headed for her house by the sea. I remember feeling quite cold and wondering how in the hell people survived here in the winter. We pulled up to a small house surrounded by cedar trees and went inside. Sitting by a large wooden table, we sipped tea. Now anyone who has been to northern Alaska knows that time is a strange bird in these parts. We just sat and sat, talking a little here and there, waiting, it seemed, for some opportune time to leave. Finally, our host announced that it was time to go and we piled back into the pickup and headed for the dock where her husband was waiting with a fishing trawler.

We took off across an amazingly placid sea. Our host sat next to a boom, knitting, and commented how unusual it was to have such a calm passing. I sat looking out at the rich, unbelievably beautiful landscape of the neighboring islands as our boat chugged along at a fairly crisp pace. Seals followed us partway.

Passing an outcropping of boulders, we came into a small natural harbor. The water was too shallow for the trawler, so we got into a dinghy and headed to shore. The scene was like something out of the Middle Ages. A group of men were on the beach burning brush, the air thick with billows of white smoke which swirled in eddies against a stark blue sky. The monks wore long beards, typical of Russian and Greek Orthodox clerics, and they were wearing long grey robes with thin ropes tied about the waist. Each one of them also wore a crucifix.

Stepping out of the boat onto the sand, we were greeted by someone who appeared to be in his early thirties and had the air of authority about him. Our host explained that I had come from Washington State to visit. The abbot smiled approvingly and proceeded to take us on a tour of the small monastery, which consisted of perhaps a dozen men or so. As we headed up a path into the shade of cedars, he noted that the monastery did not often get to host pilgrims.

He took us to several spots, including the small hut where the Saint had lived. I recall the air being musty from the old manuscripts and icons that had been in the Saint's possession. But there was also an unmistakable sense of serenity. The abbot also took us to a sacred spring reputed to have healing powers. Finally he took as to the small chapel where the Saint had been previously buried. His body had since been removed but the site was still considered holy.

The abbot caught me staring at a corner of the chapel. He asked me what I was seeing, and I said I was seeing a column of white light coming out of the floor and going up through the roof. The abbot seemed to smile a bit and said that the Saint had been buried in that corner of the church. Then he said something in a somewhat dreamy voice as if he were partway into another world; I remember his words because they sounded so odd to me at the time: "Would that we were all so sensitive."

Seeming to rouse himself from his reveries, the abbot said, "There is one more thing I would like to show you."

He guided us back down the hill to a very small chapel that had obviously just recently been built. It was quite unusual in that it was perhaps nine feet square and some twenty feet tall. The inside of the building glowed from the gold pigments of recently painted icons. They depicted the lives of saints along with other prominent figures of the Russian Orthodox Church. In the back of the tiny chapel there was a very small altar with a bible in Russian.

The abbot pointed out the various icons and their meanings, and then he said that the tour had come to an end. He motioned us out of the chapel and closed the door behind us. I remember suddenly having a question about mysticism I thought the abbot might be able to clarify. I knocked at the door, but there was no answer. I knocked again; still no sign of anyone inside.

Gingerly, I opened the door to find the chapel completely empty. For a moment I stood in shock. Then my ever-skeptical mind came in and I began to search for trap doors or other entrances. I even picked up the small frayed rug on the floor to see if there was a secret exit. Nothing.

Still in a kind of shock, I wandered out the door and out to the beach where our party was waiting. There, clearly in view, was the abbot. He was talking to my host and as I stepped up he nodded his head with a distinct twinkle in his eyes. We boarded the dinghy and headed back to the trawler. The sun was low in the sky and I stood on the deck looking over the stern as we headed back to sea. I was very quiet.

As I write these words, I find myself caught up in the feelings of awe and wonder I felt then. I had known the *siddhis* existed, had studied the physics of them, and had made it a hobby of mine to collect stories and documentations. But here on a small island off Kodiak, a humble contemplative had shown me the mystery of yogic powers firsthand.

Halfway through the ride back, the fisherman's wife

turned from her knitting and said, "You know, they do things like that all the time!"

"Things like what?" I asked.

"Oh, you know. Teleporting, bi-locating. Things like that."

"Really," I said.

"Yes", she replied, not taking her eyes off her knitting. "That island is a remote place. There is no mail service. We see them sometimes in town picking up their mail and buying things. And," she said in a most conspiratorial tone, "they don't have any way of getting there!"

*The powers of consciousness* or siddhis range from what are called the lesser siddhis to what are termed the greater siddhis. The lesser siddhis include such psychic abilities as *clairvoyance* (inner seeing), *clairaudience* (inner hearing), *clairsentience* (inner feeling), as well as *clairgnosis* (inner knowing), as in knowing something but not knowing how you know it. The first three powers, clairvoyance, clairaudience and clairsentience, are refinements of the physical senses.

As psychic powers unfold, they often first present themselves in one of these three forms, or in combination. Thus one might begin to see images in the mind that can't be physically seen—in other words, mental visual impressions. In scientific studies involving remote viewing this siddhi is most often used.

Studies show that some people can, under the right conditions, (i.e., mental relaxation) accurately report visual impressions of objects or locations hundreds of miles away without any previous knowledge of them. The reception of such visual information must presumably come from some other source than that of physical sight, since the *viewers* were nowhere near the locations they described.

Many yogis/yoginis, saints, and mystics have reported that they could see their disciples in distant locations when it was called for. In one account, the yogi Neem Karoli Baba suddenly asked for large amounts of food to be brought to him. Those present report that he consumed a mind-boggling amount of food before going into samadhi (a form of deep yogic trance). When the yogi came out of meditation, his disciples asked him what had happened. He reported that he had suddenly seen one of his disciples dying in the desert. The last desire of the dying man was to eat. Baba said that the chela (disciple) had reached a level of attainment where there was no further need to reincarnate. But with the desire for food on his mind at the moment of death, he would have been brought back into the wheel of reincarnation just through the power of this one unfulfilled desire! Baba had taken upon himself the task of fulfilling the man's last wish for food, and using his yogic powers, he transmuted the desire.

When psychic information is received auditorially, the person is called clairaudient. Such persons have subtle impressions of hearing sound and/or voices. The inner realms of consciousness are filled with sound and music that can be incredibly beautiful. It has been suggested by some that many of the great composers actually heard the music of these realms and this *music of the spheres* greatly influenced their compositions.

Some individuals feel things at a very subtle level; these persons are called clairsentients. There is often a fine line between a clairsentient and an empath. Empaths have highly developed sensitivities and often feel other persons' feelings, especially those immediately around them. Clairsentients may also be empathic, but in addition, they receive psychic impressions in the form of subtle physical sensations.

Clairgnosis is one of the more fascinating siddhis. When you have a hunch about something, but have no idea how you might know such a thing, this is clairgnosis. (That is if your hunch turns out to be true. If it turns out to be false, we call that delusion.) Some have suggested that clairgnosis is an attribute of pure consciousness which is, by nature, omniscient and omnipresent. As one rises up the ladder of consciousness, one's own personal awareness takes on some of these qualities of pure consciousness and episodes of clairgnosis increase.

The lesser siddhis also include such things as healing abilities and limited powers of prophecy. This class of yogic powers also includes the ability for awareness to become very small or very large—in other words, not confined by the limitations of the body.

The greater siddhis include such things as *levitation* (in which the body floats or hovers in air). Again this siddhi is not confined to Indian yogis or yoginis as some believe. There are well-documented sightings of St. Francis of Assisi, for one, hovering in the air. St. Francis exhibited other siddhis as well. In fact, his physical remains still have spiritual powers even after his death. While visiting his shrine in Assisi, I was transported into the spiritual realms through the emanations from his crypt! I heard a sound like wind blowing through aspen trees when I stood near his body, and when I returned to my hotel room my skin was red as if I had a light sunburn.

By the way, if you are ever at Assisi, here's a little tip. As you enter the main entrance into the basilica where St. Francis's remains are kept, turn to your left. Off to both sides, there are stairs that lead down to the crypt and it is certainly worth visiting. The problem is that there are usually throngs of people milling about, and it is difficult to find a quiet space. If you proceed further, past the stairs, you will see a large altar in the distance, the only one in this part of the church. On the floor, in front of the altar, there is a geometric figure. It sits directly above St. Francis's tomb and the emanations from this area are very strong. No one seems to know about it, so you can stand directly on the spot and receive the emanations in relative peace.

The greater siddhis also include such remarkable abilities such as *teleportation* (like the abbot I mentioned earlier) and *bi-location* (being in two places at once). There are other abilities that fall under this category as well, but the purpose of this chapter is not to discuss the siddhis in depth.

It is important to realize that the siddhis or yogic powers are attained as a natural consequence of spiritual development. There is, however, a very real danger with the siddhis. They have a glamour and a seduction for many people. The advice often given is to avoid the pursuit of yogic powers. And when they do arise, to not pay them much attention.

A short story about the dilemma of siddhis will help to make this clear. This concerns a living yogi who is quite well known, so I will avoid using his name. And although he teaches kundalini yoga there are very strong parallels with the system of Egyptian alchemy.

He is quite a powerful being, and I had the wonderful experience of studying with him at a weeklong retreat many years ago. According to a close disciple of his, who I came to know, the yogi had gone to India for a spiritual retreat in his early twenties after having attained some of the Siddhis. He was resting against a tree, listening to the beautiful music of a master musician who was caught up in the fervor of *bhakti* (divine love), and due to the intensity of devotion within the music, our yogi was transported into a deep state of samadhi and experienced great ecstasies and bliss.

The concert ended abruptly when it started to rain and the musician rushed indoors. Using his siddhic powers, the yogi caused the rain to stop, and the musician returned to his *kirtans* (sacred singing). Very quickly our yogi was transported back into samadhi, but his bliss was rudely ended by an old man kicking him in the side. The man was also a yogi, and in a furor he continued to kick the younger yogi, yelling obscenities at him.

"What are you doing?" he asked. "Don't you realize this area has been suffering from a drought? And you, you stopped the rains for your own selfish desires." The ancient yogi raised his staff in the air and pointed it at his younger peer. "Mark my words, if you don't stop this, you will pay a great karmic debt. You will spend a thousand lifetimes as a sea creature!" The old yogi then kicked some dust in the direction of the young man and left before he could respond.

Immediately the younger yogi went into meditation and through his siddhic powers returned the rains. He fervently prayed to God to take away his siddhis, and miraculously they left him. But over the years they slowly returned to a much wiser and less flamboyant man.

I believe that the siddhis are a natural expression of evolution. They are perhaps, one of our next evolutionary benchmarks. And anyone practicing internal alchemy long enough will eventually have to contend with them.

The siddhis are to us, like apples are to apple trees. Apples are intrinsic to the nature of apple trees. But it is only when the apple tree reaches a certain stage of development that the fruits appear. Until then, they are only a potential.

When an individual human consciousness reaches certain stages of development, the siddhis spontaneously appear.

Every alchemical lineage deals with the non-ordinary powers that are attained as a result of spiritual practice. And every alchemical tradition has its own methods for developing and handling these spiritual powers. In the Egyptian stream, these powers were developed as a byproduct of strengthening the Etheric Double or Ka.

## Strengthening the Ka

So let us return to the Ka for it holds such a prominent place in Egyptian alchemy. Unlike the khat (dense physical body), the Ka body can seemingly walk through walls, float in air, and cover vast distances in a moment. In yogic literature, there are many reliable accounts of saints and mystics bi-locating (being in two places at once). One explanation often given for this phenomenon has to do with the Ka body. When the Ka is sufficiently charged it can have a kind of density that can be seen by others. Because the Ka is an etheric double of the person, it looks exactly like him or her.

In the *Manuscript*, Magdalen talks about Yeshua appearing to her after the crucifixion before his ascent into heaven (spirit). This was, from the perspective of Egyptian alchemy, a form of his Ka, highly charged as a result of the alchemical practices they had engaged in.

According to the *Manuscript*, Magdalen had been assisting Yeshua in one of the primary tasks of Egyptian Alchemy: to charge his Ka body with an increase of energy. Anyone wishing to experience the fruits of the Egyptian alchemical system must engage in *power building practices* for the Ka. There are many methods used to accomplish this, but it is not in the scope of this chapter to discuss them. A couple of methods are discussed by Magdalen in the *Manuscript* itself, and I would refer the reader to them. (Note: the method of drawing in solar energy I described in the first chapter is one example of a very simple *energy building practice).*

By whatever methods used, as the Ka accumulates more energy, its magnetics become stronger. The use of these magnetic fields for the elevation of consciousness was one of the great discoveries of Egyptian alchemy.

While strengthening the Ka is a fundamental focus in this system of alchemy, it is only the first task. The second task is to successfully shift identification from the khat (the dense physical body) into the Ka—shifting, if you will, identification from the Newtonian world into the quantum. In identifying with the Ka, the practitioner does *not* disregard the physical body (khat), but in the practices of alchemical meditation, one's identity is shifted from the physical to the luminous body (Ka). This shifting of attention and the growing awareness of the Ka as an autonomous body usually takes place within a spiritual context. This is crucial; since without a mental understanding regarding the Ka, it is unlikely that one would be able to utilize its extraordinary abilities.

## The Shifting of Identification

When I teach *the shifting of identification* in workshops, I use many different methods, some of them involving movement and some of them involving inner attention. After an unusually long training session at an Egyptian Alchemical Retreat a few years ago, someone shared his startling experience. He had just finished the last inner practice and had opened his eyes. He felt someone beside him, though no one had been there when he started. He turned to his right to see himself looking back at himself, smiling. He literally jumped out of his seat. The exercises in the workshop had managed to energize his Ka to such an extent that he could see his own subtle form with open eyes!

But sometimes a person can possess a strong Ka body even if he or she has not practiced alchemy.

## A Modern Experience with the Ka

I had an unusual experience with a client's Ka several years ago. At the time, I was a practicing psychotherapist and was referred a man in his late twenties suffering from depression. In the course of our therapy together, it became clear that he had suffered extreme physical and sexual abuse as a child. I always had a strange impression whenever we met. Although he was deeply depressed, he seemed to emanate a very intense energy, as if somewhere behind those electric blue eyes there was an inferno of unbelievable power.

Now, I always make it a policy with potential suicide risks to enter into a contract. They must agree to contact me physically or at least by phone if they plan to take their own lives. And I agree not to talk them out of it, but to make sure that that is what they really want to do. In the course of trying to get me and actually speak, they usually come to their senses and the crisis is averted.

In the case of this man, I had to leave town for a professional seminar about six weeks into our work together. I gave him the phone number in Washington, D.C. where I would be staying.

Now, here is where it really gets weird. The seminar had just moved into the section on death and dying when an attendant handed the speaker a piece of paper. She asked if Tom Kenyon was present. I raised my hand and was given a piece of paper with a name and phone number. It simply identified the person as the sister of my client.

I went to the nearest pay phone and called the number. She answered and informed me that her brother, my client, had committed suicide. I was extremely grieved and pissed. He had violated our contract agreement, which had been put in place to be a safety net. Had he contacted me I could have gotten him to see that he really did not want to take his own life, but he had taken the coward's way out. He killed himself while I was out of town.

I steamed about this for several days. Then one night, I had this strange dream in which he came to me and asked for my forgiveness. In the dream, I forgave him and he went on his way.

Now, it gets very, very strange. My office happened to be next to my house, and I usually saw clients in the afternoons and evenings, never in the morning. That day, after the strange dream, I was in town and was approached by an acquaintance. He said that he was thinking about seeing me. I asked him why, since he didn't seem to be the type interested in personal growth.

He told me that he had driven by my office/house at around 5 a.m. that morning and had seen a very sad-looking person going inside. Mind you, I wasn't even awake at 5 a.m., much less seeing anyone. He said he came back around the house about a half hour later and saw the same person coming out with a smile on his face and skipping down the block. I asked him to describe this mystery person, and his description matched my client perfectly. I was stunned.

I had not yet stumbled upon Egyptian Alchemy and its ideas regarding the Ka body, and so I had no way of explaining this to myself for several years.

## Effects of Strengthening the Ka

As the Ka body becomes stronger (due to energy building practices) the powers of mind and will also become stronger. Thus, the practitioner can draw to himself or herself objects of desire much more quickly. The ability to accomplish this feat of magnetizing desires occurs as an interface between the actual strength of the Ka and one's degree of spiritual under-standing regarding the possibilities. If one possesses a strong Ka without a spiritual understanding of its signifi-cance, then the Ka cannot be fully utilized. Conversely, if someone has a high degree of understanding, but has not taken up the task of strengthening the Ka, then likewise the Ka cannot be fully utilized. In this case however, the deficit is due to a lack of energy, not a lack of understanding.

One of the side-effects of a strengthened Ka is an increased potential for spiritual illumination. In such instances, the luminous body of the Ka literally radiates more light. This *inner light* is usually not visible except in the rarest of instances. But those who are psychic can see this type of light quite clearly.

There is also an interesting benefit gained from building the Ka. Once the Ka has autonomy, it can do all kinds of things, like travel in other dimensions of consciousness to gain insight and knowledge. This activity can be quite rewarding to the alchemist. I remember my own first encounters with a master alchemist in the other realms. He continues to this day to be a great source of insight and encouragement.

# The Djed

As the Ka builds in strength there is an alchemical task that the alchemist can undertake. However, this cannot be accomplished until there is enough energy in the Ka since this act takes tremendous energy and intent. The task to which I refer involves the *djed*.

The djed is the central pathway of the chakras up the spine. As energy is progressively moved upward, there is an accompanying expansion of awareness. This movement of energy up the djed is sometimes referred to as the act of *raising the djed*. And the power that drives this energy up the djed is nothing less than *sekhem* or life-force. The term literally means "that which makes things erect."

To better understand the profound effects of raising the djed, it might be helpful to take a look at how the chakras filter perception since they are radically affected by this action.

# The Chakras

In terms of spiritual evolution and the relativity of perception, the chakras are very significant. Let's say that there are seven people at a picnic. It is a balmy day and the park is full. Each of these seven people will have a very different experience of the world based upon the activity of his or her chakras. This is a hypothetical example, since rarely are the chakras activated sequentially. Most of us have a mixture of open and closed. But for illustration purposes, our seven imaginary people will help us to better understand the filtering of perception that occurs through the chakra system.

Let's say that the first person is living primarily through the first chakra, which is located in an area near the base of the spine. This individual will be most concerned with security and survival. Forget that it is a beautiful day. This person will be anxious. All those people roaming around are possible threats, and this person would be very guarded around strangers.

Our second imaginary person lives mostly in the second chakra, located about two inches (four centimeters) above the base of the spine. This person is driven to constantly search for new sexual experiences. If he or she is not actively engaged in trying to find someone to have sex with, he or she will be besieged by constant sexual fantasies. This person may even find it difficult to have a conversation with anyone else in our group, because he or she cannot help cruising the crowd.

The third person in our group is stuck in the solar plexus, which is located back behind the pit of the stomach. His or her only real concerns are status and power. If this person engages someone in a conversation, it will only be for what that person might offer (i.e., those corporate power lunches and cocktail parties).

Moving our attention to the fourth person, we note that he or she is in the heart chakra, located behind the sternum in the center of the chest. For this individual, the world will be full of love. This love is not romantic, but is more akin to what the ancient Greeks called *agape*, or divine love. For this person, the world is love. This love can range from a soft feeling of interconnectedness to an intense experience of universal love. In some cases, such persons spontaneously enter *samadhi* due to the intensity of their *bhakti* (experience of divine love). When the heart opens, such persons often assume that those around them are experiencing the world in the same ways they are. This can be quite a disconcerting experience when he or she realizes that this is not the case.

The fifth person in our little gathering is centered in the throat chakra, located in the area of the vocal cords. This person will be highly creative, and depending upon the strength of his or her will, creations might come into reality very quickly. It is said in many alchemical traditions, that when an individual enters highly advanced evolutionary states, his or her words instantly move into manifestation.

Our sixth person is psychic and possesses the gifts of the inner senses due to the fact that the third eye is open. The third eye is an oddity in that the energy-point for this chakra is located in the forehead area just above the eyes. However, according to some yogic systems, the chakra is actually located between the eyes and back behind the bridge of the nose about an inch (two centimeters). Interestingly, this is an area of the brain where the pituitary gland (master regulator of the endocrine system) and the hypothalamus sit. The hypothalamus, the brain's information processing center, allows the brain to communicate with the rest of the body through what are called the hypothalamic pathways. The coincidental juxtaposition of this subtle energy center and such a major nerve plexus in the brain is most interesting.

The person with an opened third eye sees the world through the filter of psychic vision. He or she might easily see the auras or energy fields of those around them. He or she might even sense their desires or hear their thoughts. In some cases, he or she might even have prophetic vision in that he or she can sense the probable futures of those around them. Note that I say *probable* futures. I do not believe that the future is pre-determined. There are possibilities or choice points, and a psychic individual can sometimes sense these.

But no one can predict one's future with certainty because we all have the power of choice. And choice affects our destiny.

Finally, the seventh person in our group is centered in the crown chakra, which is located at the top of the head. For this person the world is seen as the play of Maya, illusion. Though in the world, he or she is detached from it. He or she senses the world in a way that is very difficult to imagine, for consciousness has become aware of itself. The mirror of awareness has been directed inward and the yogi or yogini has seen *the Self*, the one great being living and expressing through innumerable forms. While such a person may have compassion for the sufferings of others, he or she is not caught up in them. This person sees the world much like a shadow play. No longer affected by the dramas of life, he or she has become aware of the puppeteer and the light that casts the shadows. What was taken as reality is no longer perceived in this way. The yogi or yogini has attained enlightenment.

In reality, the situation is much more complex than this, since rarely are the chakras balanced sequentially. Thus it is possible for a person to have one or more chakras highly activated while residing in another in terms of their psychological motivations.

Many an unsuspecting disciple (chela) of a spiritual master has been disillusioned by this phenomenon. One is drawn by the obvious spiritual power and perhaps psychic abilities of a teacher, only to find out that he or she is power-hungry and manipulative. Or he or she might be promiscuous and not honoring of sexual boundaries. The conflict for a student caught in the unwanted sexual advances of a spiritual teacher can be psychologically quite difficult.

The problem is that the attainment of spiritual powers is not necessarily connected with psychological maturity. Just because a yogi or yogini has attained high states of *samadhi* and bliss does not mean that they have addressed their psychological issues. Thus someone who has unresolved issues in the lower three centers may misuse their spiritual powers.

You might, for instance, have a person who is a great teacher, but has not resolved his or her inherent psychological hostility; God help the student of such a teacher. Or you might encounter someone with extremely developed psychic abilities but with an unresolved need to manipulate others. Such a person might show all the signs of spirituality, but he or she will subtly, and perhaps not so subtly, use his or her psychic powers to sway you.

In many of these cases, the person is unconscious of his or her own psychological motivations. But just because something is unconscious does not mean it cannot do harm. In point of fact, our unconscious motivations often do more harm than those of which we are conscious. This is one reason I believe that persons undertaking the path of alchemy need to become cognizant of their own psychological history and motivations.

## Sekhem

As I mentioned earlier, the raising of the djed and the activation of the chakras takes tremendous energy. The energy that propels itself up the djed is nothing less than one's own life-force, called sekhem, or literally, "the power that makes things erect."

Sekhem is the hidden meaning behind obelisks. Obelisks are free-standing kinds of pillars except that they don't support anything, and they are pointed at the tip. They were erected all over Egypt, usually in honor of an important personage. However, they are essentially monuments to the vital power of sekhem. One of the primary tasks of the alchemist within the Egyptian system is to raise his or her excess life-force, or sekhem, up the djed. The net result of moving sekhem up the djed is that the seals or chakras become activated and strengthened. As each chakra is stimulated, latent areas of consciousness and awareness are opened.

It is important to understand that sekhem is intimately related to both one's life-force and one's sexuality. This power can be used to create a new being, as through the act of sex, or it can be used to create higher states of consciousness, as through the act of raising the djed. The primary power to accomplish both of these feats is the same. It is simply a matter of what is done with the energy that determines what is accomplished. To put this in its most simplistic terms: a major source of spiritual illumination within the Egyptian system of alchemy is transmuted sexuality.

## The Uraeus

When the energy of sekhem or transmuted life force pours into the head through the raising of the djed, there is a tremendous stimulation of the higher brain centers. This activation of these centers eventually generates what is called the Uraeus.

In sacred Egyptian art, one often sees important personages with a snake coming out of their foreheads. This serpent symbolically signifies that the person has attained the uraeus or has the authority granted by the uraeus. It often appears on the headdresses of gods and goddesses as well as royalty. I suspect the artistic use of the Uraeus eventually degenerated into a stylistic statement and the original spiritual intent was lost. However, its primary symbolic meaning is that of having attained an activation or *anointing* of the higher brain centers. This implied that such a person could see beyond the duality of the world, symbolized by another serpent form, that of Apophis. Unlike the serpent of the Uraeus, which is related to enlightenment,

Apophis represents the sine wave of all form, the dualistic play of opposite forces in creation. The gift of the Uraeus is a type of psychic vision (clairvoyance) that allows one to see beyond the veils of illusion (the play of dualistic opposites).

Activation of the Uraeus brings with it a whole host of non-ordinary awarenesses and abilities. From my own personal research I believe that, for one, it increases creativity and intelligence. For another, it stimulates some of the powers of consciousness or siddhis I mentioned earlier.

Once again, the changes created by alchemy can be tracked to changes in brain function. As yet, there are no studies on the specific brain changes created by the uraeus phenomenon but I suspect, based on personal observation, that they involve changes in neurotransmitters and increases in endorphin levels. Since the Uraeus is sensed in dream-like states of awareness, I also suspect increases in alpha and/or theta activity. Finally, I believe that there is a radical increase in non-dominant hemispheric functioning in those who experience this phenomenon. My reason for this is that in my own experiments with precursors to the Uraeus my sense of space became highly altered and there was a cessation of internal dialogue which would indicate a decrease of activity within the dominant (or talking) hemisphere.

It is not in the scope of this introduction to discuss the many interesting points regarding alchemy and brain physiology, but I will say this: the practices of internal alchemies, such as the Egyptian stream, create definite changes in brain function which, in turn, directly affect perception. By masterfully controlling these brain states through meditative practices, the alchemist is able to enter non-ordinary realms of awareness. And it is through these unusual states of inner attention that the practitioner is able affect the quantum realm (i.e., the Ka body and the Uraeus).

# Raising the Djed and
# the Myth of Horus

Through the power of intention (will), the alchemist eventually causes sekhem to move up the spine (the djed) and into the head centers creating, over time, the uraeus. As the electromagnetic force of sekhem moves upward through the chakras (seals) these centers are stimulated. This rising of sekhem up the djed is called raising the djed as I mentioned earlier. As the seven main seals (chakras) are activated through this process, the consciousness of the alchemist is radically transformed.

Symbolically, this movement of consciousness is mirrored in the story of *Horus*. There are two views of Horus. The first view holds Horus as an actual physical being who lived at the dawn of Egyptian history. The second view does not supplant the first view, but is more symbolic in nature. Whether Horus physically existed, we cannot say for sure. Legends and stories abound, as do the theories regarding the origins of his mother (Isis) and his father (Osiris). Some view these figures as aliens from another world, starseed, if you will. In this view, Isis and Osiris were geneticists and we are the descendants of this ancient science. Some starseed theorists even relate these figures to the early Sumerians. The most common view (and one that is generally accepted by academic Egyptologists) is that Isis and Osiris were divinities that existed within the living mythos of the time. They were, to use Jungian terms, archetypal realities within the collective unconscious of the ancient Egyptians.

From a purely practical standpoint in regards to alchemical practice, it does not matter if Horus physically existed or not. The story holds alchemical keys, which if understood, open up a wealth of understanding.

Horus is depicted as a hawk-headed man. As the son of Isis and Osiris, he symbolically represents the fusion of spirit and matter. In many ancient cultures, the feminine principle (Mother) was viewed as matter. Interestingly enough, our word matter derives from the Latin word mater, which means mother. In these early cultures, the male principle (Father) was viewed as spirit. Thus, at a symbolic level, Horus is a result of joining together spirit and matter.

Horus' journey to the High God Horus is allegorical to our own journey up the djed. In one form of the story, Horus must overcome evil by killing his uncle, Set, who murdered his father. The myth is very complex and has many versions. But for our purposes here, we will focus on one stage of the battle—the moment when Horus becomes the god Min.

# The God Min

In order to overcome Set, Horus must accumulate vast amounts of energy. At the alchemically symbolic level, the alchemist must rise above the lower three chakras, and this takes energy, a tremendous amount of energy. As anyone who has ever tried to rise above their own conditioning knows, the power of entropy is very strong. Entropy is the force that keeps things from moving. Psychologically it shows up as lethargy, a reluctance to make the efforts required to change a situation (evolve). Whether one is trying to stop a bad habit or activate the higher powers of consciousness does not matter. Entropy and lethargy become one's nemesis. To overcome this limiting factor in our psychological makeup requires a level of energy stronger than the force of entropy itself. This energy is in the form of sekhem, or "that which makes things erect."

In other words, Horus harnesses his procreative powers. This is symbolized by the god Min, who is shown with a large erection while holding a flail in one hand. The flail is often a piece of wood with leather strips tied to one end, and it is used to discipline a horse especially when riding a chariot. The *flail of Min* is never actually used. It is a symbol of intent, of purpose. This may be an unfortunate symbol for the modern mind since the flail carries intimations of self-abuse or harm. Nothing could be further from the intent of this symbol.

A charioteer managing a spirited horse needs to direct its attention in the direction desired. If he or she does not direct the steed, the horse will take off on its own. This can be both wasteful and dangerous. The flail allows the charioteer to get the horse's attention by whacking it on the rump. Now a sensitive equestrian knows that he or she does not need to hit the horse hard to get its attention. If rapport has been established between horse and man/woman, a slight movement of the flail is all that is needed. Thus the flail, in this sense, is a symbolic reminder to harness the procreative energies of sex.

Instead of sending his "seed" out into the world through the sexual act, Horus (as the god Min) harnesses this energy and sends it up the djed. As the energy makes its ascent into the higher brain centers, Horus is transformed by the power of the Uraeus into the High God Horus. He is no longer a god in potential; he has become a creator god in his own right. Then and only then is he able to defeat Set.

This depiction, to set things straight, is not a call to celibacy. The holding of the god Min's "seed" is symbolic and refers to the holding and transformation of subtle forces within the sexual fluids. It is these subtle forces that are cultivated and sent up the djed whether male or female.

In actuality, there is no need to refrain from the sex act in order to practice this form of alchemy. Indeed, as Magdalen discusses in the *Manuscript*, there are ways that the sex act can greatly empower the ascent of sekhem up the spine. For various historical reasons, too complex to go into here, the Church separated sex from spirit, but in the ancient Egyptian understanding, they were intimately connected.

# Misunderstandings Regarding the God Min

In the Middle Ages the flail was adopted by over-zealous monks in attempts to purge themselves of sin. The essential teaching behind the flail and the god Min had been lost. Instead of being viewed as a symbol for the attainment of god-like powers, the flail was used to inflict self-torture in sadomasochistic rituals of flagellation.

Mendicants would sit in their cells and lash themselves with flails to atone for their imagined sin. Perhaps they entered altered states of mind as a result of exhaustion and blood loss, but these macabre rituals had nothing to do with alchemy or the secrets of the great god Min.

But foolishness in regards to Min was not confined to the Middle Ages. At the turn of the last century, there was a tremendous interest among the Victorians in the lost secrets of Egypt. Egyptology was in its infancy, and many an adventurer trekked off for the deserts to discover the secrets of the Golden Age. To their horror, these stiff anal retentives discovered large statues of Min all over the place. And every one of them had a big, you-know-what. So distressed by these discoveries were they, some of the more shocked zealots cut off the offending organs. And reliefs of Min taken off to museums were, I am told, often mutilated. At the very least, a judiciously placed plaque would serve to hide the offending member from their more civilized countrymen.

The Victorians had missed the point, as had their predecessors in the Dark Ages. The ancient Egyptians were not glorifying sex. They were acknowledging it as a sacred act. It had its place, not just in the bedroom or in the bordellos and whorehouses, but in the temples, at the very center of their quest for the divine.

## Immortality

Ultimately the goal of Egyptian alchemy is immortality or, at the very least, an extension of the self after death. In this regard, there are two means available to the alchemist, one of them temporary and the other permanent.

In the first method, the energy-building practices are pursued until the Ka is virtually scintillating with energy and light. When death of the physical body (the khat) ensues, the alchemist shifts his or her attention into the Ka. Much previous experience in the *shifting of identification* insures that this process is accomplished with little effort. With the sense of self fully in the Ka, the alchemist, now an *energy-being*, is unaffected by death of the physical body. To him or her, it is like taking off an old suit of clothes.

The duration of the alchemist's existence as an energy-being depends upon how much energy was collected while alive. If the alchemist has learned to collect and conserve energy as an energy-being then the length of existence could be quite long. For whatever it is worth, I have met energy-beings who claimed to be thousands of years old.

In the second method, the energy building practices are pursued just as in the first way since charging of the Ka is vital to both methods. However, there are significant differences.

In this second path to immortality, the alchemist must align himself or herself with his or her Celestial Soul (*the BA*). This aspect of self is transcendent, outside of space and time. Some might refer to it as the Soul or High Self. But whatever one calls it, there is an alignment that takes place with the BA (the Celestial Soul) and the Ka through the djed, or sacred pathway of the chakras.

When this pathway is aligned with the BA, there is a great influx of spiritual energy into the Ka body. When this reaches a critical mass, the Ka ignites, as it were, with an *etheric fire*. This is sometimes called the *Golden Raiment* but was referred to by the ancient Egyptians as the *Sahu*. This body is immortal.

Just how an alignment with the BA or Celestial Soul creates such a metamorphosis of the Ka is a closely guarded secret. It involves the highest aspects of alchemy and is revealed to the Initiate when he or she is ready. This revelation may come directly from an embodied teacher, but more often it comes from an *Akul*, one who has attained the light body and who now lives in the realm of spirit. Sometimes this information is revealed directly from the BA to the alchemist.

In regards to survival after death, I should point out that many spiritual traditions say that there is a spark of consciousness that always survives death, regardless of the level of attainment. However, this spark does not hold the sense of personal identity in the ways of the Ka or Sahu. Thus, at death, one's personal sense of self, as well as the memory of personal history dissolves unless one of these subtle bodies has been stabilized.

## The Ammit

In addition to energy-building practices for the attainment of immortality (the Sahu), there must be a moral or ethical attitude toward one's life. One must learn the right use of energy (righteousness), and how to conduct oneself in relation to others. There is a real danger in the attainment of powers brought about through the practice of Egyptian alchemy. As one's consciousness becomes stronger, so does the ability to create manifestation of one's intentions. If an alchemist purposefully harms others in the course of his or her actions, he or she is in danger of being devoured. The sacred texts warn the alchemist of this dangerous passage through a very strange creature called the *ammit*—part crocodile, part lion and part hippopotamus. The ammit is usually shown with a representation of the djed, that depiction of the seven chakras or seals in ascending order, and sits with its reptilian snout resting ominously between the third and fourth chakra (the solar plexus and heart). This position symbolically refers to the place between power and love.

The ammit is sometimes referred to as the Great Devourer since those persons stuck in the lower three chakras will be devoured by their experiences. For instance, persons centered only in the first chakra will seek security above anything else. Those centered in the second seal will be obsessed with sex, and those in the third will be driven for power. If a person remains motivated solely by these energies without moving upward along the djed, he or she will eventually be consumed by them.

Persons engaged in the practice of alchemy can fall victim to their own misguided lusts for security, sex, and/or power. The seduction can be very strong, since the practices of alchemy build the magnetics of the Ka and desires are more quickly attained.

It is important to understand this clearly. The practices of Egyptian alchemy build the magnetic fields of the practitioner. By magnetic I do not mean the force of magnetics as in physics, though there is some relationship. Rather I mean a psycho-dynamic force that is magnetic-like in its properties. Persons with strong psycho-magnetic fields tend to draw to themselves the objects of their desires more easily than those with weak psycho-magnetic fields. Because the Ka-building practices greatly increase the psycho-magnetic force of the practitioner, he or she must be careful.

The ammit stands as a reminder of the passage from the lower three seals (chakras) into the heart. Those persons insisting on experiencing life from the lower chakras without passing into love will eventually be devoured by their desires in the lower three realms (the quest for security, sex, and power).

When someone passes through the initiatory gate of the fourth seal *(chakra)*, he or she will experience a spontaneous arising of agape (unconditional divine love). When one experiences the world from this place in consciousness, it is not possible to knowingly harm another person. Agape is all-inclusive. By nature it generates feelings of connectedness. Because the egoic-sense of *self* is expanded to include *others,* harming another person would be unthinkable.

But this sense of *harmlessness* is only present at the level of the heart. Persons coming solely from the lower three centers can easily manipulate and harm others in order to get their own selfish desires met. The ammit stands as a sobering reminder to those on the alchemical path. Those who insist upon living their lives without love will be devoured by their desires.

As if the scary prospect of being devoured by the ammit is not enough to temper the desires of an alchemist, there is another figure. This one stands on the other side of death.

## Maat

Maat is an important deity in the Egyptian pantheon having to do with the dead. *Maat* is often depicted with a scale. On one side is the heart of a person seeking entrance into the abode of heaven. On the other side of the scale is a feather. If the dead person's heart is as *light as a feather,* he or she is given entrance into spiritual paradise. If, however, the heart is weighted by regrets, guilt, and shame, the person is not given entrance and must wander through the underworld.

Symbolically, I think the figure of Maat is, as a friend of mine says, *a call to presence,* a reminder that what we do in this life will follow us into the next.

# Final Thoughts

The ancient Egyptian mentality is so far from our own, it is difficult to imagine what they really thought and felt. We have fragments of writings, a few sacred texts, and the myths of their gods and goddesses. Fortunately, we have also inherited some of their alchemical secrets, but much of that glorious civilization is lost to us. The chasm in time is too large.

By the time Magdalen had trained in the temples of Isis, Egypt had fallen, its Golden Age a long-lost glimmer. But enough of the ancient alchemical knowledge had survived along with an understanding of how to use it. By the last century B.C., the Isis cult and the secrets of sexual alchemy had spread throughout much of the ancient world.

Undoubtedly, as with all things, each culture introduced its own understandings and interpretations into the Isis mythos. Over time, churches were built upon the ruins of temples and the spiritual practices of that earliest time were often modified or forgotten. But anyone seriously looking beneath the surface of the alchemical traditions of the world can often find the mark of Isis and the alchemy of ancient Egypt.

We stand now, two thousand years more distant than did the Magdalen from the alchemists of that ancient time. For those of us working with this alchemical system, the task is clear. We cannot relive the past. For one thing, we can never truly know it. We must learn what we can from the fragments that have been left behind. We must practice the ancient alchemy of transformation as we understand it, to see where it will take us. And we must forge a new alchemical way for this time.

May the Akul, the ancient ones who have attained the Sahu, help us in our quest.

May the light of illumination guide us through our own darkness.

# A Brief
# Comparative of Internal
# Alchemies

*A primary task of Egyptian Alchemy as taught by the
Magdalen is to strengthen the Ka body. This is done
through states of high ecstasy since ecstasy and bliss
strengthen the Ka. There are two primary paths that can be
taken in this regard. For those in sacred relationship exploring the Sex Magic of Isis, the ecstasy naturally arises during
love making. But for those engaged in the solitary path
and the Alchemies of Horus, the ecstasy is self-generated.*

*For those on both the solitary and dyadic path, I
believe this section will prove invaluable by placing
the* Manuscript *within the context of other alchemical
systems. I also feel that those working with other systems of internal alchemy may find the information
below helpful in placing their own practices in relation
to the* Manuscript.

—A Personal Note from Tom

This section explores comparisons between three
of the four major alchemical systems: *Tantric
Yoga, Taoism* and *Tibetan Buddhist Tantra.*
Egyptian alchemy was presented in the previous chapter, and readers will undoubtedly recognize some common elements between the Egyptian system and the
other three lineages discussed in this section. Those
already familiar with these systems of alchemy have,
no doubt, recognized the unusual position taken by the
*Manuscript* in regards to the sex act. As a student of

comparative alchemies and mystical traditions, this
was one of the first things that struck me about the
Magdalen's material.

If I may summarize these differences, I would say that
the system introduced by the Magdalen is archetypally
female-based. According to the Magdalen, the female
holds within her nature the secrets of creation.

Magdalen goes on to mention how she was trained in
the Alchemies of Horus and how to raise the serpents
through meditative powers. But in the presence of
Yeshua and especially during their love-making, the
Alchemies naturally presented themselves. In other
words, they engaged without her having to do anything.

She speaks at great length about how the female
must feel safe and appreciated in relationship with her
Beloved. Then and only then can the alchemy of transformation she calls the Sex Magic of Isis occur. If these
elements (safety and appreciation) are in place within
the relationship, the female can *let go* and allow the feminine mysteries to express themselves through her. When
this occurs during love-making there is often a shuddering in the female. If she allows this shaking to proceed, it
will take her deeper into the mysteries.

If the male has trained himself to *nest* within the vibrational energies released by his partner then both he and
his Beloved can strengthen their Ka bodies (one of the
primary goals of this system).

The central place of the female in this alchemical system is strikingly different from many other alchemical
streams.

In many regards the main alchemical systems of the
world are male-biased. For instance, in Taoist literature
there are fewer written instructions for females than for
males. Even though Taoism is considered by some to be
matrilineal, in practice (at least in the last few hundred
years) most of the emphasis was upon male practitioners. There were, no doubt, very developed female sages
in China, but their presence is not generally represented

in Taoist alchemical treatises (with some notable exceptions). In fact, some Taoists practicing *Dual Cultivation* (the sex practices of Taoism), in previous centuries, viewed women as mere containers of *chi*. These unscrupulous practitioners would engage in the sex act solely for the purpose of extracting the female's excess chi with little regard for her comfort or safety.

In Tibetan Buddhism, although the feminine principle is deeply honored, in practice women are often relegated to lesser places of power and importance. One of the great Bodhisattvas of Tibetan Buddhism is Tara, a woman who historically lived in the general area of Tibet. When she attained illumination, legend has it that a group of lamas set out to find the new light, noting that an enlightened being had entered the world. Upon tracking the light to her village they were dismayed to discover that she was a woman. They reputedly said to her, "Now that you have attained illumination, you can be reborn as a man." To which she replied, "I will remain forever in the form of a female." To this day she resides as a feminine presence in a subtle realm of being the Tibetans call the *Samboghaya*, the realm of pure light and sound. She is known as the Swift Protectoress and is a powerful and beneficent being. Yet that attitude of inherent male superiority shows up again and again in not only certain aspects of Tibetan Buddhism but through much of Buddhism in general.

A cursory look at the history of Christianity reveals patriarchal attempts at the disenfranchisement of women within the Church and within its historical documents. In the Dark Ages, the Church formulated the Nicene Council in an attempt to edit the numerous Gospels and sacred writings of the early Church. Under the orders of the Roman ruler, Constantine, the Council was charged with choosing which of the many scriptures would become part of the New Testament. The result was that the Council threw out many of the sacred texts of the time, choosing only those that furthered their own ends.

The early mystical vision of the Christians had been shaped into the territorial and political desires of the Church and State. And in the process, many of the writings honoring the feminine were declared a heresy and the Holy Church of Rome began its long campaign to disempower women. During the Middle Ages and especially during the Holy Inquisition, the Church routinely burned women suspected of being witches. Often these women were just herbalists and healers. Indeed, any woman standing up to the patriarchal power of the Church risked a terrible death.

The disenfranchisement of women by the Church continues to this day, although it is certainly more subtle than during the Middle Ages.

I believe that religion and culture are an intimately woven tapestry. The threads of religious belief pass into the culture and the attitudes of a culture get sewn into the fabric of its religion. They are in many ways, inseparable.

So too, the mystical traditions and alchemical practices born out of religious insight, which are supposed to be above earthly issues, are invariably affected by cultural assumptions as well. Thus, one can see the threads of male dominance in the very fabric of mystical and alchemical systems throughout the world.

As a document purporting to impart an alchemical system, the *Manuscript* is unique in that its methods are steeped in the feminine mysteries. Perhaps this is because it shares roots with the Isis cults of ancient Egypt.

Some of the alchemical presuppositions of the *Manuscript* are in alignment with the major alchemical schools or lineages of the world. However, some of its views differ quite radically from other alchemical systems.

For example, the *Manuscript* holds the relationship between sexual partners in high regard. The sex act is used to activate certain alchemies within the initiates, but the emotional relationship between the male and female is viewed as the sacred foundation for these alchemies.

For another, the female is seen as holding, within her nature, certain alchemical keys for transformation. These keys cannot be forced, but are accessed only when there is safety and love in a relationship. This approach makes the *Manuscript* unique within other alchemical systems.

Believing as I do in the power of synergy, I feel that those undertaking personal experiments with the Magdalen material would do well to become aware of the other major alchemical schools accessible at this time. In other words, place the *Manuscript* in context to other internally based alchemical systems.

For this reason, I have presented a brief survey of three other major alchemical streams in regards to the sexual practices of internal alchemy. I present this in hopes that it will provide interested readers with a broader context to understand the implications of the *Manuscript* and to better utilize the practices to their benefit.

# Tantric Yoga

Tantric yoga is an ancient system of personal transformation that uses sexual energies to develop spiritual illumination. Its roots reach back thousands of years into India's past, and its goals are nothing short of divine transformation. Under the spell of Tantra, a man becomes transformed into a god while his consort is likewise transformed into a goddess. Tantra calls the divine into this world through temporary embodiment in its *tantrikas* (those who practice Tantra). And it is this potent joining of the divine and the human worlds that make this type of yoga so powerful.

This kind of yoga demands arduous training and is fraught with danger. Unless the energies of sex are mastered appropriately, one will not attain the promised liberation of consciousness. One will, instead, be deluded by the heat of one's own passions. Indeed, there are ancient cautions regarding this path of yoga. It is not suitable for everyone. Only those who can enter the fires of sexual passion with sobriety and detachment should attempt it. This type of Tantra is a far cry from the weekend Tantric workshops so popular in the West.

Tantra is a term that means energy practices, and it can be applied either to sexual practices or, as we will see in the section on Buddhist alchemy, it can refer to the energy practices of consciousness itself, as in meditation.

# Samadhi

The central piece critical to most alchemical yogas, like Tantra, is the attainment of samadhi. By alchemical yogas I mean those yogic systems that work with the transformation of consciousness through alchemical means. Not all yogas do this. For instance, Tantric Yoga is an alchemical system in that the subtle energies of sex are transformed through alchemical meditation. Raja Yoga, on the other hand, is a philosophical pursuit that may lead to a type of enlightenment but does not impart alchemical methods along the way.

The attainment of samadhi, or *inner attention,* allows the yogi or yogini to explore his or her inner worlds. During successful meditation practice, the mind turns away from the physical senses. One focuses, instead, upon consciousness (*chitta*) itself.

There are innumerable ways to attain samadhi, some of them involving concentration, mantras (words of power), yantras (visual geometries), and pranayama (breath control), to name a few.

There are varying degrees of samadhi, depending upon the depth and the phenomena that arise within the mind. In some states of samadhi, for instance, there is simply a deep sense of calm and inner peace. The yogi or yogini in such meditative states might also see lights in his or her inner mind, or experience other sensory displays, seemingly without stimulation, in other words, arising spontaneously from the mind.

In deeper states of samadhi, the sense of a separate self may altogether disappear and be replaced by an awareness of pure being (*sat*) without thought. As the yogi or yogini enters these deeper states of samadhi there is often an arising of bliss or ecstasy since the nature of consciousness is bliss (*ananda*).

## Kumbhaka and the Suspension of Breathing

As the yogi or yogini enters these deeper samadhis, there is a spontaneous retention of breath, called *kumbhaka*. In this fascinating interplay between body and mind, the breath is suspended. And as long as the yogi or yogini stays in the deeper states of samadhi, there is no need to breathe. When the awareness of the yogi or yogini shifts out of samadhi, however, into an awareness of the physical senses, the body spontaneously takes a breath. There are well-documented cases of samadhis lasting several hours or days with its attendant suspension of breath.

The phenomenon of kumbhaka is remarkably similar to the effects of Taoist *stillness-practices* in which the practitioner enters a timeless state of mind and the breath becomes very shallow or stops altogether. When we get to the section on Taoism, I will talk about a personally striking experience with a stillness-practice, so I won't go into it here. But I will say that every one of the alchemical streams has its own methods for entering stillness of mind. This is due to the simple fact that without stillness of mind, many inner alchemical reactions simply will not take place.

The practice of meditation and the entering into samadhi bring with them many developments of the psyche. One of these is a greater sensitivity to and awareness of subtle energies. This development of sensitivity is crucial for the alchemist to develop, since one cannot contain (in the alchemical container of awareness) what one is unaware of.

## Alterations in Time and Space

Next, we come to a common element experienced by all alchemists, regardless of the stream in which they are practicing— *the alteration of perceived time and space.*

While in samadhi, yogis and yoginis experience a powerful alteration in their sense of both time and space. I believe this is due to radical shifts in brain function (meditative states greatly increase alpha and/or theta activity). In these relaxed brain states, time seems more fluid and space often takes on strange attributes.

What might last an hour in linear time may be experienced as lasting for eons or for just a moment. Yogis and yoginis also report space being affected. They might experience themselves as very large, like the size of a galaxy, or very small, like the size of an atom. They might feel as if they are spinning or floating. These types of phenomena are, by the way, reported by practitioners of all the alchemical streams.

## The Three Gunas

There is another reason meditation and the attainment of samadhi is crucial to the practice of alchemical yogas (including Tantra). I call them the three stooges, but the sacred writings of India call them the three *gunas.*

The three gunas are sub-atomic forces responsible, according to yogic philosophy, for everything that exists in creation. They are symbolically represented by the Hindu trinity of Brahma, Vishnu, and Shiva. The first of these forces is called *raja* (meaning king) and is responsible for starting an action. It is associated with the god *Brahma,* who created the universe by uttering the sound Om. His consort is the goddess *Saraswati,* who is associated with the arts and with science.

The second of these forces is called *sattva* and sustains an action. It is associated with the god *Vishnu,* who is responsible for sustaining creation. His consort, or female counterpart, is *Lakshami,* who bestows wealth and beauty.

The last of the gunas is *tamas.* This rather unfashionable guna is responsible for ending an action. It is associated with *Shiva,* the Lord of Death. Shiva is also the Lord and Protector of yogis and yoginis. His consort is *Parvati,* the cosmic Mother and mother of *Ganesha,* the Destroyer of Obstacles.

When I talk about tamas in workshops, I mention that people are sometimes afraid of Shiva, frightened by endings. But without destruction there can be no creation. I point out that the three gunas operate at all levels of creation, including our breath. The impulse to take a breath is raja or Brahma. The act of inhaling is sattva or Vishnu, and the act of exhaling is tamas or Shiva. I then tell them to be Brahma by starting to take an inhale, and then I tell them to be Vishnu as they continue the inhale. But then I tell them to avoid becoming Shiva. Whatever they do, don't destroy the breath. Well, everyone usually starts laughing at the ludicrousness of my suggestion. Our body wisdom understands the need for endings, even if our minds do not.

According to one of the earliest sacred texts of India, the *Bhagavad-Gita,* the three gunas are responsible for *maya* (illusion). Yogic philosophy states that you and I are deluded. We believe ourselves to be separate beings, but in point of fact, there is only one fundamental Consciousness expressing itself through innumerable forms. Your form is only one of them, as is mine. We tend to take ourselves seriously and get upset if someone or something impinges on our little island of self. But all of this is the play of maya. There is no *you* and there is no *me*; there is only the play (*lila*) of cosmic forces.

The yogi or yogini who has attained this detached state of being is said to have attained God Realization or Unity Consciousness. But this is not just a mental attainment. It is a perceptual attainment as well. One who has attained this unified state of consciousness is no longer deluded by the illusion of maya. He or she sees through the smoke and mirrors of maya to the Self behind all things. And how is this done, you might ask? Well... we do this by getting the three stooges to go to sleep. To be more yogically correct, we might say by getting the gunas to settle into a state of quiescence.

If we enter into samadhi deeply enough, the activity of the gunas within our minds calms down. Discursive self-talk slows down and then stops altogether. Fantasies stop being generated from the deeper layers of mind, and we enter a state of deep quiescence. The three stooges have gone to sleep. Then and only then, can we catch a glimpse of our deepest innate consciousness—the *Self*.

By entering and re-entering meditation, over a long period of time, we can attain varying states of samadhi. If we enter the deepest states enough, our minds will be trained to see past the smoke screen of creation. But until we reach this lofty state of mind we will continue to experience ourselves as separate from each other, victims to the play of maya.

To bring us back full circle, the task of yogic meditation is to enter into deeper and deeper states of samadhi. As we re-experience this liberating awareness over and over again, we slip through the knot of our desires and are freed from the power of maya.

It takes a certain kind of spiritual development to even consider the need for such a radical action. Most people are quite content to pursue their own desires and are simply not interested in seeing behind the illusion.

It is crucial to understand that all perception is relative—relative to the state of the perceiver. The state of mind of a yogi or yogini who has successfully attained an awareness of the Self is very different from the state of mind of someone caught up in the everyday drama of his or her life. Maya is like a television playing a soap opera. Deluded, we continue to watch the show, convinced that it is our lives being played out. The successful yogi or yogini is one who has seen that it is just a show, enters the room, and turns off the TV.

In Tantric yoga the yogi or yogini harnesses the power of sexuality to leap through the illusion of maya, to turn off the TV of limited-mind, if you will.

But without the detached awareness of samadhi, a tantrika (someone who practices Tantric Yoga) can easily be overtaken by passions that arise through sexual contact. The goal of Tantra is a type of meditation, not hedonism. The tantrika uses sensations that arise during ritualistic sex as objects of meditation. Without being able to control their passions, tantrikas will not be able to hold the alchemical container of their awareness.

Another reason for training in samadhi is that the tantrikas must be able to still the mind enough during the sexual act to directly experience their sensory pleasures as the play or interaction of the three gunas. This takes a very sophisticated level of sensitivity, to say the least. And this level of subtle perception can only be attained through experience with samadhic states of awareness, as in meditation.

## Sexual Bliss

Let me be specific here. In the experience of sex the sensations of pleasure naturally arise. For most of us this is enough, but not so for the tantrika. He or she is not only entering the sexual experience for pleasure, but also as a means to achieve greater spiritual insight and awareness. A side-effect of Tantra is that pleasure states far exceed normal kinds of sex, but this is not the goal.

For the tantrika, the sensations of foreplay are experienced on many levels. First of all, the actual physical sensations and the release of endorphins occur as they do with most of us. But in addition, due to the mental training of a yogi or yogini, the sense of pleasure is experienced against a backdrop of mental stillness or quiescence. Discursive thought has stopped. Fantasies cease to be generated by the subconscious, and the practitioner experiences the arising of pleasure in its most subtle aspects. At its subtlest level, the practitioner senses the interaction of the three gunas as the creators of his or her sensory delight. At these very subtle levels of awareness, the slightest touch to a Tantric yogi or yogini can set off extraordinary cascades of pleasure and bliss.

As the brain secretes pleasure hormones such as endorphins and other brain chemicals induced through Tantric practice, the tantrikas become highly altered. They become intoxicated with bliss, but this bliss is not just from the sex act. It comes from making contact with *the Self*, the one behind the one who is experiencing the moment. It is the joining of these two blisses that makes Tantra so powerful. And what are these two blisses? They are the bliss of sexual touch and sexual union joined with the bliss of the Self, which is, by its nature, blissful without the need for another.

The methods of Tantric union are quite varied, but most of them require the yogi to hold his seed (avoiding ejaculation) as long as possible. This is because the cycles of arousal, sexual tension, and the dissolving of sexual tension without ejaculation propel both the yogi and yogini into powerful altered states of consciousness. It is thus not unusual for a yogi to make love with his yogini for several hours at a time. The goal of Tantra, unlike the act of sex

itself, is not to have an orgasm, per se, but to experience
the vast multidimensionality of consciousness itself.

# Ojas

There is another aspect to Tantra that I should
explain. It has to do with the transformation of sexual
essence into enlightenment. This goal of turning sexual
energy into illumination has some very strong correla-
tions to elements of both ancient Egyptian and Taoist
alchemies. In order to explain this, however, I need to
discuss yogic anatomy.

According to Tantra, there is an energy point near the
top and somewhat to the back of the head. It is generally
in the area where the hair grows out from its whorl and
some males of certain Hindu lineages shave their heads
except for a small circle of hair around this area. It is
called the *bindu* and it is a kind of energy transformer
that collects the higher frequencies available to the practitioner. Yogis would say that it is where spirit begins its
descent into matter.

This energy then steps down in frequency (slows its
speed of vibration) as it moves down towards the mulad-
hara (first chakra). Here it reaches its densest state and
becomes the sexual fluids of the individual. According to
this view, a man's semen and a woman's eggs carry not
only their genetic information but also hold the essence
of their spirituality as well.

As the male yogi practices alchemical yoga, especially in Tantra, the energetic essence of his semen, as
opposed to the semen itself, moves upward into the
higher brain centers. This spiritual process is, in many
regards, the opposite of the bindu phenomenon in
which the spiritual energy of the yogi condenses into
his sexual fluids. In this case, the energetic essences of
the male's sperm are transmuted into higher vibrational

energies, called *ojas*. The female yogini has a similar process that arises in herself.

Ojas has very potent effects of consciousness. Yogis and yoginis who successfully accomplish this alchemical distillation universally report radical changes in perception. Their sense of *inner light* is dramatically increased, and there is an increase in spiritual insight. These changes are due, no doubt, to complex alterations in brain chemistry.

## Entering the Mythic Realm: Becoming Divinity

Tantric yogis and yoginis go through elaborate preparation for tantric union, including ritualistic bathing, fasting and meditation. The space for the actual Tantra is adorned with things of beauty—flowers, fruit, and assorted foods as well as beverages believed to have aphrodisiac properties.

A crucial part of advanced tantric union is the transformation of the yogini into an embodiment of a goddess and the transformation of the male into an embodiment of a god. The deities used for this transformation vary according to the lineage that is being practiced. And the methods of metamorphosis are closely guarded. Many of them involve the use of specific *mantras* (words of power) that hold the vibratory essence of the deity being called upon as well as *yantras* (geometric patterns) also related to the deity.

In addition, the transformation is aided by complex visualizations and occasionally, though not always, through the use of psychoactive plants. Some lineages of Tantra forbid the use of such drugs, since their use during Tantric rituals can be dangerous.

Finally, before making love, both tantrikas envision themselves to be divine beings. Nothing less than full embodiment of the chosen deities will suffice. At some point, a successful tantric ritual demands that the yogi and yogini be transformed. The change is not imaginary, but is real, as real as the mythic entering this realm can be. Thus as the two tantrikas enter into the inner mysteries of Tantra they are, for all intents and purposes, making love, not with a mortal but with a divine being.

This mythic aspect has immense consequences in terms of its transformational effects. It is a key component in advanced Tantric ritual. And those who practice Tantra without this component have missed the kernel of the mystery.

# Taoism

There were two primary streams of philosophical thought in ancient China—those of Confuscianism and Taoism. Confuscianism was pragmatic and focused upon one's position in, and one's responsibilities to family and state. Taoism, on the other hand, was largely mystical, and was concerned with such things as one's relationship to the cosmos and the means to extend one's life for the purpose of spiritual illumination.

The foundation of Taoism is based upon an abstract concept known as the *Tao*. This ephemeral field of intelligence is said to be responsible for the entire universe. It continually emanates energy but is untouched by its creations. According to Taoism, mankind is blessed due to the fact that his/her deepest nature allows him/her to make direct contact with *the source of all things*. Taoist alchemy is fundamentally a means to make contact with one's deeper nature, thereby giving access to the Tao itself. Such contact is highly transformational. Those sages who accomplished this feat attained almost mythical stature, due, no doubt, to their exhibiting the powers of consciousness (siddhis) mentioned in the last chapter.

In order to comprehend Taoist alchemy, we must come to an understanding of a subtle force called *chi*. From the immense mystery of the Tao, which creates all worlds but is untouched by them, there is an eternal flow of this vital force (chi).

There are many types of chi. There is, for instance, a vital force flowing out of quasars and stars, though this is quite different in quality from the chi created by a stream. When most people think about chi, they usually think about the subtle life force in air. This type of chi is most concentrated in natural areas, away from cities. This kind of vital force is strongest in large areas of tree growth, by lakes, rivers, and streams as well as by larger bodies of water like oceans. Some individuals have speculated that this type of chi is related to negative ions and there is some evidence that this is so. But there are other types of chi as well—more subtle, more refined types of chi, and this is one of the focuses of advanced Taoist alchemy.

Traditionally, Taoist sages spent much of their time as hermits in nature. In later periods, groups of men or women would form communities to pursue their alchemical search with others. But almost always, these Taoist abodes were far from cities. They were usually located in places where the chi was especially strong, often in areas designated as *Dragon Points*.

Dragon Points are places of convergence where one form of *chi* meets another. They are most dramatically seen in mountain ranges. When two ridges meet, there is often a trench or a gorge that flows down the sides of the mountains. As *celestial chi* (the type of chi generated in the sky), flows downward, it meets the *terrestrial chi* of the mountain at the point between the ridges. This is called a *Dragon Point*.

Where two streams or rivers converge, there is a detectable increase of chi, and this too, is called a Dragon Point. Taoist sages would search for these places and put their abodes either in the Dragon Point itself, or nearby. This made their alchemical work easier since there was a ready abundance of chi that they could draw upon in their practices.

## Thought, Time, and Breath

As with Tantric yoga, the Taoist alchemist must train the mind to enter prolonged states of stillness. This quiescence of mind is crucial, since the Tao can only be experienced in mental silence. Furthermore many of the alchemical trans-formations in Taoist alchemy require a silent mind as well.

There are many classes of stillness practices, some of them involving movement, such as T'ai chi and others involving sitting meditation, such as the *Celestial Gate,* which I will discuss to some extent in a moment.

In these stillness practices, the mind is eventually led to a state of deep quietude. In actual practice, especially at the beginning, there may be a flurry of mental activity. Thoughts come and go, sometimes in a torrent, sometimes in a trickle. Eventually the practi-tioner notices that the speed of his or her thought seems to be slowing down. There seems to be more space between thoughts, and at some point they stop altogether, if only briefly.

The practitioner also notices that the breath changes during these states. There is a tendency for the breath to slow down as thought slows down. And when there is no thought there is often no breath, or it is very shallow. This is significant for several reasons.

From a neurological standpoint, we could say that this is because the brain waves of the practitioner are in the lower states of alpha and/or theta where the breath naturally gets slower. Research on meditation has noted, by the way, that these states also produce a decrease in muscle tension, heart rate, blood pressure, and respira-tion, all of which are quite positive in their stress-reducing effects. In fact, studies have shown that those who practice forms of meditation that produce these effects, as in the Taoist stillness practices, are generally less stressed than their counterparts who do not meditate.

Several years ago, about an hour before twilight, I chose to do a stillness practice known as the Celestial Gate (sometimes referred to as Heaven's Gate) in a park. As twilight descended around me I was still doing the practice, and noticed that my breathing had stopped. Not only this, but thought seemed to be arrested. My mind was clear and as calm as the surface of a tranquil lake. But most impressive to me, in the moment, was that time also seemed to have stopped, and I was suspended in a timeless dimension of mind.

I decided to walk back to my car as it was getting dark, and the trip took me twenty minutes or so. I noted that the impulse to go back to the car came as a sensation, as if it had come from deep within my body, and not as a thought. I did not think—"Now I need to get back to the car." This non-speaking state of mind seemed oddly amusing to me at the time. During my saunter, I noticed that my breath was very shallow even though the trail back to the car was over hilly terrain. That timeless feeling was still very strong and I seemed to move over the hills with little effort.

Ironically, when I saw my car in the parking lot I remembered an appointment later that evening, and I spontaneously took a deep breath. My breath had returned to normal and that feeling of timelessness vanished. I was firmly rooted back in time.

There is a fascinating relationship between the perception of timelessness and the cessation of breath. In yoga, you may recall, the cessation of breath is called kumbhaka. In Taoist meditation practice, this suspension of the breath is often encountered as well, especially when entering the deeper states of mental quiescence.

Interestingly, the idea of breath suspension can be found within Egyptian alchemy in the concept of *ankh*.

The ankh, sometimes called the Egyptian Cross, consists of three main parts—the *cross* itself, representing matter, the *shen* loop representing spirit, and the *shen knot* which represents the breath. As long as we are breathing, our spirit is bound to the matter of our bodies, our embodiments. However, when the shen knot loosens, the breath stops or gets very shallow, and we can, in that moment, enter timelessness. Once again, we see a central concept in one alchemical system repeated in other alchemical traditions. I do think it fascinating that the Taoist word for spirit (shen) is the same as the Egyptian (shen). I do not know if it is simply a coincidence of translation or if the terms really were the same. Nevertheless, it is quite interesting.

But back to the paradoxes of time, thought, and breath. As a psychotherapist who often worked in the area of psychoneuroimmunology (how our thoughts and feelings affect immunity), I find the time paradox also intriguing from the vantage point of health.

A study of patients admitted to an emergency room due to cardiac arrest reveals some fascinating information about the interplay between body and mind. During recovery, these patients were asked some questions about their perception of time. Based on their responses, researchers could predict who would recover and who would die from another heart attack. Those patients who said that they were letting things go to take care of themselves and who reported feeling that there would be more than enough time to do what needed to be done were more likely to recover and avoid a second heart attack. Those patients, however, who stated that they were under tremendous pressure to do what had been left undone and who felt that they were running out of time invariably suffered a higher incidence of death due to a second cardiac arrest.

None of this would come as a surprise to a Taoist sage. From the standpoint of Taoism, our modern time-crunch world is disturbing to both health and spiritual attainment.

We need to bring our time-bound minds back to tranquility on a regular basis or suffer the ill effects of our modern age.

I have taught a simple form of a Taoist stillness practice to hundreds if not thousands of people by now. Everyone has expressed a deep appreciation for a method of meditation that is so quick and easy to enter into. Those who have never been able to meditate due to continual thought (inner dialogue) are especially appreciative of this method since thought is not a hindrance to the practice.

I think this meditation is so effective I have included a brief description of how to do it below. If you aren't interested in experiencing this for yourself, just skip it and go to the next part.

## The Celestial Gate Meditation

The Celestial Gate Meditation practice is based on Dragon Points. Dragon Points, as I mentioned earlier, are places of convergence where one form of chi meets another.

There are several Dragon Points within the human body. The Celestial Gate is just one of these, and happens to be a place where *heavenly chi* (a very subtle form of chi) flows into the body and meets the *terrestrial (or earth) chi* of the body itself. Thus this place is an energetically *charged area,* and Taoist sages discovered a long time ago how to take advantage of it.

Sit comfortably and close your eyes. You can lie down if you wish, but this makes some people go to sleep. For a moment, just notice your breath. Don't change it in any way; just watch it. Notice the rhythm and the depth of your breath. Then after a moment become aware of the space about an inch behind the bridge of the nose. Imagine that there is an opening about one inch square in this area. This is the Celestial Gate. All you do is focus on it.

Do not concentrate on it. Just be aware of it. If you are having thoughts or fantasies, this is not a problem. Let them continue on their merry way. Just let some part of your attention be on the opening. You can think all you want about anything you want and the practice will still work, so long as some part of your attention is on the Celestial Gate (the opening).

As you continue to focus at the gate, you will notice that thoughts seem to slow down. There will seem to be more spaces between the thoughts or fantasies. And eventually they will stop altogether, if only temporarily. It is during these moments that you might find that your breath has stopped or has become very shallow. This is natural and is, in fact, a sign that you are entering the deeper states of stillness. It is in these deepest states of quiescence, where there is no-breath and no-thought that contact with the Tao takes place.

Doing it for about five minutes will usually give you a clear sense of how this practice alters awareness. Eventually you can extend the period of time for deeper experiences.

Don't let the simplicity of this meditation fool you. It is a profound stillness practice that will lead you directly to the Tao itself. Gently extend the periods of stillness so that you become acquainted with and comfortable with these deep places of quiet. As you explore your own inner worlds, you might eventually encounter celestial beings who may grace you with their guidance and instruction.

In Taoism, the deepest secrets are revealed only by the Tao itself. You cannot find these truths written in books, for it is forbidden to write about them. Thus, meditations like the Celestial Gate are like cosmic keys. Like keys, however, you must turn them to open the lock. If you wish to experience the mysteries of the Tao for yourself and not just read about them, you must turn the key.

## Cultivation of Chi

As with the Tantric yogi or yogini who attains samadhi, a Taoist practitioner will become aware of ever more subtle levels of perception. This subtlety of perception allows the Taoist to sense the flow of chi directly and to draw it into the body (called *collecting)* for the purpose of alchemical transformation (called *cultivation*).

With a heightened sensitivity to chi, a Taoist alchemist undertakes several things. First of all, he or she collects chi throughout the day, drawing this vital force into the body to strengthen organs and systems. There are many forms by which this is done. Chi Gong masters from China have recently started teaching in the West, and this is one form of chi collecting and cultivation. But there are other forms as well.

Depending upon the school and methods used, most Taoists eventually turn their attention to the chi *body.* This is the same as the etheric body of the yogis or the Ka body of the Egyptians. And like the aforementioned bodies, the chi *body* is the same shape as the physical body. It interpenetrates the physical body and there is no part of the physical body that is not within the chi body.

The development of the chi body is a crucial element in many forms of Taoist alchemy. Part of the reason for this is that it (a potent chi body) lays the foundation for more advanced practices. If either the physical body or the chi body is depleted, certain alchemical processes cannot be undertaken. And strengthening of the chi body is crucial for the attainment of Immortality.

One of the more interesting ways of cultivating chi, and thereby strengthening the chi body, involves what the Taoists call the *elixir fields.* These energetic reservoirs of chi are in three areas of the chi body itself. When they are fully charged with chi, they emit an energy that is called an *elixir* due to its strengthening effects.

The *first elixir field* is in the area of the lower organs, from the diaphragm down to the pelvic floor. This elixir field strengthens the lower visceral organs. The *second elixir field* is in the area of the upper organs of the torso, from the diaphragm up to the top of the lungs. This elixir field strengthens the lungs and heart as well as the thymus gland, one of the major sites of the immune system. The *third elixir field* is in the head and strengthens neurological function.

Certain forms of Taoist alchemy draw chi into these areas (collecting) and then circulate the chi through the corresponding organs and up towards the head (cultivation). As the chi is refined and drawn to the next elixir field, the organs within that field are strengthened and the circulating chi is refined.

The ancient Taoists also explored the subtle energy pathways of the body and mapped them out with considerable detail. The *meridians* used in acupuncture were discovered and described by the Taoists. They are similar to the *nadis* of Yoga, and scientific research on the meridians, most notably in Japan, has demonstrated that they are an energetic phenomenon.

In addition to the meridians, the Taoists described a pathway that became crucial to certain types of alchemy; they called it the *microcosmic orbit.* This pathway circulates chi from the perineum up the spine into the head and then down the front of the body back down to the perineum. As the microcosmic orbit makes its way through the chi body, it passes through the three elixir fields. By moving *chi* through the microcosmic orbit the practitioner stimulates the higher brain centers, and greatly refines the quality of the circulating chi. The refinement of chi is crucial in Taoist Alchemy since it is only through refined chi that one can enter shen, or the spirit world. It is also said in the more esoteric schools of Taoism that practicing the microcosmic orbit dissolves negative karmas (negative effects arising from past actions).

## Sexual Essence into Spirit: Jing and Shen

If we look at the transformation of consciousness through Taoist metaphor, we could say the task is that of changing water into mist. The energy of embodied life is refined through alchemical processes to the point that it becomes like mist. When one has attained this highly refined state, one's essence is now more spirit than that of man or woman. And the key to this remarkable transformation from a biological into a spiritual being begins with sex.

The transformation of sexual essence into spirit is a key component of many types of Taoism. In Taoism, the male's sexual essence is called *jing*. One's spiritual nature is called *shen*. By drawing the sexual energy of jing up the spine through the microcosmic orbit, it is refined and eventually becomes shen. This movement of chi up the spine is, of course, reminiscent of the raising of the djed in Egyptian alchemy as well as the concept of the sushumna or central pathway of the chakras in Yoga. I have not read any existing traditional Taoist writings for women in regards to the transformation of their sexual essence into shen (spirit). This does not mean, of course, that such writings don't exist, just that I haven't seen them. Nevertheless, I believe the process is similar to that of the male in many ways.

As in nature, there is always more than one way to accomplish a task. And the transformation of one's sexual essence into spiritual illumination (shen) is no exception. In some forms of Taoist alchemy, the practitioner focuses on the collection of chi into the first elixir field. When there is an excess of chi in this area, meaning not needed by the visceral organs, the alchemist will activate the *first alchemical furnace* in which the dross or impurities of the chi are removed. This refined chi is then progressively circulated into the second and third elixir fields. This movement also refines the chi, making it more subtle. By the time it reaches the head (third elixir field) it is transformed into shen, giving the Taoist access to the spirit worlds.

When a Taoist alchemist has successfully transformed his or her sexual essence into shen, he or she has attained a very exalted state of being. Myths and legends abound from ancient China in regards to these high Taoist sages. Legend has it that these beings lived in the high places of mountains (Dragon Points) sustaining themselves off of dew and herbs.

From an alchemical standpoint, morning dew collected on the leaves of plants is highly concentrated chi. A being who has transformed his or her sexual essence into shen would have no trouble sustaining himself or herself on such a refined food. For such a person, the digestive system would be highly refined and could easily metabolize the chi of dew into usable energy.

Here on an island in the Cyclades, there is a wonderful melon, a cousin to the honeydew. But unlike other melons that need watering, this melon grows on the barren, dry, and windswept soil of the island without any water whatsoever. Amazingly, it draws its water from the air. And it is one of the most extraordinary melons I have ever tasted. One can sense the intensely concentrated chi, and the taste is sweet.

There is another botanical wonder on the island that does something similar. It looks like our cedar trees in the Northwest, but like the melons it does not need any water. This is good because there is precious little on the island. These trees grow near the ocean and draw the salt-laden air to their leaves, extracting the moisture and leaving the dried salt behind. I had never thought about plants being alchemists (other than the obvious process of photosynthesis), but these two plants have obviously attained a high degree of alchemical mastery.

But let's return to our human alchemists. When a Taoist has refined his or her sexual nature into the state of shen (spirit), he or she becomes a very different order of being. And how this miraculous transformation takes

place is through balancing two opposing cosmological
forces: *yin* and *yang*.

# Yin and Yang

The deeply intuitive sages of ancient China explored
the patterns of creation within nature, and one of their
discoveries was the existence of two subtle, complementary and at times opposing forces called yin and yang. In
Taoist symbolism, the sun and moon are sometimes
used to denote these two elements of creation.

Yang (the sun) is associated with light and heat. It is
kinetic, meaning energy in motion, and it moves deci-
sively. Lightning is yang. It lights up the sky, has tremendous force, and when it strikes, there is no hesitation.

Yin (the moon) is moist, cool, and dark. It is potential
energy, not kinetic. A seed sitting under ground is under
the influence of yin. It is surrounded by moisture. It is
dark and it is cool. But when the sun (yang) comes out,
its heat warms the soil and the seed begins to grow. It is
the balance of yin and yang that produces life. Too much
moisture (yin) and the seed will rot. Too much heat
(yang) and it will shrivel up and die.

Yin and yang are not static forces. They are continually transforming into each other. Yin becomes yang and
yang becomes yin. Although we can never see yin or
yang directly, we can experience their effects.

For some reason, I am reminded of an experience I
had during my freshman year at Belmont Abbey.
Although I did not know it at the time, it is an example of
the ever-constant transformations of yin and yang.

It was October and the trees on campus were brilliant
with the mottled reds and yellows of fall. Everywhere one
stepped, the grass crackled with the sound of dead
leaves under foot. A stiff breeze was blowing across the
quadrangle, an omen of winter just ahead.

I had stepped out into the brisk air from my dormitory, en route to an afternoon soccer game. I don't remember who we were playing, but it was homecoming and the campus was humming with activity, a state rarely experienced in this Benedictine run college.

The lanes were full of parked cars with alumni returning to their alma mater. The trunks and backs of station wagons were brimming like some kind of modern cornucopias laden with fried chicken, potato salad, and iced tea. This was, after all, the South. Here and there a make shift barbecue was obscured by smoke. And the smell of hot dogs and hamburgers wafted through the air.

Students walked with their parents in a kind of spontaneous parade. Some seemed proud of being seen with their families. Some slinked back, pretending not to belong to the parents who had borne them.

This menagerie of humanity flowed into the soccer stadium like a river and I joined it on the last rung of the bleachers. As the game ensued, I remember being oddly detached, as if watching a ballet. The sky was a bright Carolina blue and the sun was hanging midway in the sky. Its warmth was just enough to be pleasant against the cold air, and I suppose it was this balanced force of the elements that created the odd effect in me.

The soccer team came onto the field and we released a hullabaloo like only a group of suppressed Catholic boys can muster. We had become yang. We were full of energy, yelling and whooping, the sound of our catcalls no doubt heard in the small town miles away.

And then the team took their positions, waiting for the ball to be tossed in the air by the referee. We stood breathlessly still. We watched with rapt attention. We had become yin.

Then our team miraculously got the ball. I say miraculously because almost every game we played that year, we lost. Not only that, but we had lost the homecoming game to this same team every year for the last five years. You can imagine the tension.

Suddenly we sprang to our feet. The aluminum bleachers groaned from the weight. We had transformed, in the twinkling of an eye, from yin into yang. We were screaming with delight as our team got closer to the goal, and then, in a moment, our glory was taken away by some blonde punk who stole the ball and the game headed off in the opposite direction. After some catcalls from a few of the alumni, we settled en masse back into our seats. Yang had become yin.

I watched this constant ballet of yang into yin and back into yang the whole afternoon. When the game was over, I watched the last glimmer of the sun as it sat behind the large oaks on campus. The air was still. The alumni had gone home and most of the students were in the pub or in their dorms. I walked the strangely silent grounds. The sliver of a new moon was rising through the last remnants of sunset. Yang had turned into yin. Oh, and the ballgame? We lost.

## Cultural Attitudes and the Cultivation of Chi

We live in an ocean of chi. Some of it is yang, full of power and direction. Some of it is yin, receptive and resting. For the most part we are unaware of it, though it affects us on many levels.

A Taoist alchemist is one who has become aware of this all-pervading sea of chi. And through the practices of alchemy, he or she learns to draw this energy into his or her body to transform consciousness and to enhance health and well-being.

Our modern lifestyle in the industrialized West is destructive of well-being. We are overly fixated on yang. We honor productivity and action. We do not, as a culture, understand or appreciate inaction. It is considered weak.

We jazz ourselves up with caffeine and other drugs. We are obsessed with speed. We are yang and proud of it.

But there are problems with this.

For one, it is out of balance, and two, it is ultimately destructive. We don't generally understand this, but yang comes out of yin.

In the state of Washington there is a powerful hydro-electric dam. There is nothing more yang, perhaps, than electricity. But the source of this yang power is watery yin. The lake that was dammed to make the hydroelectric plant is now a vast body of water. It sits absolutely still most of the time, except for little wavelets created by the wind. It is yin. It is potential power, but it is unmoving. It is *all* potential. But when the sluice gates open at the plant, this watery yin is transformed into yang and the rushing water turns the immense turbines of the power plant. This, in turn, produces another form of yang, the electricity that runs our lights and TVs and our other "time-saving" appliances. Of course, we don't have enough time to enjoy those time-saving devices, but that is another issue.

We are caught up in a cultural whirlwind of yang-madness. Fast food restaurants abound and are painted with yang colors like red and yellow to encourage customers to eat faster, making room for more customers. Mindless repetitive techno pop blares in the background and fast paced ambient music encourages us to do everything a little faster. I use the term *music* rather loosely, since this post modern crap bares little resemblance to the loftier attributes of music like healing and inspiration. But you see, music or the bastardization of it, is one of my pet peeves. So please do forgive me and let's get back to yin and yang.

To summarize my main point here, I would say that many Westerners, especially those in the United States, seem to be uncomfortable with leaving any space or moment in time unfilled.

The net affect of all this is that we are seeing an immense increase in stress-related illnesses. The body is simply not equipped to remain in yang states for long periods of time. It needs yin. It needs time to do nothing, to rest, perchance to dream.

But in our Western culture, doing nothing is seen as being lazy. Yet this is sometimes the wisest thing we can do. If you want to be yang, then you had best spend some time being yin.

A Taoist would never be caught dead having expended too much yang, if he or she can avoid it. The reason is that Taoist alchemy requires an exquisite balance of these two forces.

The ancient Taoists understood this phenomenon to a great extent, and if anything characterizes Taoism, it is the concept of poised balance. This concept becomes second nature to a practicing alchemist, since the success of Taoist alchemy requires that the forces of yin or yang be used correctly.

## Dual Cultivation

Dual Cultivation has some striking parallels to methods discussed in the *Manuscript*. There are also some very significant differences.

In order to understand this type of alchemy, we must return to yin and yang. According to Taoist theory, a healthy female possesses a virtually unlimited amount of yin-chi (chi that is yin). This is part of her nature.

A healthy male, on the other hand, has a limited amount of yang. Unlike the female, his nature does not grant him an unlimited reservoir of yang-chi.

In the advanced forms of *chi cultivation*, the female alchemist must collect yang energy in order to balance her excess yin. And the male must collect yin energy in order to balance his excess yang. In actuality, it is much more complex.

The ultimate balancing of yin and yang within a practitioner is paramount, since it is only when yin and yang have been balanced that certain alchemical practices can be engaged. Thus, all Taoists seek to balance the forces of yin and yang within themselves.

Those alchemists practicing alone must accomplish this task through elaborate alchemical meditations and energy work. Those who do this with a partner of the opposite sex can simply collect the desired chi during the act of sex.

During sexual contact there is an abundance of excess chi. The acts of stroking and fondling set off flows of chi both inside and around the body. An alchemist trained in the methods of Dual Cultivation can draw the excess chi into his or her chi body, thereby greatly enhancing his or her alchemical work.

During Dual Cultivation, the male avoids ejaculation as this would deplete his yang energy and bring the act of intercourse to an end. In this type of alchemy, long periods of intercourse are desired. The reason is quite simple and pragmatic: prolonging sex generates massive amounts of chi, and since the goal of Dual Cultivation is to collect excess chi, the more the better.

To assist in this process, the ancient Taoists developed something called the *valley orgasm*. When the male starts to feel that ejaculation is close at hand, he backs off from genital stimulation. He rests for a moment until the desire passes. Then he returns to intercourse. This continues in cycles of stimulation and rest for as long as the partners desire. The result is that both partners enter highly altered and deeply sensual states by which their sensitivity to chi is greatly increased. In addition, the amount of excess yin and yang generated from such continual sexual contact is considerable.

## The Final Attainment: Land of the Immortals

The ultimate goal of Taoist alchemy is immortality. Having attained quiescence of mind through the stillness practices, the Taoist alchemist has trained him or herself to be aware of the many types of chi. And with this knowledge he or she has been able to *collect* and *cultivate* beneficial chi through the subtle pathways of the body. He or she has learned how to distill the essence of this excess chi into energy for the purpose of increasing health and generating enhanced consciousness.

Along the way, the alchemist gets healthier and more vital, a result of collecting chi and circulating it into the major organs of the body. This is, gratifyingly, one of the key benchmarks to progress in this way of alchemy. And even if he or she does not attain the Immortal Body, the work of alchemy has been well worth the effort.

Eventually, through persistent practice, the subtle chi body is charged with vital force as well. It becomes as real to the Taoist alchemist as his or her physical body, and through it he or she can, in meditation, enter the Heavenly Abodes where master alchemists abound and one can greatly accelerate one's progress through the grace of instruction.

Finally, the great alchemical task of transforming sexual essence into spirit (shen) is coming to fruition. Long years of practice are bearing fruit and the alchemist is, in some ways, more spirit than flesh, though he or she still has a body.

The moment comes when the Taoist, now a sage, senses a moment in time. All the forces have come together in perfect timing. Yin and yang are perfectly balanced. Death might be near, or the alchemist might simply choose to leave the earth plane at will. Entering into deep meditation, the sage passes beyond the grips of time and space. The breath stops. Attention is shifted into the chi body, as it has been done so many times before. The Taoist has mounted *the Dragon*, his or her own transformed nature, and flies off into the Heavenly Abode.

The alchemist is now an *energy-being*. He or she might remain like this for a very, very long time. The moment may come, however, when no longer desiring even the subtlest of forms, the sage leaves the Heavenly Abode behind. The master alchemist refines his or her (already subtle) chi even more. Attaining the subtlest form, he or she returns to the *Formless Heaven* from which he or she originated. And as the sage slips into this primal space, all traces of the self disappear. The drop has slipped into the shining sea. There is no form; there is no sage; there is only the Tao.

# Tibetan Buddhist Alchemy

Of all the forms of Buddhism, and there are many, I personally find the Tibetan forms to be the most vibrant. Part of this is due, no doubt, to the fact that Tibetan Buddhism is actually a synthesis of both Buddhism and the Bon religion. When Siddhartha became the Buddha, the Bon had already existed for many centuries.

The Bon were known as master magicians and sorcerers, and today there are still persons practicing this ancient religion. Much of the Bon deals with the residing spirits of the primal elements (earth, air, sky, water) as well as spirits and beings that reside in places of power such as mountains and openings into the earth.

When Padmasambhava brought Buddhism into Tibet, he encountered many of these spirits. Some of the beings were quite negative, and Peme (as the Tibetans call him) transformed these demons into Protectors of the Dharma (the way of Buddhism), which is why some of the Protector Deities look so fierce.

I imagine that it is due to the Bon that the Tibetan forms of Buddhism have so many more deities (energy-beings) than do other forms of Buddhism. And the various forms of Tibetan Buddhist alchemy reflect this abundance. The idea of energy-beings may seem foreign to Westerners, since these beings are non-corporeal (meaning without physical form). However, they do have bodies of a kind. They are more energy than mass, and for the most part we are unaware of them. However, if a person's awareness is refined enough, as through meditation practice, one can, not only sense these beings but one can interact with them as well. The attributes of such beings were catalogued by lamas centuries ago in highly secret texts which, for the most part, have not found their way into the West. In certain types of advanced alchemy practiced by Tibetan hermits in their remote, high mountain retreats, some of these beings were utilized in secret Tantric rituals. I will speak more on this later, but first I think it would be good to discuss the fundamental insight of Buddhism in general, since this forms the foundation upon which the alchemical practices of Tibetan Buddhism are engaged. Indeed, without this foundation of Buddhist philosophy, the practices of Tibetan alchemy can lead to misunderstanding and abuse.

## Emptiness

From the many insights offered by the Buddha regarding *samsara* (this world of illusion), perhaps the most penetrating is the concept of emptiness. For many Westerners, hell-bent to fill every quiet moment this concept is strange indeed.

But a cursory glance at quantum physics shows that this modern science is utterly and completely in agreement with the Buddha's assessment. According to the quantum view, there is very little solidity to matter. Take your body, for instance. It has been estimated that we are comprised of +/-99.9% space. If all the actual physical matter of your body was put in a pile, it would fit on the tip of a pin! To our physical eyes and to our physical touch, we seem solid. But this is illusory, a smoke-and-mirror show created by our physical senses. In point of fact, we are mostly emptiness.

According to Buddhism, if you go deep enough into the heart of all things, there is only emptiness. And therefore no thing is ultimately real since it is, at its heart, empty and devoid of form or identity.

Take your body again. It has senses through which you make contact with the world around you. Out of these five senses you create your experience of yourself and the world around you. That wasn't a typo, by the way. You *are* the creator of your experience. You tend to identify with what you like and distance yourself mentally from those things you don't like. Perhaps you like the color of your eyes, but dislike the texture of your hair. When you see your eyes reflected back to you in a mirror, you might pause for a moment to enjoy looking at them. But when you catch a glimpse of your hair, you may find yourself feeling uncomfortable or self-critical. These emotional responses to ourselves and the world are experienced as quite real. They have a punch and a power that is sometimes difficult to avoid.

However, all of this is based on nothing. For if you go deep enough into the brain, for instance, into the neurons responsible for holding the thought and emotions of self-criticism or self-glorification, you will find that eventually there is nothing. In other words, at the deepest levels of the cells, i.e., the atomic and subatomic levels, there is no mass, no solidity, only space and emptiness.

## Relative and Absolute Existence

To summarize an essential concept in Tibetan Buddhism: "Form is emptiness, and emptiness is form. Neither is real nor unreal. They are both existing and non-existing."

To the Western mind this may very well seem like nonsense. How can something exist and non-exist at the same time? Well, what this statement refers to is both

absolute and relative existence. You and I exist at the relative level of creation. We have a common illusion of solidity, but at the deepest levels of our very physicality there is
nothing, only emptiness. Therefore, at the absolute level of
creation, you and I do not exist. We are like mirages, like
clouds; we come and go. For a moment we seem quite
real, and then we pass away. Thus not only are we essentially empty, we are impermanent as well.

## The Cultivation of Bliss

This could very well lead to depression, except that
through the practice of Buddhist alchemy we also make
contact with another aspect of our intrinsic nature: bliss.
This is one of the hallmarks of Tibetan Buddhist High
Tantra (or alchemy). Through meditative practices, the
yogi or yogini self-generates bliss. While resting within
this field of self-generated bliss, the yogi or yogini contemplates the nature of emptiness. In other words, raised
up on feelings of bliss and ecstasy, the yogi or yogini
thinks about the essential emptiness of all things, including his or her own body. This union of bliss and emptiness generates enlightenment.

The goal of Buddhist practice is to penetrate the
depths of consciousness (called *the Mind* in Buddhism).
For when this occurs, one is no longer deluded by the
play of the senses or the illusory nature of *samsara*. One
is then free and aware. In fact, when someone asked the
Buddha if he was a god, he said, "No. I am awake."

The metaphor runs very deep here. From the vantage point of illuminated consciousness, we are all in
various degrees of sleep. We think we are awake, but
we are actually dreaming. Through the power of *bodhicitta* (literally Buddha mind), we awaken from the
dream and see that we are creating our reactions to all
that we survey.

This power to recognize life as a dream, and to awaken from it, is an inherent power of *bodhicitta*. Now, it is important to understand that we all possess bodhicitta (or Buddha-mind). We are all Buddhas (awakened beings) in latent form. But some of us, due to mental and emotional obscurations (blocks), are more removed from our blissful and compassionate natures than others. And this is precisely the reason for practicing Buddhist meditations—i.e., to remove the obstacles to our essential natures.

There are many schools or lineages within Buddhism. Each lineage has its own ways of imparting the essential insights of the Buddha, and each tradition has its own ways of imparting the *dharma* (literally, the Way of Buddhism).

Our concern here is with a particular type of Tibetan Buddhist practice that is alchemical in nature. It is called *Highest Yoga Tantra* and is considered by some to be the rapid path to enlightenment. In this regard, it shares its reputation for swiftness with Dzogchen, another form of Tibetan Buddhism.

The focus of Highest Tantra is fourfold: 1) Secret Mantra, 2) alchemical meditation, 3) bliss generated from distilled sexual essence and 4) embodiment as a Buddha.

## Secret Mantra

First, let us take a look at Secret Mantra. The Sanskrit word, mantra, literally means protection of the Mind (*man* meaning mind, and *tra*, meaning protection). Within this practice, the term mantra does not mean words of power as is normally associated with this word. For instance, the bija (or seed sound) Om is a mantra, a mantric word of power. By chanting this mantra silently or out loud, one alters awareness and protects one's Mind from the delusions of samsara (the world of sensory illusion). However, the practices of Highest Yoga Tantra also protect the Mind. How do they do this? This dazzling feat of protection is accomplished by keeping the Mind free from identification with the illusion of the mundane. According to Highest Tantra, we are (in our natures) luminous, blissful beings (utterly and perfectly divine). However, one of the effects of samsara (the illusion of this world) is to defile our Minds with the impression that we are ordinary. We believe ourselves to be mortal rather than divine beings. Thus, Secret Mantra is a means to remember that we are divine Buddhas currently residing in the ocean of samsara. This is a very different strategy from that of striving to become Buddhas, and it has vast implications—one being the rapidity with which enlightenment can take place.

# The Secret Channel

Next, let us consider the alchemical meditations of Highest Tantra. The goal of this alchemical method is nothing short of enlightenment, which requires that the Mind withdraw or be freed from the sensory illusions of this world. In other words, as long as we are bedazzled by the sensory displays of our embodiment, we will not be able to make contact with our essential bodhicitta (Buddha mind). To do this, our Minds must be still, quiescent.

The yogi or yogini within Highest Tantra accomplishes this formidable task by driving the *winds* of their senses inward, away from the objects of their desires and into the inner sanctum of their energy bodies, into what is called the *Secret Channel*. The net result of this action is that the Mind is brought to a deep state of quietude. It is only within this profound stillness that *bodhicitta* can be directly experienced.

The *winds* are subtle energies that move through the energy pathways of the body (called meridians by Taoists and nadis by Yogis). My experience is that if I listen (clairaudiently, i.e. inner hearing) to the movement of life-energy through these subtle pathways, the sound is very akin to the sound of the wind.

According to Tibetan anatomy, the winds (*lhung*) are responsible for the five senses. Each sense has its own peculiar type of wind, and when the winds stop, the corresponding sense ceases. Death, from this perspective, is a dissipation of the winds. As a result, the death process is one of successive disconnection from the five senses. Ultimately, with no input from the senses, there is only consciousness. And with no sensory object to focus upon, consciousness focuses upon itself. For a moment, depending upon the clarity of the individual, there is a spontaneous arising of bliss and clear light (light without attributes). If one has been trained in the yoga of the *bardos* (states of being, especially those in the death realms), it is possible to remain in this clear light without the need for re-embodiment within samsara.

Tibetan alchemical yogas, such as Highest Tantra, are an attempt to accomplish this feat of self-realization while alive by driving the winds inward, into the Secret Channel. This subtle energy channel runs through the center of the body from the perineum up into the head. By sending the winds into this channel through the power of meditation, the senses cease to generate sensory experience and the yogi or yogini experiences *pure Mind* without dying. Repetition of this radical shift in perception eventually results in high degrees of spiritual illumination, and an ability to remain aware during death and the after-death experiences of the Bardos.

## Sexual Essence: the Red and White Drops

Another stage in Highest Yoga Tantra involves the distillation of sexual essence into bliss. One way this is accomplished is through a specific form of *tuomo,* or *psychic fire.*

In this form, one focuses on the sound *Ah* while concentrating on the navel wheel (chakra). This action causes a psychic fire to rise up the Secret Channel into the head. Here, the "heat" of the psychic fire causes the *Red and White Drops* to fall down from the crown wheel (chakra). The Red Drops are related to the sexual and spiritual essence of one's biological mother, and the White Drops to one's biological father. As the two drops join, bliss is generated. The longer the practice is engaged, the more powerful the bliss. As the bliss arises within one's mind, one contemplates the essential emptiness of all things. This union of bliss and emptiness produces a type of enlightenment.

There are dangers with this practice. According to Tibetan Medicine, *Nectar Gathering Practices*, like this, can create imbalances in the subtle bodies due to an overabundance of the fire element. For this reason, it is traditionally stated that this form of alchemy should only be undertaken under the guidance of one's tantric guru or teacher. I don't say this to discourage anyone from experimentation, but to be responsible in how it is shared. If you wish to try this practice and you do not have access to a qualified tantric master, I strongly suggest you at least read some of the available texts on Tibetan Tantra.

In the *Manuscript*, Magdalen shares a meditation that has striking similarities to the Nectar Gathering practice just described. In this case, however, the blissful states are used to strengthen the Ka body rather than to contemplate emptiness. The goals are somewhat different, but the methodologies are uncannily similar.

## Sexual Essence Initiations and Practices

The concept of sexual energy as being tied to the attainment of enlightenment shows up in Highest Tantra in other forms. For instance, one of the first Initiations is called the *Vase Initiation*, in which the sexual fluids of a deity and his or her consort are imagined. This is then poured over the head of the Initiate for the purpose of generating bliss.

In another type of Initiation, a particular mandala (a specific geometric pattern) is used: called the *Vagina Mandala*. This association of the feminine with enlightenment shows up in many forms of Tantra. The implication is clear. Without the aid of the feminine principle of consciousness, liberation cannot take place.

One of the tools of Tantric Tibetan Buddhism is the bell and *dorje*. The dorje is a stylized thunderbolt or diamond. It is held in the hand and used as a device for accumulating energy. Metaphorically, the bell is associated with the feminine and the concept of emptiness. The dorje is associated with the male and the concept of right method. When emptiness and right method are joined together, you create illumination.

But back to bliss. It is, quite frankly, one of the fundamental experiences sought after by Tibetan Buddhist Tantric yogis. The reason for this pursuit of bliss is that it is a part of our bodhicitta (or Buddha mind). When joined with awareness of emptiness, enlightenment begins to dawn. Thus, bliss is sought after not for its own sake, but as part of a larger alchemical pursuit.

In an exotic form of bliss generation (an aspect of *Deity Yoga*), some yogis or yoginis call their chosen deity into vivid manifestation within their minds. They then imagine having sexual intercourse with these highly refined beings. One result of such merging is that they take on some of the qualities of that being.

Up in the high mountainous and remote areas of Tibet, there were reputed hermits who cultivated bliss through a type of sexual interaction with energy-beings known as *dakinis*. The dakinis are feminine beings who exist in the subtle realms of existence but who have the ability to manifest quasi-physically, especially at high altitudes. The dakinis are acknowledged by Tibetan Buddhism as a reality, but some of the stories and legends about them stretch the imagination. Sexual intercourse with a dakini reportedly imparts special powers and unusual abilities to the practitioner, but it is a practice fraught with danger. The practice of Deity Yoga as described above is much safer in this regard.

In some forms of Tibetan Buddhist Tantra, a yogi or yogini would engage in these practices with an actual physical consort. But such practices were forbidden to renunciants such as monks and nuns.

As intriguing and outlandish as some of these esoteric sexual practices are, they need to be placed within the greater context of the Dharma, the Way of Buddhism. Without the tempering of these practices by the sobering task of attaining enlightenment, they can become seductive traps rather than portals to liberation. Thus, those undertaking these esoteric practices are first trained in sutra practice (the teachings of the Buddha) as well as moral codes of conduct. Without this understanding and personal ethical constraint, the more esoteric sexual practices can be quite dangerous.

## Signs of Progress

There is one final element that needs to be added here. It arises spontaneously when bliss is joined with emptiness. Somehow, as the two are drawn together within the alchemical container of the Mind, there is a reaction. Something new emerges. Although one is still embodied, one is increasingly free. One begins to see through the smoke-and-mirror show of the senses. One becomes less attached to things, for one sees clearly that all is emptiness. And nothing is worth losing oneself over.

But there is also a strange paradox. Although one begins to see more clearly and awakens somewhat from the dream, one still loses sight of it and falls back to sleep again and again. From this struggle with one's own obscurations, one develops compassion for others.

We are all in the same boat. We are all lost on the ocean of samsara. Believing ourselves to be real and fighting each other over illusions, we are like floating clouds, for a moment so vividly real and then passing away into nothing.

For those lost in the samsaric sea of illusion, this passing away of all things into nothing can be quite painful and terrifying. But for the yogi or yogini who has awakened from the dream, there is an arising of unfettered bliss and unbounded compassion.

And...there is laughter.

A friend of mine once had the honor of preparing tea for two lamas who had not seen each other in a very long time. They had been at the same monastery in their youth, and now their work took them all over the world. They had been friends all those years, and they were happy to be reunited.

She said that they sat for the longest time in silence, then chuckled, seemingly at nothing. This went on for some time. Then one of them pointed to a blossoming redbud tree, not far from where they were sitting. "And they call that a tree!" one of them said.

At which point they both started howling and slapped their thighs.

As consciousness reveals its natural bliss and compassion, life becomes inherently amusing. The horrors of samsara still exist, but they are counterbalanced by the unimaginable and unfathomable bliss of bodhicitta (Buddha-mind). Perhaps by the time one reaches this level of alchemical attainment, life must seem very odd indeed. Can we even imagine the inner life of such a person? What must it be like to know oneself as unbounded consciousness while still living in a body that is tethered to time and space? If you look at Buddhist practitioners who have attained Highest Yoga Tantra, a clue can sometimes be found. They often have smiles on their faces.

# The Alchemy
# of Relationship

Many of us do relationships the way we play poker. We do everything possible to get the upper hand. And if that fails, we bluff. We pretend to hold cards we don't have. We cheat. We lie.

And while this is the model for many a relationship in our post-modern era, it is not the model for Sacred Relationship as described in the *Manuscript*.

Let me be very upfront here. Sacred Relationship is not for everyone. In fact, I suspect that there are far fewer persons capable or even willing to undertake it than there are those who prefer to play emotional card games.

This type of relationship demands utmost honesty, both with oneself and with one's partner. Instead of hiding our cards, we lay them all out on the table. All our hopes, all our fears, all our petty and jealous thoughts, all our connivings—all of it gets laid out in the clear light of awareness for our partner to see. And he or she must do the same. It will not work if there are *back doors* unlocked with mental escape in mind. It will not work if both partners are not absolutely impeccably honest with each other.

And the reason for this radical type of honesty is that without it, the Alchemy of Relationship cannot take place. Now this may be a new term to many, even students of internal alchemy, since the dynamics of intimate relationship are rarely discussed in the four major alchemical streams (Egyptian, Taoist, Yoga Tantra and Buddhist Tantra).

So I think it might be good to define what I mean here, and to lay some type of foundation. Like all types of alchemy, this type of work is about changing one form into another. The form, in this case, is the inter-dynamics that have become habituated between two people. After a while, people tend to get into ruts. The liveliness that existed at the beginning of the relationship begins to fade. Both people become more or less unconscious. The harsh reality is that it takes continual vigilance and effort to keep a relationship conscious and alive.

Many relationships drop by the wayside because the partners are either unwilling or unable to make the efforts required to sustain them. Instead of experiencing the newness of each moment within the relationship, a kind of dullness seeps in over time; what used to be exciting is now boring. And worse, a kind of psychological and emotional lethargy sets in, and both partners succumb to the dulling effects of unconsciousness.

This type of unconsciousness is a death knell to psychological awareness and insight; and although it is rarely mentioned, this type of unconsciousness has a negative effect on one's spiritual life as well.

So the form that needs to be changed within a relationship is literally the form of interactions that habitually take place between the two partners.

Like all types of alchemy, there must be a container for the reactions to occur. And in this case, it is the container of safety and appreciation that provides the reservoir for transformation.

If there is a lack of safety or appreciation, this type of alchemy cannot be undertaken. And if you have decided you wish to try this type of alchemy in your relationship, I suggest you do an analysis first. Honestly assess if you feel safety and appreciation in your relationship. If you don't, you will be wasting your time trying to undertake this type of alchemy with your current partner. I suggest you focus your efforts, instead, on the solitary practices mentioned in the *Manuscript*. If you still want to give it a try, get your partner to talk about these feelings of danger and lack of appreciation that you are feeling. Only if and when they get resolved, should you consider taking on this type of alchemy.

So now we have two of the three elements needed for alchemy: something to be transformed (the habitual patterns of interaction) and the container (the safety net, if you will, of the relationship itself). A third element is needed; and that is, of course, energy to drive the reaction. There is usually plenty of energy in relationships in the form of neurotic patterns, hopes, fears, and desires. We'll get to those in a moment, but for now I want to talk about steel.

Our psychological selves are much like swords made from steel alloys. They have been forged in the hot searing foundry of our childhood, in the formative pressures of our early experiences. It is this early period of life that bonds the elements of our psyches together. And like steel, this was done under immense heat and pressure. Some of us were abused by overbearing or downright hostile or even destructive parents. Some of us were left to our own devices without any kind of support or guidance. And every kind of parental/child relationship falls in between these two polarities. The possibilities of childhood pressures are virtually endless, and so too are the psychological alloys that result from these types of experiences.

There is a lot of talk about *the child within* in many personal growth groups, and while there is certainly value in making contact with this *younger self*, it is not always pretty. Our cultural myth is that childhood is a time of innocence, a time in which everything is *right with the world*. For some children this is true; for many it is definitely not.

I remember being at a fellow therapist's house for a party quite a few years ago. Most of the adults were practicing therapists, psychologists, psychiatrists and several clinical social workers. I had just plopped myself in a big oversized sofa; and sipping my iced tea, I noticed a remarkable event. One of the therapists had brought his son and his son's best friend to the party. It was clear that the two boys were buds. They were playing some kind of card game and respectfully giving each other a turn. There were no attempts at cheating, and they seemed to be in a bubble of camaraderie.

Then the boy's father came into the room and asked both kids if they needed anything. They both looked up with cherub faces and smiled. No they said, in the cutest little boy voices. The father patted his son on the back and as he walked off, he nonchalantly patted his son's friend on the back as well. For a moment, his son looked at the incident in abject horror. You could see that he could not believe his eyes. And then as his father turned the corner into the other room, his son pulled back and hit his best friend in the face!

This was not childhood innocence. This was childhood rage. He was not willing to share affections from his father, not even with his best friend. This type of jealousy is typical of higher mammals, and we are, for all our self-righteous self-congratulatory delusions, still mammals. No matter how high we get spiritually, we will, for as long as we live, share traits with our mammalian brothers and sisters.

The inner life of a child is often far different than those around him or her imagine it to be. Surrounded by both dangers and opportunities, the psychological life of a child is directly shaped by how he or she chooses to deal with them. Whether it is something as life threatening as a deranged parent or a child molester, or seemingly innocuous as whom to go to the prom with, does not in some ways matter. While the impact of fighting for one's life may very well imprint a child's behavior well into adulthood, the little decisions of life, like who to socialize with or not, also have impact. All these major and minor decisions create internal psychological heat and pressure. The alloys of one's personality get bonded together or burned away. The sword has been tempered by the time we reach adulthood, and the alloy of our personalities has been set.

Some of us emerge from this childhood foundry with sharp edges, others of us are blunt. Some of us hold our edges and some of us can never seem to hold anything.

The thing about steel is that it tends to remain in its original form once it leaves the foundry. And one of the few things that can ever re-configure the alloy is if the steel gets as hot as it did when it was first formed.

In the alchemical work of Sacred Relationship, we voluntarily put ourselves back in the foundry. The heat that arises between two people when their neuroses rub against each other can get quite intense. If both people can find the courage to be *radically honest* with themselves and with each other in these searing moments, the psychological alloys can be altered. A new type of aliveness then enters the relationship fueled by the energy of psychological truth.

The thing is—most of us will do almost anything to avoid psychological heat. When we get uncomfortable, many of us get the *hell out of Dodge.* Now for some of us this means literally packing up and getting out of town or at least out of sight. For some of us it means that we are physically present, but no longer emotionally present. We numb up. We become automatons. We move and talk, almost like normal, but we have retreated far, far inside. Others of us numb ourselves with alcohol or drugs. And some of us do it with television. We humans are, after all, quite clever and creative. We can find all sorts of ways to avoid facing ourselves. In fact they are far too numerous for me to list here. But I suspect you get the idea. I guess the real question here is this—what do *you* do when things get psychologically too hot for your taste? What do *you* do when you are on the verge of feeling something that you don't want to feel?

For those in Sacred Relationship such feelings are *a call to presence.* It is a time to be *radically honest,* and for both partners to express their true feelings no matter how embarrassing or scary they might be. By speaking their truths to each other, an enlivening element enters the dynamic. Psychological honesty results in psychological insight. And with insight there is hope for awareness, and with awareness there can be change.

This chapter is hardly a manual for the Alchemy of Relationship. It's mainly, I think, a warning. Magdalen alluded to this in the *Manuscript*. She called it *obscurations to flight*. That sounds wonderfully exotic doesn't it? Well it isn't very exotic when the obscuration is clearly in your face. And it isn't very exotic feeling when the foundry of the relationship gets so hot that you feel you are dissolving (psychologically that is). It takes courage and fortitude to stay in the foundry when the heat begins to weaken the stability of one's self-perceived image. Few of us care to look foolish, scared, petty or jealous. And we will often go through elaborate means to hide these feelings from ourselves or others.

But in Sacred Relationship these things invariably float to the surface like mud that has been stirred up from the bottom of a barrel. The thing is to realize that this does not mean you are doing it (Sacred Relationship) wrong; it means that you are probably doing it right. As Magdalen said in the *Manuscript*, the power of the alchemy extrudes or pushes out the dross. This can be fascinating when the dross is being pushed out of your partner, but it is truly horrific when it extrudes out of you.

What makes Sacred Relationship *sacred* is that it is truly a holy way of being. The root of the word *holy* actually means *to make whole*. So...when we do something that creates wholeness (in this case psychological wholeness), we are engaged in a sacred or holy act.

In the crucible of mutual safety, honesty and appreciation, it is possible to forge a new kind of self. This new self is psychologically more honest, more aware and freer than its counterpart before entering *the foundry of relationship*. And like the phoenix that arises from its own ashes, this self has wings. It can fly places that it could only imagine before.

There are mysteries here, and treasures that await those who have the courage to enter the depths of themselves and their partners. It is not, as I said, for everyone.

You will probably know if you are a likely candidate because you will feel it in your soul, your heart.

If you enter this path, know that there are no manuals. There is precious little guidance out there. The path to spirituality has traditionally been one of solitude. And while times of solitude may be necessary for those in Sacred Relationship, something has turned. They agree to walk the path to godhood together, side by side, through both heaven and hell, through the brilliant summits where all things are suddenly crystal clear, and through the dark valley of psychological death where it is hard to even see one's foot in front of the other. And yet through the darkness of not knowing, a deep primordial force begins to rise up. It requires an unusual type of *holy trinity*—three things for it to do its most holy task—*mutual safety, psychological honesty* and *appreciation of the Beloved*.

Have a good journey!

# A Note to the Reader:

There is an implicit danger in writing about such things as sacred relationship. For one, some people might assume that the writer (moi) is an expert on such matters. I assure you that I am not, and I wish to place into written record this fact.

I have found myself, several times, running from the heat of the foundry of relationship. For as I mentioned earlier, when the emotional and psychic heat of sacred relationship gets really hot there is a tendency to feel that oneself is being obliterated. Of course what is being obliterated, or at the very least challenged, is our own neurosis, not our existence (which is what it feels like). Our neurotic habits are tenacious and they don't give up easily. My experience is that they often fight to the death, so to speak, rather than fade gracefully into the past. But that is just my personal experience, and I don't wish to imply that this might be your experience as well.

The art of sacred relationship, I believe, is learning how to be in the "heat" of transformation and not automatically run from it. I also think that this way of being in relationship with another is one of the most challenging and rewarding things I have ever asked of myself. Because this way of relationship is so dynamic and life-changing, I think the entrance into this path should have a warning sign, so here it is.

WARNING...ENTER THIS PATH WITH SOBRIETY AND ABANDON. KNOW THAT THOSE WHO ENTER THIS PATH WILL NEVER BE THE SAME...NOR WILL YOU. (I was redundant here for those of you who think you are an exception to everyone else.)

# One Woman's Story

Judi Sion

In this story of one woman is the story
of every woman. May you find the pathway
into the spirit by which it was written.

*—Mary Magdalen*

# Tom's Introduction to One Woman's Story

Some might wonder why we included something so personal in the last section of this book. After all, we all have our stories, and none of us is any more important than anyone else. Indeed, this is what we posed to Magdalen over and over again after she asked Judi to write "her story." And even after the book had been completed and was ready for press, we asked the Magdalen one last time, thinking that perhaps she had changed her mind. She had not. She was, in fact, quite emphatic that elements in Judi's personal story would *speak* to many women, that many of her experiences were shared by women universally. And this was, Magdalen reminded us, about the return of the feminine to a place of honor and power.

But first the patterns of abuse, betrayal, lack of honor, and disempowerment need to be owned and accepted.

Now, after sitting with the material for these many months, I think I understand what the Magdalen is talking about. It has to do with the principles of *Sophia* and the *Logos*. For those familiar with these terms, please forgive my taking the space here to discuss them, but I find many people do not understand them. This lack of general understanding about the Logos and Sophia is, I think, a result of the Church Fathers' attempt to erase the feminine from the theology of Christendom, an act that stretches back in time to the first century A.D.

Many are probably familiar with the term "Logos" as it sits at the core of the Church's two thousand-year-old theology. The Logos is the intelligence (the logic) of the cosmos itself. It is the fundamental creative force (or

God). Traditionally, theologians and philosophers have considered the Logos to be a masculine principle. This concept actually goes back thousands of years before Christ into the ancient pagan world. At a mythological level, gods were viewed as solar, while goddesses were seen as being more related to the moon (lunar). In this context, *spirit* was conceived as being in the solar realms of consciousness (male), and the *earth* (matter) resided within the lunar realms of consciousness (female). Thus the sky (heaven) became associated with the masculine while earth became associated with the feminine.

The pagan consciousness understood that all creation was the result of an interplay between the cosmological forces of the masculine and feminine (spirit and matter; sky and earth). Neither force was more important than the other. Without both of them, creation was not possible. The key to a fruitful creation, whether it be cosmic or individual, was seen as a balance between these forces.

In the earliest period of Christianity, before the political aspirations of the Church, this was commonly understood and accepted. This understanding of the place of the feminine shows up nowhere more clearly than in the concept of Sophia.

Sophia was viewed as the feminine aspect of the godhead. She was the holy bride to the Logos, and they were viewed as inseparable. When the Logos generated an impulse (the thought) to create, it was Sophia that implemented it. Without her, creation would have been impossible. They were two sides of the same coin. One remained aloof in the realms of spirit, forming the ideas of creation. But it was Sophia who received the seed (the thought of creation) from the Logos. And it was she who gave it birth into actuality in the realms of matter.

Sophia was known as the *Cosmic Mother*, and as such, she shared the same place of honor as *Isis* in Egypt and other Goddesses in other ancient cultures. According to the *Sophionic* understandings, she incarnated

as Mary, the mother of *Yeshua*. And through this embodiment the word (Logos) became flesh (Yeshua). God/man
had been actualized. But it could not have happened
without the sacred act of Sophia incarnating as a
woman. Only then could God (Logos) incarnate as a
man (in the womb of Sophia/Mary).

This understanding was common among some of the
early Christian theologians. And although many of their
writings were destroyed during the Dark Ages, a few of
them have survived.

But something ominous occurred over the first few
centuries A.D. in regards to the feminine teachings
regarding Sophia. We see a concerted effort to remove all
traces of her from Christian religious writings and thought.

Metaphorically, we could say that the Church subdued
the moon with all of her dark mysteries. The Goddess
became veiled and hidden. Not only this, but it became a
heresy to even talk about her. One could lose one's life
simply by uttering her names.

The sun was at its zenith. God (the Logos) was all there
was. Then came the mysterious Holy Trinity—the Father,
the Son and the Holy Ghost. There was no mention of
Sophia, or Mary. There was nothing feminine in the Trinity.
And the feminine was relegated to a place of unimportance.

But worse, she was scorned. In the official version of
Genesis adopted by the increasingly patriarchal Church,
the source of mankind's downfall was laid squarely on
the shoulders of Eve. She had, after all, taken the apple
from the serpent of Satan. And with this one fateful act,
she (a woman) cursed all succeeding generations.

But wait a moment. There are other versions of the creation myth. The censored version we have inherited is only
one of them. According to one Gnostic account, the serpent was a good guy. He was actually trying to help Adam
and Eve get out from under the tyrannical rule of a jealous
God (Jehovah). And in this version, the snake simply
opened the path to the godlike powers of consciousness
that were part of Adam and Eve's rightful inheritance.

The Gnostics, for those unfamiliar with them, were a long line of luminaries whose traditions, in various forms, stretched back into ancient Egypt, if not before. They believed in the power of direct revelation without the need for an intermediary (a priest). Of course, this did not fit in with the political and monetary desires of the Church, and so the Gnostics were branded as heretics and summarily imprisoned or killed on a regular basis.

In the view of the Gnostics, Eve was a heroine who, through her act of accepting the apple, raised humanity closer to ownership of its godlike powers. In the myth propagated by the Church, however, she was weak and cursed for having tricked her mate into accepting something from Satan.

Myth has power. It gets laid into the fabric of a culture and colors its attitudes and beliefs. And as a result of the officially sanctioned creation story, women have suffered considerably as the dark dangerous creatures of the moon, who by their natures consort with evil. Just read the medieval hogwash of scholars and theologians justifying their witch hunts and other admonitions against women. This incendiary madness even extended into the fledgling colonies of the United States during the Salem witch trials of the 1600s.

But I think the damage of the overly solarized mythos of Christianity extends far beyond the labeling of women as evil. All of our society suffers, men as well, and here's why.

By cutting ourselves off from the feminine aspect of creation (matter itself), there is a deep spiritual dis-ease (discomfort) that has been infecting Western culture for two millennia.

We long for the realms of spirit (heaven), but reject our experiences in the world. We have set heaven and earth at odds. Earth is, after all, tainted. We are only here because we have fallen from grace. If we are truly born in sin, just through the act of being born, then all that follows our birth is a lie. The truth lies above us, not here among us.

The expression of spirit in the form of earth experience is denied by our current cultural mythos. Thus, we
can rape and pillage the earth with seemingly little
regard. At a mythological level the earth is feminine. And
women are, after all, just to be used.

But the danger in this fallacy is that by pillaging our
earthly mother (Gaia), we are destroying the very eco-
logical roots that support us. And the biological sciences
are full of dire warnings concerning the exhaustion of
our ecosystem.

Does it dawn on us that the disappearance of animal
and plant species at its current alarming rate is a threat to
our very survival? No! We are above it all. We consider ourselves to be at the apex of nature, with an inherent God-
given right to dominate and subdue it according to our will.

The idea that other forms of life might have wills of
their own just as significant as ours does not occur to us.
And the concept of equal coexistence between us and
other life forms is barely a part of mass consciousness.
This is essentially because we do not see life forms as
expressions of spirit. At an unconscious level, we separate them. There is life and there is spirit. Heaven and
earth do not meet. At the mythological level, many view
the earth as a kind of in-between place, a test to see if
they deserve an eternal hereafter in heaven or a hellish
eternity in the bowels of—where else—the earth!

This *koyaaniqatsi* (a Hopi term for being out of balance
with the world) may very well destroy our civilization. We
must come back to a place of balance if we are to survive.
Mythologically, the moon must be unveiled within our own
psyches. The feminine principle must be put back in her
rightful place as a co-creator, not as a dominating force
nor as a subjugated force, but as an equal force.

All of this brings me back to the personal story of
one woman you are about to read. Why would this be
so pertinent?

Well, I believe, for one thing, that It goes back to the
distortion of spiritual values we have inherited. If our

life, as an embodied soul, is tainted (by the mere act of being in a body), then there is psychological discomfort with our experiences. They are, after all, of the earth, not of the spirit.

And yet, in the balance of spirit and earth, both are valued. The shimmering visions of the spirit world and the earth-caked experiences of life in a body are both seen as inherently sacred. Hanging the laundry can be just as enlightening as reading scripture.

It's all in the attitude.

Someone once asked me what "the return of the Cosmic Mother" meant. I suspect it means many things, some of which we won't recognize until we are well into it. But I imagine it will bring at least one cultural shift. We will come to recognize our earthly life and all its experiences as an expression of spirit in matter, not as a battle between the two, but as a sacred marriage.

This sacred marriage between spirit and matter is sometimes called the *Opus Magnum*, or the Great Work. It is the alpha and omega in which spirit (Logos) descends into matter (through the grace of Sophia) and returns back to itself transformed.

Our lives are forged in the alchemical furnace of experience. For those of us who willingly choose to enter the Great Work of self-illumination, our life experiences can become great teachers unto ourselves.

You are about to read the story of one woman. She shares something in common with all women undertaking the Great Work of self-illumination in this, our time. Re-storing the feminine to a place of honor in our culture begins with women honoring both themselves and their stories.

The pain and lies of the last two thousand years are brought closer to their end each time a woman takes her own power. The return of Sophia draws closer each time a man honors the women in his life as well as the feminine within himself.

Those of us striving to live this realization *are* a part of the Cosmic Mother's return. We are the moon becoming unveiled in balance to the sun, and we are the restoration of the feminine in balance to the male.

May heaven and earth be joined in this, our time.

# Judi's Preface to One Woman's Story

The first night that Mary Magdalen came through, her power and strength were as palpable as her words were audible, and it continued that way throughout the whole process. There was never a stumble over a word. Her words carefully chosen before she spoke, she spoke with authority and with definition. She was here to do a job—to set the story straight, and to go back home, which she said was a place we call heaven, but she called a "place in the soul," where she rests forever with her Beloved, Yeshua.

Hers was the most powerful presence I have ever experienced, and from her first words I was deeply moved and my consciousness profoundly altered. I typed what she brought through sitting in bed with a computer propped on a pillow, my hands trembling both with excitement and with fear that I might not get it all correctly.

When she was leaving that first night, after she had completed the information, she "turned" to me, so to speak.

I felt the definite shift to the personal, almost intimately to me, and she said, "I agree to give my story because of *you*—because you sense the importance of the relationship, the Sacred Marriage. And Metatron requested also that I give you my story." In a subsequent transmission, within the *Manuscript* itself, she stated that Isis had specifically asked that she tell her story, in this, "the beginning of the end of time."

Later we asked Magdalen for the best way to bring this information forward, considering the format of the book.

Her *Manuscript* is compact. There are no extra words. She doesn't go on and on. She clearly wants to give only the necessary coded information to awaken the memory, and those few who are ready will hear it all.

But everything you *need* to know, *all the secrets*, are here in *her* few pages.

Tom felt it was important to add an overview and to fill in some blanks, which he is well qualified to do. He is one of the most astute and erudite beings on the face of the Earth at this time regarding the entire subject of internal alchemy, as streamed from many different sources, as this has been his lifetime's work.

And me? Why am I here? Why am I privileged to be taking space to write words to you? Of what am I a lifetime student?

Relationship. And Sacred Relationship and the inherent power and mystery of the feminine are what this book is about.

And so when we asked about the format, over and over, we were told that I must write my story. I argued the point and avoided the opportunity until the book was ready to go to press and only my story was holding up publication of the *Manuscript*. The pressure mounted. I started it over and over. I wrote and rewrote. I added sections and fleshed out parts, and I still felt inadequate to the task of adding anything of value to this magnificent document, this truth that Magdalen gave.

I recapitulated my life through desert and mountains, through blizzards and sunsets that would set your heart on fire. I initially began the process under her instructions back on little Oudish, in Malta. I struggled with it in southern France and in the Cyclades, on Paros Island in Greece. I deleted and added to it like you add ingredients in soup. Too much salt. Add a little sugar. Too much drama and violence. Add the humor life always provides.

Yet, I wasn't going to include it. I still struggle over its relevance and your criticism. One day Tom said to me, "Shouldn't you be working on the *Magdalen Manuscript*?"

I said, "Oh, I just don't get it. I'm not about to include my life story. What will people think I'm trying to do?"

He handed me a card that had just arrived. It said, "Please write your story and include it in the *Manuscript*. When you write your story, you will be writing my story. You aren't writing it for yourself. You're writing it for all of us."

And so with all my flaws and fears on my shoulder, I honor what the Goddess requested.

The first section contains my story. The diary entries at the end share some of what I went through experiencing the "process" of receiving her information and the "obstacles to flight" we experienced living with this material, for it brought up, as it well should have, all my unfinished relationship issues.

In my case, these were essentially jealously, fear of abandonment, fear of betrayal, and general and pervasive unworthiness. And—to place that information in true context demands that I also tell you my story, as Metatron, my beloved advisor, has told me to do now for years.

And so I write this for Magdalen, for the Hathors, for Isis, for Metatron, for all my daughters—and for Tom who plays guitar and writes songs—because he dared to cross the dark, moist and dangerous abyss to the portal of the feminine to risk asking me to dance in Sacred Relationship, in the chalice of the Holy Grail.

# One Woman's Story

Life spit me out of my mother's womb in Appalachia, not to find waiting hands but a cold floor, as she was unattended at my birth. My mother and I shared this experience in a little clapboard house by the side of railroad tracks in Pennington Gap, Virginia. My birth name was Phyllis Elizabeth Zion, originally Sion.

Within months I was thrust into another environment, as my birth mother left home with me and my older brothers and sister to escape an abusive marriage and in search of her dream.

She wanted to be a country singer. And so when I was a month or so old, and my father was at work, she put us all on a bus, and we traveled across the state to south central Virginia where she left us with her parents while she went to find a singing job.

But as life would twist, very shortly after our arrival, grandfather's tractor pinned him underneath when he took a hill the wrong way. My older brother told me the story only a few years ago, when we found each other finally. He was running alongside the tractor so he ran to the house for help. He remembers grandmother running with her big, black nurse's bag. She took out a huge, hypodermic needle, which she filled with morphine for the pain. He watched her first squirt the liquid into the air and then inject it into grandfather. Then she tried to lift the tractor off him, breaking her back instead.

My grandfather died underneath the tractor, and grandmother never walked again.

I never knew these people. I was an infant as this drama played out, left inside the house while life and death called to its side who it wanted in the moment. We were handed out in the four directions, like leaves caught in a swirling wind.

I wound up at a motel/restaurant owned by a distant cousin while family frantically searched for someone to take an infant. There weren't many adoption agencies in the tobacco plains of Virginia in those years, and I suspect families preferred to take care of their own, as best they could.

And so it was that I was ultimately farmed out, like the tobacco I grew up around, and raised by Queen Victoria reincarnated—a staunch and severe woman, a schoolteacher, who couldn't have children of her own. At this apocalyptic juncture of fates I was still quite shy of one year, and I had already earned another equally portentous name, Judi Lee Pope.

Ruby Carter Pope loved me dearly; there is no doubt of that. Her life, and therefore the life of her husband, who became my father, centered around her Church, her family, her schoolchildren—and the constriction of me.

But her God was a fearsome and jealous thing I couldn't tolerate. And as soon as I got old enough to question, which in my instance was quite young, we came to loggerheads.

I grew up almost totally without playmates, wandering the tobacco fields of the Piedmont Region of Virginia with a St. Bernard dog and a borrowed horse. She sewed many of my clothes from flour sacks and never did anything herself but work and sacrifice. These were my models.

Oh, and judgment. They do a lot of judging in the country of Virginia.

We were very poor, though measured against the poverty of Brunswick County, Virginia; we were middle class, I suspect.

My father ran a country store that essentially served the abysmally poor black families that lived around us. I remember one barefoot woman who came in daily. She wore one single stocking over her head and ate one can of sardines and an "urnge" soda every day. It never occurred to me then that this was probably all she had to eat. And it never occurred to me then either that she never paid. Dad wrote up little pieces of paper that represented bills.

He died when I was eighteen and I found boxes of these unpaid bills, totaling well over $20,000, which was a staggering amount of money to be owed in those days. He must have fed half of Rawlings, Virginia and simply never told anyone.

I grew up being schooled in the fork of a pear tree. My teachers were a voice in the wind and whispers in the forest. I fashioned a bow and arrows myself and when the horse across the road was offered to ride, I left home for hours every day to find something. I don't know what.

I never had riding lessons. The horse taught me. The saddle and bridle anyone could figure out. And when the saddle slid underneath him, with me in it, on my first attempt, I had a little talk with him about letting the air out of his stomach before I cinched the saddle. I had to have this little talk with him often, but it worked.

And when his ears pricked up one day when he saw a fallen tree in the field, I knew what he wanted.

He wanted to fly.

And so we flew over it. I leaned into him; it was the logical thing to do. He jumped the tree; I just got to fly along with him. After that, there was nothing that stopped us. We forded rivers and trotted right down the middle of creeks. We wandered for miles through dense forests and galloped over fields and meadows, and if anything got in our way, we jumped it.

No one ever knew where I went on this horse. You could travel for days and not see another human being if you knew where to go through the forests and back roads of Brunswick County then.

I lied to my mother, of course; she wouldn't have allowed me to leave the yard but for well-crafted lies that became a necessity of life very early. She objected to everything and anything. To her, almost everything in life was either sinful or dangerous.

I never went to a birthday party or slept over at a girl friend's house. No one ever slept over at my house.

These were fantasies other people lived on the television. I had no idea people really lived like that.

My adopted mother chose my clothes and told me what to wear every day to school, even when I was much older. If I put on a sleeveless dress in June, she said I would get cold, and she added layers. If I put on a sweater in January, she told me I'd be too hot and dressed me down. The ultimate effect of this control was that I didn't have any idea what I felt or what I wanted. I wasn't allowed to date until I was 17, and she sat, stony-faced at the window, watching for me to come home even then, so she could approve my appearance when I returned, to make sure I hadn't discovered anything sinful, I'm sure.

Once, my date walked me to the door with his shirt not properly tucked in. I was never allowed to date him again. I think I was still in love with him a decade later, when we met and released each other from the fantasy we had each held, in our own way, for all those years, simply because we had never been allowed our time.

My father and mother slept in separate double beds in one bedroom. I slept with my mother until I left for college. My grandmother had the other bedroom. Ruby refused, heralding a variety of excuses, to ever finish the room upstairs. Thusly, she even managed to control how I slept at night. And she managed to never have to sleep with my father.

"Quit fidgeting," she used to say to me when I turned too often. "Lie still." Summers were endless, drenched in suspensions of tepid, stagnant pools of humidity. I lay for hours on end, too hot to sleep, not allowed to move, only my mind free to move about. Winters, I lay weighted under piles of ancient quilts, unmoving then due to the oppressions of stiff blankets from the Civil War holding me in their spell, haunting me with their visions, yet still cold in the depths of a Virginia winter.

But I had my music and dance, and I had the forest, which instructed me to dance on her naked skin barefoot, until I could waltz across the forest floor without making a sound. I had a borrowed horse, a beloved St. Bernard, named Micky, a teacher in a pear tree, a little friend in the Jack-in-the-Pulpit plant and another in the Pink Lady Slipper.

These were my childhood advisors.

There is one lesson I will never forget and now I watch it come to pass as a prophecy in my own life. From my memory, it was my first lesson delivered in the fork of that pear tree, where I wedged myself daily for years, dialoging with what I called, "words without a voice."

I was told that about every possible life experience would come to me, so that I would ultimately understand and have compassion for the human experience. And I was told that someday, when I was full of these life experiences, my voice would travel around the world, sharing what I had learned and that what I had to say would have a tremendous impact, but only when I really didn't care about such influence.

I was also told that there was another part of me out there somewhere and that someday I would meet the "mate to my being," and that our work would be together, that I wouldn't "get up in the morning and go to a job" like other people. I was told that he was part of my soul and that our work together would have a vast and beneficial influence on the world. This is, essentially, what I care to share of what I remember.

And there is one other early awareness that I distinctly remember.

I *knew* that the secrets of the universe lay in the physical experiences possible between a man and a woman—when they truly loved each other. I knew that *love* was the greatest gift you could be given. I knew there was a place you could go, a road only opened through that gateway of physicality, that few have ever walked. And I knew that was why the Church shamed sexuality and why governments had such rules and regulations to govern what they called "marriage," and why the whole subject has been both "tabooed" and regulated throughout this age of civilization.

I suspected the serpent wasn't evil, and I knew that Eve must have been brilliant to want more knowledge, and I knew it was illogical for the loving God who had created us to not want us to know everything. I suspected if there were such a beast as the devil, the smartest place for him to hide would be in the Church!

I *knew* the deepest secrets had to do with love, with what I now call Sacred Relationship. I knew that my purpose was somehow tied to reintegration of these secrets.

And I also *knew* there was another part of me out there somewhere. And I began a lifetime search for him.

I thought I saw him once, his face pressed against the window of a bus that slowly passed us on Route 1 on the way to Petersburg. For a minute, the bus and our car traveled at the same speed and our eyes met. We linked in that brief moment at some place that was holy, though we were only maybe—I don't know—eight, nine or ten years old. It would be another forty years before I touched such a holy place with a man again.

I knew *he* played guitar and wrote songs and had the voice of an angel. I always thought I'd know his voice if I ever heard it.

In terms of what shaped me, I can look back and remember the incidents that made me question the veracity of what was presented as authority. In the church I was forced to attend, I heard preaching on Sunday about love and non-judgment. I heard preaching about how God didn't care what you wore, but only saw what was in your heart. But I frequently overheard parishioners and the preacher criticizing and demeaning each other before they even got out the door!

"Can you believe she wears *that* to church," my young ears heard when my logic knew *that* was all the poor woman in question had to wear. I could *see* hearts then, and I saw purity in that old woman, but they only saw clothing.

"Well, you know where she comes from, don't you? I wouldn't expect much out of her! Her family is trash." I couldn't understand blaming someone for the actions of their parents or their distant cousins. And I remember hearing, "Always be good to your family. They're all you've ever got. And always remember that blood is thicker than water." Hmmm. That's a funny thing to say to an adopted child who had no blood around.

I simply never believed what I was told by the humans around me. And there were extraordinary events that made me look elsewhere for answers. I don't remember how old I was, maybe eight or nine. I had just gotten into bed one summer night. My mother was grading papers and my father was reading. I distinctly remember pulling a single sheet up to my chin when a glow appeared in the room. It transcended the darkness, creating an unmistakable luminescence, a pregnant "wetness" that made the very air seem visible, like floating molecules of moist light. A fear rose in me that was incalculable, beyond my wildest imagination. I had no backdrop for a mystical experience, though I am sure now that is what this was. Three lights appeared in the room, one on either side of the bed and one in the very center at the foot of the bed. A form appeared below the center light and it seemed to rock, though now I understand that was probably a pulsation.

I was frozen, completely unable to move, which exacerbated my fear. I told myself that if I could only move one digit of a finger, I could break this terrible spell and so I focused all my energy on moving one finger. It was impossible. So then I tried to focus all my will on my throat, to scream for help. I could make no sound. I thought I would surely die there, frozen to the spot. My father came down the hallway toward the bedroom, and I knew that if he came into the room he would break the spell, and I sent him every thought I could muster to please enter the room. But he stopped at the door, as if he'd forgotten something, and he turned around and never entered. I knew the "lights," whatever they were, had planted a thought to change his mind, and I knew I was dead.

I don't know how long this otherworldly spell lasted, but slowly the lights on the side dimmed. The pulsing of the center "figure" slowed in direct relation to the dimming lights. The lights on either side disappeared at the same time, blip! I was now transfixed by only the central light above the rocking figure. Imperceptibly slowly the rocking slowed, in direct proportion to the light slowly extinguishing. Finally I was held only by the unmoving apparition, a formless form, underneath a single dim light. As immediately as it had begun, simultaneously the figure disappeared, the light left, and I was free to bolt out of the bedroom and tear down the hall. I threw myself into a chair, hanging on for dear life and told my mother what had happened. I refused to go back to bed, though eventually exhaustion won out.

In the morning we received a phone call from an aunt, to say that her aged mother-in-law had died at precisely the same time as my incident occurred, and so it was that it became legend in my family that Great Aunt Somebody or Other had visited me when she passed. My only memory of her was of her sitting in a rocking chair, slowly rocking back-and-forth. And perhaps it was she, though I prefer Metatron's explanation. He says it was an Initiation from three Masters from other dimensions, and that it could only be given after I had finally decided to stay in a body; though that decision, if Metatron is right, has been questioned many times since.

I suppose that because Ruby had not allowed ordinary life to touch me for so many years, I rushed headlong into it when my father died, and I left for college at 18. I clearly began to have those "life experiences" the voice spoke to me about. I fell in and out of love like children learning to walk fall down. I was desperate for love, desperate to be touched, desperate for passion. The love "toddler" landed safely on her bottom until one night when a date refused to take me home.

I remember the feeling of fright when he drove past my street and turned instead down a dark road toward his own apartment building. His intentions were made clear when he used a martial arts grip on my arm, forcing me inside his apartment. When he turned his back inside, I bolted, running for my life. He took chase. As I ran, I had to make a choice between staying in the shadows or trying to make a phone call. The phone booth lay in light, clearly visible to anyone chasing a frightened young girl.

I chose the lighted phone booth, hoping that I could make an emergency call before he spotted me. But when I got to it, the phone was broken, and he had spotted me. I then ran toward the beach, sinking deeply into sand with each stride and exhausting myself trying to run through marsh grass and sand dunes.

But I got away.

After walking several miles along the beach, I saw figures approaching in the dim moonlight, and I panicked and took back to the roadside to cover the last five or so miles home. It was now the middle of the night, closer to dawn than night. It had been a long night of escape and terror.

A car pulled alongside me, and a voice said, "You must be crazy walking out here in the middle of the night. What's wrong? Let me give you a lift home. You're not safe out here walking like this." I peered in to see a safe-enough looking face; one I had never seen before.

I must have been crazy. Because I got into the car.

He immediately sped up to a pace that left no possibility of jumping and pulled out a blade that gleamed in the moonlight, leveling it sideways at my throat. He drove somewhere deep into the Dismal Swamp, as far as the road went then. The rest of that night and into the dawn are a blur of blood and contusions and struggling, with moonlight sharding off a knife blade.

After the battle was over he drove me back to the very street I had tried so hard to get to that night, and dropped me on the corner.

I wore a fencing mask for weeks, ashamed somehow of my cuts and bruises. As if a girl trying so hard to get home had done something to deserve the terror of that night. I ultimately went to the police, but at the time Virginia Beach had a policy of printing all rape victims' names in the local paper, and I knew Queen Victoria would hear what had happened, and I just wasn't ready for what that would create in my life. The thought of her accusations, of her screams of sin and guilt were more oppressive, more terrifying than anything that had happened to me that night.

I closed that door and went on with my life with a passion. I went to work at a radio station and moved into a phase of success in media and communication that was to continue through all the emotional turmoil of the next thirty years.

I met a handsome young man, and we began to date, getting more and more serious. He asked me to marry him. I was thinking about it, though there were signs I was ignoring, things about him and other issues with me. I had been having problems with my period, but nothing else seemed wrong. So I ignored these sporadic appearances and continued my life. Finally I sought help. Initially I was told I had a tumor. Then I was told I was seven months pregnant.

This was not in my life plan. I suppose because I had not enjoyed my own childhood, I had no intention of ever having children of my own.

Children, from what I had seen around me growing up, are what kept women from having a life. I viewed women as trapped in an endless cycle of sacrifice, not to mention that I was scared to death of the shame and the pain.

I married the handsome young man and spent a terrifying night giving birth to a girl, I was told. Perhaps it seemed the only solution at the time. My doctor had arranged a private adoption, and I never saw her. It was the best choice I felt I could make, under the circumstances. I had no money at all, and I felt she would be much better off with a family that could afford to raise her. I suppose my own childhood of flour sack clothes and few opportunities was still too fresh in my mind. And it was the only way to keep Queen Victoria from knowing and avoid sinking the illustrious and noble, but poor, southern family into shame!

I hid the last two months of the pregnancy, never leaving the apartment. I had learned at a very young age to draw the shades on things that are not supposed to be seen, and I had become that.

My handsome young husband turned out to be gay, and though he loved me as much as a gay man can love a woman, I was, after all, still a woman.

Through all of this I had managed to work my way through college in music, drama and philosophy. I had stumbled into radio as a DJ when women were first "allowed" that joy and from there I discovered the "power" of advertising. I moved into one of the most creative ad agencies in North America and worked my way into a position of authority and respect at a very young age, in what was still a man's world there as well. I won awards and honors and was highly paid. I had a magic touch that translated into high profits for my clients, and I loved what I did.

I lived what was, I suppose, a dual life. My days were filled with producing television commercials, planning campaigns, writing radio jingles, buying media, negotiating with clients and reps. My terrain ranged from the Board Room to the studio. I was a rare duck, equally adept at the creative end and the "business" end. I almost seemed to possess a psychic ability in advertising. Once I knew the soul of a client, I could "see" how the business or product or image flowed out of who he/she was and could just as easily see what ingredients were needed to position that image or message. Then I could "write" and design the "piece," whether it was print or audio or video. And much to my surprise, I could just as easily sense the budget and skew it where it belonged, holding huge traffic patterns of media in my mind. I thrilled at filling in the mental crossword puzzles, where the demographics of listeners/viewers/readers cross-matched certain words in a spot or a visual designed to reach a certain segment of a market, thus assuring sales.

But my nights were not as successful. We looked good together, and we had bought a home that was way over our heads, as all young yuppies are expected to do. It was a "Spanish Mansion" with a hand-painted tile fire-place and picture-frame molding. There was a fountain in the back courtyard, a marble foyer that ran about forty-feet-long to the foot of a staircase that could easily have been the scene for Gone With the Wind. It even boasted a servant staircase. Of course we had no ser-vants, and our nights were spent trying to clean the alter-nating black and white marble tiles in the front foyer. The roof leaked and sadly needed replacing, and the kitchen had never been brought into the 19$^{th}$ Century, much less the 20$^{th}$. The illusion was great but you couldn't cook there. And so after working all day, I worked alongside my husband to renovate this ancient mansion at night. We had lots of parties. He loved parties. But I always worried about who he'd fall in love with before the night was over. His depression seemed to get worse when he was drinking, and I knew our marriage was as much of an illusion as the Spanish Mansion.

But you never know what will break the camel's back. One morning on the way to work, I skipped along the sidewalk toward my car, trying to admire my dark green Buick Electra. It looked good in the sunlight and clients liked it, though my heart ached for my old MG.

A construction worker sat forlornly on the curb by the fender of my car. I ignored him as I stepped to the other side of the car and jumped back in shock. The driver's side had been sliced open, as if a giant had mistaken it for a can of green peas. I stood there gawking, my jaw hanging against my chest. The construction worker stood up, hardhat in hand over his chest, as if in respect for my now deceased vehicle.

"My demolition crane was on the way to a job, and when we took the corner, it just jumped off the truck and did that to your car. We had the knife on it instead of the ball. They left me behind to wait for the owner to show up."

I don't know why I cracked at that moment. But it was at that precise moment that I decided I needed to make a change. I managed to get to work only to be called into the President's office. He announced that he was leaving advertising and closing the business that month. I had been there five years, and I loved my job. I was a writer and creator. I produced radio and television commercials and planned campaigns and managed huge budgets for clients. These people were more "family" than I'd ever known.

I had just been given up for adoption again.

When I got home that night and my husband was "no-emotional-where" to be found, preferring liquor and a few ice cubes. I snapped.

Women keep score retroactively. Men erase their bad marks at the end of each day. So I was at five years and not much rope left; this was the three millionth time he hadn't been there for me. He figured he hadn't done anything wrong yet that day. Besides, he'd always gotten away with it before.

When he drank, he always threatened suicide, and I always hid the keys to his car and pleaded earnestly for him to come to his senses, which usually meant staying up all night negotiating deep passages of his inner turmoil, after which he usually celebrated by cleaning the marble tiles or stripping furniture. But it had been a bad day and that night, I was a new woman. This time I threw the keys at him, suggested he take a long drive, preferably off a short pier, packed my suitcase and walked out the door. I left him the Spanish mansion on the lake, the antique furniture, the statue of David, and a slightly damaged Buick Electra.

Luckily I had built a good reputation in advertising and was quickly offered a job in television. The day I signed my contract at the TV station, management walked out, leaving me the only person on staff at a management level. And so it was that I ran a television station for a year. I had "stumbled" into radio on bluff and bravado and gained a tremendous education, spent five years in an award-winning ad agency, and now fate had rounded out my resume quite nicely.

Fate had a few other surprises in store for me in my personal life as well. I went to a Unitarian cocktail party and saw the most handsome man I'd ever seen across the room. Judging him to probably be equally egotistical and no longer trusting very handsome young men, I spent the night crossing the room in the opposite direction he went, determined not to run into him. I survived the party without encounter and joined a group for dinner, only to find myself seated right across from him.

In the end, I took him home and ultimately we married. We were deeply comfortable together, he and I. He was an intellectual, with a great sense of honor, deeply wounded from his childhood—but who isn't.

I didn't understand the "drivers" implanted from my childhood, and I had already fully embarked on my "you need to be more giving, smarter, prettier, sexier, nicer, funnier and more talented than anyone around you to be equal and deserve life" phase. That translates to a woman headed for being Super Woman and to a potential victim.

I subbed for a late-night radio talk show host on occasion as well during those days, and I remember an incident that foretold a lot but which took another twenty years to finally make sense. The regular talk show host was a conservative and needless to say, I considered myself a liberal. I received great joy in what I considered opening the minds of his listeners when I did his show.

On one particular night I chose to talk about a very controversial legal situation. It was a court case in a nearby state in which a black woman had been jailed as an accomplice to a burglary. Her boyfriend had stolen something while she was riding in the car. During the night her white jailer entered her cell and raped her. During the rape, she managed to grab a knife from his belt, stabbed him and ran. He died, his semen splayed on the walls and his pants around his knees. She fled to another state, fearing southern justice and an extradition process was begun to bring her back to face murder charges.

Feminists were appalled. Rednecks wanted blood. I merely brought the circumstances to the attention of my listeners that evening, representing both sides of the argument, though I admit my obvious bias toward what I considered to be an enlightened and compassionate point of view.

I interviewed a local judge regarding the legal issues and also interviewed area feminists, to get the argument on the woman's behalf. When the show was over, I switched the FM to automatic, as I did every night, checked the logs, and closed down the station. I exited the side door, shutting the lights off behind me. I was alone in the station, as always at that hour. I walked out into the huge parking lot to find a row of cars down one side of the parking lot, another row of cars down the other side of the lot and a row of police cars down the middle, holding them apart from one another. The cars on the right were there to hurt me. The cars on the left were there to defend me. And the police were there to keep order. I slunk to my car and drove home and sobbed all night. How could anyone have been angry at the truth? And how could they hate me so? I was only shedding light on the dark truth. Why didn't people want to know the whole story? It was a crisis point in my southern life, a life where a woman is not supposed to offend or question.

By dawn I had come to the realization that essentially I had a power which I hadn't wanted and didn't know what to do with. People, I sadly realized, either really, really liked me, or really, really disliked me. There was, for whatever reason, no middle ground. This incident pointed this out regarding my speaking voice. I was later to realize I had the same effect on people with my writing and even my sheer presence.

That night and for many years to come, it brought me great pain to imagine having such a presence. I was frightened of power and wanted nothing to do with it. I much preferred to be loved by all, seeking only approval. It was years later and many more tearful nights before I came to respect and accept this particular power as something to *own*, something to use to make a differ- ence. It would be decades before I realized that people who make a difference usually offend someone. "People Pleasers" seldom trigger change.

My husband's government career moved us to Washington, D.C. and I began a consulting business, incorporating everything I had learned in my years in advertising.

Perhaps it was the sands in the biological hourglass and their ever-present descent from future into past, but my husband and I began to speak of children and ulti- mately had two exquisite daughters. But our life began to unravel with the intrusions into our private time. First Jennifer developed allergic reactions to milk, soy, all pro- tein, and all sugar. As I struggled with that diagnosis and some system of nutrition for her, Adrianne began a series of ear infections that continued until she was about 12 years old. Nights became a blur of shuffling from one room to another, from rocking one while she screamed in pain to cross the hallway to lift another crying infant into my arms.

These were my Superwoman days as I lived on about four hours of sleep, broken by feedings and disruption, and then served my clients during the day. My office was in my home, and I had full time help, which meant I could be with one daughter while the help was with the other. That way I could be with the girls when I wasn't on a deadline and make sure no one hurt them. The oldest, Jennifer, literally cried most of the time, due to the stomach discomfort she was in; and from ten days of age, she never napped. She finally fell asleep, crying at midnight. She woke crying at 2 AM and again at 4 AM and was up for good at 6 AM every day. The youngest simply cried all the time when she had an ear infection. She had twelve in her second year.

When I visited my clients, I frequently took the girls and the sitter along, stopping along the way at a play-ground or a Children's Museum or a mall. That way they could play while I handled business meetings.

We were living near Washington, D. C. at this point, and so it was only logical, as I was prone to stumbling through life now, that I fall into political consulting. I had a gift there too, it seems. I treated the politicians the same way I treated a shoe company. It was really quite simple. It's all just understanding what the client "stands" on and what his "soul" is made of, and how to out-pic-ture that in the marketplace.

It was during the management of a particular cam-paign that I became painfully aware of the encroaching power of the right wing evangelical agenda. The ominous and obvious portends terrified me. My crystal ball fore-told a future ahead with chiseled Constitutional Rights. I foresaw a horrible future world dominated by the kind of consciousness I grew up around, narrow and bigoted and ignorant. I saw censorship ahead and loss of freedoms, all in the name of God and righteousness, mind you. I felt totally helpless in the face of this rider, as I felt in my life in general. I was astride the back of a horse nothing like the horse of my childhood. Where this one was headed, I didn't want to go. But I was in observation mode. My "action button" hadn't yet been engaged.

The more my daughters demanded, the more my husband withdrew. He left for work at about 6 am and returned around 5 pm, to take a long, hot bath—some-thing I greatly envied. Then he either disappeared into the office at home or into the television. He emerged from one or the other hours later. I could probably count the number of times he put the girls to bed on my fingers and toes. Emotionally he became colder and colder until one day I realized it had been three years since he had touched me, and I wasn't allowed to make overtures. My attempts at dialoguing about it were fruitless. My demands for counseling brooked only one worthless marriage counselor, who could have created divorce between the world's greatest lovers. I cried myself to sleep most nights, and he never noticed.

One day I recall standing by the foot of the bed. "Why don't you ever touch me anymore?" I asked, biting my lip, steadying myself for his answer.

"I don't find you attractive any more." That was all he had to say. He went back to reading then, and I went back to keeping the girls from bothering him, which is how I spent my evenings. He didn't like to hear them cry.

However, my business life was starkly successful, and we lived in the right town, and we drove the right car. And I had oriental rugs and antiques again! And the girls were in the very best nursery school and had been tested for Gifted Programs, which was de rigueur in Northern Virginia if you were anybody who dreamed of having successful toddlers.

Then the visitations began. I was asleep in my own bed one night, and I felt a finger prodding my arm. I turned over and opened my eyes, expecting to see Jennifer standing there wanting my attention. Instead I was shocked to see no one standing there. But when I looked at my arm, my skin was indenting in cadence to the feeling of someone poking me in the arm. I looked around the room and there at the foot of the bed was a large luminous shape, rather like the shape of a human body, but with no *body*, only a glowing, pulsing pres-ence. It extended a firey "finger" and "whispered" to me, "Come and write."

And I got up and went into my office and began a series of poems I later called The Phantom Series. These

poems desperately hungered to know what this presence
was. It was a definitively male presence, a highly sexual
feeling presence. I yearned to know who had entered my
life this way, reminding me what passion was missing
from my own existence.

*"I have chased you across the paths of time. Through
birth and death and birth and death. You ignite me and I
burn,"* I wrote to him.

My childhood experience with the three lights visiting
me in my room one night had left me with a great interest in the paranormal. I'd read a book on Edgar Cayce
when I was quite young and fully accepted the understanding of reincarnation and karma. It just felt right,
and my soul knew the truth of it, for me anyway. But it
had been a while since anything had come to call,
especially anything that had changed me so. After
these visitations, which continued nightly for nine
months, I began to write a newspaper column, and I
moved back more deeply into alternative spirituality
with a growing ferocity and commitment.

My previous interest had been in the paranormal, but
now I began to contemplate God, and I knew that it was I.

My husband thought I was crazy.

But the visitations continued for nine months, long
enough to birth a newspaper column, which I wrote for the
next four years for the local paper. One of my first columns
was about the first day Jennifer went to Kindergarten. It
waxed quite poetic about a mother's hope for her child,
intending to speak about the hope we have for all children,
only using my own experience as metaphor.

I remember one line read, "May your toe shoes
never hurt." It only appeared to be about Jennifer going
to Kindergarten, but was much more about childhood
and life and loss, all couched in a mélange of beautiful
language. It spoke to all our hopes and dreams for all
our children. And for whatever reason, people hated me
for writing it. The editor was a friend, and he understood the power of columnists. He was delighted with

the controversy I had created and featured the hate
mail boldly in print.

I mean, how could they hate me for writing a sweet column about my daughter going to kindergarten and all my
hopes and dreams for her? I have read and reread that
column, and to this day I can only see it provoking tears,
not hatred. But instead I opened the paper the week after
it appeared, and there were two facing pages of hate letters about my writing. I cried all week. Next week the
paper came out and there were letters praising my writing.
I was up against my old issue of pleasing people. Why
couldn't they all love me? One day I signed a check at the
grocery store and the checkout clerk recognized my name
and commented on my column, which led the woman
behind to say how much she hated me, which led the
woman behind her to say how much she loved me. I slunk
out of the store and went home and cried again.

I told myself that if my five-year-old could grow up
and go to school, I could grow up, too. Growing up, to
me in this instance, referred to getting over my fears of
not being wanted and "not being approved of." It was the
same old, same old abandonment "why doesn't anyone
love me stuff." And you know what? It was holding me
back from being all I could be. I knew that as long as I
cared what people thought, I wouldn't be all I could be. I
was using all my energy trying to write pleasing
things...please my husband...please my children...please
my clients. I had no energy left for me.

My life is a series of stumbles and cracks. I stumble
into something, and then I crack and get out. I guess I
should have known that a fissure was opening a hole in
my marriage large enough for me to fall through. We
were traveling different roads and only meeting occasionally when we came upon a crossroads. But I don't
give up easily, and I kept trying to make things work or
pretend that it didn't matter that I wasn't happy.

One night we went to dinner with a friend who was in
town on business. He always took us out to dinner during

his visits, and on this occasion we were in Georgetown at a French Restaurant where the waiters wore roller skates and jumped on stage and did little musical numbers in-between courses. I'd had a drink, which was very unusu-al for me. It only takes one drink to make me very happy and very tipsy. Emotionally, I melted, remembering the man I had fallen in love with and married, the man I'd felt strongly enough about to have children with. And so I leaned over and ran my fingers along his neck, imagin-ing deeply luscious thoughts of sensuality. He never looked around, but he must have mistaken my fingers caressing his neck for an insect, because he slapped his hand around behind his neck, like you would swipe at a fly to shoo it away.

It felt like someone had slapped me in my heart. It was, for whatever reason, the last straw, the last intimacy rejection of the hundreds I had suffered with him. I snapped. I stood up, slipped the keys toward him so he would have the car (God knows I didn't deserve the car myself!) and walked out the door. I had 25 cents in my purse when I hailed a taxi and asked him to take me to a bank machine so I could pay the cab fare the 30 miles out to Reston where we lived. The cab driver was an Iraqi student working on his PhD. We stopped, and I picked up a girlfriend along the way. She had a trumpet, and I stopped at the house and picked up my clarinet, and we sat together on the main plaza in town, and we played music, she on the trumpet and me on the clarinet. The cab driver was on tabla and vocals. We played and sang the blues on Lake Anne Plaza until sunrise. I sang about lost love. She sang about lost youth. He sang about the horrors of war. Why no one complained, I don't know.

I intended to leave that next night, but he talked me into staying for a few weeks, saying a mother with two small children shouldn't have to go out in the cold. He said if I just gave him a few weeks, he'd find a place. But he never left. I found out later that his father had advised him not to leave, fearing I might say he deserted and claim the house. He obviously didn't know me. I walk away from houses and antiques.

*I don't deserve for anyone to take care of me. I take care of myself. No one loves me. No matter how much I give or how hard I work or how much I love, I am an orphan, and that is the way it will always be. And, after all, I am just a woman, and everyone knows we have no value. We cannot be Saints or Mystics. We are only whores. We can only serve a man. That we are necessary for the birth of children is only of temporary importance, and we about to be replaced biologically by test tubes and petri dishes.*

I wound up staying almost another six months or so after that incident, but I took off my wedding ring and no longer considered myself married. And I began to work earnestly on my spiritual life, of which he wanted no part.

I rented a cottage on Chincoteague Island and spent two weeks alone with no clock and no phone. It was my first adventure into alone time since the back roads of Virginia. I soaked in it. I sponged it. I sopped it up. I reveled in it. I splashed it on my face and bathed deeply in it, sinking into myself, anointing myself with the space to breathe and think.

I made friends with a fisherman who saved me the best of his catch of the day, and I lived blissfully on a daily ration of one huge crab, one glass of red wine, and one artichoke.

As I walked the Atlantic coast beach of the sister island, Assateague, I had what can only be described as a life-altering experience. I began a dialogue with "words without a voice" that lasted three full days as I walked the beach during a storm. This "teacher" who appeared in my head was the most challenging and powerful presence I had ever experienced at that point, and I was both awed and humbled by the power and the presence.

These "words without a voice" taught me about the illusion of perfection and about the light spectrum and our creation through it as we *fell* into matter. I was taught

about the physics of consciousness and about the perfection in what might appear to be imperfection.

He—it felt like a male presence—taught me about the
physics of soul mates, how we begin the journey into
matter as one light that splits into two lights, male and
female/positive and negative, as we "fall" through the
light spectrum to enter this electromagnetic plane of
consciousness. He told me that almost never are these
two original lights on the same plane even...that the
reuniting of these lights is extremely rare, and that if it
should happen prematurely, before each has finished its
own individual work, they might blow each other up, so
powerful are the magnetics of original lights. After these
caveats had been delivered, this voice told me that my
destiny lay in the reuniting with my original light.

A spark was rekindled in the little girl who had always
believed in true love, who had always *known* there was
another part of her somewhere out there, and though the
spark had been relit with clear warnings, my heart leapt
at the possibility. I looked deeply at my life and saw that
the foremost issue for me had always been relationship.
It was my *work*. It was my *love*. And the truth was, finding "this other half of me" was what my search had
always been about. And—if it were true that you shouldn't
meet before each of you had finished your own personal
work, then I'd better go to work on myself. And so it was
that I vowed to call forth any unfinished personal work,
so that I would be ready.

I walked those three days through a fierce Nor'easter
that blew a steady gale force at me, so that I had to walk
leaning into it. I argued with this voice of God in my
mind as I walked, railing about the inconsistencies and
vagaries of life and metaphysics.

At one point, after I'd debated vehemently over a
point, I was ordered to pick up a seashell that lay in my
path. It was cracked and barnacle-covered, slick with the
sludge of oil on one side. What had once been life was
no more and in its place, only parasites and waste and

pollution. The sky in my mind split down the middle, and for some period of time I can't describe—I saw truth. I saw it all. I saw the revolution of cosmos around cosmos, multi-leveled, multi-realmed worlds-within-worlds and layers of purpose.

Purpose and perfection were contortionists that could bend into anything they needed to be in the moment. It was *all* perfect. And even the concept of perfection was limited. And that was perfect. The imperfection was perfect!

I stayed in this place of sheer bliss for—I don't know, maybe only seconds. Maybe hours. After all, I had walked into a gale force wind for three solid days, sunrise to moonrise.

I had asked, "What's it all about?" And the Big Alfie had answered me.

I went back the fourth day at sunrise, and I asked to be able to write what I had been taught, as I had never heard such communication. I was told I'd have to "earn the words back," and that when I'd "owned" them in my own life, I could have all the teachings back—but they would come from my own mouth and heart then and not just be a repetition. And so it is that I can tell this story and not yet write the full teaching given by the wind in those three days.

Back home, I could never be the same. I had seen something, and I was different.

I loved my husband, but he was incapable of loving himself, and I should have learned one of life's great lessons by that point. You can't love someone enough to make them love you. If they can't love themselves, they surely can't love you. But I hadn't *gotten* that from my first marriage and wasn't to *get* it from my second attempt. Instead, I had lain awake at night, tears rolling down my cheeks for years, lying right beside him, and he had never noticed.

After ten years of waiting for a change in temperature, I figured he'd frozen to death and wasn't going to thaw, and so I left. I had reached a point in my growth where survival could not compensate for emotional freedom and truth. I refused to let the girls grow up in an environment that was a lie, perpetuating the myth of "mommy-daddy" based on common agreement to "stay together for the sake of the children." If this was my soulmate, he surely didn't see it that way.

And I had been called by an island in the northern sky and by a great teacher in the wind. A few months after my Chincoteague experience I saw a video that sounded a lot like my teacher in the wind.

And so it was that I packed up my daughters, closed my business, bought a van and packed it for a road trip. I was going west to write the teachings of this great Master and to work on my unfinished business, so that I would be ready.

There are memories I hold dearly from that cross-country trip with a six-year-old and an eight-year-old. We camped at night, our modest, older Volkswagen Westfalia wedged between huge converted buses and motor mansions. Linen tablecloths and silver goblets emerged from our turtle-shell, and while our neighbors stuffed themselves into plastic chairs outside their $200,000 motor homes guzzling beer, we breakfasted on eggs benedict and served our grilled cheese sandwiches with our crusts trimmed and drank our tea from silver goblets.

I sat in a pool of water beneath Horseshoe Falls in West Virginia the day my briefing was given to the Executive Branch of the White House, laughing under the pelting warm water. I could have stayed for that briefing, for the "glory" of saying I'd been there, but I chose the waterfall instead. It was the 4th of July, 1986, and it seemed a more fitting statement to make about freedom, to sit in a waterfall rather than sit in the Oval Office of the Reagan White House.

I experienced my first-ever migraine in Elk Creek, Kentucky. My head was pounding and I thought I'd better stop driving. It was early afternoon when we pulled into the Elk Creek Campground. I picked a campsite as the blinding pain sent me diving underneath covers for darkness. Next door to our camping site, Elsa permanently camped every summer. She strung Christmas tree lights and had fake grass laid out the entire breadth of her space. Her wooden sign announced her encampment to the constant stream of family and guests.

As I passed out from the pain, I held a vague memory of seeing Jenni and Adrianne wander over and enter Elsa's picket fence where she held court on a lawn chair picking beans, a little Chihuahua by her side.

I awoke hours later, electrically rewired, as I was to be for years, from these headaches that always took me down for what seemed like days. I was horrified. How long had I slept? Where were the girls? I had no intention of letting them out of my sight on this trip, having heard so many horror stories of children disappearing on their way to the bathroom at a campground. I pulled back the curtain on the van window and allowed the waning light of dusk to penetrate my optic nerve, only wincing slightly.

There were the girls, picking beans with Elsa next door.

"God," I thought. "What on earth will she think of me? I've been gone for however long, asleep in a van while my children roamed around." She was an older woman, and I had learned to be frightened of them, having been raised by one!

I stumbled my way out the door and over through the little gate beneath the "Elsa's Place at Elk Creek" sign.

The girls greeted me excitedly and begged to show me the trick Elsa's Chihuahua could do. Elsa agreed and they dispatched the little dog to "fetch a drink." The little snippet of short white hair raced into the camping trailer, and dragged out a can of beer. Ferociously, he growled and menaced and dragged the can back and forth across the fake grass, slamming it into the lawn chairs, clawing and scratching at it's pop-top until it began to leak beer. Gleefully he then lay back, pulling the can over him, catching every drop as gravity drew the liquid down his throat.

"So," Elsa said to me, "the girls tell me you're taking them off to some island way up in the Northern sky, smack-dab in the middle of nowhere. You got a good reason for doing that?"

Fear clutched at my throat. Was she going to judge me for this? Was I going to buckle under this scrutinization? Could I think of some lie to justify this action on my part?

"No," I heard myself say. "I don't have a good reason for doing this. I just want to."

"Good," Elsa said. "I never saw happiness come from anything done for a good reason."

I knew then we were on a magical journey of spirit, not mind. It continued from philosophical conversations with old folksingers on a riverboat along the Missouri to saving a frog in a whirlwind on the White River in the Badlands in South Dakota.

I liked Missoula, Montana so much that I got down on my knees in front of the van outside a Chinese Restaurant and cut it a deal. I promised my van that wherever it broke down, I'd consider that as a sign that we were supposed to stay there. Then I started the engine, silently hoping it wouldn't start. It started.

We continued until we ran out of land at the edge of a little town in Northern Washington State. We boarded a ferry on the way to the island whose call I had heard all the way back east. The three of us huddled against the wind on the bow of Kaleetan and sobbed at the recognition as home approached. Here—my heart sang. Here—my soul breathed with joy and recognized divinity. Here, where cliffs met the sea, entwined in a chain as ancient as memory, I found some sense of place I had never known before.

But no one was expecting us. There were no banners out that read, "Welcome. We have been awaiting your arrival. Sit down now and write the books you were called to write. Here's your paycheck." Reluctantly, we stayed as long as we could, but since no one made me an offer, we headed off, either to the Southwest or home. We would make that decision along the way.

But we were so close to a huge snow cone called Mt. Rainier that I couldn't see how we could be that close and not climb it. It was, after all, right there in front of us, begging for a pilgrimage. Alas, after climbing all the way up, the engine finally blew on the way down. And there we were, stranded. Or was it gifted? A blown engine would take a minimum of two weeks. I called home and had the same experience we'd had nightly when we tried to call. We got the phone machine. When I finally got through to the girl's father, telling him we were stranded, he didn't say, "Oh, let me fly out and take care of this. Are you all right? What can I do to help you? Let me fly you home right now." Instead he said, "So what does this mean to me?"

We never returned.

Through the next five years, I was a single mother, living with eagles and whales on an island in the Northern Sky. Since their father was on the other coast, he wasn't around to take them on weekends or overnights, so there were no nights off for me. No weekends alone. Life was full time. And the ear infections continued.

Through all the born-again virgin years, I had one mantra. I repeated this mantra over and over to myself. I repeated it in the bathtub, on hikes up the mountain, on the way to school to pick up the girls, everywhere. I must have said this at least twenty times a day for those five years.

*"From the Lord God of My Being Unto the Mother/ Father Within, I call forth all my unfinished business. Bring it forward. Bring forward anything I have not looked at. Bring forward my fears, my jealousies, and my insecurities. Bring it all forward and let me work on it now. So be it!"*

Occasionally, I must admit, I added a line to my mantra.

*"From the Lord God of My Being Unto the Mother/ Father Within, I call forth all my unfinished business. Bring it all forward that I may finish it, so I will be ready to meet the mate to my being."*

The girls and I were so close during those years you couldn't have gotten a sliver between us. We were all we had. We lived on $900 a month for most of those years. Once, I sat down with both Jennifer and Adrianne, and we talked about what to do. I worried constantly about money. I explained that we could move back to D.C., and I could make a lot of money again, and their clothes could come from Bloomingdales again, as they once did. Now their clothes came from Second Hand Rose. I explained that I wouldn't be as available as I now was, but that we could have help and they could take music and dance and have things they didn't have. We had managed to hang onto a nice winter rental, with large rooms and beautiful furnishings, but it was no longer in the budget, though we moved out of it every summer and sort of floated around until we could have it back in the fall. But it was still out of the price range now, and we faced a wall of expenses, especially if I was going to try to produce a book.

They listened patiently to my presentation of our financial situation, and they both intoned, simultaneously, "Oh, no! We came here so you could live your dream. You mustn't give up your dream. We can move to some-thing cheaper. Nothing will ever work if you don't live your dream!"

And so it was that we located a deserted trailer, with missing ceiling panels that allowed insulation blackened with mildew to hang down into each room. To say the roof leaked was a gross understatement. We had no fur-niture with us and couldn't afford to move our furniture from D.C., so we acquired enough to "furnish" (loosely translated, please!) our singlewide on the beach. We got our queen-sized foam mattress from the dump. It was V-shaped, with a deep crevice in the middle. We all slept together, me in the middle, one little girl on either side. I slept with little arms and legs sprawled all across me. We turned as one tangled mass, sometimes getting caught in each other's limbs. I seemed to always have a little arm across my face. I loved sleeping that way.

Of all the things I felt anger at their father for, somehow every Christmas I resented him most. He had all the Christmas ornaments and lights in his comfortable four-bedroom home in Reston, Virginia, the one his father had made sure he continued to live in. He never used them after we left, I have since discovered. But he wouldn't ship them to us. And so we had no Christmas ornaments and certainly couldn't waste money buying any. One year our dear friend, the island doctor, brought us ornaments from his tree, so we would have something to hang.

One year we couldn't afford a tree, and so a friend brought us a tree from high atop a mountain on the island where he had logging rights. It was a hemlock tree, with beautiful green branches, much prettier than the trees of Christmas past. We hung our few little ornaments on it, strung it with popcorn and Madrona berries, admired it, and went to bed. When we woke in the morning, the girls ran out to see their tree, only to find it all over the carpet. Hemlock trees drop their "green" needles inside. We were picking Hemlock needles out of that carpet for days. That was the Christmas of the Madrona branch. I thought it was quite a statement for the environment myself. No tree had to die, and a dead branch got honored. I don't think the girls shared my altruistic opinion of that particular dead branch.

We fixed the roof and slowly repaired the ceiling tiles, holding back the deadly insulation finally, but only after dozens of ear infections, and one by one we had each thrashed in the boiling temperatures of viral meningitis. I remember slipping through dimensions and twirling through the underworld, a hell of sweat and burning. My head didn't *hurt*. Hurt doesn't even come close to what that agony felt like. It felt like my marrow was being boiled while I was still in the body, and I ached beyond this world and into the next.

Two horrific storms hit the island while we were in our "trailer years." Each was labeled a "hundred year storm," supposedly so ferocious it could only happen once in a hundred years. We lived on the North Shore of Orcas Island during both of them. Power was lost early on and water followed. We had a tiny Kent woodstove in the living room of the singlewide. I filled one wall in the kitchen with wood and sealed black plastic over the inside of the windows and the sliding door and taped us in. I forced myself outside in the wind only once a day, to restock the wood. I set an alarm clock to feed the stove every two hours through the night. But we survived in that trailer when everyone else fled the North Shore. Two other single mothers deserted their huge homes in the below freezing cold, and we laid mattresses across the whole living room floor, and three mothers and six children held together through the storm in an 8' by 8' area. We cooked soup and noodles for days on that tiny stove. We thawed snow for water on the same stove that boiled our potatoes and noodles. I will always hold a special fondness for Kent stoves. It not only kept us alive, it kept us warm and fed us.

Adrianne "celebrated" her eighth birthday toward the end of the worst, and we managed to drive into town to the grocery store. The power was still off, and the store couldn't even open its door without electricity. They pried them open and forced them partially separated so that islanders could buy what few things were left on the shelves. There was one box of Duncan Hines white cake mix and we took it home. We opened the box and passed it among ourselves with a shared utensil, spooning bites of dry cake mix while we sang Happy Birthday. It is, to this day, the best birthday party I've ever been to. Three women and six children survived that storm at the point on the island where the brunt hit, better than 90 mile-an-hour winds raging down from Alaska and below zero temperatures—and we stayed warm and well fed, with no help from a man.

Somewhere, somehow, in the midst of this struggle to survive with little income, I did manage to do what I went there to do. I edited and produced three books based on the material I believed to have come from the great teacher in the wind, a consummate accomplishment for a single mother living on $900 a month. Eventually I acquired the rights back to the first two, self-published the last one, and even got it on the New Age bestseller list. Adrianne still says this is the time period she remembers when she thinks about my power, those "trailer years" when we found out that nothing could stop us.

One of these books was on the subject of male tyrants, though I did not think I had ever experienced one at the time. One was on manifestation. And one was on super consciousness.

I wish I had known I draw into my life what I edit. I would never have done the book on male tyrants.

But it wears on you, you know—the aloneness with so much responsibility. The school was dreadfully inferior, and I worried about the girls' education. I could offer them nothing beyond the most basic requirements of life, though I had become a magician in a second-hand store.

Deep in my heart, I was still lonely.

I began to lecture about the third book, specifically because it addressed a subject I thought to be sadly in need of understanding. Many people I knew held deep respect, to the point of abject reverence and subjugation, for whatever presented itself within the framework of what we considered Deity.

Send a voice and call it God or Jesus or Mary or any "known" Master and people bow in reverence. But the same people who bow to what is considered Deity within religion scoff at people who have communication with information sourced outside our current historical frame of reference, i.e., aliens. How narrow!

I decided it was my task to bridge this chasm between spirituality and what is considered "alien consciousness" and began to speak on the subject.

I have never really understood where fate meets karma. And if we create our own reality, what role does destiny play? I may never know in this lifetime. I will surely never understand how the same woman who left one man rather than allow her daughters to grow up in a loveless home could possibly get caught in what was to unfold.

I met a man at a speaking engagement who claimed to be something he wasn't. But I believed him, because I wanted him to be what he said he was...because I wanted the world to have such possibility. I wanted *me* to have such possibility.

He portrayed himself as a great teacher.

And he played guitar and he sang songs.

He told me he was Native American, a Medicine Man who had studied with the great old Grandfathers and Grandmothers. He performed ceremony and played the flute and wrote songs. He carried a sacred pipe and con-jured images deeply held within my psyche, and so began my years with the Eagle, the Bear, Spider, Raven and the White Owl and the Black Fish. I hiked deeper into the forests and spent probably two nights of every week carrying the stones into the Sweat Lodge, praying and singing. The first two years we traveled with elders, and I really did learn many amazing things. What I didn't know was that he was learning right along with me. He really hadn't known many of these things before we came together, but then, I had never experienced a real con man until him, and it took me years to figure that out. I did not know how cleverly the dark could pretend to be the light.

Slowly he began a process of tearing me down, demeaning me, cutting me off from old friends, and tak-ing my power over a period of almost five years. Until one day I awoke to realize I had become an abused woman. I had allowed a man to hit me, while I supported him.

One day I was walking behind him, on the way to the kitchen to make him a cup of coffee. All of a sudden, he twirled around and pounded a blow to my left ear. Pain so sharp it numbed shot through me, and I fell to the ground from the blow. I spent the rest of that day in bed, holding my ear, curled in a fetal position from the pain. I was deaf in that ear for six months. And I told no one. He never said he was sorry. We just went on with life. After all, he was a "great teacher" and I was just a woman. What else am I left to think about my desperation for me to allow such treatment? Perhaps because the abuse was infrequent and came literally out of the blue, I excused it. Perhaps I was too ashamed to admit it happened. Perhaps my childhood wound re-opened.

I was in the fifth grade. Right after lunch one spring day, Charlotte, the teacher's pet, saw a book lying on the teacher's desk. Charlotte was the "room librarian," and so it was her domain to check all library books found in the room. Alas, it had not been checked out at all! Ever vigilant, Charlotte promptly returned the book to the library and came back to the classroom.

The bell rang, and the teacher walked in, took a look at her desk, and asked where her book was. The room got really quiet. Mrs. Brown was especially mean to some kids and particularly nice to others. There was never a reason anyone could determine that explained her behavior or her choice of victim.

On that particular day, Mrs. Brown walked across the room and stood in front of me.

"Judi, you took my book back to the library didn't you?"

"No, ma'am, Mrs. Brown," I said respectfully. To which she drew her arm back and slapped me across the face, propelling me out of my desk and onto the floor. I was stunned and humiliated. I had done nothing!

I couldn't wait to tell Ruby what had happened. She would take care of it. Mothers always take care of things.

When I told her what happened, Ruby said, "I'm sure she had a reason. I have to teach at the same school; there's nothing I can do."

I never forgot her response and lived out the repercussions for another 30 years.

*If someone hits me, I must have done something to deserve it. If I was raped at knifepoint, it must have been because I had no business walking along that road that late at night.*

Before I finally learned my lesson, he attacked my daughter and wound up stealing everything we had accumulated between us. In the very end he almost killed me—holding me against glass-paneled doors and beating me back-and-forth across the face until I almost lost consciousness.

The truth was finally clear to me. I had fought a five-year-long battle with the dark side for the soul of a man. And lost.

We agreed to separate after the girls and I returned from studying with an herbalist. Instead, while we were out of town, he wrote obscenities on the bedroom walls with magic markers, packed everything and left. He forged my name on documents that resulted in lawsuits and cleaned out the bank account. I learned the hard lesson of a male tyrant.

We returned home and found everything gone—everything, I should say, of value. He had taken the girl's new video player bought with their child support, all CDs, all my art, my sacred bundle, all the furniture of any value, all running vehicles, including a motor home in both our names, all paperwork, even my address book. He left behind 1500 pounds of wet insulation and trash everywhere. There were threats hidden inside jars and hatbands and a notice from the landlord that we had less then 30 days to be out of the house. The girls and I cleaned the house, sealed the walls he'd covered with obscenities, repainted, and moved within that deadline.

I know how much the insulation and garbage weighed because when we shoveled it off the rental truck at the dump, they charged me $180. When I looked shocked at the cost, they said, "Hey, lady, you just offloaded 1500 pounds of trash and that's what it costs." Without a penny to my name, that was a huge sum to be charged for dumping his trash, but insult to injury had become a way of life with him. He also deserted the two dogs he had brought into my life.

I put everything left into storage, kept out one good looking outfit and took the only living space offered us— a friend's tiny motor home. We boarded the dogs at the kennel and put three cats into cages stacked on each other and moved all of us into a space only big enough to sleep in, alongside the cat cages.

I borrowed money from Adrianne, who had saved every penny she'd ever been given, perhaps just so she could loan me that money, and I went to town looking for a house. A rental agent who had clearly lost her mind rented me an expensive old waterfront farmhouse on six acres of the most beautiful land on the island. I was a woman with no job and two teenaged children. To this day, I have no idea how I got that farmhouse, nor do I have any idea how I had the courage to rent it.

We moved in slowly and invited the owners to leave their old furniture in place rather than take it to the dump! *There is a Goddess!* Thankfully, this gave us beds, a sofa from the fifties and a dining room table!

I slowly lifted my head from the paralyzing decay of shame and began to contact old friends, obtaining phone numbers one by one. I immediately discovered why he had stolen my address book. He had called many of them and told them I had stolen everything from him and left him with nothing. He told them I had taken all the money! He even told some of them that I had abused him! But here's the biggest shocker of all. Many of them believed him! He had told the most amazing lies I have ever heard. I had forgotten what a consummate liar he was! He had, after all, fooled me for years. And I had hidden the abuse from almost everyone for years. I don't know why. *It was infrequent so I justified it? I kept thinking I'd done something wrong to make him hit me? It came so "out of the blue" it was hard to believe it happened?*

This was to be my first major encounter with betrayal, and I watched many people I called friends choose to believe him instead of me. Until that experience with him, I had always believed there were two sides to every story. Now I know better. By that I mean that I understand that there are always two experiences, and in the grand "metaphysical" understanding everyone has their own truth, but there is no mitigation for abuse, verbal or physical. There is no "other side" that excuses abuse.

The final shock for me was when a girlfriend visited me one day shortly after we got our new house. She was one of the few people who knew about the abuse.

She had lived near us and had seen his hypocrisy. She was also one of a handful of people who knew that I had stood by this man through his immense legal problems, paying for his lawyers with the profits from my own books to clean up his past shady history. She told me about a telephone conversation she'd had with his mother during the months of legal battles.

He had always claimed to be a Metis, a person of mixed blood, part Native and part Caucasian. So this woman had asked his mother which side of the family had the Native blood. His mother had replied that there was absolutely no Native blood on any side, only Italian. She had confirmed that he was actually full blood—full blood Italian!

In actuality, he was nothing he had claimed to be, and until the very end, I had believed him. I had believed his version of the legal battles, which portrayed him as a victim of the system. I had believed his version of why I found different names on paperwork. I had believed his version of how awful all the other women had been in his life, betraying him, and deserting him, and leaving him with nothing. (And I swore I'd stand by him and show him how wonderful *some* women can be!) I had believed his version of where he learned and earned his medicine. And in the end, I was to discover he was not Native, not even part Native. Not only was he not *what* he said he was, but he wasn't even "who" he said he was either. I

had wondered why he had a different name from his
mother, and why his own daughter had a different last
name, and why the name I knew him by was different
from either his birth name or his only daughter's name.

He had been many different men in his life.

There is a dreadful shame that comes with being a
"victim," whether it is of abuse, or ignorance, or both,
as in my case. It is rather like being a rape victim.
There is a terrible sense that you did something to
bring it on, some horrible, awful feeling that somehow
you deserved it. In my case, this was, of course, the
result of my childhood with Queen Victoria, who had
somehow always made me feel like I was very lucky
she hadn't left me on a dung heap somewhere to
starve when she took me in as a baby. And the ideal
mating for terror is when a natural abuser meets a victim of childhood trauma. In that sense, we were made
for each other. And, if you understand the perfection of
imperfection, we both got what we chose to deserve,
as harsh and awful as that sounds. As long as we allow
it—we will be beaten. And when we value freedom
above anything and everything else, we will choose
freedom, even when it means the loss of what appears
to be *everything*.

The reason he fled when he did is because in my growing suspicions of many things, I had began to call him on
his hypocrisy more and more loudly, risking everything in
doing so—and I threatened to let people know who he
really was and who he really wasn't. Had I stayed subservient and obeying, he would still be dominating my life.

In the midst of escape from terror, I drew a friend to
my cause. A remarkable and wonderful man literally flew
to me and helped me through this crisis. He brought his
white horse to America from abroad. He told me there
was nothing I could ever do that would make him leave,
that no matter how hard I tried to push him away, he was
there to stay. I finally yielded to his pleadings, and I let
down my long hair over the castle wall.

He was the antithesis to every man I had ever known. He was grounded, both in his business life and in his spiritual life. And, he adored me! He listened intently to my feelings, valued my opinion on all matters, and he loved to touch and be touched.

He held his hand over mine one day at a café in Santa Fe, took off his favorite ring which he wore everywhere, and said, "The next ring that will go on this finger is the ring that you put there, the same day I put one on your finger. It will be the ring that binds us forever." It was a moment from a movie, and I melted. Was I finally safe enough to trust again? I let my hair down further over the castle wall.

Slowly, basking in his love and his commitment, I began to relax. He helped me unravel the messes con-straining me. He defended me. I don't think anyone had ever defended me before. We began a new busi-ness together. He adored the girls, and for the first time in their life, they had a loving, generous father. He gave Jennifer money for guitar lessons, something I'd never been able to offer her. And he bought Adrianne her own flight headset so she wouldn't have to borrow one when she went flying.

He noticed little things and acted on them. He even drove to Jennifer's college to check out her potential housemates, lovingly interrogating them, qualifying them, to make sure she would be safe in that environment, ask-ing them all sorts of silly questions only a loving father would ask. She glowed in the attention. We all did.

Love and appreciation are beyond measure. There is no yardstick long enough to measure it's importance, no scale that can weigh its immense value. I began to heal.

And so when Christmas rolled around, I was deter-mined to find the most special present I could, to thank him for choosing to be the amazing Being he had chosen to be. I wanted to give him something beyond a "thing" in a box, something beyond measure. I wanted to find some-thing to bespeak my awed and humble gratefulness to him.

And that is how I met Tom Kenyon.

A little voice in my head said to me, "You must find the tones. Give him the "sounds" for Christmas." Hmmm. What on earth did that mean? I called all my friends who sing professionally to ask them to "sing" for him for Christmas, but they were all on tour or unavailable.

Then one night a girlfriend called and mentioned Tom Kenyon's name during the conversation. My heart jumped, and bells went off in my head, which doesn't happen often to me. For years people had told me how amazing Tom Kenyon's work was, and many had said we should meet. I had actually gone home several times during my "Medicine Days" with his phone number, suggesting a meeting, only for the Great Medicine man to snarl a refusal! (Later I found out why.)

Now I was with a supportive, loving person, and I could meet whomever I felt called to meet. The words in my head—the ones without a voice—were whirring and clanging and striking chords of recognition, telling me to act— this was the Christmas present I had been looking for.

I took Tom's phone number and called his office and actually left a message that embarrasses me to this day. I recall saying something like, "I know you don't know me, but for years people have said we should meet. I don't know if they have said the same to you, but anyway, I need to find the most spectacular present for a very special man. And I wonder if you'd consider being the Christmas present?"

He called a few minutes later, and we scheduled a "present delivery" at his home up near the Canadian border.

We drove up two days later to "take delivery" of the present. I didn't even know what Tom Kenyon did! I had no idea he worked with tones. I was just listening to my guidance, something I had avoided doing for years.

We were met at the door by the largest animal I have ever seen in a house. His name was Merlin. He barely had to raise his head to look me in the eye, scanning me from head to foot. His head easily reached my chest. He was larger than a miniature horse, part Bloodhound and part Great Dane.

Merlin ushered us in, and Tom met us shortly there-after. Tom settled us on a sofa and unwrapped a crystal bowl and began to call in the archangels. I had closed my eyes, but when he began to sing, they popped open. I had to see to believe what I was hearing! This music of the spheres couldn't come from the human being sitting four feet away or from any *human* being. This was the voice of God. This was like no other voice I've ever heard, on CD, in a concert hall, anywhere, even in my dreams. No one could sound like that. Tears poured out of my eyes, and my body began to tremble. I have never known such gratitude. I was grateful that a voice like this actually existed on Earth and that I was lucky enough to be able to be in the same room with it. Such voices are locked away in cloistered palaces and hidden within opera halls and protected by guards and security. No one gets close to anyone with a voice like this, and there I was.

I slid further away on the sofa, not wanting to take these tones away from my friend. This was a gift for him; it was not for me. I was just grateful to be in the room. After Tom called in the archangels, he began a process of taking my friend into the eye of the Ibis, through it, and into another dimension, all through tone and sound. Sometimes he was an Eagle, sometimes he was a Whale, and it was all coming out of Tom Kenyon. We were both profoundly altered.

Then the Hathors came through and spoke to my friend, as if they were old, old friends. When they fin-ished their sounds and their information and directions given through Tom, Tom himself returned for a moment to announce, "The Hathor Goddess wishes to speak with you, Judi."

I was dumbfounded. I hadn't expected any attention. This was my present for someone else! I sat up straighter, feeling the intensity entering the room. I have no memory of what she said to me, nor does anyone else who was in the room. Someday the occasion will arise for me to ask her, but I know it was deeply honoring and very loving and intensely personal, so personal that none of us can remember it. I know she made reference to my recent battle with the dark and congratulated me for still being alive.

When we left, Tom caught me on the way out the door and said, "I have to tell you, I don't do this."

"*What* don't you do?" I asked.

"I don't see people privately at my house," he said matter-of-factly.

"Then why did you let us come today?" It seemed to be a legitimate question.

"The Hathors told me to let you come."

He closed the door and left me standing there, feeling very strange and elated. I knew the Hathors as interdimensional beings who had been very active and beneficial in ancient Egypt, Masters of sound and love, but I had never had an experience with them before.

Back at home on my little island I was a haunted person. I couldn't get those sounds out of my head. I had this feeling there was a connection, a deep connection somewhere. My friend had never been so affected by anything in his life, and I was very proud of myself for creating the most amazing Christmas present anyone ever received! And the sense of connection grew inside me. I was haunted by Tom Kenyon's comment, "The Hathors told me to let you come."

So about a week later I called again.

"If the Hathors told you to let us come once, would they tell you to let us come again?"

He laughed, and said he was sure they would, and so another session was set, and we went back once more. During this session I was given information about our Egyptian connections, and at the end of the session it was clear that old friends had found each other again, and I even understood why my former partner had scowled and refused to ever meet Tom Kenyon. I had been shown how I had walked a tightrope dangling above such a pit of darkness intent on destroying me that one tiny step to one side or another would have easily cost me my life.

I may not appear very logical in this very abbreviated version of my life, and perhaps I have not written the accounts of my logic, but I am a devout realist. I am logical, almost to a fault. And I am loyal, clearly to a fault, and was once very Pollyanna-ish, a trait I was quickly getting over now. I am a deductive reasoner. My greatest teacher, the friend in the wind, always used to say, "Master, reason it out." (I loved that he called us Master, rather than demanding that we approach him from a position of devotional enslavement. He always said we would never understand that we are God if we keep calling something outside of ourselves Master.)

I began to realize that the darkness isn't dumb enough to obviously look dark. It often looks like the light and discernment can be quite difficult. And when I thought about it, it made sense. If there were such a creature as the devil, where would he hide if he were smart? He'd hide in the church or some permutation thereof; he'd hide in spirituality.

And though I had long ago figured out that it was the devil himself, so to speak, at the helm of the Church of Rome and many governments, I had not looked within my own rank, within what I considered the truly sacred realms of alternative spirituality, where I was convinced the hope of the world truly lay.

And it was then that I realized that darkness was not dumb, just evil; and that darkness would, of course, attempt to permeate and use our own language to defeat our awareness in this attempt to subdue world consciousness. Darkness, the evil of enslavement, can no longer stop us from raising our consciousness through the ignorance of sin and guilt, so it has figured out how to creep, undetected, into our midst and stand alongside us, pretending to be one of us, luring us into confusion, beating us back once again from individual Christ consciousness.

Perhaps I should clarify what I consider evil. By the word evil, I refer to anything that thwarts the coming forward of the Christ Consciousness into the earth plane, anything that deters enlightenment.

My friend sat up all night that night, watching me. I went to sleep with him sitting on the edge of the bed, staring at me, tears streaming down his cheek. I asked him why he was crying, and he said he'd had no idea how close he'd come to losing me, and it broke his heart to imagine me so threatened. I woke to find him still sitting there. He swore that as long as he could help it, I would never be at risk again.

I remember the first time I met Pam Kenyon. It was several weeks after that fateful experience with the Hathors. She lit up the whole room with a glow that came directly like a light beam straight out of her heart. Her smile was sheer magnetism, her countenance pure Goddess. She was one of the most beautiful people I have ever known. She and Tom became dear, dear friends and when they moved onto the island, almost next-door, life felt really blessed, and our circle seemed complete.

Then my friend went back to Europe for a few weeks. I was to join him there soon. He called several times a day for a week, but then he discovered his European business associate had been draining the corporate funds. Then this associate emptied all the bank accounts and fled. My knight and I still talked several times a day during this crisis, and I only finally realized how serious the loss was when I asked him, pointblank, how much money he had left, and he told me he had $20 in his pocket, and since that wasn't even enough money to buy gas to get home, he was going to just leave his car in the parking lot and take a bus home.

And then, abruptly, the calls stopped, and the light in my heart went out again. This had been a very successful and powerful man who had collateralized everything he owned to the man who disappeared to get the funds to start a new business in America, so his loss was both financial and emotional. Many, many people were hurt when this occurred, and not only had my friend lost everything he had in the world, but he felt responsible for all his associate's employees who were now looking to him in their desperation.

I remember the last phone call I got from my white knight. I could hear the tension in his voice, and I could hear the only slightly muffled sobs of a man in the background. When I asked about the sobs, my friend said it was an officer in the corporation who didn't know how to make his mortgage payment, and my friend had no money to give him.

And then the phone fell silent. I slept with the cordless phone in bed every night, waking every hour or so to make sure there was a dial tone. Six weeks went by, and I was losing my mind with worry. He had come to my aid when I was at my worst. I had to do the same, but I didn't even know where to go. All the company phone numbers had been disconnected. Finally, in desperation, I called the only person I thought could get a message to my friend. I asked that he locate my friend and tell him that I was on my way to Europe to help, because he had saved my life, and now I must do the same. I just wanted him to know he wasn't alone. I asked him to tell my friend that no matter what had happened, we could work it out.

That got a response, but not the response I wanted. I got a fax that said he just couldn't be everything to everyone any longer. It said that he had taken care of too many people for too long, and now he needed to take care of himself. He said that he was going to take some time and go away and think. He said he loved me very much, more than words could say, and that someday I would look up and see him walking down my road again. He told me not to come. He told me he would come back for me, but that it would be a very, very long time before he could get here.

I have no words for the feeling of loss. I huddled on the floor, holding the slick paper in my hand. I remember it was daylight outside when night fell inside my heart.

The sun set inside me, and it would be a long time before dawn.

I had barely read the fax when Ruby's neighbors in Virginia, the good Christian ones who'd always been able to tell everyone what to do in the name of Christ, called to say that Ruby had no business living alone anymore, and that if I didn't do something to get her out of there, they would turn her in to social services. They said she was getting too mean and they couldn't be bothered with her anymore.

Adrianne and I flew to Virginia and packed Ruby's meager belongings and brought her to our little island farmhouse. I possess an immense inner strength and sur-vival will, but I was reaching my furthermost edges, and I knew it. I was adrift on an ice floe, and it was my heart.

I had survived an abuser and the loss of what I thought was the love of my life, and now I had to care-take the 95-year-old source of my childhood pain?

One night shortly after she arrived I was over at a girl-friend's house, sobbing my heart out. I drove home around 5 pm to find Ruby sitting in the window, just like she did when I was 18 years old. I shivered, took a deep sigh and walked in.

"And where have you been, young lady? How dare you come home so late," her bony finger prodded the air near my nose. She harrumphed and made little spitting sounds and shook her head.

"Good girls don't go out this late. It doesn't look good! Or maybe you don't care what people think!"

There it was. There was the source of my entire life of caring what other people thought!

Something was gravely wrong with this picture.

The words of my old teacher in the wind ricocheted in my ears, "Look around you, Master," he used to say. "Look at all the people around you. Not one single person would step in front of a bullet for you. Not one person would die for you. If they won't die for you, why are you living for them?"

I hated having Queen Victoria back in my house, and my heart ached for my friend, for someone who loved me for just who I was, not for who I appeared to be, or for how I looked, or even for what I did for him.

Jericho came tumbling down; my walls crumbled underneath me. Nothing could support me any longer. There was nothing *there*. I had just begun to touch into the anger, finally, at the abuser—at all the abusers in my life. It had taken forty years, but I had finally found my anger—and it was to become a great ally.

Now I was to learn sadness with my friend's disappearance.

It was the first time I thought someone finally actually loved me.

Now the tears of 10,000 lifetimes came in torrents. There was nothing I could do to stop the pain. I had always been able to shore up my emotional dike, but these floods could not be assuaged. There was no comfort to be found. The Eagles screamed, but I could not hear them. The great Black Fish surfaced, but my eyes could not see the wake. Even the White Owl came to comfort me, but I could feel no loving stroke.

I walked with pain and the desire to die for almost two solid years. I cannot exaggerate the intensity of this anguish. I cannot find the words in any thesaurus which, when swiped on paper, adequately capture the depth of this pool of torture. Do you know what happens when you cry for hours on end? There is a point reached in sobbing where you can only wretch until you throw up, gagging and choking on pain.

Oscar Wilde's great ballad looped endlessly in my mind.

*"Yet each man kills the thing he loves, by all let this be heard. The coward does it with a word, the kind man with a sword."*

Cowards and kind men alike had killed me.

I begged the gods to let me die. I desired death. I wanted death. I didn't have the courage to do anything about it. But I wanted it. I courted the fantasy in my mind and dreamed of having the courage to act on it.

I cut absolutely everyone out of my life except for my daughters, and Tom and Pam. Tom and Pam enfolded me in loving friendship, taking me into their inner sanctum like a wounded bird. Three other friends stayed by me. My daughters held onto me. Adrianne promised me that someday I would want to live again, a notion I couldn't believe.

And Jennifer said, "Mom, just imagine how amazing the next one will be. He's going to be even better." I thought she was insane.

"I will never let another man within ten feet of me," I railed at her. "Never. Never! Don't talk crazy!"

And so it was that I decided I needed some time myself. I had processed a lot of emotional material already it seemed to me, enough for one lifetime, and now I could handle no more. Caught between pain and anger, my death wish was growing.

I couldn't remember anyone who had ever kept a promise to me. So many promises over so many years. And so it was that a dream was born. If no one else had ever kept a promise to me, I must keep one to myself. I had always promised myself that someday I'd take the girls to Europe, on a journey of spirit. Desperate times, as they say, call for desperate measures.

I took what money I could scrape, hired someone to care take my mother, rented a car on the Internet and flew into Amsterdam with Jennifer and Adrianne. It was potentially our last summer together. Jennifer was going to India alone in the fall, and it was Adrianne's last summer before her senior year of high school. But high school could wait a month I decided. Nothing she would learn in one month of public high school would ever equal what we would learn traveling Europe together hunting Goddess sites.

We landed in Amsterdam and were met by a friend of a friend. Ron took us home, determined not to let us sleep prematurely, so that we would become acclimated to European time more quickly. Adrianne fell asleep right away, but Jen and I pinched each other to stay awake. He put on a documentary video and promised it would entertain us. It more than fulfilled his promise.

It was the story of the Priory of Sion, the story of my name, and the story of a Priest named Saunier and treasure he found. One of the few remaining clues to the mystery he left behind was a parchment that read, "The treasure belongs to Dagobert and to Sion."

I flashed to the little shack in Appalachia where I was born and my birth name, Zion, which came from Sion. I laughed at the equally portentous name I was given less than a year later when I was adopted—Pope. I had always intended to take back my birth name when the woman who adopted me died. She was now 95 and quite alive, and I was caught between names, as she was caught between dementia and sanity, this world and the next.

The documentary unfolded a story I knew to be true, a story I knew in my heart and had shared with many people. But I had no idea anyone else would ever tell such a story. I had logically deduced the truth, from little things that strung together, and from a woman's heart, which always knows the truth, or at least knows *her* truth. But here was evidence, or so it claimed, of what I had *known* for so long and felt so alone with. This documentary mentioned one name I remember, Rennes-le-Chateau, and I swore we'd find it. That's all I had written on a scrap of paper, Rennes-le-Chateau. Somewhere in France.

We took off in the morning, and I had one goal, to find this place and solve my own mystery. We drove at break-neck speeds through Germany, assaulted by hail so heavy the roof glinted with dents in the sunlight of morning. We had much to cover before France and we found ourselves in Ancona, Italy where we jumped on a ferry to Greece. We literally followed a crescent moon to Delphi. We couldn't read the roadmaps. They were in Greek! But in the middle of the night, we ascended the mountains; and when the moon set, we followed our hearts. It's a funny thing; to stand on land you once lived on and not be allowed to fully explore it. We sniffed at a little chain that said, "No Admittance" blocking entry to the spring of the Pythia. How do you tell a swallow not to enter Capistrano!

Hungrily we drank the water and climbed the ancient stairs cut so deeply into the vaginal walls behind the spring. Then we went to Hera's spring, near Nafplion, and drank and bathed where, according to legend, she returned each year to restore her virginity.

But the most haunting experience in Greece was not at a pre-supposed sacred site. We were asleep in a campground somewhere near Isthmia, along the Mediterranean. At about 3 o'clock in the morning, Pam appeared and woke me up. She told me something, but I was too groggy and still half asleep, so she grabbed me and sat me bolt upright. I stared literally into her very face, in all her splendor. She looked absolutely beautiful, radiant and literally *she was there*. She said six words to me, and I slumped back down. She grabbed me back up by the shoulders, and this time she shook me for effect, until I woke enough to really hear the six words she repeated. She extracted a promise from me, and then she released me. I looked around to find myself sitting up on a Mediterranean beach in the middle of the night. I woke the girls and told them what happened. None of us could figure out what it meant.

A few days later we took a ferry back to Venice and crossed back over Italy and entered France to finally search for Rennes-le-Chateau, but there was no such place on any map we could find.

So we decided to go to Arles, to see if the light was really different there. Van Gogh had painted there, swearing the light was different in Arles than anywhere else. And that's how we came to be just south of Arles late one afternoon as the sun hits a place of light unlike anywhere else I've been on Earth. I guess you could say I just followed the light after that. Arles itself felt too busy so instead of entering the city, we turned south. The Mediterranean wasn't too far according to the map, maybe a detour of some thirty miles. As we drove, the land flattened and marsh grass peeked up between endless fields of lavender. Rounding a corner, we almost collided with a man on a white horse, herding black bulls along the road. He wore an old, sweat-stained Stetson and a pair of Wrangler jeans. This was a working cowboy, no show pony. Lathered chaps covered his front legs. We drove on and the lavender fields yielded to full marshland with rivulets of water, and galloping herds of white horses were everywhere.

Barns on either side offered riding and we chose one. Trotting along, we rounded a corner and spooked hundreds of pink flamingos, which took to the air, leaving us behind in a stream of wind off hundreds of wings. The horses took it for granted; we were startled. I was forever enchanted.

The road ended at the sea, and we got a room for the night in a town where paella was easier to find than a crepe, and a bullfighting ring was where the town parking lot ought to be.

I hate churches. I always have. To me, they are houses of hypocrisy. But I had read about a little church here built on a Goddess site, as they almost all are, and we bumped into it walking along. And so it was that we entered the tiny church at St. Maries de la Mer. The art depicted women in a boat, the Maries, and the story I had carried in my heart for so many years began to have a location and historical validation.

Magdalen had been here.

Through the years, Mary Magdalen had rather become my patron Saint of sorts. I saw her as the lost bride, the feminine not only taken away from Christ by the Bible editors, but the woman shamed and vilified, the woman made into a whore, and hence, all women in her stead.

Whenever I asked the woman who raised me about my birth mother, she always cringed and sloughed off the question with a shudder and a less than deft air of inference as to the questionable morals of my birth mother. So perhaps I know personally the damage that can be done when a human being is so easily dismissed by even the hint of impropriety, never mind the outright label thrust on Mary Magdalen.

Somehow, miraculously, we had found the place where Magdalen landed when she entered France after the crucifixion. She had come in a boat with several historically significant people, according to the legend held there.

Among the people in the boat was a young girl, who they call Sarah. (Magdalen says her name cannot be translated into English, that it is very guttural, and that spelling it Sar'h would be more correct.) Legend depicts her as a servant. I knew her to be the daughter of Yeshua and Magdalen, called the Dark One and presumed to be Egyptian because she had to be hidden in the shadows to protect her life.

We visited the tiny crypt where Sar'h stands, all but one day a year, and were more enchanted than I ever remember feeling in such a surrounding. It is actually the only time I have ever felt holiness in a Church.

Sar'h is the patron saint of the Gypsies and every spring tens of thousands of Gypsies come from all over Europe to pay homage by taking her effigy to the sea and bathing her in an Isis Ritual. All year they visit her in her crypt and bring her new robes and gently layer her until she swells with taffeta and netting and sequins and rick-rack. They run their babies' fingers across her lips and kiss her wooden cheeks, smearing their tears into her wooden flesh. And then, on that one day, she rises high above them on a litter, led by silver-saddled white horses, snorting and prancing; and she moves through the throngs to the place at the edge of the sea where she landed with her mother.

In my brief time standing before her in the crypt, she called to me, and I found I wanted to spend time with her, waiting patiently for my turn to step close to her and honor her, over and over. I finally worked up the courage to touch her wooden cheek with my finger, and it brought tears to my eyes.

The only way I could tear myself away was to promise Sar'h I would return someday with the Gypsies, to watch her ride the clouds to the sea.

Nothing could keep me from finding Rennes now, I told myself, not after this high. You can't imagine how we felt, three women driving across Europe, sleeping at camp-grounds, in the car, occasionally taking a hotel room, searching for history, for bloodline, for that which runs through the veins, driven by something beyond under-standing. We had no tour guide, no maps beyond Michelin.

But Rennes eluded us, and we wound up at Lourdes, amid litters of sickness and palsy and aging, sagging bodies huddled together, shepherded by dozens of women in black robes. Sad, forlorn people shepherded by sad, forlorn looking nuns were everywhere! Hundreds more desperately held plastic bottles in the shape of Mother Mary under faucets, filling them, capping them and stuffing them into shopping bags to be taken home like any souvenir. Holy water in a plastic Mary.

I was disgusted. Adrianne, who has never said a bad word about anybody or anything said, "This is the dark-est place I have ever seen. You can stay here if you want to, but can you take me to the edge of town and pick me up on your way out?"

We survived Lourdes, and after exhausting myself looking for the light I never found there, we left that afternoon, leaving behind us in the rear-view mirror black-robed nuns pushing black draped litters and ancient wheelchairs back to hotel rooms and buses.

There were no miracle cures in the waters of Lourdes that day.

My heart told me that Rennes was back behind us, somewhere so close we had almost driven past it to get to Lourdes. Our time was running out. Soon we had to be back in Amsterdam. There were planes to be caught and school for Adrianne; the woman taking care of my mother needed to go home; and Jennifer was leaving to study in India in just a few days. In spite of that, I turned the car back east and we headed back for the Pyrenees. Darkness overtook us, but the full moon sang to me as she wove in and out of hilltops. And then the moon began to disappear, little pieces of her eaten away by some invading force. We pulled over and watched the full moon go into total eclipse, somewhere in the foothills of the Pyrenees.

We fell asleep that night in the car, off to the side of a back road somewhere on the way, we hoped, to Rennes. I remember waking and stretching, amazed that I'd learned to sleep curled under the steering wheel. We woke to a chill, with dew still present and cows and the sound of chickens and roosters calling dawn.

All day we drove into villages and down country roads, stopping here and there and asking for Rennes-le-Chateau. Someone gave us directions that left us in the driveway of a deserted house in the middle of nowhere. I have no idea how it is that we wound up in a little town south of Carcasonne, but here we stopped to ask directions to a hotel. I needed a bed that night.

"Well, the only place to stay anywhere around here is the old castle right back there on the river." I should have realized that after a full moon eclipse, we might be privy to some magic.

Gripped by some sense of promise, we wound the turrets, climbing stone stairs worn by the ages. Thousands of feet had trod them until one step dipped to meet the other, like ancient tango dancers. The castle dated back to the days of the Templars, when the breezes blew stories of knights and crusades through the air and mysticism filled the homes and hearths of the Cathars, one of the most persecuted sects, who were ultimately massacred by the Catholic Church.

I felt the mystery slip into my mind and wrap tendrils of a haunting that I had become so familiar with around my heart, capturing me and carrying me into dreamtime. In the morning I slipped back down the turret early and sat in the courtyard, encircled by those high walls and sipped espresso and a croissant. Life is good in southern France.

We packed the car and watched the willows weep in the rear-view mirror as we chose a direction out of town. I turned right and then left. I don't know why. I can't tell you that I "let go" and something came and took the steering wheel. I just turned left and wound up a hill, round and round and up and up and up. Prickles broke out all over my face and arms and legs and a feeling of elation took me.

At the top of the mountain we pulled into the tiniest of villages and parked. We walked in the only direction that kept us from falling off the mountain and found ourselves passing a bookstore with the obvious markings of eso-terica. I cannot tell you how out of place, in the tiniest village I have probably ever been in, an occult bookstore appeared to be.

Our pace quickened. Up a rise and then there it was, the tiny Church at Rennes-le-Chateau. The door creaked just enough for effect and we stepped inside, right past the Devil himself, or so he is thought to be by the religious ignorant, about three feet high, carved in wood with cloven feet and horns and bared teeth, holding the holy water!

On a panel, the Magdalen sat with a skull at her feet. In a painting of the Last Supper she sits under the table and as the Disciples toast Yeshua, she brushes her cheek against his ankle, her hair wrapped around his feet. The ceiling is painted blue with stars, like an ancient Egyptian tomb. I quickly sat on a pew before my legs could betray my quivering heart.

Beyond the Church lay the home of the Priest, Sauniere, and La Tour Magdala, which he built and so named, overlooking the Pyrenees. The mystery of what Sauniere found in his famous discovery was what the documentary was about, but it was not of consequence to me. I didn't want to know what he found or where he hid it. I had no urge to dig in the graveyard. My digging urges were elsewhere. I wanted the truth behind the mystery. I wanted the alchemical truth, and I knew it had to do with the Magdalen and her tantric relationship with Yeshua.

What could possibly have been so important that the Catholic Church destroyed a whole people and wrecked havoc on this entire landscape to keep secret?

That Yeshua was not celibate. That Magdalen was no whore, but the bride of Yeshua, a high Initiate, one of the highest in the Temple of Isis, well prepared for her sexual relationship with Yeshua in the Temples. That they had a daughter, and that her lineage was literally the rightful inheritor of the Kingdom, to those who believed in, or feared Kingdoms, as the Church did.

Despite the heights I scaled in Europe, despite my visions and visitations there, home ultimately demanded our presence. Life refused to be avoided, and we returned, deeply touched, but only momentarily distracted from my losses.

I suppose relationship is really not my life's work, I told myself. Perhaps I should pass the torch I carry for this work to someone who can bring it home; obviously I can't do it. I made peace with all my childhood advisors, said goodbye to all my dreams, and one night when Tom and Pam and I were driving through Hopiland, I realized what I had to do.

The love between them was the deepest and purest love I had ever seen between two people. I was thrilled to be close to it; absolutely thrilled that the closer I got, the more obvious the love was. It was real. It wasn't "put on" for show. They had loved each other from first sight. The exquisite depth of it had not lessened through the years and the experience of each other's flaws. They still held each other in the highest esteem on all levels, spiritually and emotionally.

"Maybe I'm not the one who is supposed to do this work in relationship," I gushed out from the back seat, gesturing blindly in the dark, nothing, if not dramatic.

"I've never seen two people love each other the way you do. It would be my honor to pass the Relationship Torch to you. Now I can relax and stop searching. I will never have another relationship. I pass the torch to you."

I don't know if either of them understood the depth within me from which my words came, but I leaned forward from the back seat and announced just that. I told them that I had never seen any two people love each other as they loved each other. And I babbled on that I had always been told that I came to work on balancing the male/female energy on the plane through living with my mate and through the day-to-day living/loving of each other in full and total harmony, in evenness, in truth. And then I thrust my hand forward, as if passing a torch, and summarily announced that I was out of the relationship business and that the job was henceforth theirs. Then I sat back and was quiet, to emphasize my point.

By this time, however, I had spent two years desiring to die, and I usually get what I want, in the long run. I've just noticed that I usually get what I want after I don't want it anymore. And so it was inevitable, I suppose, that the discomfort from certain physical symptoms would overtake the attention I was paying to my depression. Walking had become painful. My joints ached. I felt terrible. My strength seemed to have run out, along with my will. I had no energy. I couldn't sleep at night, tossing and turning, haunted by all the ghosts of my past.

I contacted Metatron, the archangel, through a remarkable and most genuine woman in Utah, who was also a medical intuitive. I had several readings and they, along with the information I had gotten from the Hathors through Tom, had been my only source of comfort and healing through those years.

Metatron had sharp words for me on this occasion, though. He told me I was in the early stages of Lupus and that if I didn't work immediately to counteract it, I would get my death wish. He then gave me a formula of anti-oxidants to take. I immediately called Tom and asked to speak to the Hathors. I needed corroboration or a different opinion.

When they "came in" I announced my unfaithfulness and told them that I had been seeing someone else. They howled with laughter and then, without me telling them anything that I had already been told, they launched into what was wrong with me and what could be done to heal it—if I chose to live. Then they gave me the sounds that I needed to release and heal. It was recorded, and I took those sounds home and played them over and over and over.

I credit Tom's Hathor sounds, along with the regimen of anti-oxidants, with healing me.

Now, I must tell you that though I'd had my personal healing experience with sound, I had not experienced Tom Kenyon as the teacher. Needless to say, I had issues with "teachers" and I had observed his impeccability as a human for a long, long time before I decided I would take a chance and see what he taught. But by now, the impact of sound on my life was significant, and when there was a local workshop, it only made sense for me to step in and help with registration and other facilitation needs, as a feeble attempt at "thank-you."

By the end of the first day I had discovered that my friend, Tom, not only had one of the most remarkable voices in the world, but was also the most erudite single human being I had ever experienced on a vast purview of subjects.

He understood the nuances and the intention behind the major streams of internal alchemy, including Tibetan Buddhism, Taoism, Hindiusm, Egyptian High Alchemy and esoteric Christianity; and whatever his subject, he taught with humor and humility, making the material both comprehensible and consciousness altering, simultaneously. He had distilled the essence of how each stream raises consciousness.

He literally understood the intention behind what was held as sacred within each pathway; he understood the mystery, without having to wrap the tendrils of dogma around it. He had gleaned the kernels of these streams of internal alchemy and taught both the science and the physics of consciousness, carefully and gently with no dogma attached.

By the end of that first weekend, Tom Kenyon had earned my respect in a category where I never thought I'd respect another human being—as a teacher. I was different—literally and profoundly altered from both the information and the sound.

I knew how he lived his life. I had been around the house enough to see the impeccability with which he attended his daily functions. I knew his honor. I saw how much he loved his wife, how he served the feminine, how the Mother was honored in his walk. Now I had experienced the Master Teacher, and I wanted to help him present his work to the world in the way it deserved to be presented.

As I researched his life, I discovered he was one of the pioneers in helping science accept the reality that sound and frequency can and do shift brain states, having formed Acoustic Brain Research to research the effect of sound on consciousness in 1983. He spent a decade doing the research that ultimately proved just how successfully sound could alter and affect brain states.

He had coined the word *psychoacoustic* to explain the marriage of psychotherapy and sound.

How this translated to a workshop was actually quite obvious and utterly brilliant. The left brain got the hard information it needed from the psychotherapist/scientist Tom, and the right brain got what it needed during the "sound meditations" from the mystical Tom. Unspoken material was transmitted though sound codes that came through his voice during these frequent sound meditations. The combination of both "teaching in words" and "toning in sounds" was remarkable to experience.

My intuition told me this work was going to be critical in the next decades on planet Earth. We began to dialogue about how I could help Tom put his work into the world. My years in communication and writing could be used on something that made a difference again!

But then their beautiful waterfront rental house went on the market for sale, and since they had to move, they decided to move to the Southwest. I couldn't face any more losses in my life. We were all so close, I reasoned it was perhaps time for a change in my life as well, and I made plans to join them. The Three Musketeers couldn't be separated by anything so mundane as losing a rental house, and friends like we had become don't come along often in a lifetime. I held a garage sale, and sold my favorite things, and went east to handle some old business there. My mother's care had gotten beyond my capability, and I had finally placed her in a home. My daughters were both in college. I could move anywhere.

Pam had fought breast cancer a few years before, but she had successfully beaten it. She had chosen to live. I had work to do now that felt important and no longer spent all day wanting to die. I, too, had chosen to live. And so life began to feel like springtime. There were many places within Tom's work where my business background was sorely needed. I was going to help facilitate for him. And I was heavily involved in raising the funds to build a sound healing temple the Hathors had requested in New Mexico. There was much work to do, and I genuinely felt that getting Tom's work into the world was the most important thing I could do with my talent. His work is sound, and sound and music cut across all boundaries. Sound transcends language. And he was *real*. He was no hypocrite, and he loved and honored the feminine, the

Mother. And he loved and adored his wife. And that was what really mattered to me after a lifetime of men who either abused or ignored the feminine.

And besides, we were all best friends. We all had great times together. We moved through the kitchen with ease. We traveled together well. We laughed and watched bad television together.

Pam and I had cried over the mistakes we'd made with our children. We'd looked at our childhood photo albums and sobbed that we hadn't known how beautiful we were. We cried together that we had spent a lifetime thinking we were fat and ugly. I looked at her childhood photos and saw one of the truly most beautiful women I had ever seen. She swore the same was true of me. We held each other and told each other our most intimate secrets. She had given a girl up for adoption at birth. I had given a girl up for adoption at birth.

But Pam's shoulder had begun to hurt her. And when she went to the doctor on the island before they left, they told her it was a torn rotator cuff, probably from her previous surgery. They said it would take a long time to heal and there was nothing she could do. So she did nothing. But it was getting worse. And then, just before Christmas, Tom called me on the East Coast, where I was cleaning up old business. Pam's pain had gotten so bad that he'd taken her to the emergency room.

The Emergency Room had done bone scans, which hadn't been done on the island, and they showed that the cancer had gone to the bones. Tom was told that Pam was in Stage Four cancer. Allopathic medicine offered her nothing, only a death certificate. It was jarring news, but Pam swore she could beat it. Before I could join them, they began the process of moving back. Pam wanted to come closer home.

Then they called and asked me if I would accompany Pam to Mexico to a special clinic where there was hope through a new treatment. Tom had taken care of her alone for the last several years, since the initial diagnosis and expenses were mounting, and he needed to stay behind and work to pay the bills. It would mean being gone a month, and Adrianne had just gotten home for the summer and wanted me with her. But I had made a promise a few years before, on a beach in Greece in the middle of the night, and I knew I had to go. And so it was that Pam and I spent a month in Tijuana in a clinic that used insulin comas to suspend the body in a state close to death, allowing for maximum penetration of oxygen, which ostensibly could kill cancer cells. This process was highly experimental and was not possible in North America, not with the monopoly on death that the American Medical Association has.

In that month I watched the most remarkable, desperate and genuine people come and go. I watched miracles occur, and I watched people die. When Pam initially began the coma process, after weeks of preparation, the induction process caused a terrible struggle as she moved between the dimensions. This shifting of dimensions was as exhausting emotionally as it was physically; and after her first coma Pam swore she would never do another one.

The process of both induction and the return to consciousness were extremely altering. The sense of departure was so severe on induction that panic could easily occur. And when they injected the vitamin formula that brought her back, the body was subject to horrible sweats and spasms.

The morning she was due to appear for her second coma, she refused to go. The comas were, everyone felt, her only hope. There was nothing left to try. She had been doing all the other possible protocols for weeks, to build her system, but she was in Stage Four cancer. North America offered her no hope; this, at least, offered her *hope,* and as long as she had *thought* she could handle the process, she had *believed* she could heal.

I didn't know what to do. I was alone in Tijuana, Mexico with my best friend, and the responsibility felt huge. And so that morning I seized on the only thing I could think of. I offered to try to guide her through the dimensions during the induction process, to try to guide her into the coma and back out with my voice, to lay a trail she could follow when her consciousness left her body, and I promised her I would be there for her when she returned, singing her back. She liked the idea.

I spoke with the clinic director, as he had become a friend, and he approved. I had begun the process of rewriting their medical protocols and, for all practical purposes, I had essentially started working there. He supported whatever appeared to help a patient and offered the potential of making the process easier. I reasoned that whatever belief system the patient held should be honored, as the patient was, essentially, going through the death process with each coma, over and over. So if I could sing comfort to her, honoring the Deities she held sacred, that might create a safe platform for her.

So the next morning I took along the shamanic tools I had brought with me. I had Eagle and Hawk feathers and a Tibetan rattle and other simple Tibetan instruments. I had stones that had spoken to me and asked to come. When I wheeled her in that morning, the doctors who had become my friends moved aside and let me join them. They used one side of the hospital bed, and I used the other. We laid out our tools across the sheet from each other, syringe, tubes, stethoscope on one side, Eagle, Hawk, bells on the other. I was deeply touched by their respect.

They took out syringes and the bottles of medicine that would induce the coma and the vials that would bring her back. I took out the tingshas and rattle that would lay the trail of sound I hoped she would follow, just as I had seen Tom do many times.

They injected the insulin, and I kissed her goodbye and held her hand while the insulin sunk into her veins. As it traveled through her, her journey began. The process had caused her deep panic the first time, for as she slipped through the dimensions she encountered her own underworld and the monsters of her childhood.

I called the archangels and sang her chants that represented the Deities that she revered. She loved Tara, and so I sang her the Tara chant, over and over until she slipped deeply into coma with a blissful smile on her face, unlike the first time when she had jerked and moaned so radically.

I sat by her for the time she was gone, holding her hand, as I had the first time. Then the doctors motioned to me and began the process of injecting the vial that would bring her back, having held her in the near-death state as long as the monitored vital signs showed she could handle. I picked up my feathers and instruments and called her back. I sang her the Tara chant again and other chants I knew. Her return was peaceful, and she came back smiling, without the jerking and panic.

I was ecstatic. She came back with remembrances that would eventually help her heal many unresolved issues that had haunted her. These were early childhood abuses she had hidden from her worldly view, covered over with layers of acceptability. After all, there were people to please! These were the issues that were killing her, issues that could easily cause cancer, in my humble non-AMA approved opinion. This process continued every day then, until we left. When we left the CAT scans showed a remarkable reduction of about 60% in the bone cancer.

But a 60% reduction meant 40% was left, and the clinic didn't want her to go. But Pam needed a rest; and so we went back home, which Tom had moved back to the Northwest, at her request, while we had been gone.

Once back, though, it became very apparent that she needed to take the process further, and I couldn't go to Mexico with her this time. The summer was almost gone, and Adrianne was about to return to college, and so plans were made for Pam's son to go with her instead. Expenses were mounting, and Tom had to work. She was unhappy in the Seattle area, where Tom had initially moved them, and so while she was gone the second time, Tom moved all their belongings back where Pam wanted to be, back to the beautiful waterfront house they had left behind one year before, right back almost next door to me.

I was rethinking my life. Adrianne was about to go back to college. I loved working at the clinic in Tijuana, and they really needed me there. Through my time there I had discovered a strange gift. I am good with people in crisis. I loved the edge of life and death. No wonder I had been drawn to shamanism. I was really good at ushering people between the dimensions.

I began a dialogue with the clinic about working in Tijuana full time. I would be a North American shaman at a cancer clinic in Mexico! And as it is with small towns, so it is with small islands. Word went around the island that I might go to work in Mexico. And one morning as I dreamed about how it might be to live in Mexico, Tom called.

"So, I hear you might be going to Mexico."

"Well, I'm thinking about it," I said.

"So, I guess that would mean you couldn't help me get my work into the world then."

We had all been so busy taking care of Pam, I hadn't thought about what we set out to do a few years ago. I realized that with everything going on, Tom and I hadn't had any time for a business conversation in almost a year. His work had been put on hold, and the work I was going to do for him certainly hadn't materialized.

I sat at my dining room table, staring out to sea, and I realized what this phone call really meant. He was really asking if I was going to leave them. He was asking how much I believed in his work. And he was asking how much I really wanted to be with them. And I remembered the promise I'd made to Pam on the beach in Greece, and I heard my mouth tell Tom I wasn't really serious about going to Mexico. That was all that was said. We made no more of it.

I have never regretted that decision for one minute.

Then we got a phone call from the clinic that Pam's hip had developed a hairline crack, leaving her unable to put any weight on it at all. She wanted to come home, though they pressed her to stay at the clinic where she could continue therapy. But Pam wanted to come back to the island, where she could look at the water and the Eagles and where ferryboats ply the great deep waters of Puget Sound.

Tom and I went to Seattle to pick her up. We hadn't seen her in a month, and I remember how shocked we all were when she got off the plane. She couldn't walk, and she'd lost a lot of weight.

An incoming ferry had hit the ferry dock at Orcas, and it was closed. There was no way on or off the island with a car. I located a private barge that could land without a ramp, and so we brought Pam home, like Macarthur returning to the Philippines. The boat pulled in and lowered its head gently onto the shore, and we drove off.

I could write a thousand pages about the next few months, and I could never fully or adequately tell the story. You know, you go through life, and you think you know someone from little experiences, little intimacies here and there. A cup of coffee, a tear. And eventually, you do know them, but not like we came to know each other in the next few months.

I had known Pam Kenyon about five years then, and I thought I knew her. And I thought I knew the stuff of which Tom Kenyon was made. But the two people I thought I knew became my blood in the next few months. They both ran in my veins. I watched Tom give everything he had to help Pam stay alive. He served her day and night. He made her juices and when juice made her sick, he made her grains and when grains didn't taste good, he made her curried vegetables and when they didn't taste right, he made her soup. He searched through magazines and medical books and bought anything he thought would help. The living room swelled with boxes of therapies and supplements.

In the next few months, we exchanged intimacies few people ever get the privilege to experience. I learned how to bath someone in a wheelchair. It took all of us to figure out how to dress her without putting any weight on her at all. We fell over each other learning to roll and turn the sheet as Tom and I figured out ways to move her around in bed. We propped pillows for comfort and told jokes and laughed and cried and shared deep secrets. And she had breakthroughs I will not share here. She remembered her deepest and darkest demons, the ones she had driven so far into her bones.

I arrived at their house around 7 am and I left around midnight those months. Tom handled the night shift alone, getting almost no sleep at all, for the nights were when she thrashed and relived her deeply painful child-hood. He simply never slept, and I watched his color turn beige and then gray. We were convinced Pam would live, but I wasn't sure about him anymore.

We hired several caregivers to give each of us a few breaks and Pam's other closest friends came in when he had workshops to teach. One by one, everyone she loved got to have cherished time with her. Remarkable people on the island came and sang to her and gave her massages and checked her vitals and did her hair. A doctor friend made house calls.

In retrospect, she lived with bone cancer for two years with no pain medication. Until the last weeks of her life, she took nothing. Tom held the pain off with sound and energy work, which he diligently delivered with love and humor.

One morning I went over early to find her sitting with the biggest smile I'd ever seen. Pam was bright and cheery and hungry, something I hadn't seen in quite a while. She drank a whole can of liquid food and asked for more.

Many friends stopped by that morning, and she greet-ed each of them with that smile that lit up their dark corners. But there was something different this morning.

There was a power about her, a self-affirmed, self-assured presence I hadn't seen in her before. She told us what she wanted and how she wanted it. She didn't care what the people around her wanted this morning. She knew what *she* wanted.

Tom was in California teaching and was due to return later that day, and I couldn't wait until he saw this new, powerful Pam.

I bathed her and washed her hair, and we howled at the abject ridiculousness of it all, her sitting in a wheelchair with me pouring water over her head and me sitting on the edge of the bathtub, wetter than she was.

Jennifer, my daughter, stopped by to visit. I don't remember now what Jennifer wanted to do, but I disapproved and gave her my usual parent talk, recommending my vision for her future, which, of course, differed from hers.

When Jennifer left, everyone seemed to disappear simultaneously. Pam's grown kids all went into town, and Pam and I were alone in the house.

"You have to let go of your girls, Judi. You have to let them make their own decisions," Pam said to me, cocking her head to one side and narrowing her eyes at me.

"Oh, I know," I said, "but she depends on me being the mother. I'm *supposed* to disagree with her." I tried to laugh it off, but I noticed the air was different in the room. It had that wet appearance that I had seen in a room once before. The light transfigured differently; it was moist and pregnant looking.

Pam wasn't letting this go. "Look, I'm serious. You have to let go. They have their own lives to lead. Let Jennifer go. Let Adrianne go. *Let them go.*"

I thought I'd just cajole us through this. "Well, look who's talking," I giggled at her. "Aren't you the one who hasn't let your seventeen-year-old son out of your sight for the last two weeks?"

Her eyes lay on me like clouds, lifting and floating me.

"That was yesterday. Today I see things differently."

The very air changed density. The "light" in the air was visible.

"You have to drop your agendas for your daughters. They have their own agendas. You have to allow them *their* agendas."

She wasn't going to let this go.

"Everyone has an agenda," she looked out the window toward the sparkling water. "Even my caregivers have agendas. They all want to be the 'one' who helps me feel better, or the one who takes away the pain. All the healers want to be the one who *heals* me. There's nothing wrong with that agenda, but it's *their* agenda. Not mine."

We were at one of the major issues in Pam's life. She had lived her life fulfilling someone else's agenda most of the time.

"My caregivers even have agendas for what I see when I look outside the window! she laughed. "Yesterday," she said, "I was looking out the window, staring at the water."

"And my caregiver said, 'Pam, what are you looking at?'"

"And I said, 'I'm looking at the sparkles on the water.'"

"And the caregiver said, 'Pam, what do you see when you look at the sparkles on the water? Do you see God?'"

Pam shot me a cheesy grin and curled her lip.

And Pam had said, "No, I don't see God. I see freedom."

The silence cut the air like a knife. We were at some nexus point, somewhere to the left of the last star and closing in on forever. I knew what the next question had to be, but I didn't know if I had the courage to ask it. I don't think it had ever seriously occurred to any of us that Pam might die. She was *healing*. This was just a healing crisis. She only came home for her hip to mend enough to go back to the clinic and finish the treatments, and everything would be fine after that.

But this conversation had taken on mystical proportions sounding like last words, and I didn't want to think that.

But if this was her last conversation, and I didn't ask this question, how would I live with myself?

"Do I have an agenda for you?" I bit my lip.

"You used to, before you went to Albuquerque."

"What was my agenda for you?"

"You wanted me to live." She smiled a crescent that lit the whole room. Pam is the only person I have ever met who could light up a room like that.

My hand trembled as I brushed a strand of hair from her forehead and tears popped out of my eyes, like corks bobbing to the surface.

"I want to dance with you on all the great beaches of the world."

"We will," she said.

"What? In my mind and in my heart?"

"Yes, in your mind and in your heart."

"And what about after Albuquerque?"

I had just recently slipped down to Albuquerque, under directions from the Hathors, to sink the shaft for the tone-healing temple we were building there, and it had been a deeply mystical experience in which I'd had to own my power to make it happen.

"Now you're willing to allow me my own agenda," she said with a broad smile.

"Look," she continued, "it doesn't matter if I live twenty minutes or twenty years. It's the *process* that matters."

I felt transported to some realm I had never known before. There was a palpable luminous quality between the molecules around us. The air held moisture and refracted light differently than I'd ever seen before. It looked 'wet' and Pam was literally glowing.

"Give away your animals, Judi. Find a good home for Kola Bear. You have to be free to go."

She closed her eyes. I asked her if she wanted to take a nap, and she said she did, but she was afraid she'd wake up choking on childhood memories. I promised I'd stay in the room with her, and she drifted to sleep. I sat down and began to write down the conversation. I made notes to remind the caregivers not to press their agendas on Pam in the future.

Pam began to breath strangely. I dropped the note-book and stood up by her. I put my hand on her arm. She seemed to inhale, but she wouldn't exhale. She just held her breath.

"Breathe, Pam," I said, and she exhaled.

Watching her and coaching her breathing, I remembered a teaching Tom had done on the three gunas. He had used the breath as an example so we'd understand the role of each guna.

Raja, I remember him saying, begins an action. Sattva is the sustainer, that point of continuing inhale, almost in-between breaths, the place most of us live, where we get too comfortable, where we want to stay, where we hold our breath. And then there's Tamas, who ends an action. Like breathing out and breathing in. No one wants to think about destruction—but without destruction, without letting the breath out, Tom had said, there is no room for creation.

I was thinking about the three gunas, listening to Pam breathing. She looked absolutely radiant. Her skin was ablaze with an incandescent beauty, and I had never seen her look so powerful, even in her sleep. Her breathing evened out. But then it began to slow and became shallow.

I don't really know why I began to sing, but I sang the Tara chant, standing beside her, holding her arm. If this was what death looked like, it was powerful and mystical and deeply peaceful, and all I knew to do was to sing to her. And so I sang her song, Tara's chant, for what seemed like a long time, but was only a few min-utes. And then I thought about Tom, and I wondered how to let him know wherever he was, somewhere in the air nearing Seattle, that this might be the end. And so I shifted to a chant that I hoped would call his con-sciousness. But once that was done, I shifted back to the Tara chant. This was Pam's time, whatever was happening.

I was singing her chant when she stopped breathing, exactly twenty minutes after she said it didn't matter if she lived twenty minutes or twenty years—her process was complete. She was as free as the sparkles on the water.

The rest of the day and night are a blur of the intruding assaults that land when death visits, funeral directors, police. I wanted to scream about this mystical place I'd just been with Pam. I wanted them to know how serene and peaceful and exquisite her death had been, about how powerful she was at the end. But everyone had something to do. Late that night, exhausted and hysterical, I finally went home to an empty house. I sat by the window and sobbed. That's about all I remember of the next few days—sitting by the window in an empty house, sobbing.

We had walked the long, exhausting road to the end of her life together, laughing and crying at the mysticism of death and the insulting unexpectedness of it all. Life, the process—so unvalued one day, had become so precious in the end. Power, there for the taking, had been taken, finally, but not soon enough to save her life.

I felt Pam all around me. I felt her *in* me. I felt like I *was* Pam for days.

People came from every direction. I didn't know what to do with myself. I had known what to do every other day for months. I got up early and went over to Tom and Pam's house and helped take care of Pam. I was lost and purposeless without her, and there seemed to be no place for me in this new life Tom was pulled into. No one needed me.

One morning as I sat looking out the window crying, Tom called.

Hearing the tears, he asked me what was wrong, and I remember telling him, "I don't know who I am any more. I don't know what to do. I used to know what to do. I used to get up every morning and come over to your house, but I don't know what to do now." It blurted out without a breath, a continuous wail of

exhaustion and abject frustration at the seeming hopelessness of it all.

"Yes, you do," he said, matter-of-factly, "You go back
to doing what we were going to do before Pam died. You
help me get the work out into the world."

And I remembered what I was doing before Pam got
sick. There was something to live for, something that
mattered!

I could write whole books about the next few months;
they were a textbook lesson in agendas. You'd be
amazed at what descends on a man whose wife has just
died. They came from everywhere to help him. I wondered where they had all been when we needed them;
but my voice felt rather small in those first few months,
especially up against all the raucous voices that all knew
exactly what Tom Kenyon ought to do with the rest of his
life. Everyone had an agenda for Tom. Everyone knew
where he ought to move, where he ought to spend his
time, what would heal him, what his grief should look
like, what supplements he needed, who he should be
with, and who he shouldn't be with—specifically me. I
watched people circle and surround him with agendas.
He was so torn in his grief; he couldn't see anything
beyond the paralyzing pain of losing the love of his life.

As the parade came and went, I began to plan to
move back east. I had just lost one best friend, and the
way it looked, I was going to lose another, and I just
couldn't watch that happen. Tom was completely
unaware of what was happening around him, pulled this
way and that, assaulted by so much grief, he just couldn't
see beyond it. It was quicksand, and he wasn't even able
to muster the strength to try to pull himself out, instead
latching onto whichever branch was dangled nearby.

The more I began to plan my move, the sadder I got.
I had my own grief from the loss of Pam, and the loss
of "Pam and Tom." The hopelessness engulfed and
overwhelmed me. And I felt rather lost in all the
processes happening around Tom. He had just lost his

wife. I wasn't family. I had no idea where my place was in all this twisting.

So there I was, at the bottom once more, unsure where my next breath of air would come from. Some things just bring you to your knees, and if you don't believe in a bearded old God, to whom do you pray?

I can't tell you that I got a message or that a "light" appeared and told me what to do. I just gave up. I surrendered, and I went to Mother. Metatron has always told me that I possess certain powers, which I have done my best to completely ignore, one of which is the power to *call forth*, according to him. And though I have thought this not possible, I sank to my proverbial knees and asked for help. That's all I asked for; I asked for help. Almost immediately mystical events began to unfold around me. As I slid toward sleep each night, Isis appeared. She stepped forward from a circle of ancient women, all cloaked in robes with hoods, so I never saw their faces.

She took my hand and waved us through swirling mists and what were, I can only presume, dimensions. We appeared, from this "flight" in a variety of temples. In each temple we visited, a group of Priestesses stepped forward and took me by my hand. While Isis waited, they dipped me, first in one pool of oil and then in another. Night after night this bathing ritual continued, from temple to temple and pool to pool. I was always returned about dawn. Slowly my skin began to feel softer, and I think my heart rate quickened.  I began to be conscious of my breathing. It seemed deeper and more audible, and I swear I could *hear* my heart beat.

One night they bathed me as usual and wrapped me, mummy-like, in long strips of fabric. Then they lay me down on a huge bed of giant crystal points, with dozens of different stones underneath my chakra points. I remember my "mind" thought it ought to hurt, to lie there on these crystal points. Perhaps it was the fabric wrapping that so protected me, or the careful way I was positioned, but I don't remember any pain. This specific process occurred several nights. They changed the locations of the crystal points against my body and the stones from night to night. Some nights the rose quartz was against my back at my heart. Some nights a ruby pointed directly at my throat chakra from beneath. Some nights a great blue sapphire pierced my heart from the back.

And then one night as I lay in bed a thick fog licked its way across the floor, and a giant cobra seemed to ride in on the fog. Somehow it didn't frighten me; though I remember thinking I ought to be afraid. It slithered under the sheets and across one leg and down under the other, then looping back over and under again, holding me in a human Mobius strip. Then it rose high above me and spread its hood, still firmly in control of my body.

I told no one about these new nightly visitations of Isis and friends.

I observed that I acted differently when Tom called. I caught myself twisting the phone cord, staring off into space when I talked to him. Once I blushed and giggled for no good reason.

The people telling Tom what he ought to do with his life began to bother me. I got edgy around them. I didn't trust them. I saw their agendas and began to worry that I might have one as well. I struggled to remain his friend, no matter what the price, without prejudice, without personal agenda. Leaving the island and returning East was the only solution I could imagine for the swirling emotions washing over me. I had learned to run away before the hurt, if at all possible.

I made lots of phone calls east; preparing what friends I had left there for my imminent return.

One day I drove Tom to the ferry landing, so he could take the boat to a nearby island to visit a healer. We sat in my car, waiting for the ferry to dock. It was pouring rain, not the usual spotting we get out here, but a real east coast downpour. It added to the solemnity in the air. We sat staring at the ghost ferry slipping into dock, shadowed by the rain and gray so thick it licked the land like dragon's breath.

We sat in silence. Then Tom reached over and placed his hand on my heart, and he said, "I pledge you my truth."

I felt my heart tremble in response, and I placed my hand on his heart and said, "I pledge you my truth."

It is the greatest commitment ever made. It has sustained us through everything. It has held us, like a great cord. When I think I can't possibly talk to him about something, I realize I won't be in *truth* if I don't. When I want to let something slip by and not address it, I realize I can't just let it go, or I won't be in total truth with him.

Months later two old friends went to the southwest, to see if we could assuage the pain with a dose of sun. When we returned, Tom suggested I not go back to my house. And so I moved my chair closer to his piano at his house, and he wrote a song.

*"Sometimes when I am near you, I feel like I am floating on air.*

*And it still amazes me that I do not even seem to care.*

*Sometimes when I am beside you, I feel like I am falling, tumbling into space.*

*And it seems to happen most often, whenever I see your face.*

*What is this feeling I'm feeling inside of me?*

*What is this grace coming down from above?*

*I don't know, but I feel like singing with the turtledoves.*

*Could it be that I'm just falling in love?"*

And I wrote a poem, "I long to know your taste as well as I know your song."

And I can't, and I won't, write any more of our story. It is too precious, too magical, and too potent to put in words.

Now we are living my childhood dreams, living the prophecies I have shared with no one all these years, until now. Once a psychic dodged traffic rushing across a busy street to "give me a message about my life's work." It had to do with Sacred Relationship.

One night in a restaurant in Washington, D.C. I felt someone staring at me across the room. I saw him write a note on a napkin out of the corner of my eye, and I watched it get passed from table to table. I knew it was headed for me, and I knew what it was going to say—the same thing the "words without a voice" had said in the fork of the pear tree when I was five. And I had given up hope.

Some days I feel like an old, old crone now, an ancient woman who has seen it all, and all these memories are like the pages in a detached book of life. I can view them from a distance, but they seem to belong to someone else. I feel immune from my own life story. After all, it's just another story. And I've heard them all by now. And they're all the same. And they're all different.

I know what it feels like to think you are finally safe and to step inside a car for a ride home from a long night of running from danger only to find yourself looking once again into the eyes of torment, to have the edge of cold steel pressed against your neck. I have listened to screaming and realized it was my own. And I have gasped for breath in the terror of childbirth and not slept for days on end when a precious little girl needed me much more than I needed sleep.

And I have chosen love over and over and over again.

I have fought a long, hard battle with the dark side over the soul of a man and lost.

I have laughed over dinner and shared my soul and my best red wine with a good friend, only to be fed back betrayal in his climb for what he wanted. I have been cut with knives and words. Sometimes betrayal looks like your best friend. Sometimes it looks like your lover. It wouldn't be called betrayal if you had seen it coming.

I have screamed in pleasure in a long night of ecstasy and climbed the greatest peaks of the world in another's arms, and those are the nights I will never regret. That is the closest to God, to the Goddess, I have ever been.

I had dreams for my children and forgot they might have dreams of their own. My respect and the love I hold for Jennifer and Adrianne grows by the day as they teach me about strength and integrity. And the child I gave away has found me and that sweet piece has found that vacancy in my heart and filled it. I am truly sorry I didn't have the courage to raise her, for it was only my own cowardice that made me give her up. She is exquisitely beautiful, physically and spiritually. She is Laura and I love her.

And I have held the arm of a good friend when she died and had her tell me what freedom looks like. It looks like sparkles on the water on a sunny day, like diving into shards of diamonds and becoming one of them.

I have loved and desired from such a place of desperation that I have allowed someone to hurt me, my back shoved against a door, unable to breathe or twist or contort into a direction where there wasn't a blow, fists and blood tangled in a web of horror. I have prayed and sweated and begged and intended and hoped and owned and hungered and believed and *known*. And I have wanted to die, to find freedom in the sparkles on the water on a sunny day—more than anything.

And just when there was no more breath, no more hope in me, an angel said to me, "Just imagine what the next one will be like. If you're still alive, there's hope. Remember where you come from."

I remember a place where Beings swim in blue-tinged liquid love. Where the most beautiful Fairy Princess in the whole world wears Pink Lady Slippers, and she and Jack live in the Pulpit, happily ever after. And horses can fly and so can I.

I stopped believing. But I never stopped *knowing*.

And just when everyone around me had died... and there are many ways to die...when death of another hue hungered in the far corner, salivating for more, my best friend put his hand on my heart and said, "I pledge you my truth." And I pledged mine to him.

And truth is beauty, as all great poets know.

There is no "happily ever after" in a world where beings don't yet swim in liquid love. But there is work to be done, and I have found the most dynamic and quickest way to God Realization, just where I thought it was. And I have found my Goddess, the mother of all time and space. She is returning in this, the beginning of the ending of time. And if *you* really *hear* these words, well, that is enough.

A few years ago I was sitting in the back of a workshop, running the video camera. Tom asked everyone to find a partner and tell the partner his/her life story in five minutes. No cross talk. Whatever comes out in five minutes is your life story.

I didn't have a partner so I shut the camera off and sat down, as far away from everyone as I could get. I didn't want anyone to think I was listening to their private story. I tried to hide in the wall actually; I felt so obvious and so alone back there. But no matter how far I backed away, I could still hear the stories being told around me. So I turned and buried my head in my hands so I couldn't possibly hear, but the stories around me got even louder. I looked up to see how this was possible. There was no logical way this could be happening. Then I began to hear the stories at the far end of the room just as clearly as those near me and again I tried to bury my head deeper into my lap.

I heard every story in that room.

*My father wouldn't let anyone pick me up so I lay there for months and months. They fed me and changed me and put me back, but no one was allowed to hold me...when I was three I got so sick, the doctor came and ordered them to take me to the hospital...I almost died...then she hit me and kept hitting me...and he held me down and I could feel him over me and he smelled bad, God, he was my father...and she died when I was six and no one has really loved me since...I lost my father and he was the only one who ever really loved me and I've felt so alone since...my family lost everything in the fire and we just had the awful cans of food they give you from the food banks...when my dog died, my life ended...I still miss my mother...I made millions but I wasn't happy...I was so hungry and cold...I always thought I came to do something but I don't know what it is...and he left me for her...and she left me for him..."*

I pressed my middle finger deeply into my ears. I was afraid everyone knew I could hear their stories, and then the sound waves of the Cosmos parted. There was a swoosh, like air moving through a huge seashell, like waves pounding the shore, and it seemed to open a portal of sound, and I heard it *all*. I mean, I heard everyone in the room, *and* I heard the litany of every story from the beginning of time. They spiraled out of an invisible tunnel around me. Birth, love, hope, betrayal, mistrust, anger, pity, judgment, loss, joy, laughter, tears, sweat, hard work, millions of story bubbles burst inside me. I heard it all. And it's all the same. We all have the same story. The details are different, but it's all the same story, in a strange way. We're not just one Great Being, connected divinely at a Universal level. We all have a chapter in the same story. My heart burst and engulfed everyone in that room, everyone from the beginning of time, as we know it.

Underneath it all, I'm still the little girl who believed in love. The one who knew that the secrets of the universe lay in the love that can unfold between two people. And I'm the same little girl who knew that you can get further along in the search-for-God-business if you draw to you a partner, a mate, and if you *evenly* stay in complete truth, day-in-and-day-out, in the bedroom, in the bathroom and in the kitchen. And I'm the same little girl who always believed that if you don't have a partner, you just need to stay in complete and even truth with yourself.

It doesn't matter if I live twenty years or twenty minutes. It's the day-to-day process that matters. What are you doing with your time? It may be all you have...this minute...this day. Would you rather lie in bed with someone you love for ten more minutes or get up early and jog? Do you smile on the way out the door or just turn your back and walk away? Who is your God? Is it a fearsome, jealous thing that calls you a sinner? Darling, that's not God. That's the patriarchy talking; it's either a religion or a government or an unevolved alien! It's the voice of enslavement. We have been held by such insidious entrapment for eons, through the threat of ostracism and derision, through the conjoined efforts of the ignorance around us—through lies!

My story doesn't contain any hard truths. It doesn't contain alchemical processes that if stirred and carefully followed will produce the love of your life or enlightenment. And I don't care how sophisticated we all appear to be—I know what we all really want in our heart of hearts—someone to love us and someone who will let us love them.

It is our potential.

*"Time—as you know it—is running out, and I have received permission from the Goddess herself, indeed, I have been asked by the Goddess herself, to reveal to you some of the most closely guarded secrets of all times. These are revealed to you in hopes that you will elevate yourselves in time...*

*And so it is that I reveal one of the lost secrets of the ages—that Spirit, the male principle, in order to return to itself through its journey into Matter, requires the assistance of the feminine principle, the Intelligence of Matter itself.*

*But from the solar, light-filled perspective of the masculine principle, the feminine principle carries within her a dark, moist and dangerous abyss. The solar principle feels threatened by the darkness of the lunar aspect. But it is in the joining of the Sun and the Moon, the joining of the masculine and feminine principles, in equilibrium, in energetic balance, that true illumination is attained."*

—Mary Magdalen

One night, very early on, as we had just begun to ever so gently unfold our new love, right in the midst of other people's agendas, Tom and I stood at a precipice. We stood alongside a seawall on another island. It had been a rough day, and the sea monsters were after Tom. All the sirens had turned up their volume, and I couldn't hear the pounding waves for their cacophony. They pulled at him, luring him into the sea, out, way over his head, and he was blinded by the light. Just because something appears to look like light, doesn't mean it is light. I have learned that lesson the hard way.

And he walked away from me. He just walked away with palm trees swaying gently in the night air; he left me there. Standing alone in the middle of the dark night. And I looked around and there were campfires burning all around with men huddled, drinking and partying. I didn't want to admit I was afraid to walk home across that darkness alone. And my pride stung fiercely. I had been left along a seawall on a strange island by someone who was numbed by a spider's bite and couldn't tell the light from the dark in the moment.

*I'm fine. I will not ask for help! I don't need anyone! I know how to be alone. I have rather perfected that. I love being alone. I do it well.* I don't know how to do relationship perfectly. That's the one I have to learn. And so I swallowed hard, and I called him back. And he hadn't walked so far that he couldn't hear me. And he *chose* to come back. It took both those steps. I *chose* to call him back. And he *chose* to come. In every moment, in every circumstance, from the simplest to the most sublime— it's all just choice.

In the coming years I suspect we will face choices the likes of which have never been posed to humanity. Choose freedom. Choose love. And if there is any way you can bring total, complete, *even* truth into your life— at all levels, please do it. The truth really will set you free, and there is nothing without freedom.

And to my Beloved, I adore you. May it bring tears to anyone's eyes, as Magdalen's love for Yeshua did to me, to read how it is that I love you for your willingness to cross the moist, dark and dangerous abyss to live in the portal of the feminine, in the Holy Grail, with me. Your integrity and your honor shine above all and your song will echo in the halls of forever. Thank you for allowing me to be both the Initiate and the woman in love. To me, you will always be the little boy in the back of the bus whose face I never forgot, the one I knew would grow up to play guitar and sing songs. The one I knew was my soulmate. You sing my heart. Yours *is* the voice of God.

# AfterThoughts
## A Diary After Mary Magdalen

The following entries were all written the year after we received the *Manuscript* and all the way up until publication. We felt they were pertinent, as they show a process of what this material and our commitment to truth brought forward in our lives. Be warned! It isn't always pretty. But it's the truth. It is a diary of what happened for me in living this material the best I could.

Back on beautiful little Oudish, just as Magdalen was nearing the end of delivering the *Manuscript,* I went through a torturous process, and we felt it important enough to share, to show that it isn't always the bliss that comes first.

First the man and woman come together and out of their love a child is born. In Sacred Relationship, there is always creation, a third energy is always birthed—and birth is painful. But there is a reward; a new life is created, whether it is a child, or an energy. In our case, our *work* gets birthed into the world. I'm afraid love is like that. It's a process, like all of life, and you know what Pam said—it's the process that matters.

By the way, Tom never saw what I was writing in my story until it was done, and I read it to him. When I read him the first part about when I saw the little boy's face in the back of the bus, he crooked his head and interrupted to tell me that when he was really young, maybe eight or nine, his family was traveling through Virginia along Route 1 on a bus, and he saw a little girl in a car. And the car and the bus traveled alongside each other, and he and the little girl stared at each other until the vehicles parted, and he never forgot her. It's a long shot, but I believe in long shots.

## An Obscuration to Flight
### My First Entry
### December, 2000, Oudish Island

The storm lasted at least five, maybe seven days. My storm lasted almost fourteen days, maybe more. In my paranoia, I even wondered if perhaps, somehow, the external storm had been called up by my own boiling, stewing, festering watery depths.

Externally, the sea lashed out at the tiny island with a fury akin to my own boil. Hurricanes and such identified storms are horrific, but they have a beginning, a middle, and an end. This storm blew in and swirled and stayed, blowing at my back even now as I write.

In the beginning, it was worse at night, so that days were still somehow manageable. Midway through, it was constant, with no place to go in the limestone house to escape the howling. We put towels underneath the door to stop the scraping of wood and metal on limestone, a sound akin to fingernails on chalkboard. But the wind still found enough spaces to enter, so that it whorled through the bedroom, into the bathroom and resonated down the bathtub drain, creating such a banshee sound I could never describe. We were driven downstairs, into the spare bedroom, and it took the wind longer to find us there. In Marsalforn, it escaped the sea wall in it's fury and threw huge boulders across the street, aiming for the houses that encroached on the beach and bouncing them off the limestone, like a mad bowler. They lay in such litter on the street that it was undrivable. Between Zabbat and Marsalforn, on the back road by the sea, the waves leapt at such heights that they were turquoise at the very tops as they turned to froth, pounding the rocky beach, then dragging the rocks back to the depths from which they had escaped. I had never seen turquoise illuminated waves and hope to never forget the color or the cause, or the sound of thousands of rocks being dragged to shore and dragged back into the sea with each thrust of turquoise.

Internally, I suspect this material and the timing of the presentation of this material. By that I mean that we all have little fissures, mortared over, spackled, painted a pretty, acceptable color, with throw rugs covering even the hint of anything not perfect.

A simple incident occurred, innocent and simple, but it dug down into my foundation and found a sympathetic fissure and began a process of disintegrating everything I thought I knew and believed. It grew and grew in proportion until every moment of every day was engaged in examination and torture of some aspect of this little, tiny fissure. I do not write this, nor do I choose, to detail this very personal incident, but to show how the process can work, so that I did not just rip up the very foundation of my being for only myself.

What do you fear? It will come to your door if you choose the path of the Initiate.

I feared betrayal and abandonment. I was in one of the safest places in the world, surrounded by people who love and adore me, and my fears still found me.

It was not fear of the wind. I only saw the mirror in its turbulence. And I'm certainly not saying I created the storm. I am only noticing the reflection of its fury out of the calm. And I am aware that it, like my storm, will have its season. The question for examination was, what had caused the storm? Was there a change in the barometrics, and could I determine what had changed in the pressure around me so that my own storm, the internal storm, might have its glory and then allow me to go back to my blissful state of relationship?

The incident had just occurred and it was insignificant, though it carried a message to my ears that sounded louder than it needed to have sounded. And why was that? Magdalen had just given the information about how crucial it was for the woman's *floor* to be strong and safe, how she needed to know that she was loved and that she was safe. And I had reveled in that information, knowing how sweet and clear that message would sound to such weary, tired ears as we women have. I knew we needed to feel secure to fully blossom. The poppy does not look the same that has been beaten by the wind and dashed against rocks. But look at the tall poppy that has stood in the field alongside other such poppies, flanked by supporting stalks, safely looking into the sun, with just the right amounts of moisture and sunlight and darkness. She is all she can be in that environment.

How many of us are ever safe and secure enough to be all we can be?

I was told as a little child that I would have every experience a human could have, so that when I spoke, it would be from experience and that I would have something of value to say. It was a strange thing to be told while sitting in the fork of a pear tree when you're five years old. And I never forgot it.

And so when I talk about how you can't perform under the stress of abuse, I speak from the horror of experience. I spent five years with a horribly abusive man. The abuses were slow to appear at the beginning, or I tell myself I would never have gotten caught up in such a situation. And in the beginning, they were mostly verbal. Then he began to systematically cut me off from my friends, though I didn't detect any danger in that. Then, when I least expected it, completely out of the blue, not attached to an argument or disagreement, he would strike me; leaving me almost disbelieving the event had occurred. It is demeaning, demoralizing, paralyzing and almost drove me mad. It is beyond dishonoring. The word dishonoring is so trivializing to the degree of shame and degradation that abuse creates.

I examined every aspect of every move I had made prior to those blows. What had I said? What had I done? There was nothing I had done. Did I dream it? And I was much too ashamed to let anyone know it was happening. I was far too evolved to allow such behavior and besides—thank you religion—it must have been my fault. We are, after all, such wicked creatures filled with guilt and created in sin and shame.

But that horrible relationship had ended with me still alive. I had put years and a lot of work between these incidents and *me*.

And now, here I am, in the most amazing, powerful, loving, honoring, fulfilling relationship I have ever even read about, much less experienced, and I'm feeling frightened and insignificant and jealous of nothing and every insecurity has moved into my head and taken up residence, haunting me, hounding me. All because of one tiny, little incident.

I should tell you that "nothing" happened. No one did anything to me. There was a simple communication in an email between Tom and someone else, and I took the message and extrapolated it. I boiled it, dissected it, reassembled it, recarved it, served it to all the voices in my head and published my report.

I was wounded, perhaps fatally wounded.

*"But I can handle it. I'm an Initiate. I'm living a dream life,"* I reasoned.

So I tried to put a tiny, barely visible, throw rug over the insignificant dent in the linoleum.

And then the Magdalen delivered these words, *"The next level to understand has to do with the emotional tuning of the female Initiate. For the female Initiate's receptivity is dependent upon her emotional state. This is part of her nature and cannot be sidestepped if these techniques are to work."*

And she went on, as if that wasn't enough to stir the soup.

*"Essential to the female Initiate is the authentic feeling of safety and love, or appreciation at the very least. When these are in place, something within her being lets go and allows the alchemy to occur. The alchemy is created by the joining of the male Initiate's Ka and the female Initiate's Ka. As they make love, the Ka bodies interconnect and this causes the female to open her magnetic floor."*

I froze as she continued to speak.

*"This is a strange term. It comes from the language used in the Temples of Isis. The floor is the foundation upon which one stands. When we set something to be secure, we place it on the floor. So the floor was used as a type of slang within the Temples, referring to the very basic piece that is required. So when I say 'the female's magnetic floor,' I am saying that this is the fundamental piece that has to occur."*

The light winds turned to gale force, the sea whipped, and the throw rug was blown away.

Something greater than my timidity had ripped up my floorboards to inspect the tiny fissure. Where I want to go, there can be no weakness, no fissures, and no fears. I knew some of the secrets of the ages lay in this simple, short material given with so much power and clarity. I say the word "secrets" and any woman reading this *Manuscript* will tell you she knew this. But we have been shamed and quieted for so long that we have long ago stopped trusting those inner knowings.

Magdalen was rousted from where she lay within the soul she shared with her Beloved, Yeshua, by Isis and Metatron and asked to come and tell us her story. And I had put a throw rug out to greet her. I have only two commitments. One is to the truth with Tom, and the other is to look at all my unfinished business. I have called that forward now for almost two decades. I just didn't think I could possibly have this much unfinished business.

## The Feminist Rises
### Second Entry
### December, 2000, Oudish

This material was given over a period of time between Thanksgiving and Christmas of 2000. Mary Magdalen first came through one night in Zurich, Switzerland in a small hotel in the old section of town. She continued her delivery as we zagged across the breadth of the Mediterranean, triangulated Sicily, and wound up living on Oudish, the smaller Malta Island. Magdalen completed by editing her portion herself, word by word, shortly after the above-described physical storm passed, just before Christmas, 2000.

She had chosen each word before she spoke it through Tom with a sense of power and clarity I had never heard before from any human or Spirit. She had neither anger nor pity nor any common emotion throughout the telling, but over one thing. When she spoke of the love she felt for the man, Yeshua, her heart trembled. And I cried every time she brought up how hard it had been to take the role of the Initiate, for which she had been well trained, and still be a woman in love with a man, for which there is no training under the sun.

And he was a man on a mission!

How many of these have we known?

And the job he came to do was more important than his love for her?

How many of these have we known?

And in the retelling, he is remembered as the Christ, the Redeemer, the Only Son of God; and she is remembered as a whore, though it was she who filled him?

How many of these have we known?

And she, as the unlimited vessel of energy, gave him the strength to do what he came to do. And so he did it, and then he left?

And my little, tiny fissure cracked down the epi-center, and by Christmas the fault line was above ground, visible to anyone who came near.

# Ba Humbug
# Third Entry
# December, 2000, Oudish

December continued to howl across the sparsely treed fields of Oudish, and the chill wasn't only in the air. I was still hounded by the innocent incident of the email. It was a simple, innocent email to Tom, to and from an old friend—but it happened to be an old friend who'd had an agenda for Tom, one that included a little more than friendship. This person had hurt me and almost cost us the relationship. I couldn't understand why this person was still in our life, since the original experience had brought such intense anguish.

Sacred Relationship—the way I want to do it, the way I believe it *must* be lived—must be the most important process ongoing in life. Reason is out! If I am God and my mate is God, then why would any god outside of us— any practice, any devotion, any being, anything— demand greater obedience than our love. It must be night and day, always at the heart of life, always the most important aspect of life. It must stay in total truth. No dust can be swept under the throw rug. No throw rugs covering the slight, tiny flaws. And unless it is held as the most valued and sacred experience, it will dwindle and succumb to the tendency of all relationships. This is the truth I hold in my heart. And it is the truth which no man I have ever known could handle or remain in honor to—and here I was, back at the point of truth. I felt like a jealous, scorched woman, a banshee with no compassion. I felt I *looked* like that. I didn't really think that's what was going on, but so deeply devalued is my self esteem, that I questioned my intuition. Still, if it were not so, if Tom really loved me, would he still be communicating with this person? If he knew that communication with this person hurt me, why would he continue the communication?

Perhaps I should leave.

*I am impossible to live with. My price is too high for anyone to pay. I demand too much. I give no slack. I have no slack to give after where I've been. But who on Earth can stand up to the demands of an unrelentingly demanding woman who carries a picture of relationship with colors from another universe? And I cannot find the old "governors" on my thoughts and mouth; the tricks of the southern woman have deserted me, and I cannot help but say what I think. Goddess, help me!*

Perhaps I should leave.

Oudish is said to be the island where Odysseus was held captive by the siren, Calypso, for seven years. I am captive here. There is nowhere to go. It's a tiny island dotted with fields and Catholic Churches and the sweetest, most honest people you will ever meet anywhere, and there is no escape. I am trapped here in my swirling.

Perhaps I *should* leave. Tom doesn't need this after what he's been through. He needs peace, not a shrew. I am a shrew. But I'm right. I'm a *right* shrew! Sigh.

*Do you want to be right? Or do you want to be happy?* But at what price does happiness come?

We went for a walk—a long walk. It was time for truth.

Each farmer on Oudish has a tiny little plot, maybe a acre, maybe a 1/2 acre. They are all appropriately "fenced," as it were, in oddly shaped walls of stone, hand-piled through the generations, each generation unearthing small boulders that continually rise to the surface and adding them to the stonewall. So the terrain is zigzagged by these stonewalls, like patchwork lines on a quilt of soil.

I am like a steam kettle, appearing quite quiet and passive and easy. But if something happens, like the email, I *used* to begin a slow boil, which took years to turn to steam. Now I just boil over, right away, and then I hold that boil. I mean, I can really harp over something that seems mildly out of place. I don't mean to; I can't help it. I don't see other dimensions, but I don't miss an energy exchange on this plane. Too many years in politics, I guess. I don't miss much happening energetically around me, and I could feel the difference in the air between Tom and me since I questioned this email. He was withdrawing from the dark, moist and dangerous abyss of the feminine. Her price was *pretty* high these days; I had to admit. It demanded total commitment and total truth, which he also demanded of me.

We began to talk about it all.

I thought I would die. I had to admit I was jealous of an email. I felt disrespected. I felt hurt and abandoned by an email. I thought I would die. I mean, when you cut yourself wide open to another person and talk about your fears, your jealousies, your inadequacies, your weak floor—you just *know* they can't handle it. You know your "stuff" is too ugly, too confining, for anyone to stomach. Besides, surely your stuff smells like tuna fish! No one could possibly love you through your truth.

I was afraid that it might appear that I was confining Tom, and for whatever reason, I cannot bear the thought of anyone ever confining Tom Kenyon again. I had refused to be like the people around Tom when Pam died, all vying for confinement rights!

But Tom doesn't see agendas like I do. He sees Deity and Spirits and Beings from other dimensions, and he talks to them like I talk to the waitress at a restaurant. I see agendas and politics and my prophetic abilities are limited to the human beings around me. I hear what they *don't* say, and I see what they don't think anyone sees. I see their true motives and am cursed with feeling crazy over my oddly unappreciated ability. I saw the *meaning* behind the message behind the *written* words in the email...not the one Tom wrote, but the one he received.

We walked for hours that day, over walls and fields, all the way to the Cliffs of Dwejra, a dizzying ledge of limestone hundreds of feet above the Mediterranean. I knew Tom was thinking how nice it would be to live alone. I was thinking how nice it would be to live alone. This was work!

*But the love is so intense! He takes my breath away!*

We talked it all over and over and over and over and over and over and over. Exhausted from the walk and the talk, we turned to head back. Perhaps it was time for us to part company.

Then I spotted something on the ground near my foot. It was a carved pottery shard of some kind, almost buried in the sand. It had a design, like a petroglyph, on its surface. Tom and I both stopped to look at this treasure. I reached down and dug at it with a rock, and it yielded to my pressure. We had found an ancient symbol from one of the hundreds of Goddess Temples all over the island, perhaps a message for this place where we were stuck—to love or to leave.

We almost fell down laughing when we brushed it off and discovered not an ancient amulet or shard of pottery, but the cover from a clutch pedal left in the sand decades ago. Our ancient pottery shard was someone else's old clutch pedal cover!

And so we took it as a great sign and we shifted into neutral. We had each told our truth. We stood there, in the light of that long day, and just stopped. We went home and just held each other. In truth, in total truth, no one has ever stopped my heart like Tom Kenyon. And he will learn to see agendas, and I will learn to see other dimensions. But if I don't ever see other dimensions, it's OK with me. I've got Tom to tell me the truth of what's out there. And if he doesn't ever see other people's agendas around him, that's OK, he's got me. And as long as he *appreciates* my gifts and *listens* to me, and I *appreciate* his and *listen* to him, we have total sight between us. Magdalen was right—appreciation, at the very least, is required.

# Hauntings
## Fourth Entry
### July, 2001, Paros Island, Cyclades, Greece

I am haunted by many things as I contemplate placing this material in the world at large. The responsibility for putting such information into print weighed so heavily this particular night that sleep deprived me of her peace, and I find myself sitting at the small kitchen table, palm-top in hand, so to speak, braving the mosquitoes of the Cyclades. They are small but ominously dangerous in their predatory nature; humless, they are deadly in their silence. They are truly among the little things that can really make a point in life.

The Magdalen consciousness is upon the Earth plane now, as we realize the truth of the emotion and physicality of passion and welcome the return of the feminine principal. In your journey you may encounter some of the many other visages and the voices claiming to speak for the Magdalen, or even to "be" her.

They tell different stories, these different Magdalens.

Some channels I have great respect for have been given the story that she and Yeshua were together as consorts, but had no children. Some have been given the story that there were many children. Some say that Yeshua died on the cross during his crucifixion and that Magdalen carried on the teachings alone. Some versions say he did not die on the cross, but lived with her for many more years and that the crucifixion was nothing more than a hoax, to earn his freedom, a real "crock-of-fiction."

Some say he ultimately died in Masada, during the siege. Some claim his resting place is clearly marked in

India. One recent version says he is buried in southern France, in the Pyrennees. Some channeled versions of the Magdalen story say she lived her life teaching in her own mystery school in southern France and that her bones lie there. Others say she found her peace, if you will, in England. Others say there was no such one person as Jesus Christ but that "he" was a composite of many different teachers of the time, edited together purely to create a new religion to quiet the masses under Roman government.

I am not bothered by the discrepancies, though I admit it would be far simpler if everyone were telling the same story. But they do tell the same story over the significant issues—that this Yeshua and this Magdalen were consorts and that the Church purposefully and maliciously mis-translated the word for whore to dismiss the Magdalen, to impale all of femininity with that brand, specifically to further the patriarchy and discredit passion, so that, as Magdalen put it, no one would accidentally stumble on the great truths that lie in passion.

What matters to me in this *Manuscript* is the obvious power in her words and the transcendent and palpable love she has held throughout all time for her Beloved, Yeshua.

In addition to that, the practices she gave create electrical shift. There is no doubt of that.

As I detach myself from the elation and personal "high" derived from being present when this material was given, experiencing the Magdalen first-hand, feeling her strong and even presence, listening through tears to much of her story, I find myself only now, months later, able to do what I do best, be devil's advocate, questioning it and its relevance today.

She had chosen each word with such calibrated precision. She was back to tell a story and to set the record straight. Much of what she had to do was clarify the misinformation, the lies the Church perpetrated. And Yeshua had used language that had a meaning to only a certain few, language which, when taken out of context, became supportive of something in total contradiction to what he really meant.

Just sitting down with the Master and having some bread and a glass of wine had gone from being something he loved to do with people, to eating his flesh and drinking his blood. And the Church calls others pagan?

And how would we avoid doing the same? How could we choose language and supportive commentary that couldn't/wouldn't, over time, be used to misconstrue the real meaning? Are people capable of understanding and choosing the divinity of Sacred Relationship? Or will they think this is just a great little manual on how to use sex to gain power?

And what about her role, in the light of feminism? Was she just another woman who gave her power to a man? In this case, literally *gave* her power to a man, who could not have done what he did without her contribution?

If you think this is a sex manual or the story of a woman who gave her power to a man, you have missed the point and will surely not attain the possible.

This is a story of what Magdalen called Sacred Relationship and the internal alchemies possible within the safety and devotion of Sacred Marriage.

We have been as careful as we could be in choosing words with consideration to their long-term meaning. We have tried not to use words or slang used within only certain schools of metaphysics, hoping that they will not be misconstrued, at least within our own lifetime anyway. Beyond that we can do nothing but *intend* truth and illumination.

# Pondering
## Fifth Entry
## Orcas Island, December 2001

It has been one year since Magdalen gave us this *Manuscript*. She gave it in two months. In two months she gave what she wanted of her personal story and what she wanted to share of her story as an Initiate of the Temple of Isis. In her slim volume of exquisitely chosen words she also taught what could be taught, what could be shared, for those ready to hear the beauty of it. She gave us some of the deepest secrets of the Temples of Isis and the secrets of ecstasy that have been stolen from us. It has taken me one year to come to terms with it, and to add what I have been asked to add; and I am feeling deeply humbled in the job. I have now worked with her energy on many occasions, alone and with other people and my admiration, indeed, my deepest gratitude for her beauty, her love and her genius and power awe me and always will.

I don't know what happens to us humans. We are born with all we ever need in life. We are born in beauty and genius. We are born *of* God and with God fully infused. We *are* God. There is no God outside of us. That doesn't make me any better than the next person. That next person is God, too! That's the magic. We are all God. We are all divine. We look around and we see enough land and enough hard working people to be capable of feeding everyone on the planet. We see enough bounty to take care of everyone on Earth, all the animals, and all the creatures. And we swear that when we grow up, we are going to change things. We are going to make a difference. And then something happens.

I was lucky. I grew up in the strangest of circumstances, basically away from all common influences, except for when humans tried to tell me something I had experienced differently in nature. Although I had humans telling me what to do, I had the counterbalance of deep nature, deeper than anyone I've ever met. And I couldn't see this "sin" we are all supposed to be born in. I saw beauty, despite what the people around me told me. I saw beauty in the love possible between people and I couldn't imagine how such beauty could be evil!

And then I went out in the world and I got hurt. And my *giving* nature was met equally by the *taking* nature of many around me.

And all the pain and hypocrisy and bigotry and judgment I saw growing up was caused by the belief in Jesus Christ! I didn't experience beauty coming out of the love people claimed for this Being. Then I grew in my own spirituality, and I came to understand that he was a Great Master teacher, one of many the world has been gifted to know, but indeed, a great Master, in whose name governments created a religion. How ironic then, that Mary Magdalen should use the phrase, "...were aghast that the Master would help such a one." Since that is my experience of Christianity, how ironic that this material would come to "such a one as me?"

# Fear of Flying Returns
## A Closing Entry
## Orcas Island, December 31, 2001

Just as this book was going into final edits Tom and I encountered yet another "obscuration to flight," and because it brought about such major shift and wound up affording us such understanding, we decided we had a duty to share it. You need to be aware that prickles can lie beneath the beautiful roses when you undertake Sacred Relationship. And you need to understand that we work at it every day. We live in the alchemical furnace. The more I understand and experience what Magdalen means by true Sacred Relationship, and the more I live it, the more awed I am by the process, and the more respect I have for those of us brave enough to enter the catacombs of this process.

Something simple happened. Again. It wasn't a big deal. And it *was*. It was actually quite like the simple little experience that triggered our journey on little Oudish, when my internal storm out blew the external storm. But when one partner does something that hurts the other in relationship, intentional or not, it must be respected. If it doesn't see the "light" of examination, it will darken the door of love eventually, either through atrophy or eventually through revolution. When the safety net evaporates, so goes the alchemy.

Tom invited an experience of someone into his life, someone I felt was dangerous to him, and he did it without consulting me, or I would have at least warned him about the potential for danger I "saw" in such an encounter. I am cursed with seeing the machinations of people around us, people on the street.

I "see" agendas. He sees Deity. Sigh. I see his vision as a gift. I see mine, all too often, as a burden.

When he told me about the invitation, my gut twisted. My stomach flopped and my heart raced right out the door. I made the bed, dressed, packed my emotional suitcase and left. I withdrew about forty years into my childhood. And I said nothing at first. I really tried to stuff my feelings back down. But my heart was making so much noise, I feared it would explode.

I have to tell you, I knew my discussion about this particular "obscuration to flight" wasn't going to be appreciated initially. After all, hadn't we had this experience already on Oudish?  And so it was with great, heavy heart that I sat down and began to share what was happening within me as a result of his simple, innocent, but painful-to-me action.

Tom had simply invited someone into the relationship that I "saw" as potentially dangerous. It was an innocent action, and the individual involved would hardly be considered dangerous by anyone. Intentions were altogether well meaning. But I "saw" that inviting this person into our life potentially opened portals through which, shall we say, other presences might find entry. Magdalen actually called these other presences, these other energies, demons in her day.

So what does this mean? Was I simply being a jealous woman? Or was I so intuitive that I sensed anyone who was even inadvertently dangerous? Or was I so controlling that I couldn't allow anyone into our lives that didn't meet my stamp of approval?

My initial overtures regarding the subject brooked just the reaction I expected, and so I began my emotional packing job, ready to go out the heart door. Tom does what Tom does—he numbed. And there we were. The same magnets that usually draw us together flipped, and have you seen what magnets do when they are reversed, and you try to force them together? They repel. It's very hard to talk from your heart when you are repelled, and when you know you repel the significant other in your life.

I sat down and talked with him about what I thought had been created by this action and how I felt dishonored when he didn't talk to me before opening this particular barn door and letting this horse out, which has now become my mantra.

He was appalled at my reaction. Well, of course he was! I probably initially sounded like an insane woman again. (I mean, I thought I was right, mind you. In other words, I knew I wasn't insane, but I was afraid he would think me a bit daft. I knew I was even *right*, at least for me, but I have also learned the other great truth...do you want to be right, or do you want to be happy?)

I can't stress how life threatening this business of being in total truth is to the psyche. You really think you're going to die when you first begin to speak. And there is something deeply scary about the truth, the total truth, not the clean, pretty truth, but the truth that lies under everything, the truth that we hide from everyone.

And let me tell you—it's really easy to let all this go and not tell your truth, not stir the pot. I could easily just relax and let it go. We'd have been fine if I hadn't pushed this issue—on the surface. But I knew that eventually we'd wind up just like every other couple in the world today, together, but not really together, co-dependent to each other's refusal to look at truth. You can actually think you love someone so much that you never call them on their stuff, thinking it would hurt them too much. I'll tell you what hurts—not calling someone on his or her stuff. That's what kills and creates disease and compliance to non-growth and disillusionment.

I know in my heart that those little things, those little annoyances, those little nigglings, the little truths, when *not* shared between people in Sacred Relationship build brick walls, over which there is eventually no assault. When you do not share your truth, one morning you wake up and find yourself living with a stranger, a room-mate. Read my story again. I've been there, and it is not the road to Sacred Relationship.

And I wish I could tell you that we figured out the answer by ourselves without help. And the truth is, we asked for help. I was losing my mind, haunted by the image of myself as a fearful, jealous woman. I mean, I just wrote this whole section and admitted what my fears were and here they were again! I thought we'd gotten beyond all that!

The truth was, I had another ever-so-slight crack in my foundation, and it left me fearing for my safety and for Tom's safety.

And so I approached Tom with my concerns, and "our magnets flipped" as we call it, and the always so powerful attraction between us repelled each of us, and we withdrew to our corners. I felt wounded. He felt annoyed.

We shut everything down and we asked for guidance. This possibility for transformation through relationship is the most sacred and honored aspect of life to each of us. We have each chosen this, and it is our agreement to continue to choose relationship. And we were stuck and needed help.

I know we are fortunate beyond imagination in that we have such access to guidance. And it is because I know not everyone has such access that I share what we were told.

It was explained to us that "who" we are is forged from our childhood and a myriad of lifetime experiences. The swords each of us carries into relationship are forged in the heat of pain and out of terrific smelting; we are *set*, alloyed, from such experiences. It takes at least *equal* heat to re-forge us, to change what we are, to burn off the *obstacles to flight*, as Magdalen calls them, to burn off the dross.

I want that burn, though I admit I sometimes fear the heat, and it really helped me to be told that we weren't doing anything wrong, but that, in fact, this is the process and that this experience was an indication of where we were in the process.

Tom and I have chosen to share this personal piece of guidance in the hope that it answers some questions.

*"The answer lies in the context of alchemical process. Are you showing the face of the jealous woman or the face of a woman who sees danger?*

*"It is the process between the two of you. You must speak the truth of what you are experiencing, and Tom must speak his truth from what arises within him—the conflict or the harmony. Those are the two faces. And this melding is the process of burning off the dross. So the two of you are in an alchemical process, and you are doing everything quite accurately.*

*"We understand it is a very difficult situation, and you are looking for an answer that keeps you from the heat. But the heat is required! There are psychological patterns within each of you that you might call negative, or less than resourceful, and they are melded with aspects that are positive.*

*The jealous woman is bonded with the person who feels danger, because when you make steel you bond,*

you make an alloy. And what made you was your childhood. You are taking the swords of your identities and
sticking them in the alchemical furnace, and there is no
answer to make this easier, other than to understand that
you are in an alchemical process that you willingly
chose to enter. When your swords begin to dissolve, it
feels like you are losing your identity.

"The answer is for both of you to speak the truth
about what face you have on, in the moment.

"When the furnace gets so hot that the magnets flip,
it is because the heat is so intense that it is changing
the structure of the magnets. The magnets are created
through polarizations in each of you. You are drawn to
the polarizations in each other, so there is a match.
There is a magnetism that pulls you together. When the
heat is turned up, the magnets reverse and with all the
intensity that usually pulls you together, you are then
repelled. This is temporary; just ride through it; don't
read anything into it. There is a part of you that searches for evidence, for clues that you are in dangerous territory, and you need to escape. There is no escape in
these times, only truth.

"Understand that you are in alchemical process when
you are in Sacred Relationship; and you search for pictures, and sometimes when the pictures don't match,
you get scared. You are in alchemical process. As this
heat gets turned up and you can't take the heat, go to
another place where the heat is not so strong. Pause and
let the world stop; and take each other's hands, though
the last thing you want to do is touch each other in these
times; and speak the truth about what face is showing
itself. Understand that telling the truth is not going to
break apart anything.

"Don't let anything come between you. You must live
in a fluid environment so there are no demands, so if the
heat gets too hot you can stop everything and go
through the truth process. You must live in a free-floating
environment so you can go into mystery.

*"When the feminine nature has discovered something that she treasures, she becomes a fierce protectress, and she wants to protect it at all costs. Jealousy is a face that presents itself in the course of life experiences. The problem is not with jealousy; the problem is not speaking the truth of what one needs. To go out on a limb is to speak the truth, facing the possibility that the other one may not be willing to give what you want.*

*"Relationships are rather like poker games, with everyone bluffing about who has the higher cards. When you go into Sacred Relationship, all the cards are laid out on the table for each to see. Whatever arises, it is simply put on the table; because the clarity of two people looking at all the cards allows for the possibility of transformation."*

Let me sum up.

Always stay in truth.

It's going to get hot.

Don't give up. Buy a clutch pedal cover and put it on your altar. Hold hands and walk across the burning coals. And I promise you—you will think you are going to die. And you won't.

# Post Partum
## An Afterthought

This is a story of what Magdalen calls Sacred Relationship and the internal alchemies possible within the safety and devotion of Sacred Marriage.

We do not live in times of light. "We are," as Magdalen says, "at the beginning of the ending of time." And time is short and so secrets are being revealed, in the hope that more people will wake up and make the relevant changes necessary to make a difference.

I am reminded of the story of the young man walking along the beach. In the distance, he sees what looks like tiny dots all over the beach and the shape of an old woman, bending down and then walking to the edge of the sea, and tossing something into the sea, then walking back, and bending down again, and picking something up, and throwing it into the sea.

As he approaches, he sees that the beach is littered with starfish, left behind by a quickly receeding tide. There are hundreds of star fish dying on the beach and one old woman, picking one up at a time, walking to the edge of the sea and tossing one back, and then picking up another.

He is astonished at the impossibility of her task and says, "Why on Earth are you doing that? Why are you bothering? You can't save enough of them to matter!"

She threw one more starfish into the sea and yelled into the wind, "It matters to that one."

As Magdalen said in her final transmission, "I realize in the sharing of my story that only a handful will understand, but that is enough."

In sharing One Woman's Story, I realize that many will criticize me. Some will be jealous of me. Some will call me names. Many will judge. I chose to honor the request from Mary Magdalen that it be included because I have come to, unflinchingly and without hesitation, adore her and trust her wisdom beyond my fears.

May you find your own Sacred Marriage, in balance, evenness, and ecstatic devotion with another and with yourself.

What will happen when

one woman writes

the truth about her life?

The world will split open.

—*Muriel Rukeyser*

# Addendum

We entreatied Mary Magdalen with numerous questions after she delivered her *Manuscript*. There were certain questions we knew we would be asked when we presented this material to the world. Some of the questions we asked were personal, but we felt it important to ask them when presented the opportunity. She answered some of these questions, but often her answer was, "Tell them Mary Magdalen has no comment." We share this with you to show you more of the personality of the Being we experienced. Her boundaries were clear. She had no difficulty delineating what was her personal business and what information might be of help in this time. She had no patience for questions that achieved nothing but reduce her story to idle conversation and irrelevant trivia.

Rather than write a dialogue we have presented these questions and answers exactly as they were asked and as they were answered.

**Q:** Were you and Yeshua married?

**Magdalen:** "Yeshua and I were married in a rabbinical tradition. In the Gospels they report that Yeshua turned water into wine at a wedding ceremony. What they failed to mention was that the wedding was ours. It was known.

There are two paths that sometimes overlap. One is Initiation and one is marriage.

Initiation is entering a higher threshold of understanding and ability. Initiations are given to solitary individuals.

Those in Sacred Relationship step into this through their mutual intention.

Acknowledgement by another is unnecessary. That is a cultural way of doing it. Those who enter into the heart of Sacred Relationship will go through Initiations as a result of their entering into the mysteries. What is important is not the *act* but the *process* of Sacred Relationship."

**Q:** How does the Sex Magic of Isis change for women who have had hysterectomy or menopause?

**Magdalen:** "The sexual fluids of a mature woman who has gone through either of these is, of course, different from those of a woman who is fertile. So the interaction of semen and the woman's sexual fluids do not have the same energetic constituency. However, there is a reaction and more importantly all other aspects of the Sex Magic of Isis apply. The stroking, the touch, the nesting all create the magnetic fields which can be drawn into both Initiates' subtle bodies, and so while the act may not be as dynamic as in their youth, it is still effective."

**Q:** How does Sex Magic change with men who have had vasectomies?

**Magdalen:** "The possibility of vasectomies was not a consideration during my time in the Temples of Isis. From the standpoint of the Sex Magic of Isis, the truth of the matter is that the man must rely upon stroking and touch and nesting to create the magnetic fields. The question implied is, will the Sex Magic work for a man who had a vasectomy? Yes, but with one consideration. Because the magnetics of his semen are denied interaction with the sexual fluids of his partner, he must actually stroke and touch his partner more than normal, in order to build close to the same intensity of magnetics."

**Q:** In the *Manuscript* you said that the issues that men had with their mothers might affect the alchemy between them and their partners. Does the same hold true for

women? Does their relationship with their fathers affect
the alchemy?

**Magdalen:** "To a certain extent, yes; a girl's experience
with her father, by necessity, colors her interactions with
her partner as a woman. And so to this extent, the effects
are similar. But what I wish to have pointed out in regards
to the male Initiate is the unusual vulnerability that the
male experiences in relationship to the female. A daughter
was never "carried by her father," for he does not have a
womb. Her body was not formed out of his elements.

The son, on the other hand, is carried within the
womb of the mother and is surrounded by her during his
development. And once he is born, he begins the
process of separation. Once his development reaches a
certain stage, and if there were issues with his mother
that are unresolved as a man, he may find it difficult to
nest—because to *nest* is to be surrounded by the feminine energy once again, as he was *in utero*. And this is a
different situation than with the woman and issues she
may have with her father."

**Q:** Do you have any comments about the other major
alchemical streams that teach that a man should retain
his semen during intercourse?

**Magdalen:** "You may say, 'And she laughed!'
My bias, you understand, is as a Priestess of the
Temples of Isis. The alchemy I was trained in is *feminine
based*, and we view some of these things quite differently
than the other streams you mention.

For one, we hold that the Creatrix of all time and
space, whom we call Isis, is enfolded in the natures of all
women. It is a *part* of them. Just like the seeds of a fig
are hidden within it. We also understood that alchemy
was based upon the joining of two opposites, the male
principle and the female principle. But in this way of
alchemy, the woman is understood to hold the alchemi-

cal keys. The male is needed in order to turn the keys, and it is *in* the mutual joining together of these polar opposites embodied within the male and female Initiate that the Alchemy takes place. From our perspective, the withholding of the male's semen is just another playing out of his general tendency to withhold.

It is true that a male's vitality is related to the energetics of his seed and that reckless release of his semen can affect his vitality. However, when the male releases his seed into his Beloved and he nests within her energies, he is fed and nourished by the magnetics as the door to her inner nature opens, flooding both of them with life-force. This is a different alchemical path than the other streams on the Earth at this time."

**Q:** Did you form a mystery school or teach in France or England?

**Magdalen:** "Upon landing at St. Maries my first and foremost concern was the safety of Sar'h, and so we headed north with the Druids to the Glastonbury and the Tor. When Sar'h was twelve I returned to the reeds to do the water Isis Ritual. By then Sar'h was not in danger and our return to England was more leisurely. I formed some teaching circles. After Sar'h wedded, I made periodic trips into France and into parts of England where I did teach the mysteries of the Temples of Isis."

**Q:** Is Magdalen a title?

**Magdalen:** "It was a title of spiritual recognition. There is an Order of Magdalen. It is hidden."

**Q:** What is the reason for the use of the reptilian imagery as used in the Alchemies of Horus?

**Magdalen:** "These serpentine images were used to communicate the serpent-like structure of sekhem as it

moves up the djed. As the energies released by the
Alchemies of Horus rise up the djed, they are snake-like
in nature, undulating in other words. As they enter the
head, they often tend to spread out across the hemispheres of the brain, like a cobra that shows its hood.
Thus, the serpent form is a metaphor, a symbolic element that points to the deeper structure and nature of
consciousness as it moves in the subtle body (the Ka)."

**Q:** The Gospels report that Yeshua exorcised seven
demons from you? What was that?

**Magdalen:** "Yeshua performed a rite of purification,
clearing out what you would call negativity from my
seven chakras. It was a chakra clearing. The "seven
demons" are simply negative energies that we all carry
from time to time in our fields. He cleared this from my
fields in preparation for the deeper alchemy we were to
perform together.

What is not clarified is that I cleared the seven chakras
for him as well. I preformed that same process on him.

The principal is this.

As one increases the power of one's illumination, or
spiritual nature, one becomes a magnet for many energies that are not one's own. This is true when a person is
in a lower emotional state and becomes open to negative
forces or energies, which in Yeshua's time were called
demons. This becomes especially true when one is intoxicated or altered through drug use. If one's emotional
tone (or vibrational state) is low, one opens the door to
these negative and sometimes destructive energies.

However, paradoxically, something similar occurs
when one moves upward into higher states of consciousness, because one becomes a magnet (or attractor) for
these negative energies. And we all have occasions when
we are not aware, and sometimes places are frequented
that are not in our best interest, and this is when these
energies *ride in*, so to speak.

The process was simply an ancient practice that stretches back to the Temples of Isis. It was a process for the Purification of the Seven Seals that drives out any negativity that we may carry, that we may not even be aware of. This was accomplished through the use of secret mantras, prayer, and the direction of light through intention, or will, into these centers. It is a complex process that not everyone is capable of, so to give the methodology, so to speak, to the masses would be a dis-service, because distortions would occur. It takes a level of mastery to clear the seals in the method that I used to clear him and he used to clear me.

Yet, once again, we see in the Gospel account of this, a one-sided and manipulative perspective. That Yeshua came to me for this purification as well was never reported. And yet they knew about it."

**Q:** What is meant by "the return of Cosmic Mother?

**Magdalen:** "It is a shift of collective consciousness to an honoring of the feminine. It will show up as a global and collective understanding of the sacredness of the earth itself, so that instead of raping and pillaging the earth, there will be a co-creation of the earth. And women—those souls embodied as women—will be ele-vated to a place of equality, of appreciation along with the male principal.

As you can tell, this earth has a long way to go before it reaches this."

**Q:** Do you mean it will be a long time before this happens?

**Magdalen:** "No, I mean it's a big leap in conscious-ness from where humanity is now, collectively. So thus, we can see or understand the need for purification. The need for purification decreases as each person comes into balance with the male/female within and moves to a place of honoring those externally in embodied male/female relationships."

We asked Mary Magdalen if she has had other incarnations and she told us that she has had no other incarnations.

Mary Magdalen made several references in our conversations to "those aligned with the New Earth." When we asked her what would qualify those in alignment with this New Earth, she replied without hesitation, "No guilt. No shame. No regrets."

# Glossary of Terms

**Alchemy** - the art and science of changing one form into another. Inner alchemy (like the Egyptian system) transforms the energy of consciousness and the life-force of embodiment into expanded awareness, imparting enhanced abilities to the practitioner.

**Ammit** - a mythical creature related to the djed or sacred pathway of the chakras. Part crocodile, part lion and part hippopotamus, the ammit is often represented with a depiction of the djed. It sits with its reptilian snout tucked between the third (power) and fourth (love) chakras.

**Anubis** - an Egyptian deity (part jackal/part man) associated with the Land of the Dead. Egyptian myth holds that Anubis was Osiris' guardian into the Underworld, and is thus associated with this subterranean level of the psyche.

**Ascension** - the process of raising the life-force (sekhem) up the djed into the higher brain centers, thereby activating the powers of consciousness (siddhis) and giving the practitioner access to the spiritual realms of being. The term also applies to the ascension of the Ka body into higher realms of energy and light.

**BA** - the celestial soul.

**Black Serpent** - a term used by the Magdalen to describe the lunar pathway up the spine (see ida). The Black Serpent embodies the feminine mystery of creation and is related to the Void, the source from which all things are created.

**Chakra** - an energy vortex within the subtle body. The word means "wheel" since chakras tend to spin like wheels. Science has documented the existence of the chakras, and they emit both sound and light.

**Central Column** - a subtle energy pathway that runs in front of the spine from the base up to the top of the head (see pranic tube).

**Central Pillar** - the same subtle energy pathway as the Central Column or pranic tube.

**Djed** - the sacred pathway of the chakras. The djed runs from the base of the spine to the top of the head (the crown chakra). This is the central pathway for the process of Ascension in Egyptian alchemy.

**Glorious Spiritual Body** - see Sahu

**Golden Raiment** - see Sahu

**Gold Serpent** - a term used by the Magdalen to describe the solar pathway up the spine (see pingala). The solar circuit embodies the male aspect of creation and is related to light.

**Horus** - the son of Isis and Osiris. Symbolically, Horus refers to the joining of spirit (Osiris) and matter (Isis). His story is allegorical in the sense that his journey is the same as ours as we rise up the djed to expanded states of consciousness.

**Ida** - a yogic term referring to a subtle pathway up the left side of the spine. Also known as the lunar or Chandra circuit, the ida runs from the base chakra up into the head and ends at the tip of the left nostril. (see Black Serpent).

**Isis** - the mother of Horus and one of the most prominent deities of the Egyptian pantheon. She was considered to be the Cosmic Mother, and her cult spread through most of the known ancient world.

**Incarnate** - a priestess within the Isis cult who has been trained to embody the energies of Isis.

**Initiate** - one who has passed through a portal or threshold between one level of consciousness to the next. Generally speaking, an Initiate has been trained in a sacred science and has been given access to the spiritual lineage responsible for that sacred science.

**Initiation** - the process of stepping from one level of consciousness into the next. Initiations are like benchmarks, acknowledging the attainment of some level of mastery. They may be granted or given directly from a spiritual being, or in some cases by a physical person.

**Ka** - a subtle energy body described in Egyptian alchemy. The Ka is an energetic duplicate of the physical body and is sometimes referred to as the etheric double or *spiritual twin*. Much of the focus of Egyptian alchemy is on the transformation of the Ka body.

**Khat** - the dense physical body of flesh and blood.

**Kundalini yoga** - a form of yoga that focuses on the movement of kundalini shakti, a form of energy very much related to sekhem, up the spine. As the kundalini shakti makes its ascent up the spine, the various chakras are activated giving the yogi or yogini mastery in those planes of consciousness.

**Maat** - an Egyptian deity associated with the Land of the Dead. Maat holds a scale weighted on one side with a feather. On the other side of the scale is the heart of the person seeking entrance into spiritual paradise. If the heart is weighted by shame and regrets it will tip the scale and the person must wander the Underworld. If the heart is light as a feather, the person is granted entrance into the sublime realms of spirit.

**Neter** - these are subtle powers. There are 26 neters in classic Egyptian alchemy, but the term can also be applied to anything that has energy or power. Thus the term can be related to the concept of shakti or energy in yoga.

**Pineal gland** - a gland sitting roughly in the center of the head. Its function is not fully understood by western science though, esoterically, it is viewed as holding keys to higher states of consciousness.

**Pingala** - a yogic term referring to a subtle pathway up the right side of the spine. Also known as the solar or Sureya circuit, the pingala runs from the base chakra up into the head and ends at the tip of the right nostril (see Gold Serpent).

**Pranic tube** - the pranic tube can be viewed as the center line of force within the magnetic field of the body. All bipolar magnets, including our bodies, have a north and south pole. These two poles are generated around an axis, like the axis of the earth, which is also a bipolar magnet. Within the physical body, this axis runs from the crown down to the perineum and sits in front of the spine. (see djed, central column, central pillar).

**Obstacles to Flight** - a term used by the Magdalen to describe the psychological impediments to spiritual illumination. One task of the alchemist within her tradition is to remove these Obstacles to Flight so that the Ascension of consciousness up the djed can take place.

**RA** - the Egyptian sun god. From an alchemical understanding, anything that is fire is a power of RA. Within the Ka body, there is an energy center or chakra that is fiery in nature, known as the solar plexus. A good deal of Egyptian alchemy deals with RA in its many forms as a source of energy to drive alchemical reactions within the Ka.

**Red Serpentine Drops** - a subtle energetic substance emitted from the crown that is related to the attributes of one's physical mother. These drops are generated from an alchemical meditation, given in the *Manuscript* using the Black and Gold Serpents. Interestingly, this practice is similar in many regards to a practice in Tibetan Vajrayana yoga using what are called the red and white drops. In this Tibetan practice, the drops are also used to generate bliss, but then the practitioner rests in this bliss while contemplating the empty nature or emptiness of all things. In the Alchemy of Horus, however, the end goal is different. While the joining of the drops also produces bliss, this bliss is then sent into the Ka body for the purpose of strengthening it. According to the Magdalen, ecstatic states of consciousness strengthen the Ka.

**Samadhi** - a yogic state of inner attention attained through meditation. In samadhi, consciousness is turned from the outer senses to the inner worlds. There are many ranges of samadhi, from light inner attention to profoundly altered states of consciousness. In the deepest forms of samadhi, perceived time comes to a standstill. There is no sense of it, and there is no sense of the world. Awareness becomes aware of itself, and from this deep inner recognition of the Self there is a spontaneous arising of bliss.

**Sahu** - the immortal energy body sometimes referred to as the Golden Raiment or Glorious Spiritual Body.

**Sekhem** - life-force. It means "that which makes things erect." In the process of Egyptian alchemy, one's sekhem, or life-force, is strengthened in order to be transformed into expanded awareness. It is the power of sekhem that raises the djed generating the power to *ascend* the ladder of the chakras into illumination. This highly potentized life-force is also used in specific alchemical processes to generate the powers of consciousness (see siddhis).

**Set** - the brother and murderer of Osiris, Horus' father. It is Set that Horus must overcome in the Osirian myths.

**Sex Magic** - the use of sex in relationship to magic has a long history that spans many thousands of years and numerous cultures and spiritual lineages. The Sex Magic of Isis, however, is not viewed in the same manner as magic in general. Rather than trying to affect the outside world through magical transformations, the Sex Magic of Isis focuses on the magical transformation of consciousness itself. Thus it is really a form of internal alchemy, an alchemy that draws upon the most primal and potent energies available to embodied beings.

**Siddhis** - yogic powers. These powers of consciousness cover a wide range of non-ordinary abilities. They include such things as clairvoyance (inner seeing), clairaudience (inner hearing), clairsentience (inner feeling), and clairgnosis (knowing something without knowing how you know it). These abilities also include the capacity to heal and limited powers of prophecy. The siddhis also include such truly unusual abilities such as bi-location (being in two places at once), teleportation (instantly transporting oneself over great distances), and levitation (floating in air). These powers of consciousness have been well documented in many of the world's religious and alchemical traditions, including Buddhism, Christianity, Hinduism, Islam, Judaism, and Taoism. In addition, many indigenous peoples report that their shamans also exhibit many of these abilities.

**Tantra** - a term referring to energy practices. The term is sometimes used in Buddhism, for instance, to refer to the energy practices of consciousness itself. However, the term can also be used for the energy practices of sexuality. This form of Tantra is based on the use of sexual energy for the elevation of consciousness and has many forms throughout the world.

**Uraeus** - sometimes referred to as "the anointing," the uraeus occurs when sekhem (life-force) is brought up the djed and into the brain. This movement creates a snake-like energy form, which may be why the uraeus was represented as a serpent by the ancient Egyptians.

**White Serpentine Drops** - a subtle energetic substance emitted from the crown that is related to the attributes of one's physical father. These drops are generated from an alchemical meditation, given in the *Manuscript* using the Black and Gold Serpents (see Red Serpentine Drops for a comparison with a similar practice in Tibetan Vajrayana yoga).

## Judi Sion

Judi Sion's background includes communications and advertising, as well as political consulting. Additionally she has been a photographer, a talk show host, and a newspaper columnist. Her articles have appeared in numerous magazines and newspapers. She spent seven years in a Mystery School with her teacher "in the wind" and her books from those years, *Last Waltz of the Tyrants*, *Financial Freedom* and *UFOs and the Nature of Reality* are published in English, French, Spanish and German. Her interest in Native American traditions took her into five years of intensive study and apprenticeship with the grandfathers and grandmothers of several tribal groups, including the Hopi. She has lectured on UFOs and Spirituality and taught women's mysteries both in North America and in Europe. Along with Tom Kenyon, she is taking *The Magdalen Manuscript* around the world.

## Tom Kenyon

Musician, researcher, author and therapist, Tom Kenyon has a Master's Degree in Psychological Counseling with over seventeen years in private practice. In 1983, he founded Acoustic Brain Research (ABR) to document the effects of sound and music on consciousness having realized its vast potential in his therapeutic work. For ten years he conducted brain research in the area of psychoacoustics (a term he coined, meaning the effects of sound on the psyche) and as a result developed numerous psychoacoustic recordings to increase creativity, insight and spiritual illumination.

He is the author of *Brain States* (New Leaf Publishing), a critically acclaimed guide to the brain's unused potentials. He is also co-author of *The Hathor Material* (SEE Publishing). His book, *Mind Thieves* (ORB Communications), is a visionary sci-fi novel that deals with the intricacies of quantum mechanics and consciousness.

Tom regularly conducts trainings and seminars throughout the world on the topics of sound healing, consciousness and spiritual illumination. He joins Judi Sion in taking *The Magdalen Manuscript* around the world.

## Tom Kenyon's Psychoacoustic Recordings, Books and Videos

For free information about Tom Kenyon's vast library of personal growth tools (including the ABR library) please visit the web at *www.tomkenyon.com* or, for a free catalog and newsletter, write **Tom Kenyon, PO Box 98, Orcas, WA 98280**

The library includes a diverse collection of CDs, audiotapes and videos. Most of these recordings use Tom's nearly four-octave range voice as part of sound meditations or inner explorations of consciousness. These recordings are well known for their highly transformational effects.

## Workshops, Trainings and Sacred Tours

Tom and Judi regularly conduct seminars and trainings throughout the world. These cover a wide range of topics, reflecting their interests in many areas of human potential.

Occasionally, they conduct tours to sacred places to be immersed in the culture that birthed a particular practice or spiritual tradition. On these tours, intensive inner work is part of the experience.

If you would like to be placed on their mailing list to receive yearly schedules and occasional updates, you can email *office@tomkenyon.com* or write: Tom Kenyon, PO Box 98, Orcas, WA 98280

Their schedule of events is also regularly posted on the website at *www.tomkenyon.com* for your convenience.

## Special Companion Recording of the Alchemies of Horus

As a service to our readers, Tom has produced a companion recording of the exercises from Training Protocols in the Alchemies of Horus from *The Magdalen Manuscript*.

In this recording, he guides the listener through the exercises against a psychoacoustic background designed to create receptive states of consciousness. In addition, the recording contains excerpts from Tom's toning sessions at the first Magdalen event presented in Sedona, Arizona of 2001. These tones carry the energy of Magdalen and are quite catalytic and transformative. (Note: The exercises are recorded in English.)

...ve

Spirituality

**Imagine ♥ Publications**
**Larkspur, California 94977**

# Living Life in Love

## Integrating Western Psychology and Eastern Spirituality

## by Peter Rengel

Published by:

Imagine ♥ Publications
P.O. Box 278
Fairfax, CA 94978

Phone: 415-459-3113
Fax: 415-459-5115

Cover Design by Peter Rengel, Bonnie Doyle Golden, and Pramad
Cover Artwork by Bonnie Doyle Golden,
          Transformation: Art to Lift the Spirit, Andover, Massachusetts

**Cataloging in Publication Data**

Rengel, Peter
Living Life in Love: Integrating Western Psychology and Eastern Spirituality / Peter Rengel
  p. cm.
Includes index

1. New Age movement.
2. Spiritual life--New Age movement.
3. Intercultural communication.
4. East and West.  I. Title

Library of Congress Catalog Card Number:  95-78456
BP605.N48R46  1995  299'.93  QB195-20431
ISBN 0-9647603-5-5: $17.95 Softcover

Manufactured in the United States of America

10    9    8    7    6    5    4    3

**Order more copies of *Living Life in Love* by turning to the last page of this book.**

# Prologue

The paradox of this book is that
   You are reading words to convey
      Experiences that occur in realms
         Where words do not even exist.

If you allow these words
   To be a launching pad,
      You can gently take off
         Into silent inner spaces
            Where all Hearts meet.

# The Table of Contents

## Part One: Psychology Discovers Love

### Section One: What Is Life All About?

### Section Two: Loving Yourself

## Part Two: The Leap from West to East

### Section Three: How Do You Evolve?

### Section Four: The Illusions of the Mind

### Section Five: Where Is Happiness Hidden?

## Part Three: Freeing Your Spirit

### Section Six: What Is Beyond The Mind?

# Part Four: Expressing Your Love

# The Workbook
## Meditations to Awaken Your Soul

# The Appendix

## The Delicate Dance

This book and my every breath
Are dedicated to my wife, Donna,
Who inspires me to keep dancing
With her innocence and her trust.

As we waltz our Forever together,
We discover the infinite ecstasy
Within the depths of right Now.

# Introduction

Love is as essential for human survival as food and water. Without human affection, newborn babies can die. In adults, the need to love and be loved is often sublimated because in Western society the accumulation of material wealth appears to be the most effective way to achieve Happiness. Fortunately, Life's often painful lessons wear away at this illusion until we begin to sense that the most fulfilling kind of joy lies within the realm of the Heart.

When this truth is revealed to you, the pursuit of Love becomes the central focus of your life. There are many places to look in order to satisfy the longing that arises from deep within your Soul. If you desire interpersonal Love, you may try to create more meaningful intimate relationships through learning to communicate more openly and vulnerably. If you desire a more impersonal, cosmic Love, you may seek the Truth within yourself through an inner-directed spiritual quest.

You can easily become totally immersed in this search. And rightfully so. *When you have tasted a true experience of Love inside your Heart, there is nothing else that can feed your hunger or quench your thirst.* When you are "in Love," everything comes alive. The trees and plants vibrate with the energy of creation. Everywhere you look, you notice perfection. Through eyes of compassion, you see the deep pain in people's faces as you simultaneously see their innocence and beauty.

How can you experience more Love in your life? There are as many beliefs about how to achieve this kind of harmony with the Universe as there are human beings on this planet. In the East, seekers of the more impersonal, cosmic Love or union with God (often called "Enlightenment") date back to the beginning of human history. Many of the world religions were born there. Many people's search for God in the East is the all-pervasive, central focus of their lives. The inner peace gained from generations of meditation is quite tangible. If you look underneath the material poverty, the richness of people's Souls can be seen in the shining brightness of their eyes. In the West, the search has been on more of a psychological level in order to find some contentment in a frantic world. Historically, Westerners have attempted to understand how the mind works rather than to explore spirituality directly. Each of these perspectives has something to offer. *Living Life in Love* is the marriage of these two approaches. *This book assists you to make the proper use of your mind so that you can discover your Spirit.*

You are traveling on your unique path of discovery. When you are first beginning your journey, you naturally move toward whomever you perceive has the wisdom you desire. You may attend seminars, undergo therapy, read esoteric books, and seek wise teachers or gurus. You may get up at 5:00 a.m. to meditate, or fast for days, or even walk on burning coals. Your search may lead you around the world. This is all well and fine. External pursuit is an integral part of the process. However, at some point, *you see that you must look inside yourself to discover the Love that you have been seeking from others.*

This book is designed to assist you in seeing underneath, through, and beyond the facades, appearances, and illusions of Life. As your understanding grows, you start living more of the time in the *essence* of the experience of being human. *Living Life in Love* is a conscious guide into the unconscious workings of the human psyche. It is a map showing you how to flow down the river of painful illusions until you empty into the ocean of bliss. There, you not only bathe in divine nectar, but you become the nectar itself. As your core perceptions of Reality shift, your sense of inner peace cannot be tossed around by the waves of external events.

In *Living Life in Love*, some words that usually begin with lower case letters are capitalized. These words – Love, Life, Truth, Soul, Happiness, Reality, Heart, Self – are sacred to me and worthy of utmost respect, similar to the context that has the word *God* be capitalized.

The word *mind* is used to define the mechanism that creates mental images (known as *thoughts*) arising out of discontentment or the need to achieve. Synonyms sometimes used in this context are *negative mind*, *ego*, or *desire*. The actual word is not as important as understanding that this book focuses on constructive ways to go beyond the mind, the primary creator of misery. Once the mind's destructive aspects have been addressed, the "positive mind" becomes more accessible.

One of the mind's tricks lies in its ability to make your life appear complicated so that you believe that you have to think your way through it. Every moment you are trying to figure Life out, you are not available to see the joy that emerges from the simplest events. *Living Life in Love* can help elevate you from thinking into feeling, from desiring into enjoying, from the outer into the inner, from words into silence, from doing into being. *This book is not meant to be read with your rational, linear mind. It is an experience to be absorbed into your Soul.*

The nine sections progress from West to East, from mind to no mind, from Earth to Heaven. The following outline provides an overview of this book:

## Part One: Psychology Discovers Love

Section One: What Is Life All About?
Section Two: Loving Yourself

## Part Two: The Leap from West to East

Section Three: How Do You Evolve?
Section Four: The Illusions of the Mind
Section Five: Where Is Happiness Hidden?

## Part Three: Freeing Your Spirit

Section Six: What Is Beyond the Mind?
Section Seven: Strolling Down the Spiritual Path

## Part Four: Expressing Your Love

Section Eight: Loving Others
Section Nine: Love

Each chapter within the nine sections takes on a new challenge and provides a unique perspective. Sometimes concepts seem contradictory to previous ones because, in different moments and different states of consciousness, different points of view are relevant. The approaches offered in this book to solve Life's "problems" vary from the most practical to the most esoteric. Many people want *the* formula for Happiness. What is *the* way? *There is no one way.* Life keeps changing. You keep changing. You may want to hold on to what worked last week. You assume that because it worked then, it should work now. However, one of Life's miracles is that it repeatedly finds new ways to test your ability to stay "in Love." Yesterday's solutions sometimes become today's problems if you do not let go of the past. These opportunities challenge you to reach deeper, stretch further, trust more, and let go into the unknown at the next level. *Life insists that you be newly creative as you strive to become its master rather than its victim.*

Included in this book are parables or teaching stories from various ancient spiritual traditions. If read with your intuition available, they can slip underneath your conscious mind and lift you into new perspectives. These stories have been handed down orally through many generations of seekers. A special thanks goes to the Indian mystic, Osho, whose many years of daily discourses frequently included parables. His lectures are the source of most of the stories in this book. Others came from Sufi teachers or are my creation.

The primary purpose of the prose in this book is to provide the context for the poems or aphorisms (spiritual truths). *The real transmission is within the aphorisms themselves, so be sure to pay close attention to them.* Whenever you come to a poem, slow down and read it several times. Absorb its meaning at different levels. As the aphorisms move into the more spiritual realms, there is less prose between them because the need to explain them decreases. As you evolve, words and thoughts can seem superficial. A deep joy arises as you spend more time in wordlessness, in no thought, in peaceful inner silence.

Like everything in Life, *what you put into this book is what you will receive from it.* You can read it and reread it again and again to discover, in *this* moment, which words, thoughts, or ideas strike a chord that resonates within your Soul.

Take your time. Drink it in. Taste it. Savor it. You may want to read one chapter five or six times, or to spend hours on one aphorism. Become enthralled! Imbibe it all. *This book is designed to alter your state of consciousness if you read slowly and feel into what is being said.* Allow yourself to melt into harmony with yourself and with the Universe. Many solutions to Life's mysteries can emerge from these pages if you search for the message that is hidden in the spaces between the words.

You are invited to make *Living Life in Love* into more than just an enjoyable book full of insights, ancient wisdom, and new information. Included is a Workbook that contains a series of Meditations to awaken your Soul. *This Workbook is designed be a vehicle for your own inner transformation.* It is, literally, a *Handbook to Happiness,* if you use it that way. There are a total of forty weeks of Meditations, so a ten month course awaits you. The details of this course are fully explained at in the Introduction to the Workbook on page 187. *By fully and faithfully participating in these Meditations, a "spiritual rebirth" can occur.*

In the Workbook, after each section's set of Meditations are special pages containing that section's most concise and potent aphorisms, known as *Illuminators*. They are displayed in a way that you can easily photocopy them and then cut them out and put them up in your environment as reminders. (See the copyright material on page two for the appropriate duplication of these.) The Introduction to the Workbook explains in detail how you can use these special aphorisms in the Meditations and in your everyday life.

You can also use *Living Life in Love* as you would the I-Ching or the Tarot. You may want to close your eyes as you gently place the book over your Heart. Then ask a specific question. When you are ready, randomly open the book and read its universal response. Whatever page you open to seems to magically contain the perfect wisdom for your inquiry. You can also run your finger down the Index of Aphorisms in the Appendix (pages 309-11) to find which one(s) attract you in the moment. You can then turn to the appropriate page(s) for guidance.

Approach *Living Life in Love* gently and tenderly. Let the aphorisms stir your Heart. *If you are open and available, your Soul can be touched, and your Being transformed.* Enjoy your journey!

# Acknowledgements

I feel so much gratitude for so many people who have touched my Heart and Soul.

My humble appreciation to Swami Muktananda Paramahansa, who made available an infinite energy for my first taste the ultimate of all possible human experiences.

Some of the other fellow travelers from my past who have significantly shared in my journey include Osho, Ram Dass, Ma Guru Heartleg, Bharat Mitra, Brugh Joy, H.W.L. Poonja ("Papaji"), Kathy Speeth, Henry Korman, Ernie Pecci, Luc Brebion, Lynn Lumbard, Richard Moss, Lynn Murphy, Susanne Watson, Sigi Bonnevie, Surabhi, Ajita, Maitri, Gatha, Venu, Pramad, Nartana, Sambodhi, Barkha, Alexa, Lynn M., and Franklin David Evans.

A special thanks to my parents, Joe and Betty Rengel, whose Love for me while I was growing up gave me lots of permission to explore Life.

My gratitude to Hal and Linda Kramer for publishing my first book, *Seeds of Light*, and for going out of their way to unselfishly give to me from their Hearts.

My love to my partners at the Human Awareness Institute (HAI) where we teach how to "create a world where *everyone* wins" by offering workshops around the world, including San Francisco, Michigan, New England, Southern California, Australia, and Japan. We are repeatedly blessed with weekends of facilitating people to heal in profound ways in the areas of relationships, intimacy, love, and sexuality. To Stan Dale, Anne Watts, Chip August, Tedde Rinker-Davis, Donna Spitzer, Felicia Seaton, and Sarah Jo Sand and to the members of the HAI Board: Thanks for co-creating miracles with me. I love each of you tons!

My heart is deeply touched by the HAI Interns, whose unselfish service creates a safe place for the participants to experience being loved at levels no one ever dreamed possible.

I extend my deepest appreciation to anyone with whom I have ever worked privately. By open heartedly letting me into every nuance of your inner process, you have given me the opportunity to understand the psycho-spiritual dynamics within all human beings. This book could not have been written without your trust and vulnerability.

Gratitude beyond words to the two editors-in-chief of this book, Lynn Thomas and Donna Spitzer, whose countless hours of revisions were invaluable (and fun). My awe goes to Bonnie Doyle Golden for her beautiful cover artwork and her pure spirit, and to her husband, Michael, for his patience and support. "Hurray!" to Bill Atkinson for performing magic in his creation of the two beautiful photos used in this book. My heartfelt thanks to my three other principle editors: Jim Woessner, Nancy Carleton, and Steve Levin.

Thanks to many other people whose insightful feedback is woven into this tapestry for humanity: Walter Shelburne, Michael Selby, Michael Pollack, Chip August, Bob Harlow, Katrina Davidson, Bess Greenfield, Stan, Helen, and Janet Dale, Marc Fine, Amara Rothchild, Richard and Lia Enkelis, Sonika Tinker, Debra Rein, Dayton and Renie Gnau, Todd Dworman, Sabrina Page, Sarah Jo Sand, Gudrun Zomerland, Wally Phillips, David Frost, Katherine Moler, Alison Pollack, Cherie Jones, and Wahila Minshall.

Finally, here is an "I love you!" to some very special people:

To my wife, Donna Spitzer, and to my friends, Michael Selby, Katrina Davidson, Gudrun Zomerland, Joanna Karp, Jesse and Alex Karp-Robinson, Ron Moshantz, and Cornelia Stenzel: Thanks for being my chosen family.

To Lisa and Steve Weatherly: Thanks for your generous offer and for following your Truth, which I trust is leading Donna and I to our Heart's desire.

To Sonika Tinker and Debra Rein: Thanks for enriching my life perspective.

To Alison Pollack: Thanks for your integrity.

To David Frost: Thanks for the pureness of your sincerity as you explore Love.

To Marty Fermer, Aribert and Jenise Dormann, and Wally Phillips: Thanks for being the embodiment of selfless service.

To Sabrina Page: Thanks for the dance of our friendship over the years.

To Howard Smalley: Thanks for loving the animals (and Julie and yourself!).

To Eileen and Terry Barker: Thanks for my initiation into Pastor Peter.

To our cats, Diva, Queen, and Lily: Thanks for your innocence.

# Part One

# Psychology Discovers Love

# Section One

# What Is Life All About?

### The Meaning Of Life

The meaning of life is not
   An answer revealed to you
      Upon achieving your goals.

Life is a thirst for more,
   Periodically quenched by
      Insights and revelations,
        Which are followed by
           A new thirst for more.

The meaning of life is
   Felt in magical moments
      Within the miracle itself.

## Chapter One
# The Art of Being

*Living Life in Love.* What does it mean to live your life "in Love"? When you hear the word *Love* what images come to your mind? For a moment, picture yourself "in Love." Are there certain external circumstances or situations that make it easier for you to see yourself living your life filled with Love? Are you with another person or by yourself? Do you have a particular job or house? Do you need to have a certain amount of money? Do you have a smile on your face? Are you happy all the time?

What if your capacity to be "Living Life in Love" depends *entirely* upon internal experiences instead of external events? Envision this Reality as a layering of many invisible vibrations, much like radio or television frequencies. Some of these vibrations are labeled as joyful, angry, painful, hungry, sexual, spiritual, intellectual, blissful, or sad. These are all being simultaneously broadcast, but you can only perceive the channel you have on, and your experiences follow accordingly. You perceive "Reality" as being whichever frequency you are tuned in to. You then collect evidence that Life on planet Earth is the sum total of what you experience in the vibrations that you are attuned to most frequently.

For instance, if you are hungry and walking down the street, what do you notice? Grocery stores, restaurants, or someone eating a sandwich. If you are angry, what do you notice? Two people having an argument or an adult scolding a child. If you have an urge to be sexual, you notice women's bodies or men's muscles or whatever else you are attracted to sexually. If you are "in Love," you notice a romantic couple walking hand-in-hand or two children laughing. By noticing what you see as you walk down the street, you can find out what vibration you are tuned in to or what "state of consciousness" you are in.

What you notice is no accident. When you are angry, you see the two people arguing rather than the romantic couple because you are resonating with the people's anger. The couple, on the other hand, is broadcasting on a channel that you are not tuned in to. It is as if they are on a different planet than you are in that moment, so you are not even aware of them.

Thus, many parallel realities occur simultaneously, and, in any given moment, you perceive only the channel you have on. Some important questions arise from this model.

♥ Rather than merely being at the effect of external events, what if you could always choose the frequency you want to attune to, as if selecting a television channel?

♥ What if you were to master the art of changing your inner frequency so you could alter your state of consciousness as easily as you change television channels?

♥ What if you were able to practice attuning yourself to the rhythm called Love?

♥ What if you could be living in the vibration of Love *all* the time?

♥ What if, whenever you experience frequencies that appear to be other than Love, you were able to perceive these vibrations as positive and fulfilling?

What, then, is Love?

## Love

**Love is not an idea.**

**Love is
A vibration
To attune to.**

Truly stable Happiness cannot be achieved by setting goals and then attaining them, although the never ending cycle of desiring and achieving can create transient happiness. There is a deeper joy that cannot be diminished by external circumstances. It is independent of any worldly situation. It is felt every moment you are in harmony with Love's vibration inside your Heart. *This state of consciousness is <u>all</u> you ever need to achieve.* If you agree with this perspective, it becomes apparent that you need only one goal in Life: to be in the "here and now," moment by moment, where that note of Love is always resonating.

One result of human beings not being in harmony with Love is our unconscious abuse of Mother Earth. If you observe all aspects of this planet other than the human realm, you can see that they naturally flow in Love's vibration. Nature is in a dance of perfect harmony. Have you ever seen birds too depressed to sing? The trees, animals, land, water, and sky are all joyfully humming along, except when humans interfere.

Even Nature's violence has a purity about it. When a hurricane destroys, it is part of an organic cycle of Life. When animals attack each other, there is no malicious intent. They are behaving instinctively. Violence is unadulterated for all types of animals, except for human beings (and perhaps the primates who are "almost human"). Our violence toward each other, the animals, and Mother Earth is artificial because it arises out of our neuroses, except for the rare occasion when it is provoked by the survival instinct, either to protect or feed ourselves. We strike out because we are desperately seeking some kind of relief from the pressures of being frequently thirsty for Love. *It is our unconscious fear of never finding inner peace that propels us to keep waging war with each other and the planet.*

Sensitively look for ways that you are out of harmony with the joyful rhythm of all aspects of creation that have been unaltered by human beings. You will gain a new level of understanding as to why so many people feel lost or unfulfilled. When you comprehend the source of our ignorance, you discover more compassion for our apparent maliciousness. Our suffering is compounded by our basic misunderstanding of where true Happiness is found.

## Altered States

**Most humans suffer**
**In the vibration of**
**Fear and worry.**

**Nature celebrates**
**In the vibration of**
**Joy and aliveness.**

**Which of these is**
**The altered state**
**Of consciousness?**

Mother Earth is an organism who is living in harmony except when humans interfere. In our frenetic search for fulfillment, we are the culprits who are violating this planet and each other. *The greatest form of polluting the Earth comes from insensitively playing out our inner turmoil on our external environment.* This crescendo of human chaos has hopefully reached its peak. If not, this Reality of planets and stars and galaxies may end abruptly.

Take a moment to imagine being in outer space looking down at Mother Earth, say, a thousand years ago, before humans had "overpowered" Nature and overpopulated the planet. The skies and oceans were crystal clear and sparkling blue in the year 1000. Your eyes would have been filled with purity as you looked down on this pristine gem.

The astronauts today, however, see something very different. The smoggy air and the tainted oceans are the manifestation of human neuroses. *Most humans are to the Earth what cancer is to the human body.* Unwittingly, *we* are a terminal disease for Mother Earth unless we undergo a radical operation on our attitudes and priorities.

We cannot waste a moment because the rate at which this cancer is spreading is on an exponential curve. For millions of years the planet was relatively unscarred. In the last thousand years the destruction of Mother Earth has been raging rampantly out of control.

The real cancer is the negativity within our minds. Our brains think and they think and they think. They think about the past, often with regrets. They think about the future, often with worry. Very rarely do they quiet down enough to just be in the "here and now," wherein lies ultimate contentment. We must return to our natural state of harmony within ourselves without all the dis-ease in our minds. Then we can all be in cooperation with each other and with Nature on a clean, pollution-free planet.

Some time as you drive down the freeway, observe people in their cars. How many of them appear to be enjoying the scenery, including the trees and the sky and the clouds and the sun? Most people seem to be somewhere else, lost in thoughts. They are churning and burning inside to be some place other than where they are. How often are you like that? How often are you out of tune with that ever-beckoning rhythm of Love? Every moment that you distract yourself by thinking negatively, you miss the glory of *Now*!

One human foible that often causes pain is people's need to be noticed. They want to be "seen." They need to accomplish tasks to earn recognition. Many people's entire identity is tied into what they "do" in the world. Even in the New Age community, the achievement complex still exists. The context just shifts from becoming a financial success into becoming the most evolved person or the "best" healer. Nothing is wrong with wanting to grow spiritually or to assist in the healing of the planet. But by being aware of your motives, you can discern whether or not you are in Love's vibration as you move toward your goals.

## Making a Difference

**If you are judging this world as
Having problems you must fix,
Then the difference you make
Is limited to earthly realms.**

**Working wholeheartedly while
Knowing Life is already perfect
Makes a *Divine Difference*.**

*The most important aspect of any action is not found in the results. It is within your motive.* Investment in the results of your actions can create an unhealthy attitude if you push to achieve. Do you assume that this world is a mess and you are its savior? Does your arrogance say, "I know what's best here"? Does your righteousness bulldoze whomever stands in your way? Do you lash out in anger? Or are you in harmony with yourself, with others, and even with situations that do not fit into "your plan"? Most people are so busy striving to achieve their goals that their lives are filled with "doing." They forget about "being." There is wisdom in why we are called "human beings" and not "human doings."

## The Art of Being

**Doing fills your time.
Yet, if you are Being,
Love fills your Heart.**

**Doing destroys Being
By pushing for results.**

**Open to receive Love
While you are Doing
And you can master
"The Art of Being."**

"The Art of Being" is the key to Happiness. You can have your Heart open, moment by moment, and feel Love filling you. To do this, you must stay attuned to a universal energy that is always flowing. It is a very receptive way to move through Life. It requires sensitivity, vulnerability, trust, and grace.

The irony is that chasing after Happiness, in and of itself, is one of the major obstacles to being inside Love's vibration in this moment. One of the final frontiers of inner exploration is knowing that Happiness, joy, ecstasy, bliss, God, Enlightenment are already yours. *Use your awareness to notice that your desire for Love is what often prevents you from just relaxing and being in the middle of Love.*

## Happiness

**Searching for Happiness?**
**You cannot find it.**
**You can only *be* it.**

Right now, take several breaths. Relax your jaw, let your shoulders drop, let your belly muscles relax (loosen your clothing if you need to). Feel your body being supported in its present position. Allow your focus to move from your head down to your lungs. Feel each breath fill your chest cavity. Be gentle with yourself. Be tender with yourself. Let go of any need you have to read this book or to accomplish anything right now.

Look around and notice what is in your immediate environment. Really look. Let your eyes take in the colors, textures, and shapes. If you feel more at ease, slowly stand and walk across the room in this relaxed, receptive state. Feel your belly move with each step. Notice how present you are.

You can spend *every* moment of your life this relaxed, if you learn to not be pushed around by external events. *You can "be" while you "do."*

I used to work as a waiter in a restaurant. This job can be extremely stressful, with ulcers and high blood pressure being very common among waiters. Five customers can want service right now and be very obnoxious if they do not get it. The list of what needs to be done *immediately* is always long and the priorities keep shifting from moment to moment. There is a restaurant term called "being buried," which means that it is absolutely impossible to do everything that has to be done in the next five minutes, so you are "dead."

If I would panic in these moments, three more customers would ask me for refills of coffee, their check immediately, and another bottle of wine. This added anxiety made me feel like I could literally explode if one more person asked for anything. However, I discovered an incredible secret that changed my whole waiting career (and spilled over into all other areas of my life). The moment that the first level of panic began to creep in, I learned to consciously stop, take a deep breath, and let myself know that I did not have to buy into the illusion that I needed to go faster in order to provide excellent service. If I used my will to relax and be joyfully in the present, my Reality shifted and miracles occurred. Customers would cancel their special requests and a manager would offer to open a bottle of wine for me and another waiter would make salads for me, *all without my asking*. It was as if the Universe was laughing and telling me, "Very good. You passed this test. You chose *being* over *doing*."

This story of being a waiter is a practical, everyday example of the Art of Being. In 1974, I was blessed with the gift of tasting the most profoundly cosmic experience of Love possible, often called *Enlightenment* or, in Eastern traditions, *satori* or *samadhi*. The label does not matter. The experience does, in that it altered my perceptions of Reality forever. I now know that Enlightenment is real, that it is tangible, that it is more than an idea.

This experience beyond words and thoughts occurred while I was living in Swami Muktananda's ashram (spiritual community). For about two weeks, there was no "me" inside this body. There was just a void filled with Love. When I was alone in a room, I experienced what that room was like with no one in it. The walls would be breathing, noises would be happening, insects would be flying around. But there was no human presence as I had always previously experienced. Then, if a human being would come in, the room would be filled with thoughts and desires. The room became whatever that person was thinking or feeling. And I became that person's servant, in the most beautiful sense of the word. I was just empty and humbly available to fulfill that person's every desire, every need, every whim.

As this state of grace continued, the Universe's inevitable tests to knock me out of Love became more and more subtle. Late one night someone asked me to vacuum the meditation hall. Of course, I said *yes* because *yes* was all I knew. There was no *no* in me. When I finished, I put the vacuum cleaner away in the closet and walked down the hall to go to bed.

Another person approached me and said, "Would you please vacuum the meditation hall?" I simply responded, "Sure." I went to the closet, got out the vacuum, and began contentedly cleaning again. Well, it was not really *again* because there was no *again*. There was only this moment without a past or future.

About halfway through my "second" round of vacuuming, someone else came up to me and said, "Didn't you just vacuum this a little while ago?" I responded, "Yes." He said, in a critical tone, "Then don't waste your time doing it again. Put the vacuum cleaner away and go to bed." I happily complied with no hesitation. There was no "me" inside to argue or resist. There was only a willingness to serve.

Another test occurred daily in the showers at about 4:30 a.m. The water fluctuated frequently from piping hot to freezing cold without warning. I would stand in the shower, and, as an icy cold blast occurred, there was in me only a "yes" to the experience of my body being frozen. Instantly, the water would return to piping hot. Many people complained of long, freezing showers. I am convinced that my blasts of cold water lasted only momentarily because of my unconditional "yes" to whatever came my way.

The test that I finally flunked was one hundred percent devastating. I was using twine to wrap some packages about to be mailed. There were several three or four inch pieces of string left on the table as I finished the job. Just as I was throwing them into the waste basket, a woman walked into the room and very harshly shouted, "Don't do that! We save those!" I reacted with a loud, "What?" My thought was, "This lady is crazy!"

As soon as this occurred, I felt as if I had been shot from a cannon out of Heaven. I helplessly watched my reaction destroy the delicate harmony of Love. All of a sudden there was an "I" again. My judgemental *no* created an "I" that was separate from the whole. The price I paid for "I" was feeling as if I had been yanked out of a pool of divine nectar and was instantly dying of thirst in the desert.

The next day I plummeted into a suicidal abyss. I talked to the people running the ashram, but they could not help me because none of them had had a similar experience. Muktananda was away at the time, so I finally left in despair. I struggled for many months with suicide. *If I could not live in bliss, I did not want to live at all.* From this experience, I gained deep insights into the suicidal frame of mind and found its gift. However, that is another story to be revealed later.

The following is an attempt to express in words this experience which occurred in a wordless realm, where thoughts do not even exist.

## Satori

**Love is
When
"You"
Are not.**

In retrospect, I see that at that time I could not remain in bliss forever. The "I" returned because I was not grounded enough in myself or seated deeply enough in my Heart. My journey for the past twenty years has been to clean out my inner temple, one room at a time. I am gradually moving back toward that state in a less dramatic way. As that quiet knowingness slowly grows in me, I become more solidly stabilized in the vibration of Love.

What is your deepest purpose as you participate in this enchanting mystery? Life, this precious gem, has so many aspects to be tenderly polished with Love. Whichever facet is being seen in this moment reveals this moment's reflection for celebration, just as it is. Love has no need to achieve, to improve, or to change anything. If you let go of your goals and of your need to make a difference, then you can uncover a multi-faceted glimpse of Life's absolute perfection, including its beauties and its apparent injustices.

## Life's Purpose

**When you let go of *all* purpose**
**Then you can share true Love**
**Which never needs a reason.**

Do trees have a goal? Do flowers have a need to achieve? Does the sky try to prove anything to anyone? The most meaningful moments in Life are the ones without any goals. Laughter is one of those experiences which momentarily dissolves all pursuits.

## Laughter

**Laughter lifts**
**Life's load into**
**Love's light.**

Other similarly meaningful moments may be a compassionate hug from a friend, a tender touch on the cheek, a knowing look of mutual understanding, the unspoken permission to let go and cry, the infinite exploration in your lover's eyes, and the ecstatic feeling of sexual union. Simple miracles are happening in this very moment, in a Reality that is parallel to your everyday one.

If your primary intention is to fill your life with more of these "purposeless" experiences, you discover a deeper sense of fulfillment than is *ever* possible through achieving *anything* in the external world. The more you practice "The Art of Being," the more you become Love itself. *Eventually, you become a tuning fork, making it easier for other people in your life to vibrate in Love's frequency.* What better way is there to serve this planet?

# Chapter Two
# Why Is There Pain?

In the Garden of Eden, did Adam and Eve really make a mistake? Would the path of human history been better had they not eaten the apple? Remember, the apple was the fruit from the tree of knowledge. Perhaps their sin was not in disobeying God, but in birthing the linear thinking process of the rational mind. Staying within logical realms prevents us from directly experiencing the entire Universe as being One with no separation.

*Tasting knowledge created havoc because it was the death of trust and the birth of doubt.* But, maybe it was not a sin. Maybe our fall from the Garden of Eden was actually beneficial. Perhaps it was essential to the enrichment of our human development. Let's assume that Adam and Eve were in perfect harmony before they tasted the fruit. When they (we) were cast out of bliss into the turmoil of free will, pain was born. But is that pain bad?

Today, we find ourselves far from the Garden of Eden. We have come to the brink of destroying this miraculous planet and ourselves. However, there is hope. Even though the chaos is extreme at the negative end of the spectrum, evidence of a positive direction exists simultaneously. Some of us have turned the corner and are headed back toward the Garden.

- ♥ The Berlin Wall has crumbled.
- ♥ The threat of nuclear destruction appears to be decreasing.
- ♥ South Africa is opening to equality.
- ♥ The number of dictatorships is dwindling.
- ♥ Corporate values around money, status, and power are being questioned.
- ♥ Politicians' lies are being exposed.
- ♥ People are more aware of how they are treating one another and the planet.
- ♥ Many people are seeking a more spiritual basis for their lives and their values.
- ♥ Love is recognized as being vital.

As some of us re-enter the Garden of Eden, we can drink in more of its beauty as a result of having been cast out. Remember, the Garden has remained in the same vibration as when we left it. It is a constant invitation into Love. *We* are the variable. Perhaps our journey, including our trials and tribulations, has given us the capacity to be more appreciative of Nature's peaceful vibration. *All the pain we have experienced through all the generations since the birth of humankind has carved within us a richness of character that we would not have today if we had never made the journey.*

Now we can use our free will to *genuinely* choose harmony because we have had the experience of choosing chaos. Had we unquestioningly remained in the Garden, we would lack the depth created by overcoming difficulties. This parable beautifully illustrates this:

## The Farmer's Perfect World

There was once a wheat farmer who was granted one wish by God. Without hesitation, the farmer wished that he be given the power to control the weather. With this special power, he was certain that he would be able to grow so much wheat that he could eventually end world hunger.

Thus, he created what he was sure were perfect weather conditions for growing wheat. In the spring, he willed just the right amount of gentle rain after planting the seeds. Sprouts came up abundantly. Whenever he desired sun, it was there. There were no strong winds, no thunder storms, nothing to harm his precious crop. His wheat grew taller and faster than any he had ever seen. He was sure that he was on his way to ending starvation on the planet.

When it finally came time to harvest the beautiful stalks of wheat, he felt a great disappointment. There was no wheat inside. The plants were hollow.  When he asked God what had happened, God responded, "Because there was no challenge as the wheat was growing, there was nothing to enrich it.  There was no friction, no conflict, so your wheat became lifeless, empty. Strong winds and heavy rain pounding down help give the wheat a depth of character as it rises to meet the challenge."

Review your own life.  You will likely observe that the most painful periods produce the most growth.  *The pain catapults you into places inside yourself that you would never have the courage to explore voluntarily.*  By being forced to be honest about your difficulties, you start to let go of your patterns of separating yourself from others.  As emotional pain rips you open, a kind of self-doubt arises that, ironically, is a major contribution to more fully joining the human race.  Your vulnerability allows others into your Heart and Soul.

## Beneficial Self-Doubt

**Beneficial self-doubt dissolves**
**The cornerstone of your ego.**
**You involuntarily give up**
**And feel your helplessness.**

**Out of your defenselessness,**
**You can humbly ask for help**
**Which cracks open your Heart**
**So that you can receive Love.**

This beneficial doubt leads you to your inner Home.  You may try to avoid your pain because it seems too devastating to feel fully.  However, *pain is a divine invitation to change and to grow.*  If you resist, you shrink and begin to die inside.  And the Universe does not let up.  It may even have to coerce you into facing your denial by giving you the gift of some form of personal catastrophe or disease.

## Disease

**As you evolve on this Planet,**
**Situations present chances**
**For you to embrace change.**

**Disease rears its head**
**When you do not listen**
**To the gentle tapping on**
**Your door of stagnation.**

**If you ignore the tapping,**
**Life starts knocking louder**
**And then begins pounding**
**Until you are defenseless**
**And can hear its message.**

**Either old ideas must die**
**So new ones can be born,**
**Or your body must die**
**So *you* can be reborn**
**Into another chance.**

Many people believe that suffering is the only way to deal with Life's pain. Their erroneous reasoning is that Life becomes tolerable by learning to "grin and bear it." *The irony is that running from pain is much more insidious than feeling it.*

## Suffering

**Suffering is a coating of avoidance**
**Covering your emotional pain.**

**If you allow yourself to feel the pain,**
**The pressure from your repression**
**Is released like a valve opening.**

**Both the suffering and pain**
**Now dissolve into pure Joy.**

You may be wondering, "Just feel the pain and everything will be all right? What is this guy? Some kind of masochist?" You can have different attitudes toward pain. Some are useful and some are not. Self-pity combined with a "poor me" attitude only hurts you. It drives the real pain deeper into your Being instead of releasing it. Also, feeling pain but still resisting it or judging it leaves you feeling burdened afterwards. However, if you embrace the pain without judgement as you cry, you feel lighter afterwards. You can simultaneously feel the relief of loving yourself and a bittersweet missing of not having felt Love more often.

## Types of Tears

**Tears of self-pity**
**Drive your pain deeper**
**As your "victim" wins.**

**Tears releasing pure pain**
**Lead to a smile of relief**
**As the weight of suffering**
**Lifts from your Heart.**

**Tears flowing from joy**
**Wash the dust off of**
**Your gratitude.**

The "useful" experience of feeling pain bores out a new place inside your Heart. *This carved out empty space can be filled with deeper feelings of Love than you could experience prior to feeling the pain.* Your tears melt layers upon layers of defensive ego and uncover realms of your Being that may not have ever been revealed to you.

If you have ever deeply grieved the loss of a loved one, then you probably know the beauty that can be evoked when your body is being racked with sobs of grief.

## Grief

**Out of your tears of grief**
**Arises a new depth of Love**
**That could not be felt while**
**This person was in your life.**

If you say *yes* to the feelings and head directly into them with an attitude of "I am going for it," then magic happens. *You give yourself the gift of riding that pain all the way into your Soul.* Once you touch these corners of your Being, the way you experience Reality is forever altered. Instead of living in a gray, lifeless world, you see Life energy exploding all around you. The leaves on the trees become greener and the colors of the flowers become more brilliant. People's faces become more innocent and more beautiful. Love's vibration becomes available to you if you say *yes* to your emotional pain.

## Intensity

**Feeling pain intensely**
**Increases joy immensely.**

You can choose to adopt a useful belief, if you see its wisdom. What if feeling emotional pain is not inherently an unpleasant experience? What if you were to believe that it is actually quite enjoyable? *Perhaps you were only taught that feeling pain is negative.* If you think about it, crying is a release of energy. As you open to directly experience your pain, tears flow from your eyes. It is intense, even explosive. But aren't orgasms similar? Crying may be just another type of orgasm which occurs in your Heart or solar plexis instead of in your genitals. This belief can serve you. As you feel the tears well up, you can get excited rather than resistant. You can think, "Oh boy! Here's a great chance for another emotional orgasm!" With this attitude, why would you ever need to repress anything?

If you begin to experience pain as pleasurable, then it is possible that you will encounter deeply seated guilt for enjoying Life too much. After all, weren't you taught that Life is *supposed* to be a struggle? Isn't pleasure really "of the Devil"? Ever since you were a baby, when your hands were first pulled away from your genitals as you were pleasuring yourself, weren't you being given the message that pleasure is sinful and evil? *Feeling guilty for sexual pleasure is easily generalized into unconsciously feeling guilty for enjoyment in any form.* Thus, your parents' and the church's and society's sanctimonious admonitions against sexual pleasure have not only damaged your ability to fully celebrate your sexuality. Your capacity to enjoy Life's simple pleasures, like sitting under a tree or watching the clouds, has also been diminished.

## Pain or Pleasure?

*You* **create each moment**
**As pleasurable or painful.**

**Many religions say**
**That pleasure is a sin.**
**Then to not be a sinner,**
**Must you live in pain?**

Pain is often perpetuated through guilt-inspired avoidance of pleasure. *Perhaps your most wicked "sin" is in not enjoying Life's many pleasures.*

Are you detecting some of the ways that you prevent yourself from embracing your humanness and from enjoying the simplest gifts that this Reality has to offer? *Living Life in Love* occurs as you reveal to yourself the ingrained habits that stop you from being in bliss. Being honest with yourself about your avoidance of pleasure is a significant step in breaking through harmful patterns.

One of this Reality's greatest illusions is that Happiness is elusive. The veil between you and Love may be much thinner than you think.

## Disillusioned

**To be disillusioned, in its purest sense,**
 **Means to have your illusions undone.**

**May you have the courage to risk**
 **Becoming more disillusioned with Life.**

As the illusions fall away, what is revealed underneath is your own innocence, your own purity. You have done nothing wrong. Your only problem is that you have been living outside the Garden of Eden for too long. Come back Home to the Reality of Love.

## Chapter Three
# The Magic of Gratitude

In order to rediscover the Garden of Eden, you have probably tried to understand this experience called Life. What is Life's purpose? Why are you here? Is there an ultimate meaning to existence or is this one big accident? The mind tries to decipher Life, hoping for a revelation to burst forth and show you the light. Then you've "got it"! What if your picture of how to "get it" is leading you astray?

## The Meaning of Life

**The meaning of Life is not**
**An answer revealed to you**
**Upon achieving your goals.**

**Life is a thirst for more,**
**Periodically quenched by**
**Insights and revelations,**
**Which are followed by**
**A new thirst for more.**

**The meaning of Life is**
**Felt in magical moments**
**Within the miracle itself.**

*Life's meaning is not contained within theories but within experiences.* A more rewarding alternative than trying to use your mind to search for "the answer" is to discover the place inside you that is simply enchanted with the mystery. The more frequently you are overflowing with gratitude as you feel these magical moments, the more meaningful your life becomes. The experience of gratitude is not a thought inside your head. It is a humbling feeling inside your Heart.

## Gratitude

**Feeling gratitude creates**
**Feeling more gratitude**
**For the blessing of**
**Feeling gratitude.**

The direct experience of gratitude leaves you unpretentious. It is so awe-inspiring that you may find yourself bowing down in appreciation of this clever enigma called *Reality*. Life's mysterious web is intentionally woven to remain just beyond your ability to fully comprehend. If you let go of trying to intellectually master this Reality, you can relax with a sigh of relief. You free your energy to explore other kinds of Soul-satisfying experiences. Life's simplest occurrences become wonderments because you see them through different eyes. *A quality of wide-eyed innocence opens doors into new dimensions of Reality.*

The more time you spend being grateful for the blessings already in your life, the easier it is to receive more. Feeling gratitude not only creates feeling more gratitude. It simultaneously creates more to feel grateful for. As you experience being thankful, you validate that you live in a Universe where there is a lot to be thankful for. Thus, your world becomes progressively more abundant in all ways. You become rich with Love, intimacy, sexuality, and material goods. As you allow the shower of goodness to saturate and satiate you, your need to "do" decreases and your capacity to "be" increases.

## Floating

**Row, row, row, your boat,**
**     Gently down the stream.**

**Merrily, Merrily,**
**     Merrily, Merrily,**
**          Life is but a dream.**

**Since it is all just a dream,**
**     Why make the effort to row?**

**Just float with the flow.**

This is not to suggest that you become lazy. As effort to achieve externally eases, effort to awaken internally grows fierce. Most of your attention turns inward. As you search in the deepest recesses of your inner Self, rude awakenings can shock you. With this level of self-honesty may come the painful realization that there are many more layers of your unconscious to uncover than you ever dreamed possible. You may begin to notice more subtle ways that you have been selfish or unloving or untrusting. But you can also simultaneously realize that at last you are on the right course. You are finally on your way Home to unshakable Love.

Remember, Love is the vibration that is always waiting for you in the inner depths of Now. Find as many ways as you can to attune to your inner silence and to sing in harmony with joy. When you synchronize with the vibration of Love, the monsters of fear evaporate into thin air. *When you live in gratitude, your attitude itself takes care of you.* The rational mind, your ego, short circuits because it no longer needs to be your caretaker. You are supported by something beyond the mind's comprehension. Once you have lifted the veil, you become a child of God. This ultimate parent provides all you ever need. *Life's miracles are always occurring, but remain hidden from you by your own inner disharmony.*

You cannot pretend to have found Enlightenment and then wait for the manna. If you feel that the Universe is not taking care of you, you are somehow not living in the flow of Life. When you truly surrender into the experience of Love, you let go of your need to control. You open your Being to live in a state of grace.

## Grace

**You can manipulate others**
**     To fulfill your desires or**
**          Open to receive Grace**
**               With no expectations.**

**With manipulation,**
**     There is always effort,**
**          No matter how subtle,**
**               As you *try* to receive.**

**With Grace,**
**     You are surprised by**
**          Miracles more precious**
**               Than any of your Dreams.**

*As trust takes the lead, grace enters your life.* As you melt into the unknown, the need to define yourself as a separate "I" disappears. The scope of the bliss that appears is far beyond the magnitude of any individual. You sense that *all* is supportively interconnected, from the simplest dirt and rocks to oceans and trees and animals and, finally, to all human beings, even you! The newly merging "you" is so much more than the old separate "you."

A vital step in this melting process is to recognize your needs and then ask for help. The results of your asking depend on your attitude as you make the request. For instance, you can demand that the Universe take care of you. Your reasoning may be that since you are a sincere seeker, you should be provided for. A demand arising from self-righteousness destroys any possibility of the Universe assisting you. Often pain is needed to dissolve your arrogance. *Once humbled, you can genuinely ask for support.*

In 1976, when I was a counselor in a backpacking camp in northern California's Trinity Alps, I learned a major lesson about "asking." My friend Marilyn and I were leading ten teenage boys and girls through the wilderness for two weeks. On the seventh night, we were camped in rugged mountains in unfamiliar territory. We had not seen anyone else for days. As we slept, a freak summer blizzard unleashed two feet of snow on us. We huddled together through the night to stay warm. As the sun rose, the storm was still so intense that we could barely see one foot in front of us. All the trails had disappeared. We could not see any of the surrounding mountains to read our maps. We had little food because we were due to hike to a "food drop" that day.

I was scared. No, I was quietly terrified. I felt responsible for everyone's safety. If the blizzard continued, our already wet clothes and sleeping bags would no longer keep us warm. We would either suffer from hypothermia and lose some toes and fingers or freeze to death. I remembered the near-by location of a mountain peak we had seen the day before. I left Marilyn with the kids and struggled through the ferocious blizzard which had dumped over three feet of snow by now. Breathless and frozen, I finally arrived on the peak but could not see far enough to get my bearings. I pictured those frightened kids relying upon me.

My terror intensified. Finally, in desperation, I fell to my knees and prayed. I begged God to please lift the storm just enough for me to see the path down the mountain. In that moment, I fully believed that the clouds would magically disappear. After a few minutes, nothing had happened. I began sobbing as I pictured the newspaper headlines detailing our deaths. I pleaded with God, but still nothing happened. Dejected, I finally decided to return to the others and plan a new strategy. As I was walking down from the peak, I found my feet involuntarily moving in another direction. It was strange. I felt like I was being led, for no apparent reason, to the back side of the mountain. As I came around a corner, I looked below me and saw the faintest evidence of the trail. I shouted with glee and rushed back to the others with the life-saving news.

Later I realized my picture of wanting the storm to stop almost prevented me from being able to receive the gift being offered.

## Asking

**When you finally admit**
**You cannot do it alone,**
**Asking the Universe**
**To please help you**
**Lets you bow down.**

**The very act of asking**
**Opens you to receive.**

**Then release all your ideas**
**Of how the help will come,**
**So you can see the support**
**In whatever form it arrives.**

There is generally a delay between the asking and the receiving. This period of time tests your faith. In the act of asking, you find the courage to set aside your arrogance, which has convinced you that you must do it alone. You become vulnerable enough to admit, "This is beyond my control. I cannot go on struggling. Please help." And then nothing happens for a period of time. This is when you can panic or trust. This is when you have to combat the lurking demons in your mind that whisper in your ear, "See. This stuff does not work. There is nothing here but you. So go out there and grab whatever you can." You must decide if you want to be controlled by those nagging voices or not. If you give them power over you, you may become so caught up in their negativity that you do not recognize the help when it arrives.

Most people sit in the passenger's seat of their life, feeling out of control. If you are 100% responsible for your response to every stimulus, you move into the driver's seat. If you know that you have the power to create a positive way of perceiving *any* situation, then you no longer need to be driving on a particular road in order to be happy. Instead, you learn to enjoy wherever you are, even if you have no map.

You may never entirely figure out this Mystery (Thank God!), but you are still the artist who is painting your version of Reality, moment by moment.

## Creativity

**In the creation of *your* Life,**
**You are both the artist and**
**The work of art in progress.**

**Your ultimate creation**
**Is your Life itself and**
**The Love you allow.**

You can stroll down any path, already celebrating your freedom. If you joyously watch Life unfold without having to know how it is supposed to turn out, you discover the room in your Heart that is filled with appreciation for the miracle of simply being on the Earth in a body.

## Prayer

**When your time with God shifts**
**From asking for needs to be filled**
**Into feeling grateful for all of Life,**
**You have discovered true Prayer.**

# Section Two

# Loving Yourself

## How Are You?

How you are
  Does not matter.

What matters is
  How you are
    In relationship to
      How you are.

## Chapter Four
# You Loving You

The master key to unlocking your Happiness is hidden within your capacity to love yourself. What does "loving yourself" mean? Is this the way the "me generation" is selfish? Is this egocentricity? Or vanity? Or narcissism? No, these are some of the ways that loving yourself has been misconstrued. Even the authors of *Roget's International Thesaurus* do not understand self-love. They list together under the category of "vanity," the following: "self-importance, self-esteem, self-respect, self-delight, self-admiration, self-love, self-infatuation, narcissism, autoeroticism, smugness, and self-complacency." That does not put "self-esteem, self-respect, self-admiration, self-delight, or self-love" in very good company. Nor does the inclusion of "autoeroticism" in this list cultivate a very positive attitude toward pleasuring yourself sexually. The listing of all these traits as synonyms by this well-known thesaurus demonstrates the negativity with which society misinterprets self-love. *Treating yourself with dignity and respect is in no way related to indulging yourself in egocentricity.*

Loving yourself begins by first recognizing that you are in a relationship with yourself all the time. Your thoughts (or internal voices) constantly "speak" to you in different ways. The quality or tone of your thoughts is either loving or harsh. Each moment, they treat you either with kindness, gentleness, and compassion or with anger, judgement, and deprecation. If you were to begin to listen to *only* the tone of these voices as they speak to you, you would probably be shocked to hear how cruel they often are. *Most likely, you are so accustomed to the harshness of your thoughts that you are not even aware of being abused by them.* Each thought that you let attack you and treat you with anything less than utmost respect reinforces low self-esteem. Your self-concept spirals downward.

When you focus on how your thoughts treat you, then you can create and reinforce powerful changes in your relationship with yourself. As you watch those thoughts attack you again and again, at some point you may discover a righteous indignation that says, "Stop! I don't deserve to be treated this way any more!" This insight is the beginning of the end of those cruel thoughts. You are headed Home to Love.

As you see yourself through eyes of self-compassion, you know that "you" are not those hurtful thoughts. "You" are who is being hurt by those thoughts. "You" are who is doing the best that you possibly can. "You" are the one whose deepest intentions are to be kind. Sometimes you may not treat others with as much Love or respect as you would like. But when you examine the true source of those unloving behaviors, you discover that inside yourself is a frightened little child who is desperately crying out to be noticed, to be loved. Sometimes the way you cry out does not serve yourself or others. However, what you are unconsciously doing is treating others the same way as those internal voices treat you. When you start to comprehend your innocence at a cellular level, your relationship to those destructive thoughts shifts.

You can start loving yourself right now by being aware of your many efforts to be a "good" person. Look at yourself from the level of Reality where you can see that you are a human being who may have some attitudes and behaviors which are destructive to your well-being. Rather than condemning yourself for having "bad habits," you can be in a place inside yourself that unconditionally accepts all of you, even with your "negativity."

## Loving Yourself

**Loving yourself is
Accepting yourself,
Especially
When you are not
Accepting yourself.**

If you absorb the full implications of the previous aphorism, it can absolutely transform your relationship with yourself. You no longer have to be a certain way in order to love yourself. You can see your good intentions and accept yourself even while you are still a mere mortal falling short of your ideals. *You no longer have to feel happy for you to love you.* Simply find that place inside yourself that accepts you for being *whoever* you are in this moment.

## How Are You?

**How you are
Does not matter.**

**What matters is
How you are
In relationship to
How you are.**

You no longer have to wait to become a worldly success (whatever that means) to feel good about yourself. You can even use the ways you perceive yourself to be a failure as opportunities to love yourself as you are "failing." Then you know that you are lovable whether you are a "success" or not.

In 1985, I came back to Mill Valley, California, after having spent five years traveling to other parts of the world in search of God. As I was getting re-acquainted with Western society, I decided to start my private practice again. To spread the word, I began advertising in a local newspaper and creating flyers to be distributed throughout Marin County. Meanwhile, I sat on the deck of my new home meditating many hours per day, opening my Heart to receive the people I thought would be arriving on my doorstep.

At first, nothing much happened. There were very few responses. I began to feel unsure about my private practice getting off the ground. As more time passed with hardly any "success," I began to perceive this undertaking as failing. I broke down and wept the tears of defeat for several weeks. Then, in meditation one day, a breakthrough happened. I saw "Peter," the failure, through the eyes of compassion. I began sobbing tears of gratitude for how beautiful Peter's efforts were to offer to others all the gifts that he had received in his twenty years of seeking. I also saw, in a very special moment, that Peter was lovable whether he "succeeded" or "failed" in his attempts to renew his work with people. The purity of his intentions was all that really mattered. As I fell in Love with Peter at this new level, I knew that my relationship with myself had expanded beyond a dependence on how I showed up in the external world. I discovered a whole new definition of what being successful means.

## Failure

**If you can love yourself
While you feel the pain
Of seeing your life failing,
Then you are succeeding.**

*Truly loving yourself is not about being egocentric or self-centered. It is ensuring that all the thoughts inside your head are kind to you.* As a child, you were probably discouraged from being proud of yourself or praising yourself. Parents often see this attitude as narcissistic and destructive. You may have heard, "Quit being so self-centered," or "Can't you think of anyone but yourself?" You may well have learned to turn your supportive energy outward toward others so that you would not be seen as selfish. You probably developed more compassion for your friends than for yourself.

## Supporting Yourself

**Have you noticed**
**That it is easier to**
**Give your support**
**To another person**
**Than to yourself?**

**The same voices that**
**Encourage your friends**
**Can be turned inward**
**To build self-esteem.**

Your primary relationship is with yourself, twenty-four hours a day, seven days a week, fifty-two weeks a year, for your entire lifetime. One thing is for sure. You will be with you until the day you die. *You* are your only guaranteed "Life Partner." So why not have a Love affair with yourself? You can fully love others only after you discover how to compassionately love all of you.

As you live your life, do you ever feel needy? If your answer is "no," are you fooling yourself? If your answer is "yes," is that okay with you? What do you do with your neediness when you feel it? Perhaps you feel so guilty for having *any* needs at all that you try to deny their existence, even to yourself. Or you try to get them met covertly, perhaps by having sexual intercourse when what you really want is to be touched and stroked and adored. Do you ever approach a friend and say, "I'm feeling really needy right now. Would you please give me a hug?" or "Would you please hold me and comfort me?" Perhaps this is a novel idea to you.

By comparison, do you ever feel guilty for needing a drink of water? Human beings need to be loved just like they need water. Babies can die without human affection. As an adult, you have never lost that need. You have just been trained to hide it. Once you begin to accept that you feel needy at times, then you can ask more directly to get your needs met. You may be surprised at the response you receive when you ask directly for a hug or a cuddle or for someone to just listen to you without trying to fix you. By not having any unspoken, covert agenda, your interactions become more straightforward and clear.

Another human experience that most people run away from is loneliness. *The deepest pain you can suffer here on this planet is feeling separate from God, from yourself, from others, and from Mother Earth.* When you feel lonely, why not let yourself feel the pain fully rather than distracting yourself or condemning yourself for having this human feeling? If you do not embrace this experience, your pain is driven further inside instead of being released. This denial gives birth to the greatest loneliness possible because you separate yourself from your experience. You abandon yourself when you most need support. If you gently stay with yourself, feeling all your feelings, your pain leads you to your innermost core.

## Loneliness

**Cry the tears of anguish**
**Created by your isolation.**
**Eventually, your loneliness**
**Transforms into aloneness.**

Your willingness to melt into these depths allows you to better understand this universal pain. When you have gone to the bottom of your well of loneliness, you come to terms with the fact that you are alone. Your emptiness cannot possibly be (ful)filled by another person. When you quit desperately begging for Love from someone else, you can learn to fill yourself from the inside. Then you can move toward others with a cup that is overflowing rather than with one that is empty. If you allow loneliness to become your teacher, it leads you to the true inner source of Love.

You are here on Earth having a variety of experiences so that you can embrace *all* of you. Besides, you cannot possibly be anyone other than you. As you let yourself be the unique human being that you are, you no longer have to keep trying to live into an image of who you think you are supposed to be. You can let you be you and trust that you are perfect right now.

## Trusting Yourself

Trusting yourself is allowing
　*Whatever* occurs inside you
　　To bubble up unrestrained.

Trusting yourself is admitting
　'I don't know,' if you don't,
　　For then Truth can be found.

Trusting yourself is dropping
　All your most cherished beliefs
　　When they no longer serve you.

Trusting yourself is celebrating
　All corners within your Being:
　　Both where the angels frolic
　　　*And* where the demons lurk.

Trusting yourself is enjoying
　All your own unique quirks,
　　For you can only be yourself.

One attitude that damages trust in yourself is needing to be "perfect." Having an ideal that you are supposed to be faultless creates the strife of striving after elusive illusions of perfection. As a child, your parents may have repeatedly given you the message, "You are not enough" by focusing on what you did not achieve instead of on how precious you were just for being yourself. As a result, you either tried to live up to their unattainable standards in order to win their approval or you gave up trying altogether. In either event, your self-esteem was damaged at a fundamental level. In order to try to prove your worth, you kept chasing after an ideal of perfection that could never be achieved because you had already learned that whatever you did was not enough. You could get eight A's and one B on your report card, and you would focus on the one B as a sign of your inadequacy.

With this programming, you could not possibly accept yourself when you made anything that could be construed as a mistake. What you did not know is that all human beings make mistakes. This is an essential part of being human. Growth happens by venturing into unknown territory where you stumble around in the dark for a while. When young children learn to ride two wheeled bicycles, in the beginning there are lots of falls (mistakes?). If they were to give up because they were not perfect bicyclists the first time they tried to ride, they would never learn.

What if you were to change what you now perceive as negative mistakes into positive proof that you are an alive human being instead of a machine? Then you can cheer every time you think you make an "error" because you have just proven that you are a human instead of a robot.

## Perfection

**If your ideals of perfection include
Your perceptions of imperfection,
Then 'mistakes' help you to weave
The tapestry of your own humanity.**

A traditional Zen Garden is an adventure into perfection. As you walk in the front gate, the orderliness and cleanliness are striking. Never has Nature been more geometrically pristine. All the plants are manicured so meticulously that their outlines are as straight as a ruler. Dead leaves are nowhere to be seen. Every square inch of the ground is carefully raked in impeccable, symmetrical patterns. Not even one pebble is out of place. Many visitors breathe an almost visible sigh of relief as they look because, at last, everything appears to be flawlessly in its proper place. As you walk into the back of the garden, knowing that these master gardeners have vastly improved upon Mother Nature's methods of housekeeping, a shocking scene appears before your eyes. You come upon a disheveled, unkempt area in complete disarray. Dead leaves abound. Rocks and twigs are scattered about. Contrasted to all you have just seen in the rest of the garden, the unmanicured plants look worse than someone who has not taken a bath for decades. You can become so perplexed that your innate sense of perfection becomes muddled.

This "corner of chaos" is no mistake. The Zen Buddhists wisely create this metaphor as a microcosm of how the Universe has designed the landscape of Life. Human beings can only control so much. Beyond our arrogance, which has us thinking that we always know what is best, lies an unsecable and unknowable Mystery. Chaos becomes the catalyst for the changes necessary to surrender into something greater than ourselves. In our orderly lives there needs to be a corner of chaos to invite us into a nonlinear, uncontrollable, and deeply rewarding trust for Life.

When you know you are 100% perfect even with what appears to be imperfections, then you can question the usefulness of comparing yourself with others. There is no better than or worse than, no prettier or uglier, no more evolved or less evolved. Your *only* task is to unravel your own illusions by learning from the unique lessons presented to you. They assist you in discovering how to become a more loving person. If you look to others to try to find out who you *should* be, you miss the precious gift of becoming enthralled with the unfolding of you.

## Comparison

**Comparing you with others
Keeps you in the illusion
Of better or worse.**

**If you want to compare,
Look at you a year ago
And look at you now.**

**Celebrate your growth.**

Comparing you with you gives you the opportunity to expand your sense of yourself if you look through the correct prism. If you gently focus on how far you have come, you are left with an opening into more growth. If you obsessively focus on what you have not yet achieved, then you are left with the contraction of not being enough. Haven't you listened to those critical voices of perfectionism for too long? Look at your growth as if you are watching rose petals delicately unfolding. You would never blame the rose for not yet being fully blossomed. Your harsh disapproval of yourself destroys the fragile petals of the rose inside your Heart. Evolution into Love is more arduous than seems "fair." There are many more layers and complexities than you could possibly imagine. If you learn to be in awe of the process of blooming itself, then you can enjoy all aspects of the rose, including its soft petals *and* its harsh thorns. Your enjoyment lets your inner rose relax and open at its own pace.

An image often used to describe this process of unfolding is that of an onion being peeled. As one layer comes off, there is another one underneath. The implied message in this image is that someday you will arrive at the center of the onion and will be finished. *In Life, there is no center of the onion.* This unfolding of the layers continues ad infinitum. So you might as well learn to enjoy the peeling process itself instead of trying to find the end of the journey.

Another self-destructive attitude to examine is that of being a self-sacrificing martyr. One of the unspoken rules in our society is that it is not okay to say *no* when asked to help someone. People who are learning to love themselves are sometimes judged because at times it becomes necessary to be "divinely selfish." As you begin to understand the dynamics of spirituality, one of the first discoveries is how important it is to be true to yourself. Sometimes this involves learning to say *no* to others, especially if you have habitually been a *yes* person. Resentment can easily get mixed in with the favors you do for others. It is always better to not "help" than to "help" with resentment. Saying *no* to others leads them to someone who has a genuine *yes*. It is okay to follow whatever you perceive to create more Love for you. This period of "divine selfishness" is often necessary before you can directly experience the fulfillment of unselfish giving.

## Nurturance

**When you move toward**
**Whatever nurtures you,**
**Every person benefits,**
**Even when it appears**
**Otherwise to anyone,**
**Including you.**

Let yourself repeatedly know that you are innocent. As a small child, you were dependent upon adults. In fact, you had to look to them for your very survival. Thus, you began to see the source of your Love as being "out there." You compromised yourself in order to get approval. Now you are an adult, or, perhaps more accurately, an innocent child walking around in an adult's body. And, yes, you do need Love in order to flourish. But the primary source of that Love is contained neither in anyone else nor in the fluctuations of your fickle mind. It is alive and well inside of the Mystery of your Heart.

## Chapter Five
# Victim or Master? Your Choice

There is a "Spiritual Bill of Rights" which addresses even more fundamental human freedoms than those proclaimed in the U.S. Constitution. One of the most inalienable birthrights which you can claim as a human being here on Earth is to have only the thoughts that you want to have inside your head.

If the average thought takes about four seconds, then in one minute approximately fifteen different thoughts go through your mind. That means that in one hour, nine hundred thoughts affect you. If you are awake sixteen hours a day, some 14,400 distinct thoughts occur, to say nothing of your dreams when you are sleeping. *With how many of those thousands of thoughts are you exercising your right of choice and with how many are you allowing yourself to be victimized by uninvited intruders?*

## Are You Choosing?

**As a situation arises,**
**Do you automatically**
**React out of fear or**
**Can you choose to**
**Respond with Love?**

Most people do not choose what goes on inside their heads. They do not even know that they have a choice. They unconsciously follow the internalized voices of their parents, teachers, siblings, relatives, neighbors, doctors, church, television, and lyrics from songs. They are drowning in a cesspool of destructive thoughts, with no inkling of how toxic their inner environment is, let alone with a possibility of rising out of the muck. Instead of taking action, they complain and complain, not knowing that complaining perpetuates the quagmire.

## Changing

**The same energy you use to**
**Focus on all the reasons that**
**Your life is miserably stuck**
**Can instead be channeled**
**Into welcoming the new.**

The moment you were born, you began to have many experiences of this Reality. Each experience began to shape your understanding of how Life works. You had no way of knowing that any other approaches to Life could exist except for what *you* were experiencing in your immediate environment. When you were very young, you could not possibly have had an overview of the world. You had no way of seeing what went on next door or across town or in other cultures. If your home was full of Love, then this planet became a place that is full of Love. If your home was full of bitterness or anger or sadness, then that became your underlying understanding of Reality. If feelings were rarely expressed or certain harsh behaviors went on, then this world became emotionless or cruel. *Whatever the atmosphere of your home felt like became your deepest sense of what to expect from this world.*

The ways in which you learned to cope with Life as a child became your strategy for approaching all situations. When you became old enough to venture into the neighborhood, you began to be exposed to other homes, new environments, and different kinds of people. It may have been puzzling or even shocking to see people reacting in ways that you were not accustomed to. Some of those ways may have seemed better or kinder or more loving than what you were familiar with, and some may have seemed worse or harsher or more cruel.

Through the years you began to see that no matter how entrenched you had become in "this is how it is," new evidence kept being presented. Perhaps, at some point, an inner light bulb lit up which said, "Maybe Life does not have to be the way I have always thought that it had to be. Maybe I am the variable here and I can change my attitudes and ways of thinking and perceiving. Perhaps there is a kinder and a more loving way to live here on the Earth."

As you let go of your limited ways of thinking, you see that there is more going on here than can be seen by the eye. As you open to spiritual possibilities, your intuition is strengthened. The fear that kept you confined begins to dissolve. You receive blessings from unseen resources in ways that do not make sense to your logical mind. Within each moment, the Universe is available to support you financially, emotionally, sexually, and spiritually far beyond your dreams.

## Receiving

**Receiving support requires**
**The courage to surrender**
**To Love's lead instead of**
**Being victimized by fear.**

As you unravel the elaborate illusions that fear creates, you can overcome your sense of powerlessness and impotence in the world. As you discern what is going on inside you without condemning yourself in any way, you realize that you do not have to stay stuck in *any* state of consciousness. As you see fear's traps, you can create ingenious ways to free yourself from them. You learn that there are many ways to stay open to Life's miracles.

*Become familiar with the tricks that your mind plays.* It repeatedly searches out your unique weaknesses and attacks you there. The ways you try to deal with your mind's assaults on you can be self-destructive. If you become aware of your coping patterns, you can change the ineffective ones. Perhaps you shut down completely and feel nothing. Your mind has you believing that it is a "ho-hum" world. Boredom sets in if you sit on your aliveness.

## Boredom

**Boredom is a silently**
**Boiling fury at feeling**
**Separate and useless.**

**Express your repressed rage**
**And uncover your deep urge**
**To fully participate in Life.**

**You will not stay bored for long.**

As you take control of your inner environment, you may discover that directing anger at disempowering thoughts is effective in blasting away any images that you no longer want. To get out of the powerlessness of feeling like a victim, reach inside for a beautiful kind of rage which declares, "I deserve to be treated kindly by my thoughts!" or "I deserve to think whatever I want to think!" or "I deserve Love!" This is one route to building self-esteem.

# Righteous Rage

**Expressing your rage**
**Can move your stance**
**Out of living 'in victim'**
**Into declaring yourself**
**The master of your mind.**

Find your righteous rage. Pull out a plastic wiffle bat and a big pillow and release your anger (see the Workbook Meditation for Week 5 on page 205). Yell out your right to be involved in Life as you hit the pillow with all your might. Declare from the depths of your Being that you are tired of feeling separate and watching Life pass you by. *This type of healthy anger is really an expression of your power.* It is not an irresponsible "dump" on someone if you are expressing it as your right rather than as a means to change someone else. Rage can become a key that unlocks the door to your inner sanctuary. It blasts away the muddled thoughts and creates an empty space. Out of that void arises a new depth of Love.

As you move into this process, observe how your mind wants to sabotage you. It may say, "This is ridiculous," or "How can a grown-up adult be so immature as to scream?" or "This will never work," or "I'm not really angry," or any of thousands of ways it tries to stop its own exposure. Every moment that you do not stand up to your mind and emphatically declare that you are the master of what goes on inside you, your misery gets a firmer hold on you. Your self-imposed prison walls get thicker, and you suffocate from lack of Life energy.

It is relevant here to convey the last part of the story about my starting my private practice again in Marin in 1985 (see page 34). I was continuing to love myself while I was "failing," but still nothing was moving in the outer world. One day there was a huge rainstorm. I got the inexplicable urge to go up to Mount Tamalpais. I pulled on my boots and my rain pancho and drove to the top. As I got out of my car, there were no other people or vehicles around because the storm was fierce. I walked into the middle of the chaos wondering what I was doing there. I sat down to meditate on a rock while being pelted by the rain and blasted by the wind. Once again, still without judging myself, I began to cry about how my life was failing. Suddenly, I felt as if I was struck by a bolt of lightning, which was actually an internal explosion of rage.

I started stomping around in the storm, yelling from the pit of my belly, "I'm tired of all this bullshit!" "I'm tired of nothing happening!" "I'm tired of accepting all of this and being a nice guy!" "I deserve to have clients. Now!" "I have incredible gifts to give!" "I'm tired of waiting!" "Now is the time! Not next year or next month or next week. Right now!" "All of Marin is mine! The Bay Area is mine! California is mine! The whole world is my playground!"

I pounded on my chest like Tarzan. Indiscernible sounds poured out of me. I found myself picking up rocks and hurling them. It felt as if testosterone was coursing through every cell of my Being. I loved it! I ranted and raved for more than an hour, feeling more powerful by the minute. The storm became my partner as I stepped into my fury. The wind blew harder as I yelled louder. As my anger increased, the storm picked up simultaneously. We were harmonious allies. Finally, I knew that I was finished. I thanked the raging storm which, by now, seemed like a friendly pussycat to me.

I walked off that mountain feeling more potent than ever. When I arrived back home, on my answering machine were two messages inquiring about my work. Soon thereafter, without doing anything additional, more people began calling for sessions. Finally, my private practice had been successfully launched. In retrospect, that outpouring of righteous rage was the perfect ritual to create my passage from childhood to adulthood.

*The mind loves negative attention.* It can paralyze you by keeping you bitter about past interactions. Perhaps you have felt deeply hurt by people who did not live up to their promises to you. And rightfully so. However, continuing in the pain primarily hurts *you*.

If you are ready to let go of the past, the following perspective may be useful. Breaking promises is simply one of the things that human beings do. They give their word in one moment according to the way they are feeling. Then circumstances change and they act differently than they said they would. Or they are too afraid to tell the truth, so they make false promises. In any event, you have certain expectations of them from what they have said and they do not live up to your expectations. Then you feel betrayed. Out of this experience, you may make a decision to not trust anyone and wall yourself off from future relationships. It may be difficult for you to understand this, but you were never betrayed.

## Betrayal

**It is impossible for
Anyone to betray you.**

**Betrayal's illusion occurs
If you expect others to
Never break their word.**

What has you feel betrayed is that you do not expect others to act in a certain way and then they do. Probably out of fear, they never communicate fully with you. However, if you let them be human, then you see that they are just being unconscious. You do not have to take on the betrayal. However, you may well choose to not enter into agreements with a person who is too afraid to tell the truth.

A promise with room for future variables creates flexibility. *The logical mind wants to fit Life into a neatly wrapped box instead of allowing for the inevitability of human fluctuations.* If you stop being on either end of immutable promises, then you can flow with Life. All persons involved in any agreement should understand that communication with one another is essential if anything changes.

## Promises

**The only promise
You can ever make
Is to never make
A promise that
Is set in stone.**

If you see betrayal and promises in this light, then you no longer have to put yourself in a one-down, victim position. If you hold on to resentment, you poison yourself with negative thoughts. As you let go of your expectations of others and of yourself, then you can allow for the chaos of human inconsistencies to occur without hurting yourself. You can dismantle any walls that your bitterness has built.

In summary, *the transition from child to adult occurs when you take full responsibility for your inner world.* Externally there is only one place called planet Earth. However, there are as many internal experiences of this planet as there are human beings living here. You live on your Earth and I live on mine. And it is exactly what each of us perceives it to be. You have the power to create Heaven or Hell every moment. Why let yourself get bullied around by painful experiences from the past that keep you from seeing the beauty within Now? Take charge inside you, moment by moment. You have the right to be Happy, but it is not handed to you on a silver platter. It takes every last ounce of your will to confront your mind and to claim your joy.

## Chapter Six
# Freeing Your Emotions

Have you ever noticed how uninhibited young children can be with their emotions? Take a moment to picture two three-year-olds playing peacefully in the sandbox. One of them gets angry and screams, "Stop it!" The other one gets angry back and yells, "I hate you! I hate you!" Then, if no adults are there to interfere, the storm of anger usually passes quickly, and they start playing harmoniously again. Their friendship has not been destroyed by the outburst. They do not have to spend the next hour or day or week processing what just went on between them. *They move into the next moment without holding on to the past.*

Another example of the fluidity of children's emotions can be seen when a three-year-old falls down, bumps a knee, and screams louder than you thought possible. If the crying is accepted with a gentle hug, the child's tears soon disappear and a smile comes back. The next adventure soon begins. A third example occurs when a mother leaves her child at pre-school for the first time. Often there can be lots of tears for "missing mommy." Many teachers try to stop the crying by using some form of distraction. They give the child a paint brush or cookie instead of gently holding the child and quietly whispering, "You really miss your mommy, don't you? It's okay to cry because you miss her." When the child's feelings get validated, the crying usually lasts a very short period of time. As the feeling of missing dissolves, the child begins to look around and become involved. The joyful Here and Now is available on the other side of the feelings.

As children grow older, their feelings, if they ever were okay to the adults around them, usually become unacceptable. They are no longer a "baby." They are "growing up." They must squash "childish" feelings or they will be "given something to really cry about." How might you be different today if your feelings had been accepted, validated, and even celebrated as you were growing up? What if they were seen as your friends instead of your enemies? What if you knew that every feeling inside you is trying to tell you something?

Chapter Two, "Why Is There Pain?," explores both the beauty and the necessity of consciously feeling your feelings. If you refuse to acknowledge your feelings and do not fully express them, then you create more suffering than the feeling itself ever could. It is only your upbringing that keeps you afraid of feeling. You were taught that certain emotions are "bad," so you avoid them. You resist letting go of control and limit yourself to a narrow band of experience called *thinking*. If you disarm your mind's defenses and become vulnerable enough for your emotions to flow, then you unlock the door to a precious room in your inner temple.

## Vulnerability

**Vulnerability opens
The gateway between
Thinking and feeling.**

**As you let go of thoughts
And enter into feelings,
Your Heart awakens.**

Vulnerability has a bad reputation with many people, yet it is one of the main vehicles for becoming an integrated human being. As an adult, if you want to begin to feel your feelings, there are different stages in the unfolding of this process. If you were emotionally abused as a child or are in extreme denial of your feelings, then you are probably anywhere from slightly to extremely uncomfortable around people who are crying or angry or fearful. You may try to gloss over others' feelings or quickly comfort them or distract them. You

43

protect yourself from seeing others' emotions because unconsciously you do not want your own to get triggered.

Once you have seen the wisdom of expressing your feelings, this avoidance pattern changes. It may still be too scary for you to feel your own emotions, but you begin to feel drawn to spend time with people as they are releasing theirs. After a while, these vicarious experiences let you see that it is safe to dip into your own well of feelings. You can start to directly experience the deep inner peace born on the other side of emotional release. You may even begin to enjoy the experience itself, while it is happening.

## Feeling

**If you label emotions
As being good or bad,
Your wall of judgement
Blocks your experience.**

**If you let all emotions
Explode into expression,
Orgasmic release ensues.**

Remember, if your conditioning does not get in the way, feeling your feelings can be similar to sexual release. Experiencing the explosion of your emotions is, in and of itself, enough. Recall the children in the sandbox. They can emote and then move on without hanging on to the experience. If you let go of your judgements and become fascinated by the intensity of what is taking place, you need not direct your emotional release at anyone else. You can experience your feelings and then let go without analyzing them.

However, if you do want to explore them on the psychological level, you can listen to the different emotions themselves and start gleaning the message each one is communicating to you. Those usually labeled as "negative" take on a whole new light as you begin to appreciate the wisdom being revealed to you.

Anger is often viewed as a deadly menace to be hidden, repressed, or denied. The irony is that anger becomes destructive when it is hidden, repressed, or denied. If you keep shoving anger down, it either implodes and turns into a disease like cancer or arthritis (thus being violent toward yourself), or it eventually explodes and you lash out uncontrollably (perhaps being violent with another). If you recognize and understand anger as it occurs, then it never gets stored in you and you remain clear. Feeling the heat of anger in your body does not have any inherent action associated with it. It does not necessarily lead to violence, especially if you express it appropriately. *Rather than anger being your enemy, what if you were to see it as a friendly messenger trying to tell you something for your own benefit?*

## Anger

**Anger lets you know
That you feel powerless
And want some control.**

**Listen to its message
Rather than judging
Yourself for having it.**

**Then investigate ways
To get your power back
Or surrender your need
To be the one in control.**

Fear is an example of the Universe's attempt to have you pay attention to the present rather than being run by the past. A healthy, natural fear occurs when your physical body is in imminent danger. It releases adrenaline into your system to give you the extra energy needed to cope with an emergency. This is the purpose of unadulterated fear - to tell you that your physical safety or health is in danger. Neurotic fear ignites when you innocently misperceive what is taking place around you or within you. You superimpose some negative experience from your past onto the events in the present. Your fear was probably well-founded in your childhood. It may have saved your physical well-being or even your life. But is it still serving you?

When you are fearful, the most relevant questions to ask yourself are, "Am I safe or in danger right now?" and "What do I need to do in order to make myself feel safe?" If you are in actual physical danger, you may need to take an external action to create your safety. If you are reacting to someone or some situation out of a past experience, then you need to stop and breathe. *Let yourself know that what is triggering your fear has nothing to do with what is happening in the Here and Now.* Look around and say to yourself, "Right now, I am safe."

Sadness is another emotion that often receives "bad press." The actual experience of tears flowing from your eyes can be so very beautiful. *As pain is being released, the tears are like a shower cleansing your Soul.* As you feel the pain, you gouge out a new-found depth in your Heart for more Love to come in. The irony is that you end up experiencing more richness in your Being than if you had not felt sad. You can start celebrating sadness instead of avoiding it.

## Sadness

**The beauty of sadness**
**Lies within its depth.**

**The height of ecstasy**
**That you can embrace**
**Is dependent upon**
**The depth of despair**
**That you have touched.**

**As waves of sadness break,**
**Let them wash through you.**
**Lose yourself into sadness**
**And find a brand new you**
**On the far side of the tears.**

Guilt is another often misunderstood feeling. The view of many world religions is that guilt is the best way for your conscience to control your "lower instincts." Without guilt, so this reasoning goes, you might succumb to your more basic animal nature. Uncontrolled, you might involuntarily explode into a violent or sexual rampage.

This negative perspective demonstrates a lack of faith in your basic goodness. What if you could slip underneath your guilt and release yourself from the evil spell that it has cast on you?

## Guilt

**When you feel any guilt,**
**See if you let inner voices**
**Shame you into believing**
**That your motives are bad.**

Thus, when you start feeling guilty in a given situation, ask yourself the following questions: "Have I done anything wrong" or "Are my intentions bad?" or "Is what I am wanting or doing inherently hurting anyone else?" When you find the answers to these questions, ease up on yourself! Then, after you have seen your innocence, be sure to communicate with whomever you need to clarify your motives.

Jealousy is one of the most hated of all emotions. Violence and murders are possible outcomes of not accepting this powerful feeling. People can go to extreme measures to try to control their lover so that they do not have to feel jealous. It has been described as a malignant disease maliciously "caused" by low self-esteem and the lack of self-Love.

What if you were to look for the beauty contained within the feeling? What if you were to make jealousy your teacher?

## Jealousy

**Jealousy's humbling gift is**
**Its *involuntary* explosion,**
**Which helps to clear up**
**Any illusions you have**
**About being in control**
**Of all your emotions.**
**Welcome to the Human Race.**

An experience I had with jealousy made it my friend. I had broken up with Susanne, my lover of three years. One evening about three months after our break-up, I spontaneously dropped by her apartment to see how she was doing. I knocked on the door, she opened it, and I said a warm hello to her. As I looked past her into the dining room, I saw that she had a very attractive man over for a candlelight dinner. Suddenly, everything exploded inside my gut. I was livid with anger. I was literally seeing red for about ten seconds. Then, as I realized that I was feeling jealous, I looked her straight in the eyes and said, "My God, Susanne! This is jealousy!"

As our eyes connected, there was no judgement of the feeling. No one was making anyone wrong for what was happening. *There was just a pure experience of jealousy.* In the next moment, both she and I burst into laughter. We let her new lover know what was going on and he joined us in our laughter. The three of us ended up having a wonderful dinner together before I departed to leave them on their own. Since that time, I have had little problem with jealousy as I have no need to run away from it or to judge it in any way.

A beautiful aspect of jealousy is that its explosion lets you know that you have let someone into your Heart. You care enough to be invested in what happens between you and someone else. Some people have never experienced jealousy because they have not let themselves be vulnerable enough to be affected by another human being. When that powerful feeling ignites, you know that you have let your Soul be touched so deeply that someone else has started to become an integral part of you. Your union has created a new entity called "Us." Your reaction may just be your fear of the loss of a part of "Us" that your melting with this other person has created.

Another emotion, pride, can be especially confusing. *Positive pride* enhances your self-esteem. It lets you know that you are a worthwhile human being. When you feel your genuine contribution to the welfare of others, positive pride arises in your Heart. *Negative pride* arises out of your need to prove yourself. It is self-centered, egotistical, and a haughty expression of superiority. People judge negative pride because it puffs you up into a false sense of self that tends to discount others and feed your self-importance. However, if you look deeper, you can discover what is going on underneath the surface appearance of this type of pride.

## False Pride

False pride builds a wall
To hide your insecurity.
You show a swollen chest,
Not your trembling Heart.

False pride is born
If you try to defend
Your defenselessness.

If you expose your fear,
The wall tumbles down
And innocence rises up.

The questions to ask yourself when you become prideful are, "Am I feeling insecure right now?" or "Am I trying to stop others (and myself) from seeing my vulnerability?" You can see the feeling as a friendly messenger carrying a significant communication for you or you can push it away. Instead of judging yourself for having pride, why not look for its gift?

Rejection is another great teacher. It is most people's number one fear. It ranks above the fear of death or the fear of public speaking. *Avoiding any possibility of feeling rejected may be unconsciously running you in ways you have never imagined.* This type of fear can stop you from approaching someone you would like to get to know, from applying for a job you are interested in, from asking a stranger for directions when you are lost, from asking a friend for help when you need it, or even from having any opinions of your own.

Most simply, you feel rejected when others say *no* to you. What if you were to realize that their *no* has little or nothing to do with you? Others' *no's* are either about negative judgements which they are projecting on you or about where they are in relationship to their own wants and needs in any given moment. Unfortunately, you may frequently be using someone else's *no* as an excuse to beat yourself up by taking it personally.

A female friend of mine was an assistant at a workshop when a male participant came up to her and asked her to be his partner in an exercise. She thought that it would be better for him to be with another participant so she gently said, "Thanks, but no." The man got such a hurt look in his eyes that my friend's Heart went out to him. He walked away as if he had been slapped. A few minutes later, she noticed the same man joyfully participating in the exercise with a woman who looked like his female twin. They continued to get to know each other for the rest of the workshop. Today the two of them are happily married. What if my friend had said *yes* out of duty or obligation or fear of hurting him? Or what if the man had taken her *no* in such a self-defeating way that he left the workshop rather than asking the next woman to participate? Perhaps he never would have met his wife-to-be.

The real question is, "What is rejection, really?"

## Rejection

If you knock on a door
And it remains closed,
The Universe is really
Turning you around
To go find the door
That opens to Love.

You can feel the pain of
The door being closed
And trust its perfection
All in the same breath.

Mastering rejection does not mean repressing your feelings by trying to reason with yourself. *You are the only one who can reject you by not accepting your painful feelings or by judging yourself as inadequate.* You are actually abandoning your hurt child inside whenever you do not see yourself through compassionate eyes. Keep gently feeling your pain while simultaneously trusting the *no*. Eventually, as you see how all closed doors lead you to the open ones, your pain will not arise because it has dissolved into trust.

In summary, feelings are wonderful and complete experiences in and of themselves plus they can be marvelous messengers trying to tell you something. Most people try to kill the messenger because they do not want to face their own "shortcomings." Once you see that you are innocent even with your "faults" and that everything, including your feelings, is part of your learning experience here on planet Earth, then you can listen to the message without making yourself wrong for needing to be reminded.

As you gain a deep acceptance of your humanness, you know that feeling your feelings helps bring you into harmony with Love's vibration. Also, as you learn self-acceptance, you are eventually given the gift of seeing beyond yourself and into others. Your heartfelt understanding of your own struggles allows you to experience others' pain and their joy in profound ways. Your compassion allows you to focus your attention on people's intentions rather than on their foibles.

*As you look into what motivates human beings, inside each person you start to see an innocent child who is crying out for Love.* The way adults go about looking for Love can be peculiar. As children, we wanted our parents' affection and often did not receive it. Some of us discovered that negative attention was better than being ignored. We learned how to get our parents' frustration or anger directed at us. There was some satisfaction in this because our parents' yelling was at least a confirmation that we were alive.

Have you ever noticed that when young children are being scolded, sometimes they have a big smile on their face? Often, their smile is not the result of having "gotten their parents' goat." Since they cannot yet distinguish between negative and positive energy, their smile is a genuine reflection of feeling an exhilarating rush as the Life force (in the form of anger) enters their bodies.

As they grow older, they learn the difference between positive and negative energy. However, their patterns of how to get attention are already ingrained in their behavior. They do not have the awareness to see that these ways of relating are no longer serving them, so they unconsciously act them out as adults. By this time they have become so far removed from their "original face" of innocence that they have forgotten that they are seeking Love.

As you begin to see the need for Love from the lost child inside each adult's body, it is easier to open your Heart to *whomever* you meet. Your judgements repeatedly dissolve and true compassion is born.

## Compassion

**Compassion occurs
When you feel grief
For people's suffering
*And* see the innocence
Of their cry for Love.**

# Part Two


# The Leap from West to East

# Section Three

# How Do You Evolve?

## The Game of Life

You have boundaries around
  How deeply you have accepted
    The totality of this Reality.

You are repeatedly presented
  With situations just beyond
    Your capacity to embrace.

You can reject the lessons and
  Stay in the pain of stagnation,
    Or include everything as 'you'
      And feel the joy of expansion.

## Chapter Seven
# Hurray for Risking

Most people think of taking risks as initiating different external actions – such as climbing mountains or gambling with large sums of money or leaving your old job without yet having a new one. In an interpersonal context, risking may involve telling a friend that you feel angry or talking vulnerably about a subject that is scary for you to bring up.

There is another category of risks that has nothing to do with anything outside of you. These are the most significant evolutionary steps that you can initiate. These are the risks that you take with you, internally. They are the direct result of your being willing to look at and then to change any attitudes and beliefs that are not serving you. Taking internal risks allows you to choose to grow voluntarily rather than being forced to grow through painful circumstances. When you see the many ways that you limit how much Love you allow into your life, then taking these kinds of chances becomes much more appealing, even if you become uncomfortable for a period of time.

After all, how do you evolve? By changing. And how do you change? The Universe repeatedly presents you with situations that are opportunities for you to grow. You can let go of your painful beliefs and expand, or you can let your fear paralyze you and cling to your limitations. *If you do not let go, one day your smoldering pain bursts into flames. As your ego is consumed by blazing pain, you are reduced to a pile of humble anguish.* From these ashes arise many insights into yourself and into Life. Your growth can sometimes occur involuntarily as you reluctantly expand your sense of self.

When you look back, you see that there were many signs along the way asking you to make changes earlier and in a less painful way. Risking sooner makes more sense. If you turn your back on these opportunities by allowing fear to take control, you shrink away from Life. When you cower in the corner, hoping for it to all go away, you eventually become resigned to that corner and start to die. Resignation arises out of being frozen by fear's iciness instead of being ignited by the hot flame of the desire to live Life passionately. *If you hurl yourself into the fire of risking, your frozen fear melts.*

## Resignation

**Resignation is fear of taking a risk.**
**It surpasses cancer and car accidents**
**As the number one cause of Death...**

**Except...with this kind of Death,**
**Your body does not decompose.**
**Your whole life disintegrates.**

**So be courageous enough**
**To feel the fear**
***And***
**To take the risk.**

**If you fail, so what.**
**If you succeed, so what.**
**Within the heat of risking**
**Is the essence of aliveness.**

What is your corner of dire pain? Some people's corners are obvious and some are subtle. Who or what are you avoiding? How are you stopping yourself from living more fully? What dreams are you not pursuing? Are you letting your fear keep you a victim to even the slightest degree?  What if you were to see your fear to be like a waving flag saying, "Growth Available Here!"?  Then you might perceive fear as a challenge to move toward instead of a boogey man to run away from.

If you step into whatever you are avoiding, a new "you" is born.  But you have become accustomed to yourself the way you are.  It is easier to hang on to that old identity than to embrace the new because you must let go of control.  When the caterpillar enters the cocoon, *all* that it has ever known itself to be literally dissolves in order for the butterfly to be born.  As you embrace change, the "I" that you have known dies, just like the caterpillar.

The "Death and Rebirth" process awaits you.  (To be addressed in depth in Chapter Ten, "The Cycle of Death and Rebirth.")  You may well experience anywhere from a small amount of discomfort to a great amount of pain as you go through this transformational process.  But any unexamined, repressed pain is like a death warrant.  Avoiding pain is far more devastating than feeling it.  Plus, more Love always awaits for you on the other side of every risk you take, as long as your intentions arise out of innocent and pure motives.  The mind is always struggling to stay alive.  *But anything that is left inside you which can die is only an illusion.  Your inner core of pure Love cannot be destroyed.*  The new "you" who emerges on the other side of a risk is one step closer to becoming that butterfly.

## Fear of Change

**Your resistance to change is
Your fear of the death of
Who you *think* you are.**

**Actually, change destroys
Who you are *not*
So a new level of
Who you *are*
Can emerge.**

Being willing to look inside yourself is the first step in this Life-transforming process.  The next step is to be honest about what you see.  Look at the aspects of yourself that you want to ignore, that you are denying.  It takes incredible courage not to judge yourself for what you find inside.  Remember, all humanity lies within you, from Hitler to Christ.  *When you become insatiably fascinated with the process of discovering all aspects of you without labels of good or bad, then you can accept yourself as a multi-faceted human being.*

## Change

**Conscious change occurs
By shining the light
Of awareness on
Your unawareness.**

**If you see your blindness
And then let go of the old,
You need do nothing else.
Change unfolds naturally.**

As you stand on the edge of the cliff of possibility, trying to decide whether or not to jump into the unknown, you really have no choice in the end.  You can hem and haw.  You can look over the edge and then back away.  You can say, "No, not now."  Any of these options may well be a necessary step toward your final leap. Even if your next step takes you away from the edge of the cliff, eventually you must come back to that precipice. You may need to spend minutes, hours, days, weeks, or years wandering around on the mesa before you come back to that edge again. But that cliff is always there, patiently waiting for you to return. Every step you take away from that precipice can be viewed as if you are backing up to get a running start for a greater leap.

When you do confront your fear by actually jumping into the abyss of potential bliss, the next test begins immediately. While you are still in mid-air, you are no longer the same person who was just looking over the edge. The internal change takes place, by and large, in the moment that you leap. With the risk comes the shift. However, it often takes a while for you to allow yourself to identify with this new "you."

## Allowing Change

As the Light enters to
Dissolve the darkness,
Be gentle with yourself
If you cling to the old
And deflect the new.

Even if this new you is exactly
Who you have wanted to be,
You may yet feel unworthy
To celebrate your beauty.

Give yourself time instead of guilt.
Accept yourself unable to accept.
Being a human is being human.

The other tricky part about the process of change is that it often takes some time for your internal changes to appear in the external world because the material plane is denser than your inner planes. *The period of time while you wait for the three-dimensional world to reflect your inner growth can be a test of your trust.*

## Patience

There is always a time lag
Between internal change
And outer manifestation.

With this understanding,
As you see change inside
You can knowingly trust
It will eventually appear
In your external Reality.

If you let destructive self-doubt creep in before you see the change manifest, you can regress by invalidating your growth. The beauty of this time lag is that it can deepen your inner knowingness. This test demands that you repeatedly validate your experience in a gentle, affirming way, saying, "Yes, I understand. It has not shown up out there yet, but that does not mean that I am going to nullify my growth. I'll just keep loving me, and keep my eyes open for evidence of the change to appear in my everyday life." Trust and patience are the key ingredients.

If you understand this organic process of change, then you can see where you are in the cycle without self-judgement. You can let yourself be wherever you are without thinking that you should be somewhere else.

Familiarize yourself with this cycle of:

♥ Becoming aware of a need for change.
♥ Seeing the possibility of letting go.
♥ Recognizing your fear of the new and not letting that stop you.
♥ Risking by stepping into a new behavior or attitude or situation.
♥ Feeling the joy within the risk itself.
♥ Seeing the internal change.
♥ Trusting the time lag until the new "you" appears in the outer world.
♥ Celebrating the external manifestation of your internal change.

Here is an example of the conscious process of change. Perhaps you are single and want to be in a relationship. However, whenever you are at a party where there are other single people, you clam up. You get uncomfortable or feel paralyzed, especially if there is someone who seems interesting. You stop yourself from approaching that person out of your fear of rejection. When you get home from the party, you chastise yourself for holding back. However, each time you get to the edge of the cliff of approaching someone and then do not, something does happen. Your frustration builds. You feel lonelier and lonelier until you can no longer tolerate being stuck.

Eventually, your pain motivates you to find the courage to risk reaching out to someone who attracts you. You do not have to get over your fear in order to begin the conversation. You can take your fear with you into the interaction by being honest and saying something similar to, "Hello. I noticed you from across the room. I really wanted to meet you, but I also felt afraid to approach you. In the past I would have let my fear get the better of me. Tonight, I decided to come talk with you anyway and bring my fear along with me. So, here I am, fear and all!"

*How that particular person responds is not nearly as important as the fact that you broke through your paralysis.* That person is going to think either, "What an honest and vulnerable thing to say. I'd like to find out more about you," or, "Why are you telling me all this? I don't want to know about your fear." In either case, you end up a winner. You have discovered a potential friend, or you see that this person did not respond to your vulnerability and you probably would not want to pursue a friendship anyway.

You can walk away from the interaction cheering, "I did it!" You leapt off the "shy cliff." You feel the beginning of a new sense of yourself. You are becoming a person whose fear does not stop them and who is willing to be vulnerable from the outset of meeting someone. Your honesty and vulnerability will eventually have you surrounded by people of like intention (when external Reality catches up with you).

## Meeting

**When attracted to others,**
**You may leave your body**
**To go out and meet them.**

**If you are out there**
**Looking to connect,**
**Who is left at Home**
**For them to contact?**

**True meeting occurs when**
**You invite one another into**
**The core of your experience.**

*The bravest people are not the ones who have no fear. They are the ones who do not let their fear stop them.* They go forward with their fear, trusting that as long as their intentions are good, only good will result. Risking is being willing to take a chance without knowing the outcome beforehand. If you know what is going to happen, then it is not a risk. In other words, *there are no risk-free risks.*

The best way to begin this process is to take small risks first and then experience the results. As you have some successes, then you may be willing to jump off the next cliff more readily. You may also be able to put more on the line.

Be sure to validate the ways you are already risking. This helps you to nurture your self-concept of being a risker. When you think of yourself as someone who steps into challenges rather than shrinks away from them, then your attitude toward Life shifts at a very core level. Here are some possible risks for you to look at.

First, let's look at ways you might risk being with yourself:

♥ Spend undistracted time with yourself.
♥ Notice which attitudes and behaviors serve you and which do not.
♥ Feel your emotions without self-judgement.
♥ Be total in whatever you do, just for the sake of being total, not for the results.
♥ Love the unlovable, in yourself and others.
♥ Be happy.

Now, let's look at ways you might risk being with others:

♥ Get involved with others instead of staying isolated.
♥ See others as part of yourself instead of judging them.
♥ Become intimate with others by exposing your vulnerability to them.
♥ Show your wisdom to others instead of holding back.
♥ Tell your truth to others, both "positive" truths and "negative" ones.
♥ Transform every interaction into a "win/win" situation.

Perhaps you do not see some of the above attitudes as even being risks that you could take. For instance, how is "being happy" a risk? You have to find the courage to not be a victim of negative, destructive thoughts. You have to confront beliefs that are creating you as anything other than happy. As you discover that you have the power to truly choose to be happy by being the master of your mind rather than its victim, your whole universe shifts. As you see that no one else but you can jump off your next cliff, you stop waiting for someone else to make you happy. You keep accessing new levels of realizing that you have the power to create your life the way you want it to be.

Another beautiful mystery in this process is the support that materializes once you have jumped off the cliff. *The Universe waits for you to make the first move. Conscious change cannot happen unless you initiate it.* Once you do, you step into a different rhythm. Events move into alignment to support you. The moment that you step into thin air, there is a chorus of angels there to catch you. They are cheering for you. Then they (the angels, the Universe, God, whatever label you want to use) quietly move behind the scenes to create miracles for the change to manifest.

One reward for risking may be that you meet just the right person in the oddest way. For instance, you finally decide to phone a friend to clear up a misunderstanding, dial the wrong number, and end up falling in love with the person who answers. Or you get an unjust traffic ticket and find the courage to risk going to court to fight against paying the ticket. While waiting in court, you meet an entrepreneur who wants to invest in your latest invention. The specifics of the miracle do not matter. And, yes, it often does take some time for situations to get aligned. But once you commit inside, the magic begins.

As you reap the rewards for your risks, you can never rest on your laurels. Just when you think you have taken the greatest leap, that final leap, that leap to end all leaps, you arrive at the next level and new rules apply.

# Letting Go

**Today's Truth**
**Becomes**
      **Tomorrow's lie.**
**Let go of your**
      **Sacred insights**
      **Daily.**


Whatever worked for you at one point in time was perfect for that moment, but it is not to be held on to too tightly. That leap got you onto another plateau where you may well have received a wonderful reward for having taken the risk. A deep sense of inner peace may prevail for a period of time. But then, inevitably, you begin to discover that on this new plateau are new and unfamiliar spiritual laws that you cannot quite figure out. The puzzle has again become one step beyond your ability to comprehend. *You must let go into being a beginner once more.*

Perhaps one day you will discover a plateau where insights themselves are an illusion. But do not worry. On that mesa will be a new mysterious twist that you cannot quite grasp. However, because you have embraced the wisdom of leaping into the unknown, you will intuitively reach into your Soul for the next risk.

## Chapter Eight
## The Joy of Being Total

As you see beneath the illusion of what appears to be real on this planet, you enter into "The Game of Life" whole-heartedly. The challenge is to embrace this entire Reality as being "you." Everything outside you is only a reflection of what is inside you. Thus, whatever you perceive as "other than you" inevitably appears in the three dimensional world for you to accept. If you fully embrace it, then you pass that particular test. Then the next situation/injustice/person/idea/characteristic appears. If you see it as "not you," then you temporarily flunk and are repeatedly presented with variations of this same challenge until you pass. You need not worry. You have many opportunities to master every aspect of Life.

### The Game of Life

You have boundaries around
How deeply you have accepted
The totality of this Reality.

You are repeatedly presented
With situations just beyond
Your capacity to embrace.

You can reject the lessons and
Stay in the pain of stagnation,
Or include everything as 'you'
And feel the joy of expansion.

Why would you ever choose to stay stuck in the pain of stagnation? Because of fear. And what is fear? In its purest form, it is a useful warning of imminent danger to your safety. If a ferocious animal runs toward you, fear ignites you into action. Fear arising from this survival instinct is rare because you are faced with few life-threatening situations. *Any other form of fear is a negative assumption based solely upon your biased interpretation.*

For instance, an external stimulus occurs, such as an older man with a grey beard walks toward you. You interpret the event through the filters of false fear created by painful past experiences – your father who used to hit you also had a grey beard so you feel afraid and avoid this man who could be a saint. Another destructive fear fantasy is worrying about the future. This type of fear is merely a thought that assumes something ranging from unpleasant to catastrophic is going to happen in the next few moments or next week, year, month, decade, century, or millennium. Your conclusion is not based upon fact but upon fiction within your mind. Fear creates contraction rather than expansion.

### Fear

Fear is a prison guard that
Locks you up in a cell and
Suffocates your aliveness.

Break out of your shackles
By befriending your fear.
Become so intimate that
You no longer fear fear.

Notice that fear is only a mental image passing through your mind. When you travel in fear's vibration, certain thoughts pass through your mind to validate its Reality. Remember, the picture passing through your consciousness arises out of the vibration reverberating within you. Some of those images pass through almost unnoticed. But others are very addictive to you. Adrenaline surges through your body if you obsess on certain thoughts. You can frighten yourself for hours, days, even years, making real a Universe full of reasons to be afraid. *The rush of fear coursing through your Being can be mistaken for a feeling of aliveness.* Thus, you scare yourself to prove you exist.

Another reaction to fear is to close down and feel nothing. When you do this, you deaden yourself and then justify living within your particular set of limitations. Your life becomes a "comfortable" routine. You live in a lukewarm Dream. You may even adopt or reinforce beliefs that help you to stay dead. If you do not make any waves, everything will be all right. *Each moment that you are sitting on your passion is another moment that you are already lying in your grave.* Do not let mere images passing through your mind paralyze you into mediocrity.

## Moderation

**Moderation is
The disease of
Sleeping Souls.**

**Dive into extremes.**

**Only after living on the edge
Does the true middle way
Become available to you.**

The true middle way reveals itself when you embrace *all* aspects of your humanness. You start living in a place inside yourself where you delight in *all* the situations that the Universe presents to you. You celebrate your unique reactions to those situations. Fear no longer controls you. You move about freely both in the external world and within yourself.

If you hold back from expressing your Love, your Life force begins to ebb. Perhaps you think that someday the "right" circumstances will appear and then your Heart will open. Maybe you are waiting for the perfect lover to come along. You hope that someone else will magically lift you out of your dull life into heavenly bliss. *If you are not expressing Love with whomever is in your Life right now, you are nailing the lid on your coffin.*

## Waiting

**When you hold back your Love
Waiting to find more elsewhere,
You learn how to wait,
Not how to Love.**

A woman spent an evening with a group of her closest friends who had known each other for years. They had supported one another through many crises and lover relationships. The woman, who was single, complained that she had no Love in her life. Suddenly, as she looked around the intimate circle of beloved companions, her Heart burst open with a new insight. She already had tons of Love, if she let herself receive it. *Just because the Love did not fit her picture of 'lover,' she was invalidating it.* She laughed aloud and began hugging her friends. Interestingly, she met the man of her dreams several weeks later.

If you want to "be total," dive into Life head-on. Search out newness and vitality rather than feeling trapped by your circumstances. Express your exuberance instead of tip-toeing through Life, afraid to rock the boat. Giggle with childlike innocence and excitement.

Have you noticed that when you give toddlers a new toy, they often jump up and down and wiggle every part of their body because they cannot contain their exhilaration? It is almost irrelevant what the toy is. They are waiting for any excuse to express joy. They are so full of Life that, given the opportunity, they are eager to explore and to explode. That same aliveness is inside you, probably sitting dormant most of the time. But you can tickle it and wake it up. If you do, your life will never be the same.

Start to awaken your joy. Rather than watching television in the evening, go to a dance class or take a walk and enjoy the sunset. Start painting or writing instead of only thinking about it. Volunteer with AIDS patients. Move in with your lover instead of waiting. Go back to school to study whatever *you* want to pursue this time. Quit your job and travel around the world for a year. Jump off the fence of indecision. The side on which you land does not matter as much as the fact that you are no longer sitting paralyzed on the fence.

Take the risk to put your wildest dreams into action instead of just fantasizing about "someday." Too many people have been snatched up by Death before they took the chance. You never know when Death will visit you or a loved one.

## An Appointment with Death

In the Middle Ages, there was a young man who was walking in the woods and saw the black-cloaked figure of Death near-by. Terror began coursing through his veins. He was too young to die. He ran home, jumped on his horse, and galloped into the distance. He pushed his horse to run all day long, never looking back, as he tried to put as many miles as he could between himself and Death.

Finally, at sunset, both the man and the horse collapsed in exhaustion by a stream on the other side of the kingdom. As he crawled to the edge of the water to drink, he looked up and there was Death looking down at him.

As the man cowered in his last moment of Life, Death said to him, "When I saw you this morning on the other side of the kingdom, I knew we had an appointment by this stream at sunset. I wondered how you would ever make it here on time."

Your appointment with Death may be sooner than you think. *Ask yourself daily, "If I were to die at sunset, how do I want to live this day?"* What would your priorities be? How would you spend your time? What risks would you take within yourself and with others? Would you refuse to forgive anyone? How would you live more totally?

Reach out to others instead of isolating yourself. Reveal your innermost thoughts to friends so that you can be seen for yourself instead of molding yourself into whomever you think others want you to be. Speak up in ways that say, "Here I am," without being pushy or obnoxious. Quit blaming others for any shallow conversations you have and start asking the kinds of questions that elicit genuine responses. Be the one who initiates contact with others instead of waiting for someone else to do it. Dare to approach an attractive stranger and say, "Hello. I noticed you from across the room and I feel an attraction to you. Can we talk?" Quit assuming that the world is a hostile, unfriendly place. If you consciously search for evidence that people are warm and loving, then that is exactly what you find.

Rather than being aloof, risk becoming involved in Life. Ask your closest friends if it is okay to tell them something that you believe would be useful for them to hear but you have been afraid to say. Also ask for their honest feedback about you.

What if you were to frequently say, "I love you," to family members and friends for whom you genuinely care? Why not? It may feel awkward at first if you have not said the words aloud very often. But the rewards are that your Hearts may open. Love can start to flow instead of merely being an unspoken understanding. You can invite family and friends along with you into your next level of being real. On the other hand, you must also be willing to let go of them if they do not accept your invitation.

Perhaps you were deeply hurt when you parted ways with a past lover. Perhaps you became afraid of feeling that depth of pain again so you avoid being vulnerable with others. Rather than numbing yourself and unconsciously putting yourself on hold, it is useful to notice if your life became more meaningful out of the depth of your involvement. You probably feel both pain and joy in new ways because your Heart was touched. Allow yourself to be grateful that you risked with this person because of what you learned.

"Being total" within yourself means diving fully into your own psyche. When Socrates said, "Know thyself," he was not just making polite conversation. Become fascinated with your inner workings. Look inward as you move through the external world. Notice every nuance of your reactions to every event so that you can learn the ways you separate yourself from Life. Focus your passion inward as well as outward. Let your need to uncover the Truth about your inner world be so encompassing that you become excited when you sense your next fear surfacing. Let your thirst for Truth be quenched by the most minute insight into your mind's subtle delusions. *When you are so hungry for Love that you would kill (your own ego) for it, then you are headed Home.*

## The Next Breath

A seeker came to a great Master and wanted to be initiated as his disciple. The Master told him to come back in a month. When he came back, the Master told him to wait outside for him. After many hours of sitting outside, the seeker became quite impatient but sensed that this was some sort of a test so he continued to wait.

After several more hours, the Master finally approached him and said, "Come with me." The would-be disciple followed the Master's lead to a near-by river. When they arrived on its banks, the Master walked directly into the river. The seeker followed without hesitation. As they were facing each other in the water which was up to their shoulders, the Master unexpectedly leapt upon the man and held him under the water in a vicelike grip for a long time. On the shore other disciples became extremely concerned as time kept passing. The seeker was beginning to turn blue and unable to escape. As he was fighting desperately for his life, for his next breath, he thought, "This guy is a madman instead of a Master."

Suddenly, the Master released him. The seeker sprang to the surface gasping for a gulp of Life-saving oxygen. The Master immediately looked deeply in his eyes and said to him, "When you want Love as passionately as you wanted that breath of air, then and only then will you find it."

Inner peace is born when you know that you are headed in the right direction. If you are reading this book, you have already jumped into the ocean of seekers. Sometimes you may feel as if you are drowning, but you are also gasping for that urgent, Life-seeking breath. The wisest choice is to enjoy swimming in the ocean. You can never return to the shore where you used to be drowning in the sorrow of living half-heartedly.

When you live totally, your life may be more emotionally chaotic. Yet, you will also have more depth and richness and fullness. Before choosing to "go for it," the chaos can feel like an inward, silent desperation. After jumping into the ocean, it changes into an overt cry for your right to live passionately. As you purposely dive into experiences that most people run from, you learn that you can handle anything that comes your way. *Instead of Life being a drudgery to endure, it transforms into a challenging and bold adventure into the unknown.*

## Chapter Nine
# Embracing It All!

Question:  "What did the Buddhist monk say to the hot dog vendor?"
Answer:    "Make me one with everything!"

Ah, yes!  That ancient wisdom of realizing that you are all of this, and that all of this is you.  It is exquisite to revel in thoughts of oneness.  You may even have a fantasy that someday you will have a transcendental experience that opens the doors for you to absolutely know that every molecule of this earthplane Reality is "you."  But what if it does not all happen in a flash?

I used to believe that "Enlightenment" was a one-time explosion that would catapult me into the core of Love inside my Being.  My picture was that after this dramatic experience had somehow magically occurred, Peter's ego would vanish.  "I" would forevermore be an empty vessel for Love to pour through, never indulging in human weaknesses again.

One day years ago I went to an art exhibit where there was a display of four paintings entitled, "Enlightenment," by an artist whose name I no longer remember.  Each painting depicted the exact same scene in Nature with only the subtlest change in the hues, colors, lighting, and perspective. What short-circuited in me as I kept looking at this masterpiece was that nothing dramatic was happening.  No bright white light.  No spectrum of rainbow colors carrying me into other realms.  No orgasmic realizations.  There was just a quiet, peaceful shift of consciousness allowing Life to be seen anew.  I walked away from those paintings with my ideas about Enlightenment shattered.

What if "Enlightenment" is a gradual and subtle process?  What if you are already being presented daily opportunities to embrace yet another small piece of this Reality as being "you"?  There may be many aspects of the human experience that you wish you did not have, that you do not want to "own" as being a part of you.  Other people can have some "flaw," but not you.

Do you know that recognizing a certain quality inside you does not mean that you have to act upon it?  You can acknowledge the monsters inside you without letting them dominate you.  Your recognition of them is the first step in getting power over them.  When you are in denial about their existence, then they can sneak in and covertly take over.

## Disowning

**Strong contraction or expansion**
**Shows you are lost in the illusion**
**Of being separate from the whole.**

Overcoming this denial starts by noticing what you perceive as "not you," both positively and negatively.  Judgement, contempt, or disdain toward any person or idea shows that you are pushing away some aspect of your humanity.  On the other hand, overwhelming exhilaration when you meet an enlightened person, or "fall in Love," or enter a temple, or read inspirational writings may be you perceiving the source of Love as "out there."

*Seeing all aspects of Life as being 'you' frees you from the poison of judging yourself, others, and the earthplane.*  Ironically, you may more readily push away the positive elements of yourself than the negative ones.  It is often easier to condemn yourself for the Hitler who lives inside you than to celebrate the Christ or Buddha within you.  You may think that feeling good about yourself is being narcissistic or self-indulgent.  Thus, in the name of humility, you become self-effacing.  If you recognize that you are actually degrading the God/Goddess manifest in human form, then you can rightfully question the usefulness of allowing destructive thoughts to hurt you. When you stop pretending that you are separate from any aspect of this Reality, then you can start expanding your concept of who you are.

## Expansion

The Universe taps upon
The outer edges of all
You have embraced
Of Earth's Reality.

If you hear the tap and
Open to include more,
You will experience
Exuberant expansion.

If you ignore the tap by
Clinging to limitations,
It becomes a knocking,
And then a pounding,
Demanding you open.

The pounding becomes
More and more painful
As the Universe cracks
Your brittle boundaries.

If you gently open to
The tap of the new,
You can prevent
Useless suffering.

*One of the most misunderstood sources of pain is in believing that your negative thoughts are 'you.'* As you search for your goodness, you must go underneath negative childhood programming which said that you were "no good." As an adult, you must expose the lie fed to you by your parents, society, and/or religion that your basic motivating force is evil in nature. As you begin to affirm yourself as worthwhile and well-intentioned, you enjoy a deep sigh of relief. A pure, innocent Love of Self is born. As you breathe into that newly acquired self-image, an inner beauty emerges. You finally walk on the planet not feeling guilty for being alive. At last, you experience being "okay."

*After you have enjoyed this gift for a while, the Universe gives you the opportunity to investigate a more primary negative force than parental or societal programming.* Since all human experiences are contained within each human being, you begin to get glimpses of a more fundamental evil and goodness inside you. Having recently healed your self-esteem, there can be a lot of resistance to seeing the parts of yourself that you wish were not there. You may think that you have won the ultimate war with your parents or society, but you have only won one of many battles with more encompassing cosmic forces.

Once you know that you are basically a good person, the Universe presents you with possibilities for new levels of awareness. You have opportunities to explore the positive and negative archetypal parts of you, such as the creator of beauty and the destroyer of all that is precious. Or the sensitive, compassionate benefactor who wants to save the world and the murderer who hates all other humans. Or the most tender, sweet lover who just wants to cuddle and the mad rapist who wants to plunder. Or the most honest, forthright, trustworthy person and the thief with no morals who cleverly cheats others.

Seeing these parts means that you are becoming aware of their existence inside you. You think the thoughts and have the feelings that these aspects of your humanness think and feel.  As the darkest, negative ones come forward in your consciousness, you may want to push them away because you have just claimed your basic goodness.  You may even mistake these voices as old ones from your childhood.  You may think that all your work on yourself has failed.  But, if you examine them closely, you will notice a different quality to them.  They arise from a more fundamental place, a more universal place, than do parental admonitions.  The negative ones can seem so despicable that you cannot believe anyone would ever think them.  However, as you step into meeting their challenge, you know that you are dealing with the core of your journey here on Earth.  You can frame them in such a way that you celebrate when the "worst" ones arrive.

## The Unlovable

**Loving**
**The lovable**
**Is easy.**

**Loving**
**The unlovable**
**Is Enlightening.**

There are many opportunities to embrace "the unlovable," both in the external world and within yourself.  *In the end, your Reality is not created by what you think and feel, but by how you respond to what you think and feel.*  After all, thoughts and feelings are only thoughts and feelings.  You need not "do" anything about them.  You can just observe them with fascination and curiosity.  Whatever you consider "unlovable" is whatever you judge as being inappropriate to even exist.  Are you wiser than the Creator of this Reality?

The negative is needed to be able to see the positive.  Good needs evil as a contrasting background to be perceived.  Love needs hate, peace needs war, satiation needs starvation, honesty needs dishonesty, trust needs betrayal, compassion needs cruelty.  Each element balances the whole spectrum and must be acknowledged as an essential part of the whole.

*The rewards of choosing to embrace the unembracable are often the most subtle and the most expansive.*  The challenge is for you to choose what to focus upon and to make real, especially when situations appear to be negative.

## So Be It

In ancient times, there was a highly respected sage who lived on the outskirts of a small town.  Many people came to him for counsel and were grateful to receive his gentle wisdom.  Many believed him to be Enlightened.

A young woman from the town became pregnant and had the baby out of wedlock.  The punishment for this was exile unless she named the father.  She falsely claimed that the sage was the father so that she would not be banished and could still see her secret lover.  The townspeople were outraged at the sage.  They came to his hut shouting insults at him.  They placed the baby on his doorstep for him to raise.  His only comment was, "So be it."

Soon no one came to see the sage anymore.  Everyone condemned him and avoided him.  Meanwhile, he joyfully went about the task of raising the child with all the Love in his Heart.  One day, the mother of the child saw the sage in rags begging for food.  She felt extremely guilty.  When she could no longer bear the burden of her lie being the reason that this gentle man was being mistreated, she admitted to the townspeople that he was not the father.

A humbled group then approached his hut and told him of the young woman's admission.  They took the child back from him and apologized for their haughty assumptions.  The sage's only response was, "So be it."

This wise man had no need to prove anything to anyone, nor for Life to look a certain way. He did not defend himself against injustice. When falsely accused, he accepted. When exonerated, he accepted. He just let it all unfold. He was so deeply trusting of his own integrity, he had no need for anyone else to know his Truth. His joy was not dependent upon external circumstances.

How are you at seeing perfection within what looks unfair? Are you getting so rooted in your Love that you are not knocked around by everyday events? Life is made up of a series of experiences, one after the other. *You may be so busy searching for the most 'meaningful' or the most 'transformational' experiences that you may forget that it is within the mundane that the profound awaits.* When you see a mother scolding her child in the supermarket and find compassion instead of judgement for them, then you are learning to live in harmony.

About ten years ago, I had a series of traffic violations that became a great teacher for me. The first time I was pulled over for speeding, I was so afraid of the repercussions that I barely noticed the police officer with whom I was spending a few brief moments of my life. As he drove away, I realized that I had just missed an opportunity.

## Acceptance

**Acceptance is feeling
Love in your Heart
For the police officer
Who is writing you
A speeding ticket.**

My challenge became to feel loving toward the police officer for the whole time that we were interacting. It took me several more tickets to get to that stage. By the third time, when I saw the flashing red light in my rear view mirror, I felt excited at the opportunity to love this person who was about to give me a ticket. We had a great interaction. He even told me about his recent vacation in Hawaii. I thanked him for the ticket. As we parted, there was only a feeling of goodwill on my part.

As you look at "Embracing It All" internally, there are some core aspects of your humanness that can be especially difficult to face. One that is often pushed away is the desire to commit suicide. Yet one of the most valid questions one can ask is: "Is Life worth living?" Usually when you ask such a difficult question, your experience of Life has been so painful that it may well make more sense to leave it all behind. The statement you are really making is that you would rather die than live in Hell. In one sense, that is a very powerful stand to take. When suicidal voices are shouting inside you or inside a friend, be sure to listen for their underlying message. It is so scary to let these voices speak that most people try to push them aside. If you can hear the crying out for the right to live in a happier world, then there is a healthy way to hold them.

Leaving Muktananda's Ashram after the Satori experience I had in 1974 (see page 18), I dove into a suicidal abyss. If I could not live in the state of bliss all the time, it seemed crazy to stay on this planet. As those poisonous thoughts filled me, I realized that they had something to teach me. At one point, it seemed to me that the whole point of being born onto the Earth is to see what a nightmare it is here, and then to choose to kill yourself out of self-compassion. My reasoning went something like this: Suicide is the number one taboo because it is the exact route to ultimate freedom. The bravest people are the ones who face up to this harsh realization and do something about it. The only sane act on this insane planet is to eliminate this Reality and see what is next. *I felt that the most caring choice was to kill me.* As soon as I saw the irony of destroying myself in order to love myself, a belly laugh came rolling out of me. And with that insight, the desire to take my life disappeared. I was immediately reborn into a much more loving Reality. The nightmare in which I had been living was transformed into a sweeter dream full of kindness and gentleness because I made the choice that I would rather die than continue slowly starving in the desert.

## Suicide

**Embrace your suicidal self**
**Until you feel it may well be**
**The most sane part of you.**

**Only then are you**
**Free to choose Life.**

As you progress in "loving the unlovable," many ideals of how Life is "supposed" to be on planet Earth alter radically. As you allow yourself and others to be human, the space is created for you to let go of beliefs that are hurting you. For instance, attaining "inner peace" is a worthy goal. Or is it? *What if your picture of what inner peace 'should' look like is getting in the way of your having it?*

## Inner Peace

**Inner Peace is not**
**Feeling calm inside.**

**Inner Peace is**
**Allowing your experience**
**Each new moment in time.**

**Inner Peace may mean**
**Weeping tears of sorrow,**
**Or allowing your anger,**
**Or feeling the rapture**
**Of sexual ecstasy.**

**By not judging yourself,**
**Especially when you feel**
**Turmoil churning inside,**
**Inner Peace is always Now.**

As you "Embrace It All," be open to the destruction of your ideas of what is real. *Your ideas and ideals themselves can be exactly what are in the way of being in the middle of an experience that occurs in realms where there are no ideas and ideals.* Let all your opinions and viewpoints die so that an unlimited, formless bliss can be born.

## Chapter Ten
# The Cycle of Death and Rebirth

In Western society, Death is believed to be a horrible catastrophe. People have an unspoken agreement never to mention the subject because it is too dreadful to talk about. As parents get older, families often feel awkward about discussing a will or funeral plans. When people are in the hospital dying, rarely does anyone talk openly with them about what is imminent. It looks as if the dying are being protected from a morbid subject. *However, it is really people's denial around facing their own death that keeps the subject taboo.*

It is time to break that taboo and to educate yourself about Death. By deepening your understanding of Death, you can clarify any misunderstanding you may have toward this beautiful human experience. Death is a "process," not just an isolated moment which occurs and then is over. It is a transition. It is a dropping away of all that is not permanent, of all that is an illusion, of all that is "not Love." As you dive underneath the surface appearances of this Reality, you begin to perceive the external world as an elaborate Dream. It is merely the backdrop for your classroom of learning experiences. And Death is one of the greatest teachers, one of the greatest illuminators. It frees you from all your attachments so that you become the Love you have been seeking.

In 1977, I had a brush with Death that transformed my orientation toward Life. While hitchhiking from California to Michigan late one night in the steep mountains of Idaho, I was given a ride by a cowboy in a pick-up truck. As we were driving around a sharp bend on a narrow two lane road, he started to pass a semi-trailer truck. I was shocked that he was even attempting this. Just as we were alongside the truck, speeding toward us head-on was a huge passenger bus honking its horn. There was no place for us to go. Surely death had us, or, at the very minimum, a terrible accident was a micro-second away. Suddenly, Reality seemed to be warping. *For just an instant, time and space opened a door into another realm.* The next thing we knew, we were still driving on the road, but we had somehow passed the bus and the truck without so much as a scratch. We continued to drive in silent disbelief as neither of us could comprehend what had just occurred.

Shortly thereafter, at about 2 a.m., the cowboy let me out of his truck on the freeway near Missoula, Montana, because we were headed in different directions. I followed my urge to walk into the middle of a large field and lie down. While looking up at the full moon, I began to feel the depth of what had just taken place. I found myself sobbing with terror. Then every one of my molecules was being washed with Love on a cosmic level. Suddenly, I shot up out of my body. I looked down on me and realized that I was dying. As I floated away from my body, it seemed insignificant. My Being started to expand, reaching out to blend with infinity. *Then my whole Reality exploded into a deafening Silence.* In the middle of that stillness was an endless, peaceful void with no fear. I was being loved by the most compassionate consciousness possible.

A tunnel appeared and I blissfully started down it. Then a deep, friendly voice said to me, "You can either go on to your Death or go back to Earth and let everyone there know that Death is not anything to fear." I immediately thought of my parents. Somehow, if I could let them know the beauty of Death, perhaps they could fearlessly embrace it. My next thought was, "I want to go back and let them know." With that, I came back out of the tunnel and saw my body lying on the ground below me.

I floated down and re-entered my body. I felt completely outside the realm of human time. I was afraid that I could not synchronize with linear Reality. As I walked back to the freeway, I saw a policeman who had just given someone a ticket. I immediately thought, "Who could better help me attune to Earth's Reality than a policeman?" I went over to him and started chatting. If you recall, 1977 was not long after the Vietnam War ended. Here I was, a bearded backpacker with a long pony tail hitchhiking in the middle of "redneck" territory. But the Love pouring through me allowed us to become friends instantly. I told him that I was exhausted from hitchhiking. He offered to let me sleep in Missoula's jail for the night.  I happily agreed.  He gave me a ride to the police station, where I had an uproarious time with the men on duty.  We laughed and laughed.

For the next few days, just walking down the street was an adventure.  Anyone who came within five feet of me seemed to be automatically transformed into feeling happy.  People would frequently approach me and start talking, not knowing that what they really wanted was to bathe in the energy of Love.

This experience dramatically altered me in many ways, some of which I am still discovering twenty years later.  We are so much more than we appear to be.

## You

**You are not**
**Just a body**
**With a Soul**
**Inside.**

**You are a Soul**
**Gift-wrapped**
**With a body.**

The ease with which I left my body without any earthshaking repercussions opened an incredible perspective on what is usually perceived as a traumatic event.  As I looked down on my body before entering the tunnel, it held about as much significance as a finger nail clipping in the waste basket.  Many people fear the pain that their loved ones suffer when they die.  *But the real pain is in people's resistance to Death, not in the experience of Death itself.*  Death's catastrophe lies with the anguishing loss for the people who are left behind.  They must let go of their deep attachments by facing the grieving process.  For the person who dies, there is only the joy of freedom.

## Death's Significance

**When your body**
**Drops away from**
**Your Soul,**
**Your essence**
**May or may not**
**Blink.**

A profound transformation is especially available in the final seconds before leaving your body.  The distinct alteration of time and space in those last few moments makes *anything* possible.  You are no longer subject to the limitations of linear Reality.  If you have dealt with your fear of Death, a miracle can unfold.

## Death

**Become friends with Death**
**While you are still alive.**

**If you are laughing with Death**
**As you are leaving your body,**
**You blissfully dissolve into One.**

After your body dies, you do "go on." The post-body journey begins with the exquisite ecstasy of removing the illusions of separation created by "I." When you know this, rather than fearing Death, an eagerness for the adventure is born. Ironically, the memory of my own experience of profound bliss sometimes sparks in me a desire to die because I long to quench my thirst with the depth of Love that I know awaits me.

Knowledge of your "Foreverness" can also awaken a poignant perspective on the ephemeral nature of your earthly pursuits. A wonderful fable illustrates this point:

## Beyond Death

Once there was a woman who came to Buddha in great grief. Her four-year-old son had died very suddenly. She was weeping and wailing. Her son had been the whole focus of her life. It did not seem fair that he had been taken away. She felt like she was being punished by God. She asked Buddha to perform a miracle and bring her son back to life.

Buddha said, "Go around to the people in the different houses in town. If you can find a home where no one has ever had a relative or a friend die unexpectedly, then I will use my powers to give Life to your son."

She got very excited and began to go house by house through the town. As the day passed, she started to become discouraged because in every home people had their story of Death's injustice. She kept trying and trying, though, because she so desperately wanted Buddha to bring her son back.

Finally, on the third day, it dawned on her. Someone in every house had been exposed to the sudden loss of loved ones. Everyone had to come to terms with Death, including herself. There was nothing personal going on here. God was not punishing her. She was learning to deal with the impermanence of this Reality.

Then she realized at an even deeper level that her joy had always been dependent upon the transitory realities of the external world. She came running back to Buddha and fell at his feet as she cried out, "Initiate me as your disciple. You need not bring my son back because now I know that if he were alive and then were to die again, my joy would be taken away again. I must find inside myself the place of Love that cannot be touched by Death, the place that knows and is Forever."

*As you search inside yourself for this eternal place, you begin to see that all you have believed to be 'you' has been an illusion.* Whatever you have identified with is transitory, whether it is your house, job, spouse, family, or even your body, personality, feelings, thoughts, and opinions. It is very scary to fully allow yourself to know this because everything you have ever sought other than the absolutely still place deep in your Heart must be released. All else must die.

## The Process of Elimination

**'Who you are' is
Who is left standing naked
After you have explored
All the possibilities of
Who you are not.**

Allowing yourself to be this naked beckons another kind of Death: the Death within Life which is instrumental for change and growth. Look back over the various stages of your development. Can you see that the person you are today is very different from the "you" of ten or twenty years ago? *Learning lessons from your experiences has molded and shaped you into a new human being, resembling the old but with an emerging unfamiliarity.*

One example of this process is noticing that the "you" who wanted casual affairs may have died and "you" now want a committed relationship (or vice versa). Or the soft spoken, subservient "you" may have transformed into an assertive, direct communicator. Or the "you" who never wanted to have children begins to fade as the desire to become a parent enters. Or the "you" who was always physically active has become more sedentary.

There are countless other transformations, some subtle and some blatant. Some of these transitions have been slow, some quick, some painful, some easy, some desirable, and some unwanted. In any event, if the "you" of today were in the same situations that you were in ten or twenty years ago, your reactions and decision making process would be different. The wisdom and understanding or the bitterness and mistrust you gain through living alters who you are.

When you were younger, you made certain decisions regarding what you thought would make you happy based upon what you knew then. As you grow older, whatever dreams you have chased for many years may not have brought you the deep satisfaction you had thought they would. Your priorities begin to shift. The time that has been so diligently spent pursuing money or power or a less-than-meaningful career may suddenly feel like a waste. Your previous understanding of your purpose on Earth dissolves. The courage it takes both to see this and to do something about it is awesome. *A tremendous amount of energy must be accessed to change the thrust of the essential direction of your life.*

Whereas before you were so busy being busy, family and friends may now become the priority. Quiet moments with loved ones can become tangibly precious. Intimately communicating with others becomes essential to your well-being. To make this shift, a death of the old "you" and a birth of the new "you" needs to occur. Your conscious movement toward that death makes your evolution faster, quite intense, and often painful. However, if you see the wisdom of risking these changes, any avoidance becomes even more painful. You begin to see the old thoughts and beliefs that no longer serve you. But you may experience difficulty in letting go of a part of you, even if you do not like it, because it is an old, familiar "friend."

For example, take Trust. As you pursue more satisfying relationships, you may see how your beliefs about not trusting others have perpetuated your isolation. As your desire for the end of your mistrust increases, you can see how stubborn the old thinking patterns are. It sometimes seems easier to cling to the old than to embrace the new, even when you like the new more. You identify "I" as being mistrustful. But if you feel the pain that your lack of trust has caused, you get highly motivated to change. You start to risk trusting others. As you vulnerably reveal the truth of your inability to trust and feel the depth of your anguish, magically a more trusting "you" starts to be born. It takes time and repeated awareness to let the old "you" die and to birth this new "you" who trusts. Often, the closer you are to letting go of the old "you," the more tenacious that part becomes. It does not want to die. It is afraid of Death. In a last moment of desperation, the old "you" flares up in one last attempt to stay alive. Knowing this, you can greet its last effort to survive with appreciation for its tenacity rather than with the belief that you can never change.

Many of Life's lessons involve embracing this type of Death. This is not the Death of your body. This is the Death of your ego, the Death of whomever you currently identify as "I." *This 'I' is only an illusion that keeps you separate from the whole.* Whereas before you may have identified yourself more as your role such as "I, a businessperson," or "I, a mother" or "I, a father," your self-identity begins to move inward. You may next begin to see you as "I, a feeling person," or "I, a person who is growing," or "I, a seeker of Love." As you keep on letting go of "you" on your inward journey, Love fills in the empty space that "you" have just vacated. Each Death brings forth a more loving "I." Eventually all of "I" falls away until there is just Love left. *'I' becomes and is Love.*

Once you have repeatedly seen and experienced the rewards of "The Cycle of Death and Rebirth," you can get excited each time you come to the brink of ego disaster. Stepping into what I humorously call the "perverse challenge," you might say to yourself, "Oh boy!

My judgemental thoughts are here in full force. They must be about to die because they are being so stubborn right now." You become more willing to face and feel the pain of letting go. *You know that if another portion of you dies that there will be less 'I' and more Love.* You are well on your way to discovering that you are so much more than your thoughts and desires.

## Ego Deaths

**When an old idea of
'Who you are' dies,
A new you is born.**

**These deaths repeat
Until no *you* is left
To be annihilated.**

      Integrating Death into Life is essential. Death is a vital force in the transformation of your Being. Death destroys anything that is not real, including your toxic thoughts and desires, your false personality, and finally your body. What is left is pure light, pure Love. So give up your resistance to the process. Quit hanging on to the security of your identity. Let your thirst for Love make you totally irrational. Within illogical madness, you discover the Death of who you think you are and the birth of a magnificent void known as Love.

## Deepening Your Commitment

**You came to Earth to die
While still in your body.**

**If you are not willing to
Put your ego on the line
In order to find Love,
Love can't find you.**

# Section Four

# The Illusions of the Mind

## Beyond Beliefs

When you go beyond beliefs,
You discover that Truth is
A state of consciousness,
Not an idea.

### Chapter Eleven

# That's You in the Mirror

One of Earth's most pervasive illusions is that Reality exists outside you. In fact, the *only* place where you experience the external world is inside yourself. Vision takes place inside your eyeballs, as objects register on your optic nerves and then are interpreted by your brain. Hearing occurs inside your ears, as three tiny bones vibrate and pass on their messages for translation. *Every* experience you have of Reality occurs *inside* you. What you see, hear, feel, taste, or smell is deciphered through your own unique filtering of whatever appears to exist externally. You are living in your *interpretation* of Reality, rather than in Reality itself.

It seems as if you are on the same planet as the person next to you. You are not. If three people are on the beach admiring a seashell, each person has a different experience of it because of past history with shells and varying predisposed propensities to receive through the five senses. One person may notice the shape of the shell, another may primarily enjoy the color, and the third feels its texture. If it is the first time one person has ever seen a seashell, no sentimental memories color that person's experience. Whereas if another has spent summers vacationing on the beach, then that person may well get nostalgic to the point of tears. All three may agree, "The shell is beautiful," but for completely different reasons. Three different shells are being experienced.

Chapter One, "The Art of Being," explains that one way to discover where you are inside yourself is to observe what you notice as you walk down the street. *What registers in your mind from the myriad of external stimuli is always the reflection of the vibration you are attuned to internally.* The eyes are not only "the windows of the Soul."

## Eyes

**If you observe what**
**Your vision notices,**
**Your eyes become**
**The mirror for your**
**State of consciousness.**

Your perceptions of Reality create your unique Dream. *The external world is neutral. You are the variable.* You provide the color, tone, flavor, and texture by your choice of how you interpret the stimuli.

When interacting with people, you can consciously cultivate attitudes that help you to pay attention to their Souls rather than to their personalities. What you see is dependent upon how deeply you look into others. Knowing this, you can start creating more meaningful connections with people by not letting yourself be distracted by unrewarding superficialities.

## Personality

**Humans are both**
**Neurotic and Divine.**

**Why would you focus on**
**The level of personality**
**And miss your chance**
**To see God?**

77

*Since you are the sole creator of your interpretations of this Dream, you can choose whether to live in a nightmare or in paradise.* You can examine any beliefs or attitudes that create the pain of separation rather than the joy of joining.

Most religions, which could be sources for unifying all human beings, instead create rivalry and disharmony between people of differing faiths.

## Sameness

**Religions create labels such as**
**Jewish or Christian or Hindu,**
**Making paths appear different.**

**The holy mountain favors no one.**
**The same Truth is revealed to each**
**As Love's universal secrets unfold.**

**If we stop believing these labels**
**And start listening to our Hearts,**
**Then we can join together as One.**

Some beliefs can have you unconsciously hold back your Love. The concept of "Soul Mate" may keep you waiting for just the "right" person to appear rather than seeing that whoever is in front of you is a person to love. Similar to the woman who complained that she had no Love in her life as she was surrounded by loving friends, the idea that there is only one special person to love can cause you to miss the beauty within others.

## Your Soul Mate

**If you risk looking deeply**
**Into the eyes of *any* person,**
**You'll find your Soul Mate**
**For that moment in time.**

As you move through the external world, you can make many choices that create Heaven here on Earth. *You can be open to finding teachers in different forms who lead you into experiences of the Now rather than perpetuate your mind's illusions.*

Young children can be incredible teachers. They are frequently very close to the source of joy. If you are at a party and feel bored, spend some time with the children who are there. Allow them to become your vehicle into experiencing a zest for Life. As you let go of "you" and tune into the kids, they show you the treasures within an innocent Now. You will discover a very different party than if you only talked with other adults. When you get home, you may feel a certain lightness because the kids helped you attune to the present tense. What is more important than this?

## Through a Child's Eyes

**Look at the world through**
**The eyes of a two-year-old**
**If you want to see Now.**

Nature is another profound teacher. Remember, the natural world is already traveling in Love's vibration. It beckons you to tune into its rhythm of bliss. I had a life altering experience with a fly who landed on my hand and began rubbing his head with his front legs. If I had listened to my linear mind, I would have shooed it away as a dirty insect. Instead, I listened to my Heart and allowed this fly to become my teacher for a little while. I became fascinated with watching him. I began feeling Love for him and felt his Love flowing to me. Then he quit rubbing his head. I felt disappointed because I wanted him to continue. As my desire for him to be different entered, he flew away because I was no longer loving him unconditionally. I quickly recognized what I had done and asked him to forgive me. Instantly, he flew back onto my hand and started rubbing his head again. The next time he stopped, I simply kept admiring him without my own agenda. In that moment, our connection grew deeper, and I still feel Love for him today.

An ordinary tree also blessed me. I was on a meditation retreat and had been diving into inner realms for several days. At one point, I went for a walk on a hillside and sat down beneath an everyday California oak tree. Suddenly, I felt the tree literally showering me with Love. As I looked up in gratitude, light was pouring down from the tree's limbs onto me. We were vibrating in the same rhythm. For a short period of time, I was open to the energy that is always present, but that I often distract myself from attuning to.

Flowers are another beautiful reflection of our innermost nature. They can become your sex education teacher. *Do you realize that flowers are the sex organs of a plant?* They are the equivalent of the plant's genitalia. A flower is a plant's expression of an extended orgasm. What if everyone perceived their own genitalia to be as beautiful as a flower?

You can celebrate your orgasms with the same explosion of joy that creates flowers. Imagine if the world's negative distortion of sexuality's tender expression could be healed.

## Flowering

**Buds burst into flowers
As green plants bloom
In an orgasmic miracle.**

**May you divinely cherish
The flowering beauty of
*Your* sexual blossoming.**

Inner and outer Reality? Neither exists as independent from the other. Me versus you. Us versus them. These are all destructive, painful illusions. So why not just melt?

## Perceptions

**Arrogance
Perceives
Others as less.**

**Humility
Perceives
Others as more.**

**Enlightenment
Perceives
No other.**

## Chapter Twelve
# The Trap of Psychological Processing

Here you are on Earth with an incredible mystery to solve: How can you unlock the door to Happiness? You may have delved into this question for years by trying to understand the workings of your psyche. Perhaps you have analyzed and re-experienced your childhood traumas. Perhaps you have seen the sources of your negative thinking patterns. Perhaps you can honestly communicate your feelings to others. Yet, you still feel something is missing.

You may be ripe for a quantum leap in consciousness. You may be ready to spend more time in other dimensions of your Being than in the realm of linear thoughts. You may see the trap of psychological processing. Mental insights are beautiful, even orgasmic at times. And yet, they can keep your experience of Life limited. There are many other divine chambers in the palace of your Being to explore. But if you do not know that there are secret doors leading into new rooms, you can remain at the level of thought forever. You do not need to know the blueprint of your inner temple in order to find these rooms. You only have to let go of the ingrained habit you may have of thinking your way through Life.

## Choice

**Your most profound choice**
**Each new moment in time**
**Is whether you are**
**Lost in thoughts**
**Or lost in Love.**

*An extremely valuable insight into the exploration of consciousness is to see the trap of trying to solve your problems by using your mind.* The negative mind is the creator of problems. It wants you to have problems because as long as you are identified with your negative thoughts, it stays alive, vibrant and in control of your inner state.

## Simplicity

**The mind distorts**
**Truth's simplicity**
**Into mental complexity**
**For its self-perpetuation.**

Cogitating is similar to mental masturbation – without the satisfaction of an orgasm. You are tickled and teased into many possibilities. Yet, you are still inexplicably agitated. Something unnamable is missing. You sense that inner peace lies just beyond your grasp.

## Peace of Mind

**Peace of mind**
**Is impossible.**

**Where Mind is**
**Peace is not.**

81

*You cannot cure the mind's negativity by using the mind.* That is like trying to clean your clothes by rubbing them with dirt or trying to end violence by waging war. When you are vibrating in the level of consciousness where problems seem to be real, your sole task is to use your awareness to observe that your negative mind has tricked you into believing that something is wrong. Once you have clearly discerned this covert manipulation, your next challenge is to take the quantum leap from your mind into Love.

## Problems

**Resolutions to problems
Can never be found within
The state of consciousness
Called *worry* which only
Perpetuates all problems.**

**You must shift your very vibration,
By looking inside with awareness
Or meditating to open your Heart
Or feeling the problem's pain
Or moving into sexuality
Or receiving a hug
Or dancing
Or singing.**

**It takes the utmost use of your will
To live in the problem-free Reality
Which awaits you with open arms.**

Do not worry. If you miss your problems, you can go back to visit them. They are always there, waiting for you in the vibration of concern, worry, anxiety, or even panic. They relish it when you to drop by because then they become the center of attention. Every time you hobnob with them, their self-esteem improves and their grip on you tightens. Be aware that whenever you visit your problems, you will probably stay much longer than you had planned. They have clever ways of distracting you from joy.

*Most people have an extremely 'codependent' relationship with their problems.* They sacrifice their own Happiness by fueling the reality of worry. When you distill all the possible ways to use your mind, you end up with a bottom-line option: to focus on your problems or to focus on your joy. Which do you choose?

Are you becoming upset with what is being stated? Are you thinking that it is not so simple? If so, perhaps those very thoughts are your negative mind's struggle for survival. The possibility awaiting you is very simple, but not necessarily easy. Your mind does not want to become useless. It panics whenever you approach the realization that on the other side of its negative existence is thought-free bliss.

## The Ultimate Solution

**The *only* problem is that
Your mind is terrified
To have no problems.**

**Without any problems,
Your negative thoughts
Would have no excuse
To gather their forces.**

My deepest spiritual quest is to be a pure, innocent expression of Love. *When I surrender into being an energetic phenomenon rather than my personality, then everything that is not a manifestation of Love dissolves.* This entirely internal process has nothing to do with anyone else. I repeatedly look inward to notice if my mind is fooling me. If anything other than Love is present, then comes the most challenging task I have while here on Earth. I must reach inside for the courage to confront my mind. I must access a fierce, swordlike energy found in the depths of my will to cut through that which is taking me out of Love.

*Wielding this sword is the most aggressive action I ever take.* In the past, 99% of me wanted to give up. I went unconscious to hold on to "Peter" as I had always known him. But a deeper wisdom knew that another level of "Peter" had to die for more Love to be born. Harnessing the courage within the 1% in order to transcend the 99% keeps me choosing Love again and again, regardless of how many times I fall into the negative mind's traps.

Love arises out of emptiness. *When thoughts are absent, Love is present.* You do not have to "do" something in order to Love. Everything else just has to be out of the way. But the mind conjures up many ingenious mental images that seem too enticing to ignore. It tricks you into believing that the next thought is the one that will solve all your problems and make you happy. What if you knew that Happiness exists outside of the realm of the mind? How long would you tolerate the endlessly looping trap of those alluring negative thoughts?

Do you doubt whether you can win the war with your mind? If so, this doubt is exactly how your mind wins. You have a right to think whatever you want and to reside in any room of your inner temple that you choose. Use your will to defeat your mind. A beneficial way to express your power in order to claim your right to choose your thoughts is outlined in the Workbook Meditation for Week Five on page 205. This Life-saving declaration is a proper and effective use of your anger. It moves you from being a victim of overpowering thoughts into proclaiming yourself the master of your inner Reality.

## Destroying Doubt

**Rather than trying to think**
**Your way out of the doubt,**
**Directly blast it with anger**
**For stealing your Freedom.**

This is one of many methods for dealing with doubt. Notice if you are trying to cling to "the solution." Each moment needs to be addressed anew. Other alternatives include:

♥ Watch the ebb and flow of doubt without "doing" anything about it.

♥ Say to the doubt, "Thank-you for sharing," and then focus on another subject.

♥ Listen for how the doubt is trying to take care of you by protecting you. Let it know that you no longer need to use fear as a way to take care of yourself.

♥ Appreciate the doubt for its deviousness and how it has again hooked you by saying to it, "Great job! How did you ever come up with that one? I really believed you for a while."

♥ Joke with the doubt by exaggerating its effect on you: "You are right. If I wear the wrong outfit, I should commit suicide."

♥ Do not pay attention to the subject matter of your doubt. Instead, notice what doubt feels like – its texture and quality. Trace that feeling as it transfers from one topic to another. Become fascinated with the parasitic nature of the feeling itself instead of trying to resolve whatever topic is serving as doubt's temporary host.

Become so familiar with doubt that it is no longer some mysterious enemy draining your power. *The more you are in relationship to doubt rather than lost in it, the freer you become.*

There are an infinite number of ways to stay engaged with your mind until the day you die. You may even feel a certain level of contentment within the realm of thinking. But an underlying discontentment reveals a conscious or unconscious knowing that you are missing out on Life. If you want to surrender into Love's emptiness, you must find the courage to confront your mind. You must take the risk to die into Love. You must let go of the stubbornness that makes "I" a separate Being. Feel both the pain and the joy of letting go of control. It is within your decision to risk that a deep inner peace begins to be born.

A whole new identity awaits you. How you relate with others dramatically shifts. Have you noticed that you have less to talk about with your closest friend when you are feeling great? If you are feeling horrible, the two of you can go on for hours complaining to each other. But if you are feeling wonderful, there is little to say. Then the scary part emerges. You have a possibility of just being present with each other and sharing Love. You could look into each other's eyes or gently touch each other's face and say, "I love you." But this terrifies most people. *It is much safer to commiserate than to be tender.*

For you to free yourself from the trap of psychological processing, you have to go through the discomfort and fear of being in the Here and Now. Your primary way of relating to yourself and to others has likely been through the filter of discontentment. Are you ready to leap into a new identity? Are you ready to end your intimate, codependent relationship with problems? Are you ready to perceive yourself as being happy? Are you ready to let go of friends who insist on staying stuck in misery? These questions are not asked lightly. One of the most frightening cliffs is at the edge of joy's abyss. For you to leap into the Reality where nothing is left to "fix" inside you or others can be frightening. However, what awaits is the discovery of unconditional Love.

## The Final Frontier

**The only thing**
**Left to work on**
**Is the concept that**
**You have anything**
**Left to work on.**

## Chapter Thirteen
# Questioning Your Questions

Have you ever looked at the quality of the questions you ask yourself in order to solve your problems (or "process yourself")? I frequently assist others to see Life's challenges through spiritual eyes. Rather than providing answers, my focus is to ask the types of questions that enable others to shift levels of consciousness as they search for solutions. The conclusions they reach are not nearly as important as the perspective that is born when their stubborn stance wobbles while seeking answers. *The questions themselves must arise from the place where problems do not exist.* Most people do not know how to ask themselves these kinds of questions. Thus, when they try to free themselves from the quagmire of problems, they have no point of reference to help elevate them into other realms.

Examine any beliefs that encourage you to remain at the level of "processing." You may think that the way to achieve growth is by talking about the many nuances of your inner experiences. From one perspective, this may well be true. However, your clever mind can also trick you into obsessively dissecting every experience. If your bottom-line goal is to have a quiet mind, then your primary motivation is to discover ways to be in the Here and Now. *Every moment involved in self-analysis is a moment not spent in the silence of Love.*

One common belief that can keep you in the trap of processing is the notion that you must complete past experiences – that you must repeatedly examine your childhood/birth traumas, or your relationship with your parents, or past-life karma, or whatever else is "unfinished." This is an endless process unless you see that the very concept of "completion" is an illusion that keeps you chasing after an unattainable goal.


## Completion

**Life ongoingly unfolds
With many loose ends.
The need to complete
Keeps the past alive.**

**Completion occurs
By letting go of *all*
Ideas of completion.**


The trick is to be able to discern between glossing over or repressing something and being ready to move on. Notice if you have a belief (as many therapists do) that you must continue to scrutinize the past in order to heal yourself. You can become so engrossed in your history that you keep missing the joy within Now. If you cannot remember an incident or scene from your childhood, you can compulsively pursue it without a moment's inner peace until you find it.

A much healthier approach is to make it your intention to be in the present tense as much as possible. Then, if an incident or a pain flashes before you as you are in the Now, feel that pain as it arises. *The image that comes forth from your unconscious must be dealt with because it is between you and the present tense, not because you are chasing after your past.* After you fully feel the pain, it dissolves and you can return to the Now until something else arises. This way, your whole orientation toward Life is to just be. Remember, the vibration of Love exists only in the Here and Now, not in the there and then.

The following questions are designed to get you out of processing as quickly as possible and back into your Heart. By asking them and then gently allowing your response to arise, you create an elevator to lift you out of the level of consciousness where problems are perpetuated. Be alert to an inherent danger in this process. You can easily fool yourself into providing the answer you know is "spiritually correct," thus repressing your true response.

After you ask a question, only when you feel an "Aha!" resonating deep inside your Being do you know that you have discovered a true resolution. Thus, utmost inner awareness is requested as you proceed. To clarify the source of your pain, begin with the first question below, as it is the most encompassing. Take plenty of time to allow any insights to arise. *If you get an "Aha!," then quit reading and go enjoy Life.* If no release occurs, then continue with the second question, then the third, etc. As you proceed, notice that you are not focusing on the problem itself, but on the underlying false assumptions which created the perception that you even have a problem. Let these questions guide you to your own inner peace.

♥ **Right now, am I lost in thoughts inside my head or am I in Love inside my Heart?**

Take the quantum leap out of thinking and into being present in your Heart.

♥ **Have I been too happy too long? Am I letting my mind destroy my bliss? Am I creating this problem to escape joy?**

Truly see the illusion of your "problem" and feel the "Aha!" of exposing the tricks of your mind.

♥ **Am I taking Life too seriously? Or can I just see the joke in this whole situation and allow cosmic humor to lighten me up?**

Freedom lies within you capacity to overcome the disease of seriousness.

♥ **Right now, am I desiring or enjoying?**

Let go of thinking that you will find joy when this or that desire is fulfilled and enjoy this moment, where Love lives.

♥ **What am I feeling right now?**

Allow yourself to vulnerably melt into experiencing whatever you are feeling without judgement. Cry until your tears lead to a smile of relief as your Heart opens again.

♥ **Am I giving away my power to external events to determine my Happiness? Can I shift my inner attitudes to allow Happiness to bloom from the inside out, regardless of the external circumstances?**

If you genuinely realize that you can let go of altering the external to find joy, then you can re-connect with your inner peace without wasting your energy trying to control.

♥ **Am I saying "Yes" or "No" to this moment? Can I find the "Yes" which accepts *all*, including both my silly little "No" and the perfection of the Universe exactly as it is?**

If you let go of your self-righteousness and your need to know the unknowable, then you can breath a sigh of relief born out of simply saying "Yes."

♥ **Am I making my thoughts too real?**

If you see how thin thoughts are, then you no longer need to give them power over you.

♥ **Am I being tricked into believing my mind's negativity instead of standing firm in my Love?**

See your mind's trap and appreciate its clever deviousness.

♥ **Let's now become more specific by focusing on any attitudes that hurt you. You can consciously shift destructive attitudes by gently being aware of them.**

1. In this moment, can I transform my judgement into acceptance?
2. In this moment, can I shift from being a victim to being a master?
3. In this moment, can I let my need to control melt into surrender?
4. In this moment, can I convert my doubt into trust?
5. In this moment, can I transmute my complaints into appreciation?
6. In this moment, can I stop struggling and start flowing (even flowing with the experience of being out of harmony)?
7. In this moment, can I let my stubbornness melt into co-operation?
8. In this moment, can I see through my illusion of scarcity and validate the Truth of my abundance?
9. In this moment, can I end my greedy grabbing and start trusting?

♥ **Am I denying or embracing a disowned belief?**

Challenge yourself to love whatever aspect of yourself you have tried to deny, no matter how deplorable. *All* human experiences are contained within you.

♥ **Am I holding on to or letting go of a self-limiting belief?**

As you truly see how you limit your potential, the walls of your self-imposed prison melt. Feel yourself expand into the next level of your Being.

♥ **Am I convinced that a negative thought is more real than a positive one?**

Both are an illusion, so why not choose the positive one?

♥ **If you still feel stuck, take your pain to a friend and ask for a hug. No more words. No more processing. Just a long, silent, comforting snuggle. And let yourself fully receive your friend's Love!**

If these questions have helped you gain some perspective on how to more effectively be with yourself (or with a friend), then you need not stay lost in the endlessly looping trap of psychological processing. *In order to be elevated into Heaven, either you need to climb a ladder or you need to learn how to fly.* These questions help to create the ladder. Your good intentions, vulnerability, and trust help you to sprout wings!

## Chapter Fourteen
# Beyond All Beliefs

*This chapter may challenge you more than any other.* It invites you to look at *all* your beliefs in new ways. The mind does not like to be questioned about its assumptions, so it will likely try to find ways to sabotage you. You may repeatedly fall asleep while reading this chapter. Or you may have a strong urge to go for a walk and then not get back to reading again. Or you may even feel like throwing this book out. In order to receive *Living Life in Love's* gifts, you may need to overcome your mind's resistance.

Use utmost awareness as you proceed. Right now, renew your commitment to take up residence in that inner place which is beyond polarities and thoughts. *You can discover and let go of how you limit your perception of who you are as a spiritual being.* Good luck as you venture into the new.

There are many different paths to Enlightenment. If you walk down a variety of them, you find that each one has its own special flavor, texture, and aroma. Each one has a different set of beliefs, which, if followed one hundred percent, will theoretically lead you to the promised bliss. Each path appeals to a different type of ego, so what attracts one person does not necessarily attract someone else. Or, at a certain stage of your own development, one discipline is appropriate for you, but at another point in time may not draw you at all. The common factor is that the goal of all these paths is exactly the same - ultimate Truth or Enlightenment. *The problem is that it is virtually impossible for you to be in a human body <u>and</u> comply with all your chosen path's spiritual rules to achieve the goal.* This illogical madness has you chasing after that which is humanly impossible. The way through this enigma is to know that the place you are seeking exists underneath the mind and "Beyond All Beliefs." It is an inner place of perfect silence and harmony that cannot be disturbed or even touched by *any* thought.

## Beyond Beliefs

**When you go beyond beliefs,**
**You discover that Truth is**
**A state of consciousness,**
**Not an idea.**

Can you bypass all these paths winding up the holy mountain and fly directly to the pinnacle of consciousness? Yes. The most basic tool is a knowingness deep inside your Heart that *all* beliefs are a compromise of the ultimate Truth. Why? Because all beliefs inherently involve the creation of a position or a stance which divides consciousness from "One" into "Not One." *The most useful beliefs launch you into the place of no beliefs.* You must dive so deeply inside your Being that you not only live in the place where there are no polarities, but that you actually become that place.

The mind is a pendulum which swings from one extreme to the other. As you observe the vacillations of your thoughts, you can begin to let go of your attachment to any one position. In one moment the mind states with conviction, "Quit your job," or "Get married," or "Have a baby." Then, just minutes or hours or days later, it tells you exactly the opposite. If you live out on the end of this pendulum, you repeatedly swing back and forth as you search for "the answer." But, if you live right at the fulcrum of the pendulum, then you can peacefully watch the mind's variables and eliminate the inevitable chaos created by taking its fluctuations seriously.

The more you can enjoy the mind's vacillations without holding on to any one viewpoint as the final Truth, the freer you become.

## Vows of Celibacy

There was a very wise spiritual teacher whose whole effort was to destroy his disciples' points of view. One day he began speaking on the beauties of celibacy. He extolled on the virtues of the monastic lifestyle. He lauded the ability to witness sexual desires without needing to act upon them in any way.

His disciples listened attentively. Their Master had never made any proclamations about sexuality. By the end of a month of these "virtuous" lectures, all his disciples had become celibate. Couples split apart, and everyone knew they had finally entered the "advanced" stages of spiritual development.

However, the main topic for the Master's next series of discourses was the magnificence of sexual expression. He graphically described the ecstasy of sexually devouring your beloved. The newly self-proclaimed celibates squirmed in their seats as their desires awoke at new levels. During the next month of tantalizing and titillating lectures, one by one they sheepishly abandoned their vows of celibacy to experience their lust.

After this second month, the Master came out one day and launched into another round of accolades on the virtues of celibacy. The disciples burst into laughter with him. They began to recognize the absurdity of trying to live up to external spiritual ideals rather than listening to their own internal Truth.

Spiritual freedom does not depend upon which choices you make in the external world. It makes no difference whether you are celibate or sexual, whether you have a baby or not, or whether you work as a waiter or a healer. *Your freedom lies within your capacity to recognize the mind's fickleness.*

As you become more stably seated on that still point of the pendulum, you can begin to release your most basic assumptions about this Reality's mysteries that are beyond your logical mind's comprehension. You discover that no one has the final word on what is good or bad because no human being can see all the long range repercussions of any event. This is the beginning of trusting the miracle of surrender.

## Good or Bad?

In the Fifteenth Century there was an old man who lived on a small farm outside a village. He was a poor man materially but a rich man spiritually. One day a beautiful wild horse wandered into his corral. By the law at that time, it became his. The people from the town heard the news and said to him, "This is so wonderful. The eyes of fortune are shining on you."

His response was, "This is neither good nor bad. All we know is that this horse has come."

About a week later, the horse ran away in the night. The townspeople were upset, saying, "This is terrible. Now he is gone and you are back to nothing again."

His response was, "This is neither good nor bad. All we know is that he is no longer here."

A few days later, the horse returned to the farm with a whole herd of wild horses, making the old man wealthy because horses in those days were extremely valuable. The townspeople said, "How lucky you are. Now you are rich."

His response was, "This is neither good nor bad. All we know is that these horses have come."

His son began training the horses to be ridden and fell from one of them. He was crippled for life as a result. The townspeople said, "What a catastrophe! Your son's life is ruined."

His response was, "My son's fall is neither good nor bad. All we know is that he can no longer walk without crutches."

As it turned out, their country went to war. The son's condition exempted him from going. Almost all the other young men were killed in battle. The townspeople said, "Your son's fall was so very fortunate. He was not killed in the war."

The old man just sat there silently, feeling utmost compassion for the townspeople's pain caused by perceiving Reality as a duality.

The townspeople never understood the old man. They continued to be swayed by the momentary appearance of events. The old man sat on that still point of the pendulum, not pulled into the fluctuating illusions of the moment. He surrendered by trusting the ebb and flow of events without labeling them as good or bad.

Not only did the old man let go of judging the events that appeared to be negative, but he also did not get pulled into the ones that appeared to be positive. They can be an even more subtle trap than the negative ones. At a certain stage of your spiritual development, you discover the power to externally manifest your desires. With this power, you can get intoxicated by the material plane in new ways. Use your awareness to navigate these waters.

## Beyond Positivity

**As your negative self-image is healed
And your positivity begins to bloom,
Even beautiful blossoms must die
For the tree of Life to bear fruit.**

Positive thoughts and a positive self-image are only a steppingstone to freedom from all polarities. First you need to heal your negative view of yourself and the world. Then, as the blossoms of positivity appear, the next step takes you into the fruits of a quiet neutrality.

Examine any unexamined beliefs and attitudes which hold you in a particular place, not in order to change them or to make them better, but to be free from all beliefs. When you release your most fundamental beliefs at the very core of your Soul, you automatically heal any other distortions surrounding that core. *Question all your beliefs, especially the ones that seem to be beyond questioning.*

## Conditioning

**You are beginning to fathom
The depth of your conditioning
When you question whether
Even beliefs as basic as
'Your body must die'
Were loaned to you
After you arrived
On this Planet.**

When you wonder whether the thought, "Your body must die," is inherently part of this Reality or is just a belief that is not necessarily so, then your very questioning becomes the basis for transformation. It shakes the mind down to its roots. As the mind spins and doubts, then the "you" who is not the mind can find some space to emerge. By scrutinizing each belief or attitude that holds you in a particular place, you are on your way to freedom from all beliefs.

For instance, many health advocates and New Age people have the belief, "Sugar is bad for you." Their experience is that when they eat sugar, they feel a short-lived, artificial "high." Within about fifteen minutes, their energy becomes depleted and they feel depressed. However, when I lived in Muktananda's Ashram, the belief there was, "Shakti (Life energy) loves sugar." Before the 4:00 a.m. meditation, many devotees ate sugar-coated cinnamon rolls. On their birthdays, they handed out sweets to one another. Chai (a common kind of tea) had lots of sugar in it. No one judged it negatively. Everyone had fun consuming it with no ill effects.

While we are on the subject of eating, diet is a wonderfully controversial topic. There are many beliefs about eating properly for spiritual evolvement. Vegetarians know that meat eaters are gross and insensitive to animals. But how does a broccoli plant feel about being murdered? Food combiners know that certain categories of food need to be eaten separately from others in order to be healthy. But what about people who consume only wafers and water and live to be one hundred years old? Many health food advocates worry so much about what they eat that it can be painful to be around them at meal times.

## A Healthy Diet

**What you eat cannot**
**Make you more evolved.**

**When you and all your ideas**
**Stay out of the way of Nature,**
**All food becomes pure energy.**

Notice if you are reacting to any of the above statements. If so, what is your reaction about? Are you invested in holding onto a certain set of beliefs or values that are limiting you in any way? Let us continue.

Another New Age belief is that crystals can heal you. Some people believe that certain stones have the power to heal physical, spiritual, and emotional wounds when placed on certain chakras (energy centers in the body). And sometimes it works. Other times it does not. Perhaps the combined strength of the faith of the healer and healee is the primary factor in producing results.

## Crystals

**Crystals are**
**A clear expression of Love**
**From the mineral kingdom.**

**What if their ability to heal you**
**Depends more upon your beliefs**
**Than upon their inherent power?**

A distinct set of beliefs surround people who "channel entities." Many people believe that these entities exist independently from their channelers. This is absolutely true at one level of consciousness. But what if you look from the perspective that sees the channeler through more empowering eyes? What if you believed that the wisdom being spoken comes from the depths of the channeler's own psyche?  After all, if you believe that the whole Universe is contained within your own Heart, then those entities must be inside you somewhere.

## Channeling

**Channeling an entity's wisdom is
A self-illusion created to deny that
*All* Truth lives within your Heart.**

**Say goodbye to your entity.
And say hello to listening to
The voice of *your* inner wisdom.**

What about past lives?  Many people who receive past-life readings find them to be very valuable.  Many people believe that when you have developed enough spiritually, then you begin to experience your past lives.  But what if that experience is just another figment of your imagination?  Might the only reason that past-life visions appear at all is because you believe in them?

## Past Lives

**You were a priestess in Greece
And an emperor in Rome
And a harem girl in Egypt.**

**Your present lover was
Your son in Babylon and
Murdered you in China.**

**Your mother was
Your lover in Atlantis and
Your twin brother in India.**

**These are wonderful triggers
To elicit deep emotions and
To perpetuate imagination
And to build spiritual pride.**

**But do they
Bring you closer
To this moment?**

Again, do not try to throw out a wrong belief and replace it with the "correct" one. *Question the validity of having any beliefs at all.* The more you see the trap of holding on to any perspective, the freer you are to choose which beliefs serve you and which do not.

Money is another great topic.  Maybe you believe that people with money have big egos or are greedy, mean, and dishonest.  Or you may have an idea that the only way to get an abundance of money is to work hard for many hours at some tedious job which you make tolerable by seeing it as a "spiritual challenge."  Or perhaps money is "anti-spiritual" to you. If so, then the covert message you send to yourself is that it is a sin for you to be wealthy. Questioning these beliefs can help you to see why you do not have more financial abundance. When you fully understand that money is energy and not pieces of paper, then you can have a positive feeling about it.  You also transform your relationship to work and to play.

## Money

**The day you let go of the idea that
Money is compensation for work,
Your orientation toward Life
Can dramatically transform.**

**Receiving money is the natural result
Of allowing your Heart to lead you
To do whatever makes you happy.**

There are many other beliefs that are worth examining. Again, the whole idea of this exploration is not to try to find the "right" belief, but to see that all beliefs are just beliefs. They can run you only if you have not carefully looked at them and questioned the usefulness of their existence. Briefly, here are a few more often held assumptions for you to examine.

♥ **There are no available, sensitive, attractive men (or women) around here.**

Keep this belief and you will never find a mate!

♥ **You are 100% responsible for creating your Reality.**

How Egocentric! You are responsible for your response to your reaction to Reality.

♥ **Everything that happens to you means something.**

A great way to become obsessed with analyzing insignificant events and miss Now.

♥ **Breakthroughs and insights are solutions that last forever.**

If it were only that easy. The rules keep changing.

♥ **The only way to heal childhood traumas is to keep reliving them in therapy.**

You had better have a lot of money for therapy for the rest of your life.

♥ **Relationships are a struggle.**

Then why would you ever want to be in one?

♥ **Life is empty without a mate.**

Then every moment that you are single it is impossible to be happy.

♥ **Hot, lusty sex isn't spiritual.**

Then why did God create lust in you?

♥ **Enlightenment means going beyond sex and your emotions.**

This kind of Enlightenment must not be for human beings.

Continue looking inside your Being. Search for any beliefs that do not serve you. Question all the corners of your mind. There is a bumper sticker, "Question Authority." You have probably given your mind much more authority over you than you could ever give to any politician or policeman or anyone else. *The place to question authority is inside yourself.* Whenever a disempowering thought arises, ask yourself:

♥ "Why do I think that?"
♥ "Does that thought serve me?"
♥ "Do I want to change the belief that gives rise to that thought?"

If you challenge and then passionately tackle your beliefs one by one, you will eventually win your freedom.

Hopefully, you realize that you and you alone create your interpretation of Life's experiences. If looking to others or to your mind for answers is not making you happy, try diving more deeply into your inner Self to explore the uncharted and unchartable territory, where the mysteries of Love reside.

## The Answer

**When your mind asks a question,
Rather than seeking the answer,
Delicately follow that question
Back into the pool of silence
Out of which it has arisen.**

**There, no answers are needed
Because *all* questions dissolve
Into the wisdom within Now.**

Now you are ready for a bumper sticker reading, "Question Reality!" Rather than putting this bumper sticker on your car, place it in the spotlight of your awareness as frequently as possible. Let it remind you that you need not be pulled into the illusions of the external world. Your internal experience of Love can then become the totality of your Reality.

# Section Five

# Where Is Happiness Hidden?

### Lost and Found

To think that
   You can find
      The Answer
         Is to be lost.

To embrace
   Life's mystery
      Not knowing
         Is to be found.

## Chapter Fifteen
# Yes!

"Yes!" The most powerful word in the English language is *Yes*! *Ultimate freedom is to experience a 'yes' to everything that occurs, both internally and externally.* You have arrived at the pinnacle of human consciousness each moment that you can see, know, sense, feel, perceive, realize, understand, grok, comprehend, fathom, appreciate, digest, and discern the perfection of what you cannot see, know, sense, feel, perceive, realize, understand, grok, comprehend, fathom, appreciate, digest, and discern. Bliss is yours when you are not resisting this Reality in any way. You have given God your stamp of approval for her creation. *You* are *yes.*

Thus, the *only* relevant question to ask yourself is, "How do I find my true *yes*?" The answer to this question can be very tricky. Your *yes* has to be pure. It has to be total. It has to emanate from the core of your Being without any hidden or repressed *no's* mixed in.

To uncover your deepest *yes*, begin by closely examining your *no's*. To your ego/negative mind, *no* seems like a powerful position to take. *No* defines a "you." *No* states, "I exist." *No* declares, "I am here to exert *my* will." *No* brags, "I have power over you." *No* seems to have so much freedom in it. But it is really the childish freedom of a rebellious teenager. You taste mature freedom when you can honestly say *Yes!* without feeling trapped. *You must see the illusion within the contraction of the mind's 'no' to fully embrace the expansion of the Spirit's 'yes.'* One way to get beyond *no* is to explore your understanding or misunderstanding of power.


## Power

True power is not
   Exerting your will to
      Get what you want.

True power lies within
   Surrendering your will
      To flow with changes.

This expression of power
   Transforms your reality
      From Doing into Being.


In your attempts to flow gracefully with the "Yes Dance," you may sometimes awkwardly step on some *no's*. You may try to get rid of your ego by ignoring it. You may think that all you have to do now is "just say yes." You may reason, "If I just bow down and surrender by saying *yes* to everyone else's whims and desires, then I will live in bliss. My desires are merely an illusion so I will just be of total service to others. That's the key!"

In the short run, this strategy may work. But in the long run, it will not. It is not that easy. Your decision to always say *yes* pushes your *no* underground for a period of time. You may *temporarily* experience the bliss of surrender. But eventually, your *no* explodes into rebellion. And when it does, you discover how desperately your ego wants to be in control.

When you were a newborn baby, you were a pure *yes*. You were not yet separate from the whole. You had no self-concept as being distinct from other people or even from the material world. You wanted to touch, taste, and sense everything within your sphere, whether it was another person or a toy or even some dirt. Whoever or whatever came your way, you experienced as an integral part of yourself with no judgement. You were merely exploring "you" in different forms within this Reality.

After being in a body for some months, you began to develop a sense of Self as being separate from the whole. "I" came into existence. Ego was born. The most potent way for you to assert that "you" existed was to say *no*. At the age of about two, it was so wonderful (and scary) to discover how quickly people noticed you when you stubbornly declared, "No!"

Unfortunately, most parents do not understand this process of individuation. Your parents probably took your *no* personally. They reacted to it and tried to stop it. They scolded you or punished you because they heard your *no* as a defiance of them rather than as the birth of your ego. They were frightened because they did not know how to control you. Thus, they clamped down on you in their unique ways. Rarely, if ever, did anyone embrace and accept your *no*.

*Before you can find your true 'yes,' you must first fully express your deepest 'no.'* One effective way to do this is to find a place alone where you can uninhibitedly make noise, like your home or your car. You can also muffle your voice by placing a pillow over your mouth. Begin by directing speaking your *no*! to any mental images that elicit deep feelings – parents, siblings, other relatives, teachers, lovers, society, the Church, God, environmental rapists, politicians, or anyone who has ever violated you in any way. Let your *no* get as loud as it wants. Notice how good it feels to freely shout, "No!" Repeat this process until you feel empowered and are satisfied and in Love with your *no*. It may take only several times or it may take years. Then, on the other side of this *no*, your Spirit's *yes* emerges.

## Yes After No

**After you declare *No* and
Affirm your right to exist,
You discover a new *Yes*
That satisfies the Soul's
Deep craving to merge.**

What if you were to respond to people's requests of you with a *yes* or a *no* depending solely upon how you honestly feel? Your answer need not be logical nor fit into any preconceived notion of who you should or should not be. Most people look for the one rule that they can apply to every situation. Then, hopefully, they can always be ethically and morally correct. One of the many beautiful mysteries of this Reality is that hard and fast rules do not work. You must be alive, awake, and aware as you discern the unique circumstances of each situation. *Instead of always being a 'yes' to others in order to be a loving person, you have to repeatedly let go of your ideas of what a loving person's responses 'should be.'*

## Yes or No?

**Yes or *No* to someone else
Does not ever inherently
Enhance or diminish Love.**

**Look through selfless eyes
To find out which response
Deepens both your Hearts.**

Let's take another look at surrender from an unusual point of view. What does surrender mean to you? Prostrating to others? Existing only to serve? Having no wants or needs of your own? *What if your whole concept of surrender included even your own ego as an integral part of what you are surrendering to?*

## Surrender

**Surrender is observing all
Without any investment,
Including your own ego
As it is lost in illusions.**

**By allowing you to be yourself,
And others to be themselves,
And the world to be itself,
Control turns into trust.**

You can reside in an inner place of trust which is deeper than your ego. It is the birthplace of all thoughts and perceptions. This is the Home of the "witness" (to be explored more fully in Chapter Nineteen), which has no need for you to be a particular way in order to be "spiritually correct." This revolutionary concept eliminates the requirement of having to obey certain spoken or unspoken spiritual rules to be Enlightened. All externally imposed pictures of how you are supposed to be dissolve. You gain the permission to just be human as you let go of having to control yourself. You experience unconditional acceptance of even your ego. *You discover that 'you' are not your ego, but that 'you' are that place which is in relationship to your ego.* With this freedom, you do not have to wait, to change, or to accomplish anything in order to be loved, lovable, and loving.

Where does all this leave us in the dance between control and surrender? At times, you may choose to take control. You may use your will to prevent negative thoughts from dominating you. Thus, you are taking positive control of your mind and attitudes in order to create more joy. At other times, you may choose not to interfere with your process because you see the wisdom in moving deeper into negativity, where certain lessons can be learned.

No blanket rule exists about control and surrender. You have to be aware of how each situation touches you. In one instance, you may intuitively sense the perfection of a bigger picture beyond your comprehension. You surrender into that unknown and take no action. In another instance, you may make every effort to move things in the direction that you feel they need to go as you simultaneously know that everything is perfect, including your effort. You can even be attached to the results *and* trust that any outcome is perfect, even if it does not seem perfect from your limited perspective. If you consciously try to control any situation from a place of unconditional acceptance, then you are still surrendered.

Take war as an example. Should you do everything in your power to end the insanity of people killing each other? Or do you need to surrender into letting those who need to participate in violence do so? War and violence, as with everything on this planet, exist for us to learn and grow from. Your lesson may be to experience killing another person, or to be killed, or to lose a loved one, or to protest the travesty of it all, or to fully feel the pain of human ignorance and then to love everyone involved. If you give yourself full permission to be you, however you are, then you are surrendering to "what is." You can become involved in whatever way is appropriate for you, including not being involved.

To attain the freedom within surrender, you have to risk knowing that knowing is not the answer. You have to risk letting go into the mystery behind the veil of illusions called Reality. *You have to find the place in your Heart where paradoxes are embraced as invitations to expand your awareness, where 'positive' and 'negative' are perceived as complementary forces rather than opposites, and where the cycle of Life and Death are celebrated as essential catalysts of change.* In that place, control and surrender are partners in a dance which births trust.

# Trusting

**Trusting means**
**Letting go of control**
**By allowing yourself**
**And others to move**
**In *any* direction.**

**Trusting means sensing**
**When to surrender to**
**The unseen mystery.**

There are no linear techniques to teach you how to surrender because surrender is a non-linear process. By its very nature, it has to be. It involves trusting Reality to be other than it appears. You can learn to trust when the doors you want to be opened are closed. You do not have to try to smash down those doors. Your motivation would probably arise out of a kind of arrogance that has you think *you* know what is best. There exists a grander scheme beyond most human being's ability to see. If you try to fight against it, you become tired, angry, and stressed. Instead, you can open your Heart and trust that certain doors are closed because they are leading you to open ones, behind which lies a treasure.

## Closed Doors

In ancient times, there was a tradition that if a wandering monk who had renounced worldly ways were to come into your town, it was an honor and a blessing to have him stay overnight in your house.

One rather cold, moonless evening a female renunciate came into a small town looking for lodging. However, at this time in history, almost all monks, with very few exceptions, were male. She knocked on the door of a cozy-looking home, only to have the owner slam the door in her face when he saw that she was a woman. She said a blessing for him and went on to the next house only to have a similar response. House after house she had doors slammed shut when the owners saw that she was a woman. Each time she felt utmost compassion for their rudeness and ignorance.

Finally, she wandered into a field on the outskirts of town. In the darkness, she stumbled and fell down, exhausted. As she lay there, she prayed for all those people who had been so cruel to her, until she fell fast asleep in the cold. A few hours later she awakened and rolled over to see a most magnificent sight. The full moon had risen and she looked up to see that she had fallen underneath a cherry tree bursting with blossoms. She marveled at the beauty of the pink blossoms illuminated by the full moon behind them. She again blessed those townspeople, this time for their ignorance which led her to this majestic scene. As her Love poured forth, her Heart opened to receive the light of God. In that moment, she became Enlightened.

Ironically, the townspeople's *no* became the perfect vehicle to lead the woman monk to Enlightenment. However, the townspeople missed an opportunity to become more loving. They did not know that when you relate to others, it is vital to treat them as an integral part of yourself. Or, perhaps the townspeople were merely exercising their right to say *no*, which ultimately benefitted the woman monk. Judging others' actions is dangerous, especially when their behavior looks unloving because you cannot see the bigger picture.

At times, it is important to take a stand for what you feel is right by saying *no* to others. At other times, it is essential to the well being of everyone involved to let go of being right and melt into something more encompassing than the individual self. *To achieve any goal, if you take others equally into account, all decisions can be made as if everyone is one entity.* Spiritually, the completion of any task is of less importance than the people being in harmony every moment they are working together. Then everyone can reap the rewards of feeling connected.

## When to Surrender

**If you create useless pain**
**By clinging to your ideals,**
**It is time to give up control**
**By letting go of *your* way.**

As you master the mind's dance between *yes* and *no*, you discover a more encompassing *yes*. This *yes* gives birth to all other *yes's* and *no's*. This *yes* frees you from having to control yourself, others, or situations. This *yes* overflows with a depth of surrender that opens the gateway to experiencing Heaven here on Earth.

## Yes

**Are you *Yes* or *No* to Life?**

**If you melt into being**
**\*Yes\* to the external,**
**\*Yes\* to your yes's,**
**\*Yes\* to your no's, and**
**\*Yes\* to 'I don't know,'**
**Then you are here, now,**
**Inside a *Yes* to Life**
**And inside Love.**

At the level of the mind, there are always polarities – good/bad, right/wrong, yes/no. *No* always arises from these polarities, as does a certain type of *yes*. If you surrender into a deeper source within, you discover the *yes* which arises from Spirit. Real Love lives within this realm. *This 'yes' expands you into celebrating all of existence without resistance.*

## Chapter Sixteen
# Quantum Leap into the Abyss

One of the most powerful motivators for the inner journey is discontentment. Do you ever feel that Life is futile, yet you sense that it cannot be an aimless journey? Do you intuitively know that Life has to have meaning, but feel frustrated because you have not found fulfillment? The existential crisis of "What's it all about?" can be immobilizing, yet it is also one of Life's greatest gifts. Its pain can motivate you to question the core assumptions upon which you base your life.

## Imprisonment

**Longing for more to Life
Allows you to discover
That you are in prison.**

**Trusting your yearning
Lets you risk changes
And unlocks the door
To inner freedom.**

When you respond to your deep inner longing, the embers of your spiritual craving burst into flames. Your rigidity melts. In the depths of your Heart, you finally admit that you do not have all the answers. From this realization arises an excruciatingly painful yet exquisitely essential process, often called "the dissolution of the ego." *Your desperation disintegrates your arrogance, and humility is born.* By questioning your knowingness, you unveil a deeper orientation toward Life. As you bow down and surrender to the unknowable, your innocence is reborn.

## Knowing

**To know you know
Is not to know
Through arrogance.**

**To know you don't know
Is not to know
Through false humility.**

**To not know you don't know
Is not to know
Through ignorance.**

**To know you cannot know
Is to know
Through wisdom.**

**To know you need not know
Is to know
Through trust.**

**To let go of knowing
Is to know
Through innocence.**

Your rational mind stifles you into a narrow approach to Life. The linear nature of the thought process limits your range of experiences. As a human being, you have a vast array of ways to touch into the multiple dimensions of this Reality. Out of habit and comfort, you spend most of your time within a narrow band of those possibilities. You think and you think and you think.

You hope to eradicate negative thoughts by attacking them with other thoughts. *You attempt to find answers to problems by utilizing the greatest problem creator: your mind.* Like a caged rat going nowhere on its endless squeaky wheel, you repeatedly try to think your way to "The Answer."

Once in a while, almost by accident, you may step off the wheel. You have brief excursions into other experiential realms such as emotions, sexuality, or Love. But you quickly return to the wheel of thoughts and run yourself ragged because it is familiar and feels safe. The price you pay for this false security is that your Spirit gets buried alive.

## The Cup of Tea

In ancient times, a seeker found a great Master after years of searching. When he arrived at the tiny hut in the Himalayas, he expected the sage to impart to him the wisdom of the ages. He started asking many questions about God, meditation, and Enlightenment. Instead of answering, the Master invited him to have a cup of tea. The seeker thought it was a bit strange, but reluctantly agreed. He was eager to resolve his inquiries into Life's mysteries.

As the Master finished preparing the tea in silence, he started to slowly pour it into a cup. The seeker watched attentively as the cup became halfway full, then three quarters, then right up to the brim. The Master kept pouring and the cup overflowed, spilling tea all over the table and onto the floor. The seeker thought, "What a stupid man. He is so unaware that he cannot even pour a cup of tea. I must have come to the wrong man."

Slowly and deliberately, the master looked deeply into the seeker's eyes and said, "You are just like this cup of tea. You are so overflowing with thoughts and desires about God and such that nothing can be imparted to you. From the moment you walked into my hut, its silence has been filled with your thousands of questions. Go empty yourself and then come back to me."

The Western mind is so busy with unnecessary thoughts. If the mind does not rest, stress increases. If you could send your thoughts on vacation, wouldn't you breathe a sigh of relief? One of the key elements in "The Art of Being" discussed in Chapter One is to be in an empty, receptive mode while doing tasks. This attitude is magical because your battery is constantly recharging as you move through Life. Energy is not leaking because you are not over-exerting yourself. Your goals are easily accomplished because they are the natural consequence of the Love you receive each moment, rather than of your strenuous effort.

Thinking yields few long lasting rewards. Recall your most fulfilling experiences. You were probably accessing non-thinking domains within your Being. What is more meaningful than crying tears of joy as you see your beloved at the wedding altar? Or feeling the awe of the miracle of a child being born? Or bathing in the ecstasy of being sexual? Or feeling your Heart burst with compassion as you embrace a tearful friend? All these very human experiences tap into non-linear dimensions. Usually, external events propel you into these deeper realms. *What if you could access transcendent experiences by having certain attitudes and intentions independent of all external events?*

## The Sunset

Once when Swami Muktananda was visiting Hawaii on a world tour, his devoted chauffeur, Jayananda, decided to give him a special treat. They were driving near the beach just before sunset. Jayananda took a detour so that they could stop at a cliff above the ocean at one of the most beautiful overlooks in all the Hawaiian islands.

As they pulled over, the sun was dipping into the ocean. The sky was aflame with more colors than the chauffeur had ever seen.

There were tears of gratitude flowing down Jayananda's cheeks for the miracle of creation. He turned to Muktananda in the back seat and noticed a blissful smile on his Master's face.

Jayananda said, "Isn't this sunset magnificent?"

Muktananda replied, "What sunset?"

Muktananda was so deeply seated in his inner bliss that his joy did not need any external trigger. When I lived in his ashram, sometimes I would see him walk from his room to the meditation hall. I often wondered if he remembered the route or if he had to find his way anew each time. I kept having the amusing fantasy that one day we would all be waiting for him to arrive for the afternoon meditation, and he would never show up because he had made a wrong turn in the corridors. In my imagination, he ended up stumbling upon the kitchen where he helped prepare the dinner. To him, it made no difference whether he cut vegetables or sat in meditation because he had taken his final leap off the cliff of bliss. He lived floating in mid-air, never needing to land in earthly illusions again.

## Lost and Found

> **To think that**
> **You can find**
> **The Answer**
> **Is to be lost.**
>
> **To embrace**
> **Life's mystery**
> **Not knowing**
> **Is to be found.**

You find your true Self when you surrender into the unknown. The door to your Heart's desires opens when you realize that Life's mysteries cannot be figured out. A leap of faith is needed to unequivocally know this in every cell of your Being.

Your vitality diminishes if you have a picture of how Life is supposed to unfold, and then you become frustrated if it does not follow *your* plan. What if you had a sense of your goals in Life and simultaneously knew that eventually they would all land in your lap? Furthermore, what if you were not invested in the way they were achieved? As you "open to receive," you develop a knowingness that the world is already giving you exactly what you need. Eventually, you learn to let go of your scarcity consciousness and to trust. Then you no longer feel like a beggar chasing after your next meal because you already know that the Universe has given you a free lifetime ticket to its gourmet banquet.

One of the best ways to reverse the energetic flow created by external pursuit is to meditate. Just the word *meditation* can open a can of worms. What does meditation mean? How can you do it right? What are the best techniques? Does your posture matter? Is there a secret mantra that really works?

For clarity, let's define meditation as sitting down, closing your eyes for a period of time, and having the goal be to unlock the magical room of Love inside your Heart. The key to meditation is in your intention. Aspire to fall into the deepest recesses of your inner Self who lives underneath *all* thoughts. Then, whenever you notice that you are lost in thoughts, nonjudgementally remind yourself of your purpose. This awareness gently guides your meditation back on course by quieting your mind. Luxuriate in the stillness. If the noise of your thoughts sweeps the silence away again, simply notice and refocus on your Heart.

Something significant happens when you close your eyes for some time every day. Finally, you have begun the quest. You have started to search for Love inside your Heart. At first, you may perceive that you are only thinking without any silence for the entire period that your eyes are closed. Remember, this is the first stage. At least give yourself credit for sitting with your eyes closed. This is a 180° change in the direction of your attention. Let your whole effort be to fall back into your Heart. If you seek inner silence, you are headed Home. *Open to receive Love from within yourself instead of from outside yourself.*

## Meditation

**Meditation is not a technique**
    **Because your mind would only**
        **Become attached to the method.**

**There are no guided fantasies**
    **Because imagination is perpetuated.**
**There are no solutions**
    **Because problems do not exist.**
**There are no answers**
    **Because questions are not relevant.**

**There is only this moment,**
    **With an opportunity for you**
        **To discover the inner Silence**
            **Where Love always awaits you.**

As you meditate and as you move through your daily life, you can cultivate an inner awareness that increases your ability to quiet your mind. *Your mind's ears can either listen to thoughts or listen to sounds, but it cannot do both simultaneously.* If you use your awareness to pay attention to this internal listening mechanism, you will find yourself in the present tense more frequently.

## Listening

**If your awareness flows**
    **Down the river of sound,**
    **All thoughts become still**
    **And you are Here, Now.**

Gurdjieff, a Russian mystic, espoused a principle he called, "Clocking in Time in the Present Tense." This theory proposes that the more time you spend in the "Here and Now" rather than in the past or future, the happier you become, *regardless of other variables.* Psychological processing or any other discipline is unnecessary. Your *only* goal is to "be" in the Present. Everything that the mind does to divert you from that intention is merely a distraction. Rather than paying attention to the content of your thoughts, which gives them a lot of importance, the object is to use your awareness to notice whether you are thinking or not. If you notice thoughts, then you use your mind's ears to listen to the sounds around you rather than to pay attention to your thoughts. Each moment that you are non-judgementally listening to external noises, you are also clocking in another moment in the Now. This awareness helps you to not give credence to the endlessly looping trap of the thinking process.

You are most available to exchange Love with others when you are soft and receptive inside yourself. Going through Life with a receptive attitude heightens your sensitivity and allows you to be responsive in tender-hearted ways. You can touch something special with each person you meet, from your mate to parents to children to in-laws to the check-out clerk at the supermarket. This point of view can create more Happiness than you ever dreamed possible. *The trickiest part of understanding receptivity is that it seems too simple.* The ego tries to complicate simplicity because it has to take a back seat for this attitude to work. And what do all egos hate? Being unnoticed.

Right now, picture yourself standing at the edge of a cliff which is your challenge to let go at the next level. You look into the abyss of change, trying to decide whether or not to jump. After you step off into what appears to be thin air, the cliff often turns out to be nothing more than a curb. Then you simply step down onto the next avenue of your journey without any traumas. That short step may often feel like a long, scary free-fall. Only if your trust is deeply rooted can you know that when you step off, either the ground will gently rise to support you or you will sprout angel wings and instantly fly.

To jump into the unknown, you have to let go of control. Unwilling to surrender, your mind engages in very convincing negative thoughts. You contract in fear. Then, your fear escalates into panic which creates paralysis. *The mind will not release the old 'you' so that the new 'you' can emerge.*

There is a joke about a man who accidentally fell off the top of the Empire State Building. About halfway down a woman who had her window open saw him falling. As he arrived at her floor, she yelled to him, "How are you doing?" He responded, "So far, so good." Truly, he was in the moment. He did not let his thoughts about the future control him in the present.

Do not misconstrue what is being conveyed about thinking. Thinking is not wrong. It has its place. However, it usually forces itself to center stage about 99.9% of the time. If you were to live only 5% more of your time in other-than-thinking realms, your exploration of other dimensions of Life would dramatically increase. The key is for you to make that leap of faith into the unknown when Life challenges you with a cliff. *Take the initiative to be a pioneer into your inner frontier.* When you explore your inner abyss, you repeatedly discover the sweetness of Love.

## Quantum Leap

**Empty your mind,**
**Fill your Heart.**

**Don't settle for less.**

**Chapter Seventeen**

# Inner Over Outer

As you dive deeper into Life's mysteries, you can feel more reverence for the Creator of this masterpiece. When you are sure that you have Life all figured out, it changes. When you have solved one mystery, you are presented with a whole new puzzle which you did not even know was a part of the game. You are repeatedly asked to readjust and readapt.

God has given human beings a very special quest here on Earth.

## The Secret Treasure

God was trying to decide where to hide the most highly valued human treasure so that Life would have challenge, purpose, and mystery. At first God considered the bottom of the deepest oceans but realized that some day human beings would invent submarines and would find it too easily. The top of the highest mountain was also entertained, but eventually airplanes would allow access to even the peaks of the Himalayas. The moon was a possibility, but God foresaw that space ships would land there.

With a giant "Aha!" God joyfully chuckled about the place where most humans would think it was a waste of time to look, the place where few would search with the persistence necessary. The answers to the deepest mysteries of Life were hidden in a secret room inside the temple of each human being's Heart. In that room is the ultimate treasure chest overflowing with the elusive and most precious of all gems, Love and Happiness.

You may not even be aware that this inner room exists. Thus, you seek Happiness externally. Or if you do discover the door, it *seems* as if it can only be opened by finding out the combination to the lock. Naturally, you may look to others for the combination. Sometimes some person or event can crack open the door, and you are granted a glimpse inside. Ultimately, however, it appears that you must discover the combination in order to enter the room *whenever* you want, independent of external circumstances. It is an inside job.

Here is the paradox. No combination is necessary because your Heart has no lock. The gentlest nudge swings it wide open. Unfortunately, most people never even approach the door. They are so busy searching outside themselves that they never knock. Others who have tasted the room's treasures may deny that they discovered them within themselves because they have been so thoroughly indoctrinated to look externally.

*What if what you seek is not in any of the places where you are looking?* What if your quest is fruitless because the treasure is not within the domain you have been exploring?

## Where to Look

One dark night a woman who was walking through the friendly streets of her small town came upon a man obviously looking for something. He was down on his hands and knees underneath a street light diligently searching.

She asked him, "What is it you are looking for?"

He responded, "I am a tailor and I dropped my favorite needle and cannot find it."

She asked, "Do you know where you were when you dropped it?"

He answered, "Yes. I was way over there in the middle of that field."

Very puzzled, she asked, "If you dropped it way over there, then why are searching for it here?"

"Because it is too dark in that field to find it. There is a street light here, so this is where I'll be able to see it."

Most people are similar to the tailor. Having lost their Happiness, they search for it in a well-lit, obvious place – the external world. Most of their energy flows outward, hoping to find some contentment through material objects or relationships with others. They scan their outer environment in a desperate attempt to discover *anything* that might alleviate the painful gnawing inside their Souls.

Most people have developed eyes like a hawk's. If they catch sight of whatever they perceive as a "Happiness-maker," they hone in on it. They start stalking their prey, and cannot relax until they have captured it. If they finally succeed, they find pleasure in their "victory" for only a short time. Soon they start the cycle again by chasing the next illusion. And most people are running after many concurrent pursuits, with each one distracting them from being in the Here and Now.

When you recognize that your joy has been lost in the depths of your innermost Self, the real "Pursuit of Happiness" can begin. This inward search can be very scary. There are no lights or maps to show you the way. You must search blindly because the usual modalities of sight and thoughts are not very effective. The clarity of vision necessary for this journey is found within your Heart's intuition. *The key to open the door into new realms is to learn to trust that anything which appears to be other than Love is an illusion.* With this simple tool, you can discover the nooks and crannies where fulfillment is hidden.

This inner pursuit is often a very shattering experience. If you have been looking externally for Happiness, your whole thrust, consciously or unconsciously, has been to control others to ensnare what you think you need. If you achieve one goal, there is momentary joy, and then you focus on the next goal. The act of "chasing after" makes you a beggar because you have abandoned the joy of your connection with your Self to look "out there." *Your life ends up in pursuit of what you lack rather than in enjoyment of what you already have.* Every moment you are discontent with "what is," you are out of harmony with Love's vibration.

The inward path can also be very lonely because your current friends may not support you. They may try to dismiss your quest, invalidate your feelings, or accuse you of being self-centered, or even crazy, all because they are avoiding their fear of venturing inside themselves. *You must find the courage to dive into your internal infinity alone.*

Goals achieved in the material plane are easy to see. You either have them in your possession or you do not. Inner achievements are more elusive. They are more subtle and difficult to measure. One minute you feel joyful, thinking you will be happy forever. Then an inner shift occurs and your bliss disappears, often without your knowing why or how.

The challenge is to become so familiar with the most minute change inside yourself that you do not permit *any* thought or *any* circumstance to knock you out of Love. *A major step in stabilizing your joy is to unquestionably know that ultimate contentment comes from inside, not outside.*

## The Outer Death

Discovering that nothing
  Outside yourself can lead
    To ultimate fulfillment is
      Devastating and exquisite.

Devastating
  Because you lose
    Your desire for
      Worldly pursuits.

Exquisite
  Because you find
    A new Freedom
      To fly inward.

If you know that nothing is more important than learning how to permanently reside in your Heart, you start to reverse the current of your awareness by focusing inward.

## Diving In

**If you seek outside yourself,**
**No one is left at Home to**
**Receive Life's blessings.**

**When you dive into your Self,**
**You are a magnet attracting**
**All you ever need...plus...**
**Love you can't conceive.**

Rather than "diving in," most people are "chasing after," which creates an anti-magnet that literally repels what they seek. As you relax into your Heart, you may feel as if a cheerleading squad of angels is shouting, "Hurray! You are headed in the right direction! How can we further support you?" The Universe yearns for you to discover that secret room.

As you consciously leap into the inner abyss, more subtle nuances of spiritual laws come into effect. Unseen forces assist you by aligning events so that your life runs smoothly. This frees you to devote your attention to stabilizing yourself in the temple of your Heart. "Coincidences" help you to receive what you need to further your inner journey. You experience both little and big "miracles" which tell you that you are on track.

As you continue to explore your inner world, you begin to appreciate its infinite dimensions. You may begin to ask questions like, "What do thoughts consist of?" or "Where do emotions originate?" or "What creates sexual arousal?" You may challenge yourself to choose thoughts that nurture you rather than ones that hurt you. Instead of repeatedly focusing on the next goal, you become excited about each step of the journey. The awe you have for the whole process tickles your desire to mine for more inner treasures.

## Fascination

**Fascination turned inward**
**Keeps you forever exploring**
**The infinite inner blossoming**
**Of the mystery called 'You.'**

As you pioneer your inner frontier, you realize that you do have some control over where you reside inside yourself. The more you consciously choose to be centered in your Heart, the less you need to exert control over anyone or anything.

For instance, on different days you might encounter the same grouchy bank teller. One day you might react by becoming upset. Another day you might notice the teller's emotional pain and reach out from your Heart. *By knowing that your awareness rather than the bank teller's mood is the variable, you can rise above being a victim of external circumstances to become the master of your inner world.*

Your ideals probably tell you that you "should" always be compassionate and understanding with the bank teller. In fact, reactions to events happen so quickly that it is virtually impossible to control them. True, the more centered you are, the more likely you will perceive other people's pain as *their* pain and not react defensively. Yet, the real reward is in your choice to not judge your reactions. You have the freedom to change once you know that *all* reactions arise from whatever inner vibration you are attuned to (your state of consciousness) when the stimulus occurs.

## Inner Over Outer

**Your inner joy becomes real**
**When you are not a victim**
**Of your reactions to events.**

**You gain power over the external**
**By celebrating *all* of the internal,**
**Without judgement or repression.**

**Instead of being lost in reactions,**
**You now become free to choose**
**Your response to your reactions.**

For example, if you react defensively, in the next moment, you can choose not to judge that reaction. It has already occurred. There is nothing that you can do to change it. Instead, you can place your awareness on how you want to respond to your reaction. This is the moment of choice, the moment of exerting your will, the moment of potential freedom. *You can choose to respond by unconditionally accepting your reaction, whatever it is.* When you are enthralled with exploring your humanness, your curiosity and fascination make it impossible to judge yourself. Without self-condemnation, you are free to remain in Love's vibration every moment.

As you embrace all your reactions with self-compassion, you diminish the need to look outside yourself to validate your Love. *The less power you give external events, the more stable your Happiness becomes.* If you perceive "Reality" as having no more substance than a movie projector's light shining on a screen, then your circumstances cannot toss you around. When you stay centered in your Heart, you can simply enjoy the unfolding of any event, be it comedy or tragedy, romance or mystery. You are the *only* one who chooses how real you make this illusion.

## External Reality

**External Reality**
**Can be either**
**Thick or thin.**

**The thinner**
**The external,**
**The more joyful**
**The internal.**

Let's look at this paradigm from the innermost vantage point. Your reactions are not "you." They are external to your true Self. As you spend more time in your Heart, you increasingly perceive that calm and peaceful center as "you." Consequently, personality traits that you previously identified as "you" become external to the new "you." From this perspective, you can observe what you used to think was "you" with compassion, not needing to change a thing. As you perceive your reactions as external to the real "you," your unloving deeds and thoughts become "thinner." Thus, they cannot affect you so negatively.

The Universe supports your inward journey. As you gain experiences of "helpful coincidences," you breathe more easily. Trust is born. If you realize that your only essential survival needs are food, water, and shelter, then you can stop using energy to chase other non-vital illusions. Your need to try to control the outer world diminishes dramatically. This frees you to learn more about how to effortlessly receive.

## The Tree of Life

**When efforting matures,**
**Patience blossoms and**
**Drops the fruits**
**Of allowing**
**Into your lap.**

As you fall deeper into your inner infinity, many secrets are revealed. As the outer dies, the inner comes alive in ways that are more fulfilling than *any* externally oriented experience could ever be. You are bestowed with the privilege of seeing behind the veils of "Reality." It is no longer just a spiritual theory that this world is only a dream. You *know* in every cell of your Being that it is all an illusion. The Earth, the stars, the galaxy, the Universe all become an elaborate classroom where your *only* homework assignment is to stay centered inside Love.

*Eventually, the illusion of any separation between inner and outer, or internal and external, dissolves.* As you let go into your Heart, you discover the hologram from which this movie is projected.

## Full Circle

**As you fall into inner infinity,**
**You discover that every atom**
**Contains the whole Universe.**

You entered this magnificent dream through the birth canal and will exit through the Death tunnel. When you depart, what you take with you depends upon how clearly you have seen behind this Reality's veils. *In everyone's innermost core is the pure light that is the source of the illumination for the cosmos to project this marvelous movie called Life.* Once you merge with this light, earthly illusions vanish.

## Coming Home

**Being confined in a box called Reality**
**Makes this Universe much too tiny.**

**Falling into your infinite inner Self,**
**You find the Truth of this illusion:**
**There is no birth, there is no death,**
**There is no pain, there is no joy.**

**You will finally come Home**
**When *you* dissolve into All.**

# Part Three

# Freeing Your Spirit

# Section Six

# What Is Beyond the Mind?

## The Witness

The witness
Floats in the middle of
The stream of thoughts
Without ever getting wet.

## Chapter Eighteen
# Desiring No Desires

What are "thoughts"? From where do they arise? What are they made of? How do they influence your ability to be in Love? How can you stop your thoughts from pushing you around? How can you choose them instead of them choosing you?

If you are not your thoughts, then who are you?

## Who Are You?

**Just as the clouds are not the sky,
Your thoughts are not you.**

**You are the empty space in which
Your thoughts are floating.**

You may have become so identified with your thoughts that even the idea that you are something other than your thoughts can be terrifying. Right now, your thoughts may vehemently declare, "This guy is crazy. Of course I am my thoughts." Then, *exactly who is the thinker of those thoughts? Who remembers your experiences but is not your experiences?*

The mind is the ultimate egocentric. It keeps you focused on it. Your attention is the food that keeps it thriving. However, Love arises from a place where there are no thoughts. When you are in harmony with another person or are exchanging Love with someone, you do not need to talk. You need no words because you are beyond thoughts and concepts. You tenderly touch each other's face, gently stroke each other's hair, or silently look into each other's eyes without words. *Being in Love is expressing and exchanging energy.*

♥ What if you could feel Love with no need for a Love object outside yourself?

♥ What if you could be in Love each moment, regardless of external circumstances?

♥ What if you were so empty that thoughts could not get in the way of your Love?

You could easily be wondering, "Now this guy says to stop thinking. That is not possible. I need to think. Without my mind, I could not function. I would be a zombie."

Yes, you do need to think. Your mind can be an effective tool. However, *are you using your mind or is it using you?* Probably, you are the breeding ground for its demons – demons who have gained control over you. They are having a heyday, from their point of view. But from your point of view, they are destroying the very fiber of your life.

You can stand up to them and say, "Stop!"? Brugh Joy, healer and author of *Joy's Way*, tells a poignant personal story to illustrate this point. I have turned it into a parable.

## Who Is in Charge?

A man was taking a walk through the English countryside when he came upon a beautiful, large, fenced-in pasture. He climbed the fence and started strolling across the flower-laden field. Just as he was approaching the center of the pasture, a herd of raging bulls charged at him in full force. Terror shot through his veins as he desperately scrambled toward the fence.

As he ran, he looked over his shoulder and noticed the bulls gaining on him so quickly that he knew he would never make it to the fence. Fear kept his legs pumping at maximum speed. All of a sudden, he got a giant "Aha!" He instantly stopped running, planted his feet firmly on the ground, and turned around to face the charging bulls. He deliberately pointed his finger at the lead bull, looked him straight in the eyes, and shouted, "Stop!" And they all did! He then walked calmly to the fence in a state of bliss.

121

Those charging bulls are the demons of your mind. They all too frequently "bully" you around, but most of the time you probably do not even know it. *You may be so accustomed to being the brunt of your mind's abuse that you are not even aware of being violated.* Your mind races at such a fast pace that you rarely have the opportunity to drink in the serenity that is possible. Negative thoughts are like a swarm of hornets busily buzzing behind your head as they constantly menace you. You do have the power to turn around, look them right in the eye, and order them to "Stop!" You can learn how to access that power effectively.

What makes a thought arise inside your mind? Almost all thoughts are a message to you that some illusionary desire needs to be satisfied. Probably about 98% of your thoughts state, "I am not content with some situation(s), person(s), or myself, and I need to do something to change it, them, or me." You may well want to change yourself. However, self-critical thoughts are devious because they can disguise themselves as friends. They ardently try to convince you that they will help you by "improving you."

Actually, these thoughts are covertly poisoning your well-being. They taint you with the color of self-negation. Their underlying message is, "Something is wrong with you. You could be happy if only you would do this. Or this. Or this." They imply that you are not lovable exactly the way you are.

Each moment that you try to satisfy your mind's demands by jumping through its endless hoops, you miss the beauty within you right Now. Instead, you can use your will to direct your awareness toward feeling thankful for how miraculous Life already is. When you have appreciative thoughts, nurturing people or beneficial situations spontaneously appear in your Reality to confirm your gratitude.

You do have a choice as to where you place your attention. *Whatever is in the spotlight of your awareness increases in magnitude.* When you are in desire, you chase after what you perceive you lack. When you are in enjoyment, you can appreciate what you already have.

## Desiring or Enjoying?

**Desiring creates pursuit.**
**Enjoying creates gratitude.**
**The one you focus on grows.**

You can stay engaged with the mind forever as it screams for negative attention, similar to a child who acts out. You must use your will to choose to see the perfection within Now. The more perfection you perceive, the more you can trust Life. *You discover that this Reality is 'user friendly.'*

Without this trusting attitude, your ability to live full of wonder is stifled. If you keep chasing after what you think you lack instead of appreciating what you already have, the attitude of scarcity causes greed.

## Greed

**Greed is**
**A desire for more**
**With an underlying**
**Sense of unworthiness.**

**This combination causes you**
**To grab instead of allow,**
**To push instead of trust.**

The desire/thought cycle is worth a closer examination. *The mind stays alive by thinking. It is terrified to be quiet because it fears dying.* It grabs the center stage of your attention by making each thought seem important, even urgent. Your mind has successfully tricked you whenever you needlessly think.

But what are thoughts? They are images floating in your consciousness, like clouds floating across the sky. Thoughts are a filmy layer between you and the Present. The energy to create them arises from the same source as emotions and sexual feelings, except it ignites in the head instead of in the solar plexus or genitals. They usually begin from a desire.

## Desire

**Desire lies between you**
   **And utter contentment.**

**When a desire arises**
   **From the pool of serenity,**
      **You have a micro-instant**
         **To make a choice.**

**You can relax in the pool**
   **And watch the desire rise**
      **Like a soap bubble until**
         **It floats out of sight...**

**Or you can grab onto the desire**
   **As it breaks through the surface**
      **And ride away on it until**
         **The pool of serenity is**
            **Out of sight.**

There are Life-enhancing desires and Life-destroying ones. A positive one might be the desire to become more loving, to be of service to others, or to be more truthful. A negative one might be the desire to smoke cigarettes, to compulsively overwork, to seek revenge, or to earn exorbitant amounts of money. Negative desires lead you down the path of self-destruction. Positive ones do distract you from the present, but they also give you the motivation to move your life in a fulfilling direction. They also motivate you to go to a particular location where Life's lessons await you.

Positive desires also create your long-term goals or "North Star." As you sail on your life's journey toward your North Star, know that your route will zigzag, no matter how well you have charted the course. No plans can anticipate Life's unpredictable storms. You must tack back and forth when you veer off the mark. *You must learn the art of 'being with' the perfection of what seems like imperfection while you navigate toward your goals.*

## Goals

**If you have goals left to attain,**
   **Let them be directions to walk,**
      **Not obsessions that run you.**

**As you stroll through Life,**
   **Goals come to you easily**
      **If you stop chasing them.**

**The greatest achievement is to**
   **Penetrate the illusion of all goals.**

Trust knows that Truth wins in the long run. Goodness always finds you if you stay in Love, even when the external world does not match your pictures of how it is "supposed" to be. It is relatively easy to be in your Heart when things are going "your way." The real test occurs when Life takes an unexpected turn and disintegrates your cherished plans. This is the time to be especially gentle with yourself. The Universe is challenging you to feel what you need to feel without judging yourself or the external circumstances. If you are able to simultaneously experience your own pain and the perfection of it all, then you have risen to the occasion. *Being in harmony with apparent disharmony creates freedom.*

As you surrender into Love, a profound Truth is revealed: Every moment that you spend seeking Happiness in the future, an underlying pain persists in the present, whether you are aware of it or not.

## Desiring No Desires

**Fulfilling any desire brings joy**
**Because the pain of yearning**
**Is relieved....temporarily.**

**Soon, a new desire tempts you**
**To chase after the next carrot,**
**Crushing the fragile Now**
**With yet another Dream.**

**If you focus on desire itself,**
**Not on the object of desire,**
**You can break this cycle.**

**Desiring no desires takes you Home.**

When you face the Truth of this trap, you begin to search for what creates unhealthy desires. As you dig inside, you uncover mistrust and insecurity. You want your longing to be relieved by an unknown something. Even if you have already discovered that you are seeking Love, you may have forgotten that God hid the ultimate treasure inside your Heart. *When you know that you are Love, the external search ceases.*

There was a period of about six months in my life when I lived in a small cabin in the woods of west Marin County. I had set aside this time to explore consciousness. I spent most of my waking hours sitting in a chair watching the flames of the fire in the fireplace. I decided to become aware of which thought motivated me to get up from my chair. I wanted to discover the true origin of each urge to move. Was it really *my* desire or was it someone else's from my past?

As I observed, it became obvious that, almost every time, some historic source created my "need" to move. My motivation arose from my mother's desire to eat chocolate or socialize with friends, or my father's desire to be a success in the world or not waste time, or society's desire for me to buy material things or fulfill my "social obligations." Even the foods I craved were my parents' favorite choices, except for my desire for carrot juice, which seemed to be my own. Or was even this urge influenced by my neurotic need to appear to be a consciously evolving, healthy spiritual seeker? The more I witnessed my desires without judgement, the freer I felt from being at their mercy. I became more aware of watching the energy of desire itself rather than automatically acting upon any one of them. This process greatly diminished desire's power over me.

Are you eager to confront these nebulous distractions called "desires"? Do you want to be free of desires' illusions? Well, you cannot just declare, "That's it! No more desires! Starting in this moment, I am living in the Here and Now forever."

*Or can you?* This is a very powerful intention. Your mind will probably attempt to undermine this declaration, particularly if you make it from the depths of your Being. It will pull out all its big guns.  It hates to be cornered.  It may retaliate by trying to convince you with thoughts like, "This book is stupid.  Put it down now."  Or, "I'm tired.  Let's go to sleep."  Or, "With no desires, I would be a vegetable sitting under some tree for the rest of my life."

The mind needs to panic.  It is a good sign when it protests, or even shouts at you. *The mind yells the loudest when you are the closest to a breakthrough.*  Generally, immediately prior to a part of your mind dying, it screams bloody murder (it's own?) as it desperately tries to seduce you into believing its illusions.

What can you do with these desires when you have seen their destructiveness?  You need to *do* nothing.  Your task is to watch each desirous thought with awareness.  Watch with fascination.  With curiosity.  With amazement.  Become more seated in that internal place that can observe the mind in action but *is not* the mind.

## Dieting Your Desires

**Feed your desires
And you end up with
An overinflated ego.**

**Starve your desires
And you end up with
Imploding repression.**

**Witness your desires
And you end up with
Freedom.**

*Living Life in Love*.  It is an inside job.  As you become more aware of your desires, the most useful attitude is to compassionately observe them without any need to get rid of them.  Ironically, as you unconditionally accept them, destructive desires dissipate.  By shining the light of awareness on them, the illumination itself dissolves desires organically. The secret pathways to your Heart are revealed once you see behind their illusions.

## Discovering Love

**Desire's absence
Creates space for
Love's presence.**

## Chapter Nineteen
# Developing the Witness

As you evolve consciously, you become aware of how thoughts determine your inner Reality. You notice how your well-being can be destroyed by "negative" thoughts. You may try to reprogram yourself to think "positive" thoughts. As you enter this process, it is easy to chastise yourself whenever you discover a negative image passing through your mind. You can become afraid of your thoughts because you believe that when you have a negative thought, you create a miserable Reality for yourself, making your life Hell. From this point of view, you must be extremely careful to control every thought that comes into your head.

What if you were to embrace a whole new perspective that frees you from having to fear what goes through your mind? What if you could permanently reside in an inner place that experiences *all* thoughts as having no more substance than thin air? *What if the next level of your evolution involves knowing that thoughts themselves are an illusion?* Then you would not have to focus on trying to control either your mind or the external world.

## Thoughts

**Your thoughts**
**Can't bully you around**
**If you don't empower them**
**By believing they are real.**

There are different stages of human evolution. At first people are unconscious of the power of their thoughts. Then they become aware of the influence thoughts have over them, and often decide to not remain a victim of the mind's whims. They reach inside to strengthen their will in order to determine which thoughts enter their head, as addressed in Chapter Eighteen, "Desiring No Desires."

Now it is time to learn yet another approach to mastering the mind. This attitude has nothing to do with controlling your thoughts. *Ultimate freedom is attained by using your will to take up residence outside the mind's sphere altogether.*

## Mastering the Mind

**The objective is not**
**To control the mind.**

**The objective is**
**To stop the mind**
**From controlling you.**

**You master the mind**
**By giving it free reign**
**As you enjoy witnessing**
**Thoughts' infinite variety.**

What is this witness? As stated before, the witness observes your experiences but is not your experiences. It recalls your memories but is not your memories. It compassionately comprehends the psychological and emotional subtleties inside yourself and others. The witness perceives the nuances of every experience with no judgement or comparison. It is the eternal part of yourself which existed before you arrived here on Earth and will go on after you leave your body behind. It *knows* that this Reality is only a temporary dream and that the only thing which is real and forever is the Love inside your Heart. *The witness is the all-compassionate beam of light at the very core of your Being that is not touched by the painful illusions of this Earth's supposed 'Reality.'*

As you consciously observe your thoughts, you begin to identify yourself (known to you as "I") as being the witness rather than the thoughts. You become the watcher, the still point inside, out of which the whole earth plane Reality arises. You *become* the centermost core of your Being. You *know* that you are the dreamer of this dream rather than the dream itself. As you stabilize in the heart of your Heart, your sense of inner peace profoundly deepens. This unshakeable foundation of Love lets you watch with sheer delight as the mind dances back and forth between polarities.

## The Witness

> **The witness**
> **Floats in the middle of**
> **The stream of thoughts**
> **Without ever getting wet.**

Without the witness, you stay lost in reactions to experiences with little chance to learn. You repeat the same painful patterns. The witness provides a self-reflective quality so that you can be in relationship to not only your thoughts, but also to your feelings, your experiences, and external events.

The primary motivation for developing the witness is usually *pain*! The witness lets you see that you are 100% responsible for your response to your reaction to every event. It brings awareness to the ways in which you are stuck in harmful patterns. It keeps you from repeatedly banging your head against the wall. *As you develop the witness, you no longer have to make an effort to change because you are already watching yourself unfold organically.* Rather than being at the mercy of your thoughts, you know that their power over you is equivalent to a breeze instead of a hurricane.

You become free to discover within yourself the many layers of consciousness. Since the witness is not judgemental, you are free to look directly into the face of *all* aspects of you without self-condemnation. You can dance underneath your denial mechanisms. You can go into your darkest corners to shine the light of awareness and heal all parts of your "inhumanity." Most people are so busy denying they have any negativity in them that they resist fully facing their "shadow," or dark side. The witness frees you to embrace *all* of you, from your divinity to your devilry.

## Choiceless Awareness

> **'Choiceless awareness'**
> **Watches thoughts without**
> **Preferencing their content.**
>
> **'Choiceless' lets all aspects**
> **Of humanity's kaleidoscope**
> **Arise from your unconscious,**
> **Set free by no self-judgement.**
>
> **'Awareness' lets the witness**
> **Compassionately see *all* of you**
> **With unconditional acceptance.**

As you become stably seated in the witness, you can take the lid off your unconscious and let "Pandora's Box" open. The Universe never gives you more than you can handle, even though it can *feel* like too much. *That extra stretch exercises the muscles of your inner awareness.* If you passionately face Life's "perverse challenges," the inner victim dissolves. Eventually, you know that you can handle *anything* that comes your way. Your stance becomes, "Let's go for it. Is this all? So far, I have lost my job, my mother died, and my lover left me. Give me more. I am here to get Enlightened."

As you realize that experiences are just experiences, no matter how intense they are, you can embrace whatever crosses your path. Instead of trying to turn others into who *you* think they should be, you simply love them exactly as they are. *You discover that Pandora's Box is filled with toys to play with instead of monsters to battle.*

The witness frees you from trying to control your mind or the external world. As you feel safe to look at "what is," a kind of curiosity arises which allows you to uninhibitedly delve into the human condition - both yours and others'! The development of the witness is the underlying commonality of many of the therapeutic techniques that have been born over the past thirty years. Psychosynthesis, Gestalt, Psychodrama, Alchemical Hypnotherapy, Voice Dialogue, The Option Process, The Enneagram, and other methods give people the opportunity to be in relationship to their inner process rather than be lost in it. If you know that the common thread running through all these techniques is the refinement of the witness, then you do not have to be limited by one particular modality. Instead, you can use any of them to further your ability to go beyond the mind itself. It is easy to miss this essential point and then get bogged down by believing that one technique has all the answers.

Does cultivating the witness make you a mere observer of Life rather than a full-on participant? Actually, the opposite occurs. As the witness matures, you directly experience unconditional acceptance. With this safety, you relax into enjoying your humanness. As you feel free to be you, you blossom into a full experience of *all* parts of yourself that you were avoiding before because, through your eyes of self-judgement, they were not okay. The witness allows you to let go of controlling and unduly exerting yourself. It knows that you are already taken care of. *As you become the witness, you begin to trust instead of try.*

One of the more subtle inner "devils" is doubt, a paralyzer that keeps you on the fence of indecision. Every moment that you are stuck on that fence hoping for a clear answer, you miss out on moving freely through Life. Doubt is one of the mind's most powerful ways to disable you by keeping you captured in its fluctuations. If you try to battle doubt, you immerse yourself in inescapable quicksand. The whole time you are waging war, the mind celebrates because it has you in its clutches. You can spend hours or days or weeks or even years trying to decide about some issue, lost in the clever trap of doubt.

Rather than paying attention to the content of the problem, observe the energy of doubt itself. You can trace a certain negative attitude that tries to attach itself to different subjects. Notice that the same negative flavor of a "problem" you are trying to resolve gets transferred to a new topic when you clear up the first dilemma. If you witness the flavor of the energy itself rather than being pulled into trying to logically solve each problem, you take a genuine step in raising yourself out of the muck. You discover that it is useless to try to resolve problems from the level of consciousness in which they were created because the same negative energy jumps from one subject to another.

## Doubt

**The dark mind thrives on**
**Your giving credence to**
**The voice of doubt.**

**Transcendence occurs**
**When you are neither**
**For nor against doubt.**

The witness helps you to discover that doubt thrives when you lack trust, either in yourself or in another person or in the Universe. You spin negative fantasies about the many possible outcomes of your decisions. You assume that things will go wrong rather than right. And you blame yourself for disastrous results before anything has even occurred. As you try to sort things out, the voice of doubt is so loud that you cannot hear anything else. What if you were to intentionally search for a subtler, quieter voice that is simultaneously speaking to you?

## Inner Voices

**Listen very sensitively
To your inner voices and
Choose which to empower:
The shout of doubt...
Or...
The whisper of trust.**

As you let yourself be led by the whisper of trust, Life begins to change. You gain concrete experiences of trust benefitting you and those around you. You start to relax as you feel the Universe supporting you. Then you can transfer your trust to a new subject. Just as the negative flavor of doubt bounces from problem to problem, so does the positive flavor of trust. The difference is that doubt destroys and trust enhances.

The witness is also extremely helpful in expanding your capacity to be happy. You are accustomed to spending a certain amount of time in certain states of consciousness. If you were to make a chart each week of how many hours you spend being happy, sad, angry, forlorn, blissful, vengeful, hopeful, sexual, lost in thoughts, confident, or insecure, you would find that, week after week, you spend a similar amount of time in each one, unless there is a dramatic change in external circumstances. If an unusual event occurs, such as finding a new job or meeting a new lover or moving into your dream house, all of a sudden you are happy more of the time than you normally are. *But you cannot stay happy for too long because you are addicted to a certain amount of pain or anger.* As you fall back into your old habit patterns, you become doubly discouraged because you believe that you have failed. You thought that you had finally found the key to unlocking your Happiness. Unfortunately, the only way to permanently open that lock is from the inside, independent of any transitory external changes in your daily routines.

Be aware of how often you feel happy. You can increase joy's frequency by strongly declaring that you are expanding the amount of time you feel good. The main thing that takes you out of joy is that you are unaccustomed to identifying with it.

## Bliss Quota

**What is your Bliss Quota?
An hour per day? Per month?
What are the limits of your joy?**

**Monitor how long you can feel
Exquisitely contented...then
Allow that time to increase.**

**Observe your discomfort with
Feeling more bliss than usual.**

**This awareness alone allows
More Love into your life.**

The negative mind often deliberately contaminates bliss with the contagious disease known as "seriousness," which has reached epidemic proportions in today's society. One way to immunize yourself from the malady of solemnity is to giggle frequently. Humor is an instant cure for seriousness. If you start to become infected with heaviness as you expand beyond the previous limits of your "Bliss Quota," lighten up by asking yourself, "What's wrong? Have I been too happy too long?" The smile in your Heart in response to this question can be a panacea for your dis-ease.

As you fall into your Self so deeply that your self-image becomes the witness itself, you relax. When you identify "I" as being the witness rather than all the other "stuff," you can enjoy the uncensored movie arising from your mind. As *you* become "compassionate choiceless awareness," you free yourself to embrace *all* of you, unconditionally, without judgement. You discover that *nothing* is wrong with you. Love, hate, pain, joy, lust, grief, emotions, and thoughts are all in you - the same as what is in every other person. You can finally celebrate this human being being human!

Quit empowering your negative mind. Give up trying to find "The Answer." Stop asking yourself that ever-so-dangerous, thought-perpetuating question, "Why?" It deludes you into seeking a solution which cannot be found where you are looking.

## Why?

**Any answer to 'Why?'**
**Must always be a lie.**

**You cannot find**
**Truth in your mind.**

As Rumi wrote: "Out beyond all ideas of wrongdoing and rightdoing, there is a field. I'll meet you there..." He is pointing to the field where the witness lives, or, more accurately, plays. May that place in your deepest core become your playground for dancing with bliss.

## Chapter Twenty
# The Ecstasy of Emptiness

Worship silence. Aspire to become nothing. Dive into the inner void. Seek that which is infinitely indefinable. Inside emptiness lies the entire Universe. *Where there is nothing is where there is everything to be gained.*

These words are not written out of spiritual ideals or theories. They are written out of my direct experience of the depths of compassion within Silence. The exquisite encounter I had with Death discussed in Chapter Ten (see page 69) gave me a profound personal teaching about the ultimate power of the void. When I was blessed with the gift of going beyond words and ideas and thoughts, what greeted me was the infinite Love within emptiness.

Look at the most meaningful connections that you have with another person. Words are not needed. In fact, they are generally a hindrance. When being sexual, at the very moment of orgasm and immediately afterwards, often a soothing silence emerges and allows *all* of you, including your body, emotions, and thoughts, to deeply relax all the way down to your Soul. These experiences are clues in solving the bigger mystery.

## In Between

**Truth lives where there is no 'I'...**
**In the spaces between thoughts.**

**Let your whole effort be**
**To fall into this void...**
**Forever.**

Why is this so difficult? Because it goes against everything that your Western mind has ever been taught. You have been indoctrinated from the moment you were born to be important, to be somebody. Society's foundation is built upon needing its members to achieve, to get ahead, to consume, to spend money. The seeds of destruction of all that is deemed important in the Western world are contained within the concept of seeking silence. As you get to the edge of the abyss of emptiness, the logical mind shouts, "No!" It then invents your next project or problem or part of your personality to work on so that you must continually stay engaged with it.

## Emptiness

**The mind fills emptiness**
**With *any* thought form**
**Instead of stepping aside**
**To create the silent void**
**From which Love arises.**

You are invited into an illogical process that may directly oppose what you believe to be the main purpose of your life. You have been trained to pursue knowledge by filling your mind with more and more facts and ideas. The assumed progression is that the more you can cram into your brain, the smarter you become. The smarter you become, the more successful you become. The more successful you become, the happier you are. The most deceiving part of this lie is that it is true...at the material level of Reality. Within this narrow perspective, there is no way to dispute this claim. However, the best way to see through this lie is to observe how unfulfilled many people are who have successfully walked this path, perhaps including yourself. Maybe, just maybe, another kind of Happiness is more fulfilling and longer lasting than the joy created by acquiring knowledge.

## Learning

**Learning
Inspires
Your mind.
Unlearning
Frees
Your spirit.**

The journey becomes an unravelling of the complexities you have made of your life. *It is a process of simplifying. It is taking away from rather than adding to. It is letting go of rather than holding on to.* Your mind believes that it has to figure Life out. It desperately tries to keep everything together. Paradoxically, when everything falls apart, a mystical "something else" can happen. The route to that "something else" is terrifying because your mind, as you have known it, has to dissolve.

## Spiritual Insanity

**As you transcend linear limitations
And feel like you are going insane,
Know that *all* Enlightened beings
Have deliberately lost their mind
And have no need to find it again.**

Not until you go beyond the mind can you discover ultimate Happiness. Your Soul repeatedly cries out to you. It urges you to return to one of the most basic questions that you can ask yourself: "Who am I?" There are an infinite number of answers to this question. The more you define yourself in linear ways, the more limits you place upon yourself. If you see yourself as only a human body walking around on this planet, then that is who you become. If you see yourself as the different roles you play, then that is who you become. If you question these self-limitations, then you can take the lid off who you perceive yourself to be. The more you cannot put your finger on who you believe yourself to be, the more fully you discover your infinite nature. *The more you can honestly say, 'I have no idea who I am,' the more you become the magical mystery itself.*

## Identity

**When you lose your identity as
Father/son, mother/daughter,
Secretary, lawyer, waiter,
Rich, poor, good, bad,
Sad, happy, angry,
You find you.**

The "you" that you find beyond your mind is so much more than you ever dreamed you could be. When you strip away all your self-limiting beliefs, you feel a magnificent and humbling Life force flowing through you.

Trying to understand how this miracle works is enticing. And fascinating. A certain joy is born when you seek the Truth. However, after you have been on the path for a while, you see an infinite number of places to look for answers. This process can become so engulfing that you could spend a thousand years in just one corner. And you will probably discover that what you seek cannot be found where you are looking, much like the tailor and the lost needle. To expedite your search, you can eliminate the vast realm of unfruitful, barren territory known as "logic." If you explore elsewhere, you eventually explode into an "Aha!" that launches you into nonlinear aspects of Reality, such as trust and awe.

## Understanding

**The desire to understand
Can imprison your Spirit
At the level of Thinking.**

**Understanding fills the mind,
But cannot awaken the Soul.**

Once again you are left with a non-answer. The key to the Universe always seems to be just out of reach. *No techniques can be given.* There is only an invitation into your intuition and into the vast realms of your inner Self. You may already be looking for the space between your thoughts. You may already know how to feel yourself falling back into your Heart as you search for that secret room. Hopefully, you no longer pay much attention to those puffs of imaginings called "thoughts." If you shine the light of awareness on your innermost darkness, you illuminate your uniquely unfolding Self. Your primary commitment effortlessly evolves into watering "The Seed of Silence" within your Soul.

## The Seed of Silence

**To use a linear technique to
Change your belief system
Absolutely misses the point.**

**You merely substitute
One thought for another,
And you are still trapped
At the level of the mind.**

**Dive in deeper to discover
That tiny *Seed of Silence*
Buried under *all* thoughts.**

**Water that delicate seed
With your gentlest Love
So that it can sprout.**

**As the *Seed of Silence* grows
And the mind's grip on you
Becomes weaker and weaker,
Your flowering Heart can
Fully blossom into Love.**

So far, the focus has been on seeking internal emptiness. However, on a practical level, disarray in your external environment can easily distract you from your inner silence. Chaotic surroundings can agitate your inner harmony.

Dr. Eleanor Griffith, a brilliant child psychologist and pre-school director in Berkeley, California, has shown that children feel calmer when their environment is orderly. Her classroom is kept tidy. When a child finishes with a toy, either the child or Eleanor returns it to its designated place on a shelf. If kids start to get upset, she first straightens up the toys. Frequently, they immediately calm down, without her doing anything else.

Cleaning up external clutter can also give you the space to clarify internal turmoil. If your energy is primarily focused outward in order to cope with Life, you are not free to look inward. *You may unconsciously create outer muddle because then you can avoid facing your inner confusion.* Although true joy is not dependent upon your environment, outer chaos can certainly be a distraction. Thus, if you want to minimize the need to place your attention on external Reality, you can clean up your environment.

Close your eyes for a moment and envision your home right now. Do you have dirty dishes in the sink, an unmade bed, clothes strewn about, unpaid bills, scattered papers, messy closets, an uncared for car, or a disorganized attic or garage? This kind of chaos can trap your awareness in suspended projects or unresolved problems.

If you see the wisdom in this perspective and decide to clean up your clutter, your attitude as you proceed is essential. If a messy home is your way of rebelling against your parents, you need to let go of this belief. On the other hand, you cannot straighten up your home as a way of pleasing your parents or anyone else. Your fundamental intention must be to clean for the sake of clearing up your life and enhancing your spiritual evolution. *Clean with Love or do not clean at all.* If you are not energized as you clean, then you are doing it for the wrong reasons. If you feel a glow inside your Heart as you proceed, then you are in harmony with the underlying purpose of this task.

Unfinished business with other people can also prevent you from dropping into the void. Cleaning up relationships clears up agitation in your mind. Every negative judgement or resentment that you hold onto hurts *you* more than anyone else. *You poison yourself every time you think harshly about others.*

Close your eyes and envision anyone with whom you are upset. What stops you from seeing that the negativity occurred between you because of a misunderstanding or reactive egos? Why do you give that person (or your mental image of that person) the power to take you out of Love? When you find compassion and forgiveness for yourself and for the other person, you are also making the statement, "I am the master of my mind, and I choose Love." Why would you ever let your negative mind win? For your own sake, look deeper into what is really going on. Let go of your stubbornness and melt into Love.

If you clean up your clutter on the material plane and with other people, then you can continue your inner journey unencumbered. Once you have completed one major "spring cleaning," then everyday maintenance becomes easier. On the material plane, you can beautify each room you enter by picking up a piece of clothing, straightening a pillow, or changing a burned out light bulb. You can keep your relationships clean by communicating vulnerably the moment that any interaction feels sticky or unloving.

Underneath each human being's neurosis is a deep longing for everyone to be happy. When you discover the infinite quantity of Love inside your Heart, your ability to support others increases because you no longer need to fight against anyone for a limited commodity. Knowing this, competition can melt into cooperation.

## The Human Race

**When the human race**
**Decides to stop racing,**
**Love can take the lead**
**And then *everyone* wins.**

# Section Seven

# Strolling Down
# The Spiritual Path

### The Spiritual Path

If you are marching down
The spiritual path searching,
You can miss the stroll itself
Wherein lies *all* that you seek.

## Chapter Twenty-One
# The Spiritual Seeker Must Die

Once you know that you are "on the path," you must deal with a new set of illusions, known as "spiritual belief systems." *In an attempt to achieve 'Enlightenment,' your mind may construct a false spiritual ladder to climb.*

## Spiritual Pursuits

**If your life purpose is
To evolve spiritually,
Then free yourself
From chasing after
*All* spiritual goals.**

You can easily be fooled into focusing all your attention on trying to live up to high-sounding spiritual ideals that, in fact, subtly destroy your Love. You can become so attached to perceiving yourself as "a seeker" that your spiritual identity itself prevents you from knowing that you are *already* Divine.

## Knocking on God's Door

There was once a man who sincerely sought God for over forty years. He renounced the world when he was eighteen years old. He became celibate at twenty. He joined a monastery soon thereafter. He meditated every day for years. He traveled to visit the ancient sages in the caves of the Himalayas. Everyone who came in contact with him quickly learned what a dedicated seeker he was.

One day as he was walking in the deepest recesses of the untouched forest, he came across the House of God. There was no doubt in his mind that he had at last arrived at the place he had been seeking for his whole life. Now he only needed to walk up the steps to the front door and knock. He knew that God would open the door and his journey would be finished.

He walked up onto the porch and raised his arm to tap on the door. Suddenly, a great fear arose in him. He could not make himself do it. He slithered away from the House of God. He had become so identified with being a "seeker" that he could not fathom who he would be if he found that which he had been pursuing for all these years.

The path itself has so many nuances. You must uncover different levels of illusions along the way. Spiritual teachers or gurus can be a wonderful vehicle to point you in the right direction. However, you can also become snarled in their briar patch of holiness if you look to them for all the answers. The true guru repeatedly invites you into your inner Self to discover whatever it is you are seeking.

## Gurus

**True spiritual masters
Show you how to be you,
Not how to worship them.**

There are as many routes to God as there are human beings on the planet. You can learn from others' experiences only up to a certain point. You cannot duplicate what works for them because they are not you. In the end, you awaken by walking down your own path filled with your unique challenges. You must deal with your illusions by facing them instead of hoping that they will disappear if you run away into a spiritual cave. As you consciously explore all the dead end alleys of your desires, you learn that Enlightenment is available within each moment, no matter what road you are on.

## Dead Ends

Many dead end alleys
   Tempt you to exit from
      'Enlightenment Freeway.'

Chasing after Money, Sex,
   Power, or Spiritual Goals
      Seems to lead you astray.

However, by denying ones
   That repeatedly attract you,
      You will always look back,
         Wondering what you missed.

You must explore each of
   Those apparent dead ends.

As you re-enter the Freeway,
   The alleys are no longer exits.
      They are an essential part of
         Your journey going Nowhere.

The original inspiration for you to step onto the spiritual path is often a genuine, heartfelt experience. Once you have tasted the divine nectar, your insatiable thirst lets you risk in many ways. *However, even your desire for Enlightenment must eventually be seen as an obstacle to being in the Now.* But before you give it up, let yourself honor this very special desire. It changes the whole thrust of your life.

## The Seeker

Desiring Enlightenment
   Is not different from
      Desiring a new car.
         Both destroy Now.

And yet,

If your desire for
   The car is fulfilled,
      It is replaced by
         An endless stream
            Of new desires.

If your desire for
   Enlightenment is fulfilled,
      *You* are replaced by
         An endless stream
            Of Love.

Spiritual beliefs can be very tricky. They can covertly manipulate you into judging yourself because they disguise themselves in a veil of holiness. Nothing is more spiritual than searching inside your Heart for forgiveness and then finding it. But do you know that the most Enlightened beings never need to forgive?

## Forgiveness

**Feeling forgiveness is**
    **A beautiful release from**
        **The prison of the past.**

**But, the very need to forgive**
    **Shows that you have judged.**

**Let go of all judgements**
    **And you will never need**
        **To forgive anyone again.**

*The above aphorism is a deliberately created, clever spiritual trap.* Did you fall for it? If you try to live up to the ideal of letting go of all judgement so that you will never need to forgive again, then you have just set up another spiritual goal for yourself. The trap lies within the belief that if you can somehow get to the place of never judging, then you will become Enlightened.

Sounds great, eh? But don't worry. You will need to forgive again because you will judge again. You are still human. Sometimes, goals disguised as spiritual ideals can craftily destroy your acceptance of who you are *right now,* including your judgemental aspects.

*Let every thought, whether you label it as 'positive' or 'negative,' be a mere whisper on the horizon of your consciousness instead of a bellowing directive from center stage.* Ironically, as you lose yourself into inner bliss, your mind loses its control over you. You have seen its tricks and do not bite at its bait. Eventually, the mind rarely even bothers to cast its line in your direction because the fishing is better elsewhere.

The wisest teachings inform you that there are no teachings. Spiritual goals dissolve as your ego disappears into the vibration of Love within Now.

## The Spiritual Path

**When you boldly march down**
**The spiritual path searching,**
**You can miss the stroll itself**
**Wherein lies *all* that you seek.**

When you stop searching, then you can remove the blinders that have prevented you from seeing that you have already arrived.

## Seeking God

**Seeking God**
**Keeps you from**
**Seeing God**
**Inside Now.**

### Chapter Twenty-Two
# Dissolving Spiritual Idealism

Spiritual ideals can inspire you to new heights of ecstasy. They can also be the most deadly murderers of bliss. Ideals originate in the realm of thoughts, which are the layer of illusion between you and Now. *In the end, all your pictures of Enlightenment must be destroyed.* All methods of finding God must be released when the technique itself stands in the way of being in the Now. You must be free of goals to become the energy of Love.

## Two Pathways to God

One day God sent a female angel down to Earth to see how everything was going, especially among the dedicated seekers. The angel first came upon an older man sitting under a tree meditating. As she flew down, the man opened his eyes. The angel said, "I have been sent from God to see how you are doing. Is there anything you want me to ask God for you?"

The old man replied, "Yes. I have been meditating for hours each day for the past forty years. How much longer until I am Enlightened? I must be getting close, and I do not have many years left this lifetime."

The angel responded, "I will go ask God and return with an answer."

On the way back up to Heaven, the angel flew over a clearing in the forest where there was another man joyfully dancing and singing. As she approached, he barely noticed. But the angel wanted to be sure to take care of each of God's seekers, so she also said to him, "I have been sent from God to see how you are doing. Is there anything you want me to ask God for you?"

The man was lost in the bliss of his dancing and singing. He waved a friendly hello and called out to her, "No, not really. Just pass on my gratitude for being given a human body in which to celebrate Life."

The angel flew on back up to Heaven and talked with God. Later she returned to Earth and found the first man still meditating underneath the tree. As she approached, he opened his eyes and said, "It is wonderful to see you. I have been waiting for your answer for days now. What did God say?"

The angel replied, "God said that it will only be three more lifetimes for you to achieve Enlightenment."

The man flew into a rage and shouted, "Three more lifetimes! I cannot wait that long. God must be wrong!"

Having delivered her message, the angel flew off and came across the other man still dancing and singing in the forest. She approached him and he greeted her with a friendly, "Hello again. Do you want to dance with me?"

The angel responded, "Thanks, but not right now. I know you did not request it, but I did ask God when you would get Enlightened."

The man replied, "That's great. What did God say?"

The angel conveyed the message: "You will achieve Enlightenment in as many lifetimes as there are leaves on the trees in this forest."

The man continued with his joyous celebration and exclaimed, "How wonderful. That gives me all the more time to sing and dance."

In the next moment, he became Enlightened.

God is not the anthropomorphic projection frequently envisioned. No humanlike embodiment of energy sits up in Heaven or anywhere else. God is so much more vast than this limited interpretation. If you can let go of trying to comprehend God through your mind, an opportunity becomes available for you to directly experience in your Heart the infinite Light out of which this Reality arises.

# God

**God is a vibration**
    **Showering Love**
        **Indiscriminately.**

**God is an empty void,**
    **Open to receiving all**
        **That flows from you,**
        **Be it pain, joy, rage,**
            **Love, hate, or sex.**

**If you pour *all* of you**
    **Into God's emptiness,**
        **You attune your Soul**
        **To be in harmony with**
            **The angels' Love Song.**

Unfortunately, you cannot find God within the dogma of religion. God does not live in doctrines or beliefs. God is no more accessible in a church or temple than anywhere else. God is directly available within a special feeling, not within a physical or mental structure.

# Religiousness

***Religiousness* is**
    **Feeling a sacredness**
        **Overflowing with awe**
        **For the miracle of Life.**

***Religion* is**
    **An artificial structure which**
        **Contaminates religiousness**
        **By creating a middleman**
            **Between you and God.**

Many people try to find God by disciplining their mind and desires. *It is not actions, but the intention behind the actions, that creates divinity.* As your innocence emerges, an attitude of surrender allows you to open your Heart to Love.

# Discipline

**Discipline is**
    **A misunderstood**
        **Spiritual concept.**

**Discipline is *not***
    **Meditating each day or**
        **Exercising your body**
        **In the 'correct' way.**

**Discipline is being**
    **Courageous enough**
        **To see through your**
        **Most elusive illusions.**

One of the greatest illusions is within the realm of time. Most people have structured their lives so they do not have enough time. They are usually so busy hurrying to the next place or project or person that they miss the magic within the present moment.

## Time

**You can worry about
Spending time or
Saving time or
Wasting time.**

**Or you can just relax
And have a good time.**

You can miss out on the simplest expressions of bliss if you look for spirituality in all the wrong places. Even your nose can offer you a moment of ecstasy if you allow it to.

## Sneezing

**A sneeze is
Your nose
Exploding
In orgasm.
So be total and enjoy.**

If you let go of your pictures of where to find Love, you can celebrate everything. Being present with "Jello" can open the doors to tasting the sublime.

## Jello

**Jiggle.
Wiggle.
Squiggle.
Giggle.**

## Chapter Twenty-Three
# Shining a Light on Enlightenment

Let's play with more of Enlightenment's elusive illusions.

## Enlightenment's Trap

*Enlightenment* is only
    Another concept that
        Keeps you imprisoned.

Trying to achieve
    *Your* idea of liberation
        Keeps you trying.

If you quit pursuing
    All spiritual ideals,
        Love pursues you.

When ambitious people become seekers of God, they often mistakenly translate their need to achieve material success into a need to accomplish spiritual goals. They do not understand that the laws of cause and effect in nonlinear realms are very different.

## Enlightenment

Enlightenment
    Is like Death.

Both are already
    On their way to you.

So why not have fun
    Until one...
        Or the other...
            Or both arrive?

As you relax into the inevitability of your own Enlightenment, the loss of your identity as someone trying to go somewhere can be scary. How you move through the world shifts at the most fundamental levels. *You realize that the place you are trying to get to is no more rewarding than where you already are.*

## Nowhere

Do you realize that
    *Nowhere* is both
    *No where*
    And
        *Now here*?

Where was it that
    You were headed
        In such a hurry?

High-sounding spiritual ideals often fog up the window of Truth's clarity by making Enlightenment seem so unattainable.

## Ordinariness

**An Enlightened ordinary person is
Easily missed as you search for
*Your* image of divine wisdom.**

**As you keep letting go of
*All* preconceived notions,
You see Enlightenment
In many people's eyes,
Even in your own.**

Seriousness is one of the attitudes that can make your task here on Earth seem to be of utmost and urgent importance.  If you are dedicated to doing "God's work," you may believe that you should receive special dispensations.  *What if your seriousness is a malady that wilts the blossoms in you Heart?*

## Spiritual Seriousness

**Spiritual seriousness is
A holy-veiled hautiness
That makes you believe
*Your* purpose on Earth
Is greater than a flower's.**

The veils between illumination and ignorance are so very thin.  A slight shift of the cornerstone upon which your perceptions of this Reality are built allows your illusions to come tumbling down.  When the foundation of your core beliefs erodes away, then you have nothing solid left to stand upon except the trust in your Heart.  When all your points of view evaporate, your ego dissolves and Enlightenment appears.

## The Awakened Ones

**The only difference between
Enlightened persons and
Unenlightened ones is that
The enlightened ones
Accept themselves
Exactly as they are:
Unenlightened!**

# Part Four

# Expressing Your Love

# Section Eight

# Loving Others

## Unconditional Love

Love can only be
    'Unconditional.'

If your Love has
    *Any* strings attached,
        Then it is not Love.

## Chapter Twenty-Four
# Friendship

The first seven sections of *Living Life in Love* have dealt primarily with your internal world and how to create a loving relationship with yourself. This section focuses on ways to love others. As your understanding of your psyche deepens, an appreciation for your humanness develops. You also begin to see others through new eyes. You notice how much you have in common with people rather than amplifying differences. You see that all human beings are doing the best that they possibly can. You feel empathy for their plight because you know that their pain is your pain. *Even though people's anxiety is attached to different subjects and appear to have different causes, everyone's experience of feeling pain itself is identical.* All the rivers of humanity flow into one ocean.

## All One

Each moment you see people
As separate from yourself,
Ego is reborn.

If you can feel the despair that
The illusion of *other* creates,
Your walls disintegrate and
Communion is born.

If you notice the petty ways you keep yourself apart from others, your "I" begins to melt as you feel the pain of separation. *You see that you have created an emotional chasm between you and others to protect yourself from feeling the depth of your own pain.* The deeper you let go into this abyss of agony, the more sensitive you become to the common threads that tie all human beings together. You also discover that your isolation does not serve you or anyone else. You become your own best "ego buster."

## Blaming

The ego sees faults.
Love sees Love.

Which are you
Looking for?

As you become more vigilant, you uncover ways that you have refused to swim in the vast ocean of humanity. You can no longer overlook the behaviors and/or attitudes to which you have been blind in the past because you see how much these have hurt you. You know that your judgements must dissolve for your own sake, as well as for others.

## Judgement

Whenever you judge others,
You give them your power
By polluting your purity
With poisonous thoughts.

Also, notice the ways you try to be helpful. *The intention with which you reach out to others is more important than the act of reaching out itself.* Sometimes being concerned about someone can be more destructive than constructive.

## Concern

**An unhealthy type of concern**
  **Appears to be humanitarian,**
    **But is a cancerous disease.**

**This concern pressures others**
  **To not feel their pain because**
    **It makes *you* uncomfortable.**

**Your judgement can block**
  **The releasing of their pain**
    **As fear of your own feelings**
      **Disposes them to hold back.**

**If you are *caring and trusting*,**
  **Without this sticky concern,**
    **Expectations disappear and**
      **Transformation is available.**

As you look from new perspectives, the ways you fool yourself surface. The reasons you enter into relationships can be explored anew. As you examine your relationship to your relationships, you may discover that your underlying motives arise more from selfishness than from unselfishness. You may be trying to fill your emptiness through someone else.

Because of society's lies about who you are *supposed* to be, it is almost impossible to feel okay just being you. You cannot let others know about your insecurities or neediness because you are not even supposed to have them. You hide from others what you consider to be unacceptable. *When you relate, the underlying modality is often one of self-protection.*

As a child, the best way for you to be safe was to hide the truth of your experience or you would be punished, either psychologically, physically, sexually, or some other way. You protected yourself by burying your vulnerability underneath mask after mask for your very survival. This was an intelligent thing to do because adults did have power over you.

However, eventually *you* could not distinguish your truths from your lies. You came to believe your lies, not out of maliciousness, but out of ignorance. Now, as you unravel this process of lying for self-protection, the "little white lies" that you have been telling yourself and your friends become intolerable because you no longer want to hide anything.

## Deceit

**A lie's greatest deceit is**
  **How it fools its creator**
    **Into believing it is true.**

As you tell the truth to yourself and others, you see that your self-protective device has been isolating you. It may have served you as a child, but now it only creates an invisible wall of separation around you. As you risk telling the truth about being a human being, you discover that others feel free to let down their walls, too. *Instead of relating lie to lie, you relate truth to truth.* You not only feel the beauty of joining through sharing common human experiences, but you also discover the strength of vulnerability.

As a child, learning to tell lies may have saved your life, or at least saved you from unjust punishment. However, what was wise then can become an obstacle now if you want to bridge the chasm separating you from others. It is time for you to redefine strength.

## Strength

**Vulnerability unveils**
**The potency of softness**
**By disarming battling egos.**

Have you noticed that vulnerability is an invitation for both you and your friends to access the sweetness inside your Hearts? As a child, it was impossible for you to know that your protective masks were creating a facade. Eventually, when you observed yourself, you could see only the false masks. Very likely, you did not like what you saw, so you ran away from yourself. You lost sight of your true Self, especially your innocence. *You abandoned yourself and hid from others by not allowing your vulnerability to show.* But now it is time for joining by laying down your defenses, both within yourself and with others.

## Protection

**Your best weapon is**
**To let yourself become**
**Totally vulnerable to**
**Your enemy's sword.**

**If you bare your underbelly,**
**Your enemy needs no sword.**
**No one has to feel defensive**
**And you can explore peace.**

Perhaps your mind is saying, "Is this guy crazy? If I am totally vulnerable, I will be taken advantage of or abused. My enemy's sword will kill me!" Just like everything else in this book, this aphorism arose from personal experience.

One day I was driving along and saw a warehouse on fire. About a half mile down the road was a fire engine going in the wrong direction. I quickly made a left turn to catch the fire engine and redirect it. I cut in front of someone coming from the opposite direction. He had to brake quickly as I turned. I signaled the fire engine to pull over, ran over to its driver, and told him where the fire was. He thanked me, turned around, and sped off.

As I walked back to my car, I saw that the man I cut off had followed me. Waving a tire iron in his hand, he angrily ran toward me, ready to slug me. He looked muscular and enraged. I calmly walked toward him, knowing that I had done the right thing and thinking that it was appropriate for him to be upset. When we got within a few of feet of each other, I looked him straight in the eye and sincerely said, "I'm sorry I cut you off. I needed to catch the fire engine and show it where the fire is."

My calm directness obviously affected him. Completely disarmed, he stopped, took a breath, and said, "Oh. I'm sorry." He lowered his tire iron, turned around, quietly got into his car, and left. Vulnerability works!

As you discover new attitudes that help you love people more, you begin to see what real friendship is. Most people do not make friends from a clear choice. They assume that a person is their friend merely because circumstances have thrown them together.

Who are your best friends? Why do you consider them "best friends"? Are your friendships primarily based on shared activities? Does real intimacy open between you? Do you tell *everything* to one another? Do you walk away from your time together feeling good about yourself? Do you know if your friend feels uplifted by you?

When I worked as a waiter, I often overheard what people discussed. Frequently, I noticed them complaining, either about a situation or a person who was not there. They were unconsciously colluding to blame others for their woes. My pain in overhearing these conversations was that this modality seemed to be about 95% of how "friends" spent their time together. To me, this did not seem like the best way to create intimacy.

## Joining

**Friends can often create
A false togetherness by
Judging others as wrong.
If mutual complaining is
Replaced by vulnerability,
Then real joining is born.**

Loving others involves developing the capacity to look into people's Hearts through compassionate eyes. If your friends are judging themselves, you can point out the goodness which is underneath their neuroses and petty concerns. *If you look for the innocence within others' intentions, then you can experience genuine friendship.*

## Friendship

**A true friend keeps
Seeing your Love,
Especially when
You do not.**

Western Society reinforces the idea that "doing" is a higher value than "being." Yet, an invaluable gift is exchanged when one person does nothing except attentively listen to the other. What is the secret to exchanging a gift in each interaction? Do not be fooled by the following answer. As with all spiritual truths, its simplicity does not mean it is simplistic.

## The Greatest Gift

**The greatest gift
You can ever give
Is to truly receive
Another Human Being.**

How do you "truly receive another human being?" Recall your closest friends who have shared tender, intimate moments with you. Why do you like them? You probably feel that they care about you. They are not self-centered and talk only about themselves. They also ask questions about you. They are interested in you. You feel respected by them. They do not try to solve your problems with suggestions. True friends give you the space to sort through what is necessary by supportively listening until you find your own solutions.

One of the most gifted modern day therapists was Carl Rogers. His clients blossomed into their power and self-confidence. He primarily used one therapeutic technique, now known as "active listening." He simply reflected back to his clients what he heard them say, listening for the feelings underneath their words.

Probably, no one taught you how to effectively assist someone else. Unfortunately, schools rarely offer any courses on how to be a friend. You learned how to "help" by watching others, who may or may not have known what they were doing. "Helpers" jump in with lots of advice, often being insensitive to how disempowering they are. If you want to spiritually and emotionally support someone, you need to be in a very receptive mode.

## Helping

**Helping is not about**
**Providing solutions.**

**Helping occurs when you**
**Ask the kind of questions**
**That allow others to look**
**For their own answers.**

**If you then listen with**
**The ears of your Heart,**
**They find *their* wisdom.**

If you truly hear, understand, and accept what others say, they can open to their next level of vulnerability with you and within themselves. As they reveal their innermost thoughts, whatever has kept them from finding their own solutions unravels. As they feel safe to feel their feelings, the door to their Heart opens. They feel loved *and* empowered.

## The Gift of Receiving

**Most people are stagnating with**
**Hearts full of unexpressed Love,**
**Dammed up behind walls of fear**
**With no safe place to let it flow.**

**By opening to receive them,**
**The dam disintegrates and**
**Their goodness floods forth**
**In waves of Love bathing all.**

People have infinite amounts of Love inside their Hearts, but often do not feel safe enough to let it out. In today's high pressure society, people's pace is frenetic as they pursue what they believe will make them happy. Their internal world is chaotic as they needlessly spin the wheels of their minds with endless worry. Very few people are able to stop their thoughts long enough to really receive someone else. *If you become a person who listens, who sees, who understands, and who unconditionally accepts others without trying to fix them, then your presence alone is an invaluable gift.*

People are full of thoughts and desires. Their energy is literally overflowing with no room to receive any input. What you say to them cannot be heard until they empty some of their overflow. Most people want others to show a genuine interest in them, yet someone has to be the initiator of the receiving. If you empty yourself by meditating or by practicing being present each moment, then you are available for many healing exchanges with others.

## Healing

**Healing is not 'doing'**
**Something to someone.**

**Healing appears as**
**Human beings Be,**
**Melting into Now**
**With each other.**

**Love arises as all are**
**Emptied of darkness**
**And filled with Light.**

If you relate superficially, little of true value is exchanged. Someone needs to lead the way into uncharted territory. If you trust by being receptive and vulnerable, you create a favorable environment to transform many inner caterpillars into butterflies.

If you ever feel drained by being with someone, then you are probably trying too hard to give or receive something. If you feel as if you give and give and are not appreciated, then you are not really *giving* in its purest form. You are subtly seeking something in return. Maybe you want to be appreciated, acknowledged, or liked. These are all traps if you want to learn to love unconditionally. *Inside your Heart is a place where giving is receiving and receiving is giving.* Fulfillment means you are being filled as you are giving.

## Giving

**True giving occurs when,**
**After having given,**
**You have more**
**Instead of less.**

This "more" is the key to all human interaction. If you can find the extra awareness to listen to people with ears of compassion and without trying to fix them in any way, then you will be filled by those interactions. You will walk away from your time with others feeling happier and deeply satisfied. What is more valuable than this?

Intimate friendships are rewarding because you let go into something more vast than your individual self. As you uncover your own innocence, you see the child crying out for Love inside each person's eyes. As you learn to treat yourself and others with dignity, respect, understanding, trust, kindness, and compassion, the dormant buds of your Love awaken. Your friendships start to flower as the delicate petals within your Heart unfold.

## Blossoming

**Love is a seedling**
**When you feel it**
**All by yourself.**

**Love blossoms when**
**Your Heart touches**
**Another Soul.**

### Chapter Twenty-Five
# Opening to Intimacy

Being intimately involved with another person turns up the flame of the holy fire. Your ego burns up faster. When you are single, you do not receive the instant reflection of someone responding to every subtle change in you. You can be more unconscious since it is more difficult for you to see your own energetic subtleties than it is for your lover to feel them. *In an intimate relationship, it is essential for you to take 100% responsibility for the accuracy of the mirror image which your partner reflects back to you.* The ego's tendency is to try to protect itself by pointing an accusing finger at your partner instead of looking within to see how you are involved in the creation of *whatever* occurs. If you are at all defensive or in denial, then you will have a difficult time being in a successful, loving, sexual relationship.

If you genuinely know that you are one another's mirror, then each of you can take full responsibility for whether Love is flowing between you or not. If my wife, Donna, feels safe enough with me to be herself totally, whether it is with a smile on her face, or by chatting aimlessly, or with tears flowing down her cheeks, or by feeling sexually juicy, or by being whoever else she needs to be in the moment, then I know that I am in harmony with my Self and with Love. If I am looking inside honestly, I know in my Heart if I am being present with her and loving her exactly the way she is or if I am wanting her to be different in any way. *By continually letting go of my ideas of who I think Donna should or should not be, I get to discover who she actually is, without my own agenda.* Our being together is rejuvenated by my fascination with watching our spiritual unfolding. I repeatedly have the opportunity to see my beloved through new eyes. One of the greatest gifts of our relationship is that I am learning how to unconditionally love another person.

Actually, the phrase *Unconditional Love* is a misnomer because it is an unnecessary repetition of synonymous terms.

## Unconditional Love

**Love can only be
'Unconditional.'**

**If your Love has
*Any* strings attached,
Then it is not Love.**

If you place any covert demands on anyone, no matter how seemingly insignificant or subtle, then you are involved in manipulation instead of facing your own insecurity. If you feel diminished after being with people, then you have not loved them. You have wanted something from them. When you truly give your Love away, you feel fuller. *Most relationships are based upon compromise and barter because both people try to fill a lack in themselves rather than showering the other with an overflowing abundance of Love.*

Even using the word "relationship" is dangerous. By categorizing your interactions with another human being with a stagnant label, there is an implied contract that can destroy the beauty of spontaneity. When you meet someone, you have no obligations to one another. You have separate lives tentatively touching for a moment in time. Then, if you feel attracted to one another, plans are made and you see each other again. If all goes well, more dates are set up. At some point along this time line, you may share your sexuality together. Your lives begin to intertwine. You each bring to the relationship your own ideas of who the other is supposed to be. In order to get your "needs" met, you begin to either subtly or blatantly try to control each other. You make demands upon one another. What gets lost in this process of bargaining and maneuvering is the curiosity that was born when you first met.

# Relating

*Relating* **is real because**
**It unfolds in the moment**
**Between free individuals.**

*Relationship* **is an illusion**
**Created by your own fear**
**To promise some security.**

**If** *relating* **becomes** *relationship*,
**You have built a false structure**
**Dissolving Now's freedom into**
**Hopes, dreams, expectations.**

**When you transform your concept**
**Of relationship into relating-ship,**
**Both the past and future dissolve.**

*In a 'relating-ship,' the fresh eyes through which you first saw this person stay open so that you see your lover as an intriguing unknown instead of a boring known.* When you perceive someone as a "familiar stranger," you are inside the spontaneous creation of Now.

Usually, as a relationship "progresses," you both compromise your freedom in the hope of receiving the Love that you have always craved. *You mistakenly make your lover the source of your Love instead of remembering that it originates in your own Heart.* The fear of losing that source grows as your lives become more intertwined. Then you try to control your lover in unhealthy ways. If you can get them to "commit" to you, then you will not have to face your fear of abandonment or the pain of your loneliness. Ironically, the more you cling to your lover, the more likely he or she will feel trapped or suffocated and leave.

# Lovers' Paradox

**A lover whom you imprison**
**By your fearful limitations**
**May seek somewhere else**
**In order to find freedom.**

**A lover whom you let fly**
**With your heartfelt trust**
**Repeatedly returns to you**
**In order to find freedom.**

**Allowing total freedom**
**Creates total commitment.**

The last two lines of the above aphorism are also true in the reverse order: Total commitment creates total freedom. If you have a difficult time committing, you miss the bliss created by being 100% total. Closing your "back doors" of escape opens the window to a freedom much vaster than the inner prison of contraction created by resisting Love.

Often in a relationship, one person wants freedom while the other wants commitment. If both people stubbornly hold on to their own perspective, neither one feels satisfied. If your jealousy or insecurity makes you try to control your partner, then your opportunity for growth lies within offering your lover freedom at a pace that challenges you, but does not terrorize you. If commitment is your nemesis, then your gift is contained within closing all your escape hatches, one by one. You can use the next few paragraphs to assist you. It is up to the two of you to understand your basic differences and to work together as partners, or else your egos lock into a power struggle that strangles your Love.

True commitment has nothing to do with compromising yourself or limiting yourself in any way. It arises out of profound experiences you have with someone who is an integral part of your Soul. *Commitment is a feeling to be cherished, not a contract to be endured.* You cannot force it upon another person from the outside. Nor can you convince yourself to make a commitment by using your will. It has to repeatedly arise from inside your Heart.

When you share the deepest recesses of the present tense with another person, the walls of separation crumble. When the two of you merge into one, you have a direct experience of feeling committed as your lover becomes you. A problem can develop when you both leave the depths of Now and return to the illusion of separateness. Often, the sense of commitment dissolves and you are left not knowing what is real.

# Commitment

**Commitment is a quality
To be felt in the Present,
Not a promise for the future.**

Within each moment of true commitment, a feeling of expansion explodes inside each person. *If either of you contracts or feels claustrophobic, then you are not experiencing commitment.* You have agreed to an artificial contract containing obligations arising out of fear or guilt. If you succumb to this type of false "commitment," you end up feeling imprisoned. Your resentment toward your partner will eventually destroy the "relationship." Love cannot be forced. You can only honor whatever is true for you, whether or not it makes logical sense. Let go of trying to control the future with your lover. *Let commitment arise organically out of deep and repeated experiences of intimacy.*

Sharing your sexuality with another person is one of the most powerful ways to enhance commitment. It also creates fertile ground for spiritual transformation. *Sexual intimacy is a holy invitation into your lover's inner temple.* You create what the Greeks called "Temenos," or a safe space for the exploration of consciousness.

Do not minimize the power of being sexual with someone. You are playing with fire. Often in today's fast-paced world, you can be tempted to become sexually involved very quickly. When genitals are shared in a vulnerable context (versus casual sex's usual lack of vulnerability), the dynamics of how the two of you relate change dramatically, whether you want them to or not. *You can go too far too fast and then not know how to retreat because you have already bonded emotionally.*

If you seek intimacy through sexuality, when you meet someone who is a potential lover, wait a while before being sexual. Get to know the person thoroughly first. See where and how they live, meet their friends and family, find out about their work. Get a sense of their whole life and who they are in the world. Then, if you do choose to open those sexual doors, you join with all of their Being, not just with their genitals. If you each cherish the vulnerability and the trust that it takes to allow real intimacy, then your attitude opens those innermost doors. If you dive into each other totally, the entire Universe becomes available to both of you. Ultimate, infinite Love awaits you.

Often when you first are sexual with someone, the two of you spend a lot of time riding the wave of passionate bliss. As your Heart and sexuality open, you can easily project your repressed archetypal "knight in shining armor" or "goddess of infinite beauty" onto your new lover. Your projection of ultimate mate onto someone else is really more about you than the other person. The door to a very precious room in the temple of your Heart involuntarily flies open. Your squelched ecstasy soars as you surf together on the wave of Love.

However, you cannot stay on the crest of that wave forever. *At some point, it begins to subside and the opportunity to love another human being who is less than perfect arises.*

In a long term relationship, the wave of passion retreats, and then returns. You can dive into your lover for hours or days or even weeks at a time. But then the ocean calms down again.

It is easy to make either you or your partner wrong for this natural cycle, especially when the energy subsides.

## The Wave of Passion

**Lovers can easily enjoy riding**
**The crest of the wave of passion**
**As it breaks forth into the new.**

**You also need to learn to accept**
**That the wave must then recede**
**In its rhythm of ebb and flow.**

**As you each return to**
**Your individual selves,**
**Rather than doubting,**
**Trust that you are both**
**Gathering momentum**
**To ride the next wave.**

Entering into sexuality can catapult you into exquisite nonlinear realms of Reality. Notice how your sense of time gets lost while being sexual. Two hours can easily seem like fifteen minutes. The more totally you let go of control, the more profound the timelessness becomes. *As you melt into Love, 'forever' occurs within each endless moment that you are together as one.* However, when you return to linear time, the mind wants to reconstruct the *forever* into promises for the future. But *forever* cannot ever be found in the future.

## Lovers' Illusion

**Chasing tomorrow's promises**
**Keeps you from being inside**
**The true *Forever* within Now.**

True *forever* is similar to commitment. It takes place in the depths of the present tense. As time dissolves, a thought can pass through your mind that clearly says, "Let's get married." This thought indicates the depth of your connection. It does not necessarily mean that you need to "do" anything about it. You may or may not choose to act upon it.

An experience of *forever* can be so powerful that you want to recapture it. You can fastidiously reset the external stage by lighting the same candles and playing the same music. You can make overt or covert "relationship agreements," trying to assure yourself that your lover will never leave you so that you feel safe enough to revisit those feelings. However, you can never duplicate any experience, no matter how hard you try. You must be willing to repeatedly risk your Heart and Soul for unblemished experiences of timelessness to emerge.

This process of the two of you merging must also include the need for each of you to be alone at times. The more completely you melt into another person, the more you may want to spend time by yourself to re-establish your own sense of Self. You may need to rediscover that you are the center of your Universe and that the source of your Love is within.

Often, couples do not realize that this dynamic is natural. One partner may not honor the other's desire for "alone time," or may not recognize his or her own need for being alone. Out of this misunderstanding, time apart is often achieved in a less than ideal way.

# Lovers' Alone Time

**Arguing with your lover**
**Can be a painful way to**
**Create time by yourself.**
**Hurt hurdles you apart.**

**Sensitively listen for**
**Your need to be alone**
**And directly ask for it**
**Instead of indirectly**
**Walling yourself off.**

If you want "alone time," first reassure your partner that you are still in Love. Then give an approximate time to check back in with each other. By creating space in this way, your lover need not feel abandoned while you are apart. If each of you can respect the other's need for "alone time" without interpreting it as rejection, then you do not intertwine in an unhealthy way. You will not need to ask, "What happened to those two free individuals who enjoyed relating to each other?" or "How did I lose my myself in this relationship?" The more you stay an individual, the more profoundly you can merge into shared bliss.

As you melt with your lover, a profound spiritual quality can emerge. I have spent time with three spiritual teachers. As I bowed down to the divinity in each of them, I had ecstatic experiences of egoless surrender. I was available to humbly be of service by stepping into whatever role was needed. I always assumed that the spiritual Love which showered down on me as I bowed to my gurus' feet came from the depths that they had touched inside themselves.

One day I bowed down and kissed Donna's feet to symbolize my surrender to her. As I prostrated, her feet seemed to become those of an ancient Indian master. I broke down and wept because in that moment I realized that I could explore the same inner infinity with her as I had with my gurus. Everything we needed to go "all the way" was within ourselves. I did not have to hold anything back while waiting for my next spiritual master. Ironically, as I kissed her feet, our "relating-ship" became my guru and continues to be my path today.

If you surrender into being spiritual teachers for one another, a deep reverence can blossom. When your lover offers psychological or emotional perceptions of you, always look for any possible grain of truth (and vice versa). Listen to each other with respect, as if God is talking. By honoring each other when you are together, you are empowered to be dignified individuals in the world when you are apart.

You are co-creating a new Being, called "Us." The same way that it is important for you to listen to all the voices inside yourself when trying to make a decision, you can treat each other as an integral part of "Us" when discussing anything. If either of you have any hesitation, do not try to bypass it, gloss it over, or push for a result. Trust the hesitation, knowing that it ultimately leads to the best possible solution. *Continue in dialogue until all parts of 'Us' are satisfied. This way, you both 'count' and you both win.*

One key attitude can fundamentally alter the way you talk about your relationship problems. When you discuss a difficult "issue" with your partner, each of you probably unconsciously places the problem *between* you, as if you were on opposite sides of a fence. Each unsolved problem becomes the equivalent of a brick in a wall of separation between you. Then you both talk *at* the bricks instead of *with* each other. What if you could take those bricks from between you, let down your defenses, and stand arm-in-arm with your mutual challenge *in front* of the two of you, looking at it together as partners. Isn't your ideal to be friends 100% of the time, even while you are discussing the most volatile subjects? Don't you hate seeing each other as enemies when differences come up? *What if you were able to make 'staying on the same side' with each other a higher priority than either one of you being right?*

# On the Same Side

**Being in harmony while**
**Exploring differences**
**Creates Love that is**
**Beyond agreement.**

*This feeling of togetherness is more precious than finding the solution to any problem.* As you talk, if either of you begins to feel separate, that person says, "I'm seeing you as my enemy right now, and I want to see you as my friend," or "I don't feel like we are on the same side right now." Then stop, look into each other's eyes, and let go of any stubbornness that sustains your separateness.

*This act of surrender takes utmost awareness. Each of you has to call upon your deepest trust of the other's intentions.* As you get your priorities straight inside your Hearts, a hug and some tears can help melt any defensiveness. Then you can return to your discussion from a different perspective.

In our relationship, this framework allows Donna to feel safe as she talks with Peter, her friend, about Peter, the insensitive "klutz" who did not treat her lovingly in a previous interaction. If I start to feel defensive, I take a deep breath, and know that if I can understand Donna's point of view, we can always resolve whatever is disturbing our peace. And she does the same with me. If we can let go of our obstinacy, and listen to the other's experience as being real and valid, we spend as little time as possible "out of Love." By cultivating this attitude, we have been able to stay in harmony while dealing with core issues, such as having opposite views about having a baby and about being monogamous.

Through lovers being together in all these nurturing ways, a sense of devotion, in its purest form, grows. As you learn to melt into something that is bigger than either one of you, you can start to worship the god/goddess within each other. *Out of your reverence for each other, a sense of awe for all of Life is born.*

# Devotion

**Devotion is not**
    **Having the courtesy to**
        **Put your beloved first.**

**True devotion is**
    **Having the courage to**
        **Put your Truth first.**

**If you treat your beloved**
    **As an integral part of you,**
        **Both of you will discover**
        **Devotion to the Divine.**

May you find the courage to see your lover as your absolute mirror. May you see your lover as your vehicle to Enlightenment instead of an obstacle to your Love. May you drop your defensiveness and go to your lover's feet. *As you bow down and surrender, you discover your own Divinity.*

## Chapter Twenty-Six
# Sexuality: Upping the Ante

*Sexual intimacy is one of the most sought after and the most avoided of all human experiences.* Most people want it and are terrified of it at the same time. Lying in bed with your lover, you can be in varying degrees of intimacy. You can talk about the day's events, your problems, or your hopes and fears. This creates bonding at the level of ideas.

Yet, a deeper intimacy can occur when the words stop. If your Hearts, emotions, and sexuality open, energy flows between you silently. A new level of communication begins.

## Useful Words

**The most useful words**
**Help launch you into**
**The bliss of no words.**

This leap from words into a nonverbal exchange of energy can be terrifying. As you merge with your partner, you can be swept up into waves of "irrational" emotions. Your identity starts to wobble as your ego boundaries disintegrate. The two of you are becoming interdependent. You both have the opportunity to learn how to surrender into the blending of "I" into "Us."

Risking the dissolution of your ego is scary but does have its spiritual rewards. The illusion of being separate from the whole vanishes. *As 'you' dissolve into divine union with one other human being, you feel vitally connected with all human beings, all creatures, and all of creation.*

An important distinction needs to be made here. The beauty of surrender has been tarnished by people's misinterpretation of the concept known as "codependency." *You are codependent only if you 'give to get.'* When you give anything to your lover, if you feel diminished, disempowered, or compromised in any way, then you must be looking for something in return. Giving unconditionally leaves you feeling filled rather than depleted, regardless of your lover's response. You are probably forgetting that the source of your Love is within you.

In true surrender, on the other hand, the act of giving arises from an internal place that needs *nothing* in return. To be capable of surrender, you must first be able to define and set your boundaries. Once this has been mastered, then the next challenge is to let go of your boundaries. This allows you to surrender, not to your lover's ego desires, but to whatever allows the Love between the two of you to prosper. A mature awareness is necessary for you to look beyond your self-imposed limitations and discover something much greater than either you or your partner. As you create this new Being, "Us," your Heart's capacity expands. Embracing the spirit of unselfishly serving "Us" opens you to experiences of limitless Love.

If you take responsibility for your fear of losing your identity as an individual, you also take a quantum leap in your ability to be intimate. *To truly merge with another human being means the Death of who you have perceived yourself to be.* When you care deeply, you feel your lover's pain as your own. This union is an essential ingredient for Love to flow. Without it, you stay safely untouched in your box of isolation. Ironically, in a healthy relating-ship, the more completely you melt into your partner, the stronger and more independent you become when you are apart, leading your individual life.

You can work with your fear of intimacy. Recognizing the feeling as it occurs is the first step. Then, rather than running away to protect yourself, communicate to your partner that you are scared. Stay "on the same side" and ask your partner to gently hold you without trying to fix you. If you feel the fear without needing to *do* anything, it eventually evaporates. Soon, the next level of intimacy emerges. *Instead of fear running you, you are in relationship to it.*

How do you protect yourself from letting your lover more deeply into your Heart and into your sex? The world is full of distractions, such as newspapers, books, television, movies, socializing, and earning more money. If you let go of these external diversions, you can look for the more subtle, internal self-deceptions. You may unconsciously pick a fight the moment before you have an opportunity to spend quality time together. You may get tired and fall asleep. You may escape into hot, lusty sex to safely sidestep a softer, more vulnerable connection.

Talking about a "significant issue" can also be an avoidance of intimacy. You stay at the level of words instead of allowing more profound modes of relating to unfold. If you can find the kind of words that lead both of you out of your heads and into your Hearts, then walls come down. You each feel safe enough to express a Love beyond words.

## Communication

**Words from the head**
**Perpetuate thinking.**

**Words from the Heart**
**Melt you into intimacy.**

Telling each other the Truth can be a "turn-on." As Isadora Alman (sexologist and author of *Aural Sex and Verbal Intercourse*) says, "Communication is the best lubrication." Safety is created by having absolutely no *withholds* from one another. *Nothing* is held back. You get to know one another all the way down into the deepest, darkest corners. *You are only as separate as your secrets.* Thus, speak the unspeakable to each other.

The most difficult things to say may be, "I'm feeling sexually attracted to someone else," or "I'm not feeling sexually turned on by you," or "I'm thinking of leaving you." No matter how scary, always speak any thought that could create separation if left unsaid. *Always communicate with the intention to join with your lover.* Also, remember that thoughts are merely thoughts. They lose their power if you share them without censorship.

If you go to this depth of truth telling, you will not have walls between you. This blending of your naked minds can create psychic harmony. Someday you may not even need to use words to communicate. But, for now, when you want to be intimate, make your whole intention to surrender into the energetic flow of Love that arises from Silence.

You can become quite adept at getting out of the trap of words and into energy. Learn how to stay vulnerable to your lover the whole time you are being sexual. The moment after an orgasm, notice if you unconsciously pull away from your lover. Orgasms can leave you so vulnerable that you may be afraid to stay open. You can easily put up a subtle wall to protect yourself and avoid intense feelings. If you recognize this pattern, carefully observe the moment right after orgasm. You can make a conscious choice to leave your wall down. You might sometimes cry with your lover after having an orgasm because you feel so naked. Ironically, those post-orgasm tears are such a precious invitation into the depths of intimacy that you may not ever want to stop their flow.

Individuals allow sexual intimacy in different ways. Some people need to feel connected in their Hearts before they feel safe enough to open sexually. Others need to feel that their sexuality is accepted before opening their Hearts. In heterosexual relationships, often the man needs to feel free to express himself sexually before offering his Heart; whereas, the woman needs to feel the safety of the man giving her his Heart before she can share the depths of her sexuality to him. God's joke seems to be that we human beings are supposed to create intimacy out of these seemingly opposite approaches.

## Two Routes to Bliss

**Does the Heart open
The doors to sex, or
Does great sex create
The intimacy for Love?**

**If you can find harmony
Within your differences,
Ecstasy will pursue you.**

People often do not understand the implications of this dynamic. They cannot figure out why they have less than completely satisfying sexual relationships. Men often believe that either they are too sexual for any woman to handle (and feel guilty about that), or that they are somehow attracting women who are not sexual enough for them (and felt frustrated about that). There needs to be a sensitive dance to create the safety for the woman to open her sexuality and for the man to surrender his Heart.

Throughout the ages, "respectable" women have not had permission to ask for what they want sexually. Until the 1960s, women were not supposed to have *any* sexual desires, or they were considered sluts or nymphomaniacs. Because of the historical programming that men should always want sex and women should not, women can easily feel as if they are being sexually used solely to satisfy men's desires. *This myth often creates women who are in sexual situations feeling as if they are being taken from rather than given to.*

Men can unconsciously perpetuate this disempowering myth because as teenagers they are programmed to believe that women must be tricked into having sex. Men think that they have to ply women with alcohol and drugs to break down their inhibitions. Then they can slyly manipulate women into getting so turned on that they cannot stop themselves. It is time to put an end to this craziness. Both genders can claim their right to pleasure.

Another very destructive, unspoken fantasy is that men are supposed to know exactly how to turn a woman on without ever asking her what she likes. In fact, according to this romantic fable, it spoils the mystique if there is *any* talking involved.

To further complicate matters, men frequently have an extremely sensitive "male ego." They have been programmed that they must "do it right" or else they are not a "real man." Yet, each man and each woman enjoys being sexual in their own unique manner. In order to end this insanity, you must bring everything out in the open by talking about it. Then, if both of you ask for 100% of what you want sexually, you can eagerly learn how to please one another.

Educate each other about what you enjoy. *If you know that the only goal of talking about your sexuality is to increase each other's pleasure, then you can more easily let go of your defensiveness.* Let your partner know what arouses you and what makes you feel less sexual. "This feels great" leads to more pleasure. "Let's try something else" also leads to more pleasure. In the long run, you both win by communicating. If you feel sexually loved and accepted, you naturally want to satisfy your partner's desires. Each of you becomes more eager to participate because you have increasingly positive experiences.

Another frequent male/female difference is that as the two of you move into being sexual, the woman may want to be touched and stroked all over first. She usually does not want a man to go straight for the "target areas" – the breasts and genitals. Yet, a man may well be just the opposite. He can become bored by being touched all over and would prefer that his penis be given attention right away. An intimate connection is virtually impossible if the man tries to give the woman what he enjoys by going straight for her target areas, and the woman tries to give the man what she enjoys by slowly stroking him all over.

Understanding this difference, the two of you can create mutual pleasure by giving to one another what the other one really wants. A beautiful exercise is to set up a whole evening for one of you to completely serve the other by responding to your lover's every request. Another evening, the roles can be reversed. Defining yourself as the receiver or the giver for the entire evening makes it easier to ask for 100% of what you want or to surrender into giving 100%. After you have participated in this exercise a number of times, it also becomes easier to spontaneously dance back and forth between being the "giver" and "receiver" when your roles are undefined.

Sexual energy is renewed if you relate tenderly as you go through the routine of your lives. If you make it a top priority to stop, hug, and say "I love you" throughout the day, then Love never becomes an assumption. You can easily take your lover for granted. Love springs to Life by expressing it. You can frequently speak aloud all the ways you adore each other. You can buy each other flowers or cards to say, "I'm crazy about you." You can be insatiable romantics.

You can also be sexual healers for each other. Donna helps to heal parts of me that I find hard to accept, and vice versa. As we unconditionally accept the other as a sexual being, we each become more whole. An example of this is that I enjoy watching erotic, adult movies. I used to feel a bit guilty about that. Donna has nothing in particular going on about my watching the movies. Sometimes she joins me, sometimes she does not. Since she does not judge this harmless activity, I have become more accepting of myself.

You can make it a priority to create "sacred time" or "empty time" together. Do not let "activities" like television, movies, sports, work, or socializing get in the way of diving into each other's Souls. You can spend time together each day in uninterrupted intimacy. You can deeply nurture yourselves by creating an atmosphere in which you can soar together.

How frequently you are intimate is not nearly as important as whether the amount of time each of you wants to be together is similar. If one wants an hour per day and the other wants an hour per month, then you are in trouble. But if your "intimacy quota" nearly matches, then you can choose to make uninterrupted time together a high enough priority to satisfy your mutual needs.

If you do not carve out the time, other activities can easily consume you. *Society is designed to lure you away from being intimate because you are not spending any money during this time.* Intimacy is the enemy of consumerism because your sense of well-being is so greatly enhanced that you do not need to buy material goods to be happy.

*Another helpful attitude is for each of you to be willing to enter into the possibility of being sexual, even when you may not be feeling sexual in the moment.* Beautiful experiences of intimacy are potentially available when you are vulnerable together. Thus, be open to melt into sexuality, no matter what your defensive mind says.

Sometimes you may not be aware of how much of a sexual charge has built up within you. *Tumescence* is a term for this unexpressed sexual energy. If it is not recognized, it can create undercurrents of confusion.

## Tumescence

Tumescence occurs if you have
An overabundance of energy
And nowhere to channel it.

Tumescence expresses itself
In the form of bitchiness,
Either blatant or covert.

If you and your lover quarrel
Without any apparent reason,
Stop, as you smile knowingly,
And cry out, "Tumescence!"

Then let your lust explode
Until you are both satiated,
Glowing with contentment.

When being sexual together, feel free to give both verbal and nonverbal feedback. *Break through the myth that if you talk during sex, you spoil the magic.* If you do not communicate about something that comes up during sex, a *withhold* comes between you, just like a brick in a wall. The sexual energy cannot flow freely. It is extra important to have *nothing* in the way when you merge sexually with your lover because sex turns up the volume of energy. Any little speck of misunderstanding quickly becomes a pebble, then a rock, and then a boulder between you if it is not cleared up.

Learn to communicate in ways that do not hurt. Instead of focusing on what is not working, make positive suggestions about what you want. Rather than saying, "I don't like the way you are touching me," say, "I'd really like you to touch me very gently right now."

*When one of you brings up any difficulty, hold sacred that the underlying intention is to make your sex life better for both of you.* Be sensitive to whomever makes a sexual request, knowing that it is a delicate invitation into new levels of intimacy.

## Sexual Intimacy

**Do you ever hesitate**
**To enhance intimacy**
**By sharing your Lust?**

**Hot sexual energy,**
**Bursting with Life,**
**Needs urgent release.**

**To create the safety for**
**Sexuality to flow freely,**
**Take the risk to expose**
**Your fear's inhibitions.**

Give each other full permission to change the direction of the flow at any moment. Stop what does not feel good, either by nonverbally guiding your lover to a different part of your body or by vulnerably talking about what is going on. Feeling connected emotionally is more important than satisfying your immediate sexual desires. Rather than forcing your sexuality to continue, trust when the energy dies. Let go and see what feelings need to be expressed. *Rather than tears being a distraction to be tolerated, honor that they are an enhancement of your lovemaking.*

You can also enjoy being "sexually creative." Share all your sexual fantasies. Do not screen or judge any ideas. Have fun acting them out or verbally turning each other on with whatever fantasy arises. *Find new parts of the body to eroticize.* The breasts and genitals are such a small portion of the areas you can explore. Almost any part of the body loves to be turned on. The soles of your feet, toes, calves, back of your knees, fingers, armpits, ears, and neck eagerly celebrate when you give them attention.

Laugh a lot and do not take sex too seriously. An awkward, heavy silence can sometimes pervade people's sexual exchange. The mood will not be spoiled by humor. A well-timed tickle or giggle can lighten you up. You can then express your innocent joy, which adds fuel to the lust rather than diminishes it.

Communicate about your sexual desires and experiences in an everyday context, outside the bedroom. Talk about what you did and did not like about your last lovemaking session in a friendly, unthreatening way. Speak in specifics rather than in generalities. For instance, you might say, "The way you used your tongue on my neck last night really turned me on. I would love more of that" or "I loved the way you sucked my toes. Next time let's worship our toes for a long time," or "You really turned on my breasts last night. Would you spend more time stroking the rest of my breasts before you touch my nipples?" This reinforces the fun you are already having and informs one another about your future desires.

*Since you are really making Love to each other only one time (for the rest of your lives), there is no need to pressure yourselves to have an orgasm in any one session.* Notice if you feel a need to orgasm so that you do not feel lonely afterwards. When you choose not to push yourself to orgasm and to feel the loneliness instead, your tears may open a new corner of compassion for yourself and for the rest of humanity.

Create opportunities to go to the next level of your sexual exploration together. Be total in your sexuality by risking. This lets your *relating-ship* be reborn frequently. There is a hierarchy of sexual experiences to be explored. By opening to new areas or by enjoying more subtle nuances of previously perused places, you discover your sexuality anew.

## Sexual Hierarchy

**You have an outer limit
On the sexual experiences
You have allowed yourself.**

**If you explore the unknown,
You drink in the ecstasy of
Innocent participation in
The freeing of repression.**

Understanding sexual hierarchies can enhance your spiritual evolution. You have probably allowed yourself to sample only a portion of what is possible in the realm of human sexuality. There is a vast array of imaginable adventures. *You have your own unique progression of what is increasingly risky for you to participate in.* If you share all your sexual thoughts with your partner, then you two can mutually design ways for each of you to repeatedly open to your unique sexual expansion. Sometimes, while being sexual, you may have a fleeting thought about what you would like, but fear or embarrassment stops you from sharing your idea. When you take the risk of speaking the unspeakable to your lover, you open the doors for both of you to express your sexuality in new ways.

Any sexual routine is deadly. After couples have been together for a while, they can become accustomed to having sex in a certain way. They may wait until they are in bed, then begin kissing, and then fondling each other in a specific order that leads to intercourse and perhaps to orgasm. If they just keep repeating the same sexual pattern, eventually it becomes boring because there is no spark of creativity to ignite the flame of joy within Now.

When most couples are first sexual together, they have very profound experiences. Sexual attraction creates you being drawn to each other for you to take one another to new depths of sexuality and intimacy. However, you can become lazy after you have explored the first layer of these new experiences. You may unconsciously be afraid to open to deeper levels. If you do not allow new ways of being together to emerge, then your sex life and your relationship are destined for a premature Death.

## A Sexual Secret

**Sex is renewed
By risking *all*,
Each moment.**

The *all* that you risk is not only your sexuality. You need to also risk the vulnerability of your Heart to repeatedly revitalize your connection.

*The bottom-line purpose of intimate relating-ship is to be in Love every moment.* That's it! You need not be together to accomplish great tasks or to change the world. It is more than enough for the two of you to be in the vibration of Love, moment by moment.

People often want "techniques" to improve their relationship. *The only 'technique' that repeatedly works is softening your attitude.* Your willingness to let go of stubbornness and the need to be right allows you to melt into harmony instead of staying stuck in the illusion of separation. Feeling the pain of isolation motivates the dropping of the ego and invites the joining of Souls. If you could cultivate this attitude, the need to run from one relationship to the next would soon end.

Love is the state of consciousness where you are in harmony with yourself, others, and your environment. Every person and every situation in your life is born out of your Love for one another. The spiritual growth of the people around you is the natural by-product of your Love.

Sexual intimacy can fill and satiate you. Then your abundance of Love effortlessly overflows to others.

## Touching Souls

**Touching Souls**
**In silent union,**
**Mind becomes empty,**
**Heart becomes full.**

## Chapter Twenty-Seven
# What Is Spiritual Sex?

If you are here on the planet to become more loving and to evolve spiritually, how does sexuality fit into your picture? In most spiritual traditions, sex has long been held as an obstacle to Enlightenment. It has been seen as something to overcome, to transcend, or to go beyond. Vows of celibacy have often been praised as seekers try to conquer the "burdens" and "illusions" of earthly desires. *The underlying and usually unquestioned assumption is that sexual denial eventually leads to Enlightenment.*

But isn't Enlightenment the realization that *all* the Universe is contained within the infinite depths of your Heart? And doesn't *all* the Universe include your sexuality and your lust? Are you supposed to somehow cast out an integral part of your own humanity in order to become a fully-realized person? Celibacy may occur in a natural, organic way as you embrace all aspects of your sexuality and go through to the other side. But to try to force it upon yourself is destructive. It may be a by-product of your evolution, but it is not the goal.

## Celibacy

The spiritual vow
To give up sex
Creates repression
Instead of celibacy.

Lust no longer smolders
When the hot flame of
Your sexual desires
Easily and effortlessly
Becomes a cool breeze.

When sex is nonflammable,
Celibacy will surprise you.

*Sexuality can be a vehicle into spirituality rather than an obstacle to it.* One way to express your desire to be reunited with God is by merging with another person through sharing your sexuality. The more deeply you feel the longing to return Home, the more deeply you may want to free your sexual nature. And that very expression, when realized as such, adds fuel to the most significant fire there is: the burning up of the human ego and the subsequent dissolving of the illusion of separation. *The gift of your sexuality is that it is a profound modality for the ecstatic affirmation of human Love.* Why not include sex and God in the same breath? Why would you ever want to see them as opposing forces rather than as partners?

## Sex and God

Transcending your sexuality
To become more spiritual is
An Enlightenment illusion.

When God touches your Heart,
Your sexuality is awakened.
Your body lights up and
Your life lightens up.

173

Sexual expression can be frightening. It is a movement from everyday limited levels of consciousness into an expansion of your energetic aliveness. Two activities that challenge the ego structure down to its very core are meditation and sexual/emotional expression. Both require letting go of the negative mind's usual control over you. The mind/ego has power over you whenever you make negative thoughts real by focusing on them. In meditation and in sex, in order to become the master of your mind, you must escape from its traps that keep you absorbed at the level of thought. You achieve ultimate freedom if you can access a place inside yourself that lives only in the present tense, not trying to go anywhere or to accomplish anything. In this receptive state, Love happens. Fulfillment happens. Happiness happens. Union happens.

The mind wants you to be at its every beck and call. It becomes very threatened if you surrender into the flow of sexual energy. Therefore, it tells you that sex is wrong, or a waste of time, or an addiction, or not spiritual enough. Or it starts a fight with your lover when the possibility for a new level of sexual intimacy is available. Listening to your mind's negativity has you miss the bliss that you could be experiencing if you were to truly let go into the formless. Dive in underneath the superficial motivations of your sexual desires to the deepest stirrings within your Soul. *Approach lovemaking with an attitude of reverence and awe because untainted sex is the sharing of divine nectar.* With the safety created by this underlying context, all avenues of pure sexual expression open to mutual exploration.

## The Lovers' Dance

**Sexual seduction can be
A lovely dance between
Tension and relaxation.**

**If you frolic together
In a free form flow,
You start waltzing
With your Divinity.**

What, then, is "spiritual sex"? Take a moment to envision your ideal of two people engaged in "spiritual sex." Do you picture candles and incense burning? Do the lovers bow to each other, kiss one another's feet, and then sit in the yab-yum position (cross-legged, one on the lap of the other)? Do they see the whole Universe in each other's eyes? Do they gently breathe together, barely moving? Have they transcended the trappings of hot, animal lust? Are they beyond the need for genital orgasms?

Whether your pictures are similar to these or not, notice if you do have any ideas of what spiritual sex is *supposed* to be. What experiences are spiritual lovers supposed to have? Just notice what your beliefs are. Then, see if the following questions challenge those ideas.

♥ What if spiritual sex has little to do with how spiritual it appears to be?
♥ What if spiritual sex is much more encompassing than you have envisioned?
♥ What if holding on to your pictures of spiritual sex limits the possibilities of other profound experiences?
♥ *What if spiritual sex has more to do with the intention of the lovers than with the activity itself?*

Spiritual sex arises out of both partners' desire for union through uninhibited self-expression. What if you are here on earth not to transcend your humanness, but to revere yourself exactly as you are right now? You are a fascinating combination of a heavenly angel/god/goddess and an earthly animal/beast. As you let go into the formless with the intention to become one with your lover, what can emerge is a dance back and forth between your god/goddess and your animal urges. As your animal nature releases into an uninhibited expression of lust, perhaps the absolutely perfect spiritual union becomes available to you in that moment. Then, in another moment, when you are softly touching and looking into one another's eyes, you have included your human, animal lust rather than trying to bypass it. As you surrender to your lover's feet in devotion, you can worship each other's divinity and each other's humanness. In fact, as you let out your lust, you create the foundation upon which to build your temple.

## Spiritual Sex

**When your sexual roots**
**Explode into the Earth,**
**Your spiritual wings can**
**Fly freely into Heaven.**

Are lust and Love enemies waging war against one another or friends complementing each other? When sexual energy begins to flow, you can be overpowered by your genitals if you let them sweep you into actions that you regret later. *You need not do anything about your sexual arousal unless your Heart is in agreement with your genitals.*

## Lust

**Lust disguises itself as Love**
**Only when you have failed**
**To know Lust intimately.**

**Enjoy the burst of Life**
**From Lust's explosion,**
**But do not be fooled**
**By a fickle turn-on.**

**Lust needs no Heart,**
**But Love is enhanced**
**When it includes Lust.**

Sexuality can be a doorway into bliss instead of a stumbling block to be overcome. Embracing both soft, cool sex, and hot, lusty sex creates more colors with which to paint a richer self-portrait. "Spiritual sex" includes the entire spectrum from Life's rainbow, such as:

- ♥ Diving into each other's eyes.
- ♥ Tenderly touching each other's face.
- ♥ Experiencing the pain of having any walls between you.
- ♥ Holding each other Heart to Heart and letting your energy flow.
- ♥ Being of total service to your lover.
- ♥ Rutting like wild animals.
- ♥ Crying as new doors open to deeper levels of intimacy.
- ♥ Following your sexuality's own expression without preconceived pictures.
- ♥ Allowing yourself to be created into whoever your partner wants you to be.

More magic happens if you allow yourself to be seen as an archetype. You can be the most beautiful or handsome person in the history of humankind, or the sexiest, lustiest human on the planet, or a Greek God or Goddess, or more in Love than any couple has ever been.

As you surrender into the unknown, new possibilities arise from the innocence of your creativity. The reward for your risks is a surprise that delights you and relights your Love.

If you let go of your thoughts about how sex *should* be, new experiences become available to you. Pure sexuality arises out of a more fundamental core within your Being than your mind. You can enhance your arousal by using energy from thoughts. For instance, you may turn yourself on with phrases like "I love you!" or "This is really hot!" or "This feels great!" or "Jesus!" With an enticing mental image, "Shazam!" – an orgasm is triggered. As you further explore the dance of sexuality, you may be blessed with orgasms that arise from a place beyond thoughts. There, you touch the source of all Life.

## Ultimate Orgasms

**Profound orgasms unfold when
"You" dissolve into Love's void.**

**If you allow a thought-free energy
To pulsate throughout your Being,
You are swept into a Reality where
Time is not and Perfect Silence is.**

Do you know the tantric secret about orgasms? *While releasing into orgasm, you can perform 'white magic' by visualizing ways you would like Life to be.* You can picture anything, such as being deeply in Love forever; or money flowing abundantly in your life; or the healing of a friend or relative; or finding relief for the hungry or homeless; or the whole world living in harmony.

What you envision at the moment of orgasm plants a seed within that level of consciousness. Because you are so open, your picture filters down through all the other layers of consciousness. It eventually shows up in your outer world, if you do not let doubt get in your way. You can actually change your everyday Reality through this "white magic."

With this additional incentive, what are some ways that can you take yourself deeper into Love and into sex?

♥   By embracing all sexual acts.
♥   By integrating the lust-filled, sex-hungry animal and the soft, gentle angel.
♥   By being sexually creative and not settling for a sexual routine.
♥   By being sexually curious and discovering what you want to explore next.
♥   By being willing to ask for 100% of what you want.
♥   By allowing the energy to freely dance between talking, emotional vulnerability, soft, cool sex, and hot, lusty sex.

What are the actual experiences that are available out of diving into intimacy? They are boundless and infinite. Donna and I feel more in Love than any other couple in the history of humankind; and we want every other couple to have this same feeling. We are head over heels in Love with each other about 99% of the time (or is it "heels over head in Love"?). After ten years of intimate sexuality, we feel like we are at the very beginning of exploring infinite realms of relating. We have psychic experiences which indicate that we are attuned to one another in the natural way that all of us are meant to be. We are often moved to tears of gratitude for being in each other's lives and touching each other's Soul. We know that at least one other person on this planet accepts us completely, loves every deep, dark corner of us, and lets us feel absolutely safe. *We sometimes see each other as all men or all women, so that we can fall in Love with all human beings through each other.* Through our respect for each other, we feel a sense of reverence and awe for all human beings as gods and goddesses. We have the opportunity to worship another god/goddess disguised as a human being from a place of true surrender and devotion.

As you fully embrace your animal nature, a profound integration of Heaven and Earth emerges. As you celebrate the gift of your sexuality's unique expression, you discover that you do not have to wait until you die in order to be liberated. As your Hearts and your sex soar together, you free yourself to celebrate in Heavenly bliss while still in your body.

## Freedom

**Death is freedom**
**From time and space.**

**Sex is freedom**
**From time.**

**Love is Freedom.**

With Love, there is nothing to free yourself from. There is no place to try to get to nor anything to accomplish. Love includes and embraces the entire Universe. *Nothing is an obstacle to overcome because you have already arrived.*

# Section Nine

# Love

## Love

Love is not an idea.

Love is
    A vibration
        To attune to.

# Chapter Twenty-Eight
## Love

**– The Beginning –**

# The Workbook

## Meditations
## to
## Awaken Your Soul

## Illuminators

### Deepening Your Commitment

You came to the Earth to die
While still in your body.

If you are not willing to
Put your ego on the line
In order to find Love,
Love can't find you.

# Introduction to the Workbook

This workbook contains specially designed Meditations to open your Heart and to develop the compassionate witness of your thoughts. To derive maximum benefit, you will want to fully participate in the Meditations as they are outlined in the week-by-week format. You may want to read through the whole book once and then go back to spend additional time reading each section as you are involved with the corresponding Meditations.

This is a forty week course, making your decision to participate a very significant commitment. Ten months is a perfect period of time for you to gestate as you gently turn your attention inward. A genuine spiritual rebirth awaits you if you dive in totally.

To involve yourself in the Meditations, you must be clearly committed to spending twenty minutes with yourself daily. *This commitment, by itself, begins to move something in your Soul.* You are making some powerful statements to yourself and to the Universe, such as, "I care about myself enough to make my inner exploration a top priority," and "I am seeking Love within me instead of trying to find fulfillment from someone else."

You can enter into this transformational process on your own, with your lover, or with friends, perhaps by forming a weekly support group. Many of the Meditations can be done once a day by yourself and once a day with a partner. Discover what way works the best for you.

The text's most concise and potent aphorisms, known as Illuminators, are repeated at the end of each section's Meditations. An Illuminator is printed on its own page five to seven times in such a way that you can easily photocopy it (see the copyright page in the front of the book which describes how you can do this). *These particular aphorisms from the text are especially effective in by-passing the linear mind and opening the Heart.* You can make use of these Illuminators in several ways to more fully integrate *Living Life in Love* into your moment-to-moment consciousness.

Each week's Meditation is linked with one particular Illuminator. Turn to the page with multiple copies of that aphorism on it. Photocopy that page two or three times, cut out ten or fifteen copies of the Illuminator, and then tape them up in different places as a gentle reminder. You can put them on your bathroom mirror, your refrigerator, the dashboard of your car, visible places at work, your front door, and even the back of your toilet seat. Repeatedly seeing them assists you in waking up to Love. Display only the one aphorism for each week's Meditation in many different places, and then replace it with another one the next week. *By focusing on only one Illuminator per week, you allow its meaning to spiral deeper and deeper into your Soul.*

Many of the Meditations involve asking a "repeating question" to yourself in the mirror. A repeating question is just what it sounds like. While in eye contact with yourself in the mirror (or with another person), you will be asking a question, for example, "Where is Love?" After you breathe and take it in, feel into your Heart or your body (versus your head) for your response. Do not ponder the question. Respond spontaneously by speaking aloud the first word or phrase that arises in you. Keep your response concise (the maximum length being one sentence). Then receive that answer by saying, "Thank you" out loud, take a breath, and repeat the question, "Where is Love?" Again, say the first word or phrase that comes to you after breathing and letting the question sink in. Allow each response to arise spontaneously in the moment. Do not become rote in your answers.

Always receive the answer with a "Thank you," and then take a breath before asking the question again. *Wait a moment until you find the place in you that is really curious to know the answer and ask it from there rather than asking in a routine manner.* This attitude helps the question penetrate the deepest levels within you. Do not worry if you are doing it "right" or if you are getting anything out of it. This process does not need to make any sense or be logical. Have no goals. Just allow it to unfold in its own way. Most importantly, stick with your commitment and the question, *especially* if you get bored. *Often, you are the closest to a new insight or awareness when your mind tries to escape into boredom.*

To receive the most benefit from participating in these Meditations, the following guidelines are offered:

♥ Do these Meditations in a private room, such as your bedroom, with the door closed. Do not answer the phone or let anything else interrupt you. If you want to get the most out of these Meditations, create the time to be fully with yourself. You are worth it!

♥ Have a full length mirror situated in such a way that you can comfortably sit in a chair or cross-legged on the floor directly in front of it. In order to have maximum eye contact with yourself, sit so that there is only an inch or two between your knees and the mirror. If you keep the mirror clean, you will not be distracted by smudges.

♥ Set a timer to ring automatically after ten or twenty minutes so that you do not have to think about how much time has elapsed. Many watches have this feature. A portable stovetop timer can work if it does not tick too loudly. Continue the Meditation until the alarm rings.

♥ Tape the aphorism connected with the current week's Meditation to the mirror just above the reflection of your head. This visual reminder assists you to stay focused.

♥ Repeating questions are usually done for ten minutes at a time, twice a day. Choose the times of day that work for you. For the most benefit, be sure that you honor your twenty minute per day commitment, *regardless of what your thoughts say to try to convince you otherwise.* A key element of the power you gain over your mind is that you do not let your commitment to yourself be swayed by the momentary fluctuations of your thoughts.

♥ If you have a friend or a lover who is also participating in this process, you can do the Meditations once a day by yourself in the mirror for ten minutes and once with each other for ten minutes. Be sure that you both sit close enough to see deeply into each others' eyes. A good way to do this is to each sit on a small pillow on the floor with one person straddling the other's legs and your arms around each other's waist.

♥ When you do the Meditation alone in the mirror, stay in eye contact with yourself at all times. View your reflection as if it is another person sitting directly across from you. Whether you are participating in this with yourself or with someone else, know that "the two of you" are being as intimate as possible. *Please honor your partner by staying connected at all times, even if you are emotionally uncomfortable.* Do not go away from your partner in any way. We have all experienced enough abandonment in our lives.

♥ **Each week as you move through your everyday life, let the current repeating question become your mantra.** As frequently as you can remember, ask it to yourself wherever you are. Notice if any changes occur in your interactions with others and to your perceptions of Reality.

For some Meditations, you refer to an Illuminator without a repeating question. As before, the aphorism corresponding to the Meditation needs to be taped to the mirror just above the reflection of your head. You may be asked to look back and forth between the Illuminator and your eyes. Spend about thirty seconds reading, absorbing, and imbibing the aphorism. Then gaze deeply into your eyes for about the same length of time. Return to the aphorism for about thirty seconds, then back to your eyes, etc. When you look into your eyes, choose one eye to concentrate on. Look directly into the blackness of the pupil, which is the window to the Soul. It is easy to be distracted by the beauty of the iris or to just "space out." *Focus on the infinity within the pupil.* A very lovely integration of the Illuminator and the depths of your Soul can occur from these Meditations.

Other types of Meditations are offered. They are designed to be integrated directly into your external, everyday life. One of the bottom lines in Life is to be in the "here and now," and the intention of these Meditations is to find ways to do that. Some are "pattern interrupts." They can awaken you from sleepy routines and bring you into the present tense. Once you sense the flavor of them, you may want to design your own pattern interrupts. You may be surprised at your own creativity. Sometimes these Meditations are so enjoyable that people dismiss them because they are not serious enough. *It is possible for you to evolve spiritually and to have fun at the same time.* You have the opportunity to joyfully dance with the play of consciousness.

If you do not want to participate in all the Meditations, there are alternatives. If you want to spend only one week on each section instead of four or five, there is an asterisk beside the Meditation that I recommend. Or you can do only the ones that attract you. If you dedicate yourself to participating fully in these Meditations, whether it is for all forty weeks or for eight weeks or for some amount of time in between, your internal life will transform.

You may want to utilize the Illuminators in other ways that benefit you. You may want to cut out and tape up only the ones that especially touch you. You may want to frame your favorite one(s) for daily inspiration. The Illuminators are arranged in this workbook after each section's Meditations in the same order as they appear in the text. The upper right header of all Illuminator pages tells the text page number on which that Illuminator appears. You can then easily refer back to the text to review its context. The Illuminators are wonderful vehicles for you to receive additional value from this book, whether you participate in the Meditations or not.

*Living Life in Love* is designed to be more than just interesting and insightful. It is a "Handbook to Happiness" that can open your Heart and give you access to direct experiences of your Soul. Enjoy!

# Section One

# What Is Life All About?

## Meditations and Illuminators

### The Meaning of Life

The meaning of life is not
　An answer revealed to you
　　Upon achieving your goals.

Life is a thirst for more,
　Periodically quenched by
　　Insights and revelations,
　　　Which are followed by
　　　　A new thirst for more.

The meaning of life is
　Felt in magical moments
　　Within the miracle itself.

**Meditations and Illuminators**

# What Is Life All About?

**\*Week 1:**   Put up copies of the Illuminator **"Love"** (page 194) in many places, including one above the reflection of your head in the mirror.

Do the Repeating Question in the mirror for ten minutes twice a day (or if you are with a partner, once a day by yourself and once a day together, asking and answering for five minutes each):

### "Where is Love?"

**Week 2:**   Put up copies of the Illuminator **"Gratitude"** (page 200) in many places, including one above the reflection of your head in the mirror.

**Part One:**  Once a day for ten minutes, write out a list of everything for which you feel grateful.  Be sure to include specifics, such as any supportive relationships, any recent nurturing interactions, the food you eat, your shelter, your favorite music or hobbies, any material objects that are meaningful to you, etc.  You might also want to include the often overlooked miracles arising out of being in a body, such as breathing, enjoying your five senses (seeing, hearing, smelling, touching, tasting), moving your toes at will, celebrating sexual pleasure, etc.  You can include ways that you enjoy Mother Earth's gifts of sunshine, wind, rain, water, sky, oceans, trees, flowers, grass, land animals, fish, and dolphins.

**Part Two:**  Once a day for ten minutes, do the Repeating Question in the mirror.  If you are with a partner, do the question together one day, asking and answering for five minutes each.  The next day do it by yourself in the mirror:

### "What are you grateful for?"

**Week 3:**   Put up copies of the Illuminator **"Life's Purpose"** (page 197) in many places, including one above the reflection of your head in the mirror.

Do the Repeating Question in the mirror for ten minutes twice a day (or if you are with a partner, once a day by yourself and once a day together, asking and answering for five minutes each):

### "What is your purpose?"

**Week 4:**   Put up copies of the Illuminator **"Satori"** (page 196) in many places, including one above the reflection of your head in the mirror.

Do the Repeating Question in the mirror for ten minutes twice a day (or if you are with a partner, once a day by yourself and once a day together, asking and answering for five minutes each):

### "Where is 'I' ?"

\* If you are choosing to do only one Meditation per section, this one is recommended.

# Love

## Love is not an idea.

## Love is
## A vibration
## To attune to.

### Love

Love is not an idea.

Love is
  A vibration
    To attune to.

### Love

Love is not an idea.

Love is
  A vibration
    To attune to.

### Love

Love is not an idea.

Love is
  A vibration
    To attune to.

### Love

Love is not an idea.

Love is
  A vibration
    To attune to.

### Love

Love is not an idea.

Love is
  A vibration
    To attune to.

### Love

Love is not an idea.

Love is
  A vibration
    To attune to.

# Happiness

## Searching for happiness?
## You cannot find it.
## You can only *be* it.

**Happiness**

Searching for happiness?
You cannot find it.
You can only *be* it.

**Happiness**

Searching for happiness?
You cannot find it.
You can only *be* it.

**Happiness**

Searching for happiness?
You cannot find it.
You can only *be* it.

**Happiness**

Searching for happiness?
You cannot find it.
You can only *be* it.

**Happiness**

Searching for happiness?
You cannot find it.
You can only *be* it.

**Happiness**

Searching for happiness?
You cannot find it.
You can only *be* it.

# Satori

## Love is
## When
## 'You'
## Are not.

### Satori

Love is
When
  'You'
    Are not.

### Satori

Love is
When
  'You'
    Are not.

### Satori

Love is
When
  'You'
    Are not.

### Satori

Love is
When
  'You'
    Are not.

### Satori

Love is
When
  'You'
    Are not.

### Satori

Love is
When
  'You'
    Are not.

# Life's Purpose

## When you let go of *all* purpose,
## Then you can share true Love
## Which never needs a reason.

### Life's Purpose

When you let go of *all* purpose,
Then you can share true Love
Which never needs a reason.

### Life's Purpose

When you let go of *all* purpose,
Then you can share true Love
Which never needs a reason.

### Life's Purpose

When you let go of *all* purpose,
Then you can share true Love
Which never needs a reason.

### Life's Purpose

When you let go of *all* purpose,
Then you can share true Love
Which never needs a reason.

### Life's Purpose

When you let go of *all* purpose,
Then you can share true Love
Which never needs a reason.

### Life's Purpose

When you let go of *all* purpose,
Then you can share true Love
Which never needs a reason.

# Laughter

## Laughter lifts
## Life's load into
## Love's light.

### Laughter

**Laughter lifts**
**Life's load into**
**Love's light.**

### Laughter

**Laughter lifts**
**Life's load into**
**Love's light.**

### Laughter

**Laughter lifts**
**Life's load into**
**Love's light.**

### Laughter

**Laughter lifts**
**Life's load into**
**Love's light.**

### Laughter

**Laughter lifts**
**Life's load into**
**Love's light.**

### Laughter

**Laughter lifts**
**Life's load into**
**Love's light.**

# Intensity

## Feeling pain intensely
## Increases joy immensely.

### Intensity

**Feeling pain intensely**
**Increases joy immensely.**

### Intensity

**Feeling pain intensely**
**Increases joy immensely.**

### Intensity

**Feeling pain intensely**
**Increases joy immensely.**

### Intensity

**Feeling pain intensely**
**Increases joy immensely.**

### Intensity

**Feeling pain intensely**
**Increases joy immensely.**

### Intensity

**Feeling pain intensely**
**Increases joy immensely.**

# Gratitude

## Feeling gratitude creates
## Feeling more gratitude
## For the blessing of
## Feeling gratitude.

### Gratitude

Feeling gratitude creates
Feeling more gratitude
For the blessing of
Feeling gratitude.

### Gratitude

Feeling gratitude creates
Feeling more gratitude
For the blessing of
Feeling gratitude.

### Gratitude

Feeling gratitude creates
Feeling more gratitude
For the blessing of
Feeling gratitude.

### Gratitude

Feeling gratitude creates
Feeling more gratitude
For the blessing of
Feeling gratitude.

### Gratitude

Feeling gratitude creates
Feeling more gratitude
For the blessing of
Feeling gratitude.

### Gratitude

Feeling gratitude creates
Feeling more gratitude
For the blessing of
Feeling gratitude.

# Prayer

## When your time with God shifts
## From asking for needs to be filled
## Into feeling grateful for all of Life,
## You have discovered true Prayer.

### Prayer

When your time with God shifts
From asking for needs to be filled
Into feeling grateful for all of Life,
You have discovered true Prayer.

### Prayer

When your time with God shifts
From asking for needs to be filled
Into feeling grateful for all of Life,
You have discovered true Prayer.

### Prayer

When your time with God shifts
From asking for needs to be filled
Into feeling grateful for all of Life,
You have discovered true Prayer.

### Prayer

When your time with God shifts
From asking for needs to be filled
Into feeling grateful for all of Life,
You have discovered true Prayer.

### Prayer

When your time with God shifts
From asking for needs to be filled
Into feeling grateful for all of Life,
You have discovered true Prayer.

### Prayer

When your time with God shifts
From asking for needs to be filled
Into feeling grateful for all of Life,
You have discovered true Prayer.

# Section Two

# Loving Yourself

## Meditations and Illuminators

### How Are You?

How you are
  Does not matter.
What matters is
  How you are
    In relationship to
      How you are.

## Meditations and Illuminators

# Loving Yourself

**Week 5:** Put up copies of the Illuminator "**Righteous Rage**" (page 212) in many places, including one above the reflection of your head in the mirror.

It is time to declare yourself the Master of your mind. Buy a sturdy wiffle bat and a large pillow. Find a place where you feel safe to make as much noise as you want. Before you start, you may want to let your neighbors know that you will be yelling and that everything is okay. If you have some physical injury to your body that does not allow you to hit the pillow with the bat, you can squeeze the pillow with your hands or just yell. If you cannot find a safe place to make noise, screaming into a pillow works, too.

1. Kneel before the pillow with bat in hand and close your eyes. Envision all the ways you hold back in your life or do not fully express yourself. If your job or relationship or any situation is not fulfilling, feel your frustration. See your life passing you by without living it how you want to. Know that you could go to your grave never fully participating in Life unless you take charge.

2. As the tension builds, find a sentence that expresses your frustration, for instance, "I'm tired of nothing happening!" or "I don't want to die without _____" or "I won't sit on the sidelines anymore," or "I hate being poor." Find a short sentence to express the essence of your holding back.

3. Start to hit the pillow and say the sentence with conviction. Let the volume of your voice increase until you are yelling. Allow the sentence to change if it wants to. Do this for five or ten minutes or longer if you feel to.

4. Now it is time to move from the first stage, releasing your anger, into the second stage, declaring your power. Close your eyes again and this time find a sentence that declares what you deserve, for instance, "I deserve to be loved," or "I deserve a fulfilling job," or "I deserve a great relationship," or "I deserve plenty of money."

5. As you begin to feel how much you want this, hit the pillow again and shout your sentence with conviction. Even if you do not believe it at first or if a phrase comes out that is filled with the tone of doubt, still shout it. Repeat it until you find yourself feeling powerful. Continue for another five or ten minutes or more, until you feel finished.

6. Close your eyes. Sit in a powerful position with your shoulders back and your chest out. Feel a sense of potency coursing through your body. See if any voices try to invalidate what you have just declared, for instance, "This will never help!" or "You'll never get it!" or "You did it wrong!"

7. If doubtful voices arise, close your eyes and envision these voices as a gremlin or a demon or a devilish character attacking you. Then pick up the bat, look the demon in the eyes, and direct your anger at it, telling it to get out of your head. Counter its negative thoughts with positive declarations, such as, "This is helping!" or "I am getting it!" or "I am doing it right for me!" *You have a right to have whatever thoughts you want to have inside your head.*

8. Declare the new you with short, powerful phrases, such as, "I am a loving person," or "I am rich," or "I am enough," or "I am attractive and sexy." Keep doing this process until you feel uplifted and powerful as you sit there with

your eyes closed. Then open your eyes and look in the mirror and see your powerful self, including whatever qualities you have just declared.

Do this Meditation for at least twenty minutes, every day for a week (or longer if you want - I did it frequently for about a year). If your body feels sore or stiff, keep going as long as you have not aggravated an injury. If you feel stuck or too frightened to participate, get professional help by describing to a counselor what you want to do. Be sure that this person understands the purpose for this type of release and has had experience working with it. Although this looks like "anger work," it is really a declaration of your power.

**Week 6:**    Put up copies of the Illuminator **"Changing"** (page 211) in many places, including one above the reflection of your head in the mirror.

Do the Repeating Question in the mirror for ten minutes twice a day (or if you are with a partner, once a day by yourself and once a day with your partner, asking and answering for five minutes each):

**"How are you changing?"**

**Week 7:**    Put up copies of the Illuminator **"Compassion"** (page 214) in many places, including one above the reflection of your head in the mirror.

**Part One:** There is either Love or a cry for Love. This week, look for the innocent child within every adult you encounter. Look into their eyes or at the way they hold their body or whatever else assists you to find the little boy or girl who lives inside each adult's body. Watch the ways that the child is reaching out to be noticed or loved.

Sometimes the person's method of crying out for Love can be self-defeating and tends to push people away rather than invite Love in. *As you begin to see the innocent child's cry for Love within every behavior, compassion is born.* This is particularly rewarding when you can emphathize with the people who would normally bother you the most because you can see that they are the ones who are the most self-defeating and thus the loneliest.

**Part Two:** Spend at least ten minutes a day looking in your eyes in the mirror as you search for your own inner child's cry for Love. Look for the loneliness in your eyes and find compassion for the ways you try to find Love that are not serving you.

**\*Week 8:**    Put up copies of the Illuminator **"Loving Yourself"** (page 207) in many places, including one above the reflection of your head in the mirror.

Do each of the Repeating Questions in the mirror once a day for ten minutes (or if you are with a partner, one day ask both questions to yourself in the mirror and the next day be with your partner for both questions, asking and answering for five minutes each):

For the first ten minute period each day ask, **"What do you love about you?"**

For the second ten minute period ask, **"How can you love you more?"**

\* If you are choosing to do only one Meditation per section, this one is recommended.

# Loving Yourself

## Loving yourself is
## Accepting yourself,
## Especially
## When you are not
## Accepting yourself.


### Loving Yourself

Loving yourself is
  Accepting yourself,
    Especially
      When you are not
        Accepting yourself.

### Loving Yourself

Loving yourself is
  Accepting yourself,
    Especially
      When you are not
        Accepting yourself.

### Loving Yourself

Loving yourself is
  Accepting yourself,
    Especially
      When you are not
        Accepting yourself.

### Loving Yourself

Loving yourself is
  Accepting yourself,
    Especially
      When you are not
        Accepting yourself.

### Loving Yourself

Loving yourself is
  Accepting yourself,
    Especially
      When you are not
        Accepting Illung yourself.

### Loving Yourself

Loving yourself is
  Accepting yourself,
    Especially
      When you are not
        Accepting yourself.

# How Are You?

**How you are**
**Does not matter.**

**What matters is**
**How you are**
**In relationship to**
**How you are.**

### How Are You?

How you are
   Does not matter.

What matters is
   How you are
      In relationship to
         How you are.

### How Are You?

How you are
   Does not matter.

What matters is
   How you are
      In relationship to
         How you are.

### How Are You?

How you are
   Does not matter.

What matters is
   How you are
      In relationship to
         How you are.

### How Are You?

How you are
   Does not matter.

What matters is
   How you are
      In relationship to
         How you are.

# Failure

**If you can love yourself
While you feel the pain
Of seeing your life failing,
Then you are succeeding.**

### Failure

If you can love yourself
While you feel the pain
Of seeing your life failing,
Then you are succeeding.

### Failure

If you can love yourself
While you feel the pain
Of seeing your life failing,
Then you are succeeding.

### Failure

If you can love yourself
While you feel the pain
Of seeing your life failing,
Then you are succeeding.

### Failure

If you can love yourself
While you feel the pain
Of seeing your life failing,
Then you are succeeding.

### Failure

If you can love yourself
While you feel the pain
Of seeing your life failing,
Then you are succeeding.

### Failure

If you can love yourself
While you feel the pain
Of seeing your life failing,
Then you are succeeding.

# Perfection

## If your ideals of perfection include
## Your perceptions of imperfection,
## Then 'mistakes' help you to weave
## The tapestry of your own humanity.

### Perfection

If your ideals of perfection include
  Your perceptions of imperfection,
    Then 'mistakes' help you to weave
      The tapestry of your own humanity.

### Perfection

If your ideals of perfection include
  Your perceptions of imperfection,
    Then 'mistakes' help you to weave
      The tapestry of your own humanity.

### Perfection

If your ideals of perfection include
  Your perceptions of imperfection,
    Then 'mistakes' help you to weave
      The tapestry of your own humanity.

### Perfection

If your ideals of perfection include
  Your perceptions of imperfection,
    Then 'mistakes' help you to weave
      The tapestry of your own humanity.

### Perfection

If your ideals of perfection include
  Your perceptions of imperfection,
    Then 'mistakes' help you to weave
      The tapestry of your own humanity.

### Perfection

If your ideals of perfection include
  Your perceptions of imperfection,
    Then 'mistakes' help you to weave
      The tapestry of your own humanity.

# Changing

## The same energy you use to
## Focus on all the reasons that
## Your life is miserably stuck
## Can instead be channeled
## Into welcoming the new.

### Changing

The same energy you use to
 Focus on all the reasons that
  Your life is miserably stuck
   Can instead be channeled
    Into welcoming the new.

### Changing

The same energy you use to
 Focus on all the reasons that
  Your life is miserably stuck
   Can instead be channeled
    Into welcoming the new.

### Changing

The same energy you use to
 Focus on all the reasons that
  Your life is miserably stuck
   Can instead be channeled
    Into welcoming the new.

### Changing

The same energy you use to
 Focus on all the reasons that
  Your life is miserably stuck
   Can instead be channeled
    Into welcoming the new.

### Changing

The same energy you use to
 Focus on all the reasons that
  Your life is miserably stuck
   Can instead be channeled
    Into welcuming the new.

### Changing

The same energy you use to
 Focus on all the reasons that
  Your life is miserably stuck
   Can instead be channeled
    Into welcoming the new.

# Righteous Rage

**Expressing your rage
Can move your stance
From living 'in victim'
Into declaring yourself
The master of your mind.**

### Righteous Rage

Expressing your rage
  Can move your stance
    From living 'in victim'
      Into declaring yourself
        The master of your mind.

### Righteous Rage

Expressing your rage
  Can move your stance
    From living 'in victim'
      Into declaring yourself
        The master of your mind.

### Righteous Rage

Expressing your rage
  Can move your stance
    From living 'in victim'
      Into declaring yourself
        The master of your mind.

### Righteous Rage

Expressing your rage
  Can move your stance
    From living 'in victim'
      Into declaring yourself
        The master of your mind.

### Righteous Rage

Expressing your rage
  Can move your stance
    From living 'in victim'
      Into declaring yourself
        The master of your mind.

### Righteous Rage

Expressing your rage
  Can move your stance
    From living 'in victim'
      Into declaring yourself
        The master of your mind.

# Vulnerability

**Vulnerability opens
The gateway between
Thinking and feeling.**

**If you let go of thoughts
And enter into feelings,
Your Heart awakens.**

### Vulnerability

**Vulnerability opens
The gateway between
Thinking and feeling.**

**If you let go of thoughts
And enter into feelings,
Your Heart awakens.**

### Vulnerability

**Vulnerability opens
The gateway between
Thinking and feeling.**

**If you let go of thoughts
And enter into feelings,
Your Heart awakens.**

### Vulnerability

**Vulnerability opens
The gateway between
Thinking and feeling.**

**If you let go of thoughts
And enter into feelings,
Your Heart awakens.**

### Vulnerability

**Vulnerability opens
The gateway between
Thinking and feeling.**

**If you let go of thoughts
And enter into feelings,
Your Heart awakens.**

# Compassion

**Compassion occurs**
**When you feel grief**
**For people's suffering**
***And* see the innocence**
**Of their cry for Love.**

### Compassion

Compassion occurs
When you feel grief
For people's suffering
*And* see the innocence
Of their cry for Love.

### Compassion

Compassion occurs
When you feel grief
For people's suffering
*And* see the innocence
Of their cry for Love.

### Compassion

Compassion occurs
When you feel grief
For people's suffering
*And* see the innocence
Of their cry for Love.

### Compassion

Compassion occurs
When you feel grief
For people's suffering
*And* see the innocence
Of their cry for Love.

### Compassion

Compassion occurs
When you feel grief
For people's suffering
*And* see the innocence
Of their cry for Love.

### Compassion

Compassion occurs
When you feel grief
For people's suffering
*And* see the innocence
Of their cry for Love.

# Section Three

# How Do You Evolve?

## Meditations and Illuminators

### The Game of Life

You have boundaries around
How deeply you have accepted
The totality of this Reality.

You are repeatedly presented
With situations just beyond
Your capacity to embrace.

You can reject the lessons and
Stay in the pain of stagnation,
Or include everything as 'you'
And feel the joy of expansion.

## Section Three
## Meditations and Illuminators

# How Do You Evolve?

**Week 9:**     Put up copies of the Illuminator **"The Process of Elimination"** (page 226) in many places, including one above the reflection of your head in the mirror (and on the back of the toilet seat!).

For ten minutes twice a day, make eye contact with yourself in the mirror. Become curious as to where "you" are within what you see. Very slowly and deliberately speak the following into the depths of your pupils as you search for "you":

> **"I am not my body."**
> **"I am not my thoughts."**
> **"I am not my emotions."**
> **"I am not my sexuality."**
> **"I am Love."**

**\*Week 10:**     Put up copies of the Illuminator **"Waiting"** (page 221) in many places, including one above the reflection of your head in the mirror.

**Part One:**  For ten minutes twice a day stand on a chair facing a wall. Place the chair close to the wall so that, as you stand on it, your nose is no more than six inches from the wall. Do not physically touch the wall in any way.

Your task is to repeatedly fall in Love with the wall, moment by moment, instead of waiting for some outside source to trigger the opening of your Heart. See if you can simply appreciate the wall's color and texture. Moment by moment, notice if you are "loving" or "waiting to love."

Also, be sure to put a copy of the Illuminator "Waiting" about six inches above your head on the wall where you are standing on the chair so that it is on the edge of your peripheral vision as you are falling in Love with the wall.

**Part Two:** Every moment as you move through your life this week, keep noticing again and again, "In this moment, am I loving or waiting to love?" See if you can let your love flow to whomever you come in contact with no expectations of receiving anything from anyone.

**Week 11:**     Put up copies of the Illuminator **"Letting Go"** (page 220) in many places, including one above the reflection of your head in the mirror.

**Part One:**  Choose one of your most precious treasures, such as a piece of jewelry or a momentum from a special occasion that you hold near and dear to your Heart. Sometime during this week, go into the woods by yourself and bury it or go to a large body of water and throw it in. Feel all your feelings as you say goodbye to the past.

217

**Part Two:** Do the Repeating Question in the mirror for ten minutes twice a day (or if you are with a partner, once a day by yourself and once a day with your partner, asking and answering for five minutes each):

**"What are you holding on to?"**

**Week 12:** Put up copies of the Illuminator **"Deepening Your Commitment"** (page 227) in many places, including one above the reflection of your head in the mirror.

Do the Repeating Question in the mirror for ten minutes twice a day (or if you are with a partner, once a day by yourself and once a day with your partner, asking and answering for five minutes each):

**"How much do you want to be Love?"**

**NOTE:** This does not say "Love_d_." It says "Love" without the "d" because ultimately you are Love. Keep looking for the depths of your desire to return Home to God.

* If you are choosing to do only one Meditation per section, this one is recommended.

# Fear of Change

**Your resistance to change is
Your fear of the death of
Who you *think* you are.**

**Actually, change destroys
Who you are *not*
So the next level of
Who you *are*
Can emerge.**

### Fear Of Change

Your resistance to change is
Your fearing the death of
Who you *think* you are.

Actually, change destroys
Who you are *not*
So the next level of
Who you *are*
Can emerge.

### Fear of Change

Your resistance to change is
Your fearing the death of
Who you *think* you are.

Actually, change destroys
Who you are *not*
So the next level of
Who you *are*
Can emerge.

### Fear Of Change

Your resistance to change is
Your fearing the death of
Who you *think* you are.

Actually, change destroys
Who you are *not*
So the next level of
Who you *are*
Can emerge.

### Fear of Change

Your resistance to change is
Your fearing the death of
Who you *think* you are.

Actually, change destroys
Who you are *not*
So the next level of
Who you *are*
Can emerge.

# Letting Go

## Today's Truth
## Becomes
## Tomorrow's lie.

## Let go of your
## Sacred insights
## Daily.

### Letting Go

Today's Truth
Becomes
    Tomorrow's lie.

Let go of your
    Sacred insights
    Daily.

### Letting Go

Today's Truth
Becomes
    Tomorrow's lie.

Let go of your
    Sacred insights
    Daily.

### Letting Go

Today's Truth
Becomes
    Tomorrow's lie.

Let go of your
    Sacred insights
    Daily.

### Letting Go

Today's Truth
Becomes
    Tomorrow's lie.

Let go of your
    Sacred insights
    Daily.

# Waiting

## When you hold back your Love
## Waiting to find more elsewhere,
## You learn how to wait,
## Not how to Love.

### Waiting

When you hold back your Love
Waiting to find more elsewhere,
You learn how to wait,
Not how to Love.

### Waiting

When you hold back your Love
Waiting to find more elsewhere,
You learn how to wait,
Not how to Love.

### Waiting

When you hold back your Love
Waiting to find more elsewhere,
You learn how to wait,
Not how to Love.

### Waiting

When you hold back your Love
Waiting to find more elsewhere,
You learn how to wait,
Not how to Love.

### Waiting

When you hold back your Love
Waiting to find more elsewhere,
You learn how to wait,
Not how to Love.

### Waiting

When you hold back your Love
Waiting to find more elsewhere,
You learn how to wait,
Not how to Love.

# The Unlovable

Loving
The lovable
Is easy.

Loving
The unlovable
Is Enlightening.


### The Unlovable

Loving
The lovable
Is easy.
Loving
The unlovable
Is Enlightening.

### The Unlovable

Loving
The lovable
Is easy.
Loving
The unlovable
Is Enlightening.


### The Unlovable

Loving
The lovable
Is easy.
Loving
The unlovable
Is Enlightening.

### The Unlovable

Loving
The lovable
Is easy.
Loving
The unlovable
Is Enlightening.

# Acceptance

## Acceptance is feeling
## Love in your Heart
## For the police officer
## Who is writing you
## A speeding ticket.

### Acceptance

Acceptance is feeling
Love in your Heart
For the police officer
Who is writing you
A speeding ticket.

### Acceptance

Acceptance is feeling
Love in your Heart
For the police officer
Who is writing you
A speeding ticket.

### Acceptance

Acceptance is feeling
Love in your Heart
For the police officer
Who is writing you
A speeding ticket.

### Acceptance

Acceptance is feeling
Love in your Heart
For the police officer
Who is writing you
A speeding ticket.

### Acceptance

Acceptance is feeling
Love in your Heart
For the police officer
Who is writing you
A speeding ticket.

### Acceptance

Acceptance is feeling
Love in your Heart
For the police officer
Who is writing you
A speeding ticket.

# You

## You are not
### Just a body
#### With a Soul
##### Inside.

## You are a Soul
### Gift-wrapped
#### With a body.

**You**

You are not
  Just a body
    With a Soul
      Inside.
You are a Soul
  Gift-wrapped
    With a body.

**You**

You are not
  Just a body
    With a Soul
      Inside.
You are a Soul
  Gift-wrapped
    With a body.

**You**

You are not
  Just a body
    With a Soul
      Inside.
You are a Soul
  Gift-wrapped
    With a body.

**You**

You are not
  Just a body
    With a Soul
      Inside.
You are a Soul
  Gift-wrapped
    With a body.

# Death's Significance

## When your body
## Drops away from
## Your soul,
## Your essence
## May or may not
## Blink.

**Death's Significance**

When your body
  Drops away from
    Your soul,
      Your essence
        May or may not
          Blink.

**Death's Significance**

When your body
  Drops away from
    Your soul,
      Your essence
        May or may not
          Blink.

**Death's Significance**

When your body
  Drops away from
    Your soul,
      Your essence
        May or may not
          Blink.

**Death's Significance**

When your body
  Drops away from
    Your soul,
      Your essence
        May or may not
          Blink.

# The Process of Elimination

'Who you are' is
Who is left standing naked
After you have explored
All the possibilities of
Who you are not.

## The Process of Elimination

'Who you are' is
Who is left standing naked
After you have explored
All the possibilities of
Who you are not.

## The Process of Elimination

'Who you are' is
Who is left standing naked
After you have explored
All the possibilities of
Who you are not.

## The Process of Elimination

'Who you are' is
Who is left standing naked
After you have explored
All the possibilities of
Who you are not.

## The Process of Elimination

'Who you are' is
Who is left standing naked
After you have explored
All the possibilities of
Who you are not.

## The Process of Elimination

'Who you are' is
Who is left standing naked
After you have explored
All the possibilities of
Who you are not.

## The Process of Elimination

'Who you are' is
Who is left standing naked
After you have explored
All the possibilities of
Who you are not.

# Deepening Your Commitment

## You came to Earth to die
## While still in your body.

## If you are not willing to
## Put your ego on the line
## In order to find Love,
## Love can't find you.

### Deepening Your Commitment

You came to Earth to die
   While still in your body.

If you are not willing to
   Put your ego on the line
    In order to find Love,
      Love can't find you.

### Deepening Your Commitment

You came to Earth to die
   While still in your body.

If you are not willing to
   Put your ego on the line
    In order to find Love,
      Love can't find you.

### Deepening Your Commitment

You came to Earth to die
   While still in your body.

If you are not willing to
   Put your ego on the line
    In order to find Love,
      Love can't find you.

### Deepening Your Commitment

You came to Earth to die
   While still in your body.

If you are not willing to
   Put your ego on the line
    In order to find Love,
      Love can't find you.

# Section Four

# The Illusions of the Mind

## Meditations and Illuminators

### Beyond Beliefs

When you go beyond beliefs,
You discover that Truth is
A state of consciousness,
Not an idea.

## Section Four
## Meditations and Illuminators
# The Illusions of the Mind

**Week 13:**     Put up copies of the Illuminator "**Eyes**" (page 233) in many places, including one above the reflection of your head in the mirror.

Go for a ten minute walk twice a day, looking with your eyes in a new way. Make it your intention to only experience the colors and hues and textures of whatever touches your optic nerve without labeling the objects in any way. Perceive your eyes as manufacturers of the colors rather than as the recipients of them.

**Week 14:**     Put up copies of the Illuminator "**Choice**" (page 237) in many places, including one above the reflection of your head in the mirror.

Sit in front of the mirror and spend about thirty seconds reading, imbibing, and absorbing the Illuminator "Choice." Then be with yourself through your eyes for about the same length of time. When you are looking into your eyes, choose one eye to concentrate on. Look directly into the blackness of that eye's pupil, which is the passageway into the Soul. It is easy to get distracted by the beauty of the iris or to just "space out." So really focus in on the infinity within the pupil itself. Let yourself get "lost in Love."

Go back and forth between the Illuminator and your eyes, spending about thirty seconds on each, until the ten minutes has passed. If you do this Meditation twice a day for a week, this Illuminator can create a very lovely opening into the depths of your Soul.

**Week 15:**     Put up copies of the Illuminator "**Simplicity**" (page 238) in many places, including one above the reflection of your head in the mirror.

Do the Repeating Question in the mirror for ten minutes twice a day (or if you are with a partner, once a day by yourself and once a day with your partner, asking and answering for five minutes each):

**"How does your mind fool you?"**

**\*Week 16:**     Put up copies of the Illuminator "**Conditioning**" (page 242) in many places, including one above the reflection of your head in the mirror.

This week you are going to explore the underlying assumptions from which your beliefs arise. Each day choose one topic to focus on. Some possible examples are: Men, Women, Power, Thoughts, The mind, Emotions, Love, Anger, Compassion, Sadness, Joy, Happiness, Creativity, Enlightenment, Sex, Penises, Vaginas, Relationships, Friendship, Marriage, A wife, A husband, Children, My mother, My father, Work, A boss, Money, Wealthy people, Old people, Teenagers, Asians, Blacks, Hispanics, Religion, Christians, Jews, Arabs, Muslims, Russians, Politicians, "I" (or write "your name"), etc.

Spontaneously write out your completion to the following sentence:

**".....(today's topic).....is/am/are ........................."**

Write this sentence out for one topic quickly as many times as possible for 10 minutes twice a day. At the end of the day, go back and read each sentence about that day's topic. After each sentence, ask the questions, "Who said so?" and "Why is that so?" until you see the underlying assumptions that created that sentence's point of view.

The next day, choose another topic to focus on and repeat the above so that you will have focused on seven areas by week's end.

After seven days, gather all the sheets of paper on which you have written about all your topics. Crumble them up in a fireplace and light them on fire. As they burn, watch all your beliefs and points of view go up in flames.

**Week 17:**    Put up copies of the Illuminator **"The Final Frontier"** (page 240) in many places, including one above the reflection of your head in the mirror.

This week, every time you feel stuck, depressed, in pain, or want to make a decision, use the series of questions in Chapter Thirteen (page 86). Sit in front of the mirror for twenty minutes a day. Focus on a topic and then ask one question at a time as you look into the eyes and Heart of the reflection of your life partner in the mirror. Let yourself be vulnerable as you allow each question to penetrate your Soul.

Or, if you are with a partner, spend one day focussed on one of you, another day on the other, and another day both do it separately in the mirror.

Let this be an exploration to see if this series of questions works for you. Many people find it profound. You may or may not. Do not judge yourself either way. If you find them useful, then you have one more tool to assist you in your transformation. If you do not feel drawn to these questions, let them go and focus on other routes to your Heart. But try them for a week to find out for yourself.

* If you are choosing to do only one Meditation per section, this one is recommended.

# Eyes

## If you observe what
## Your vision notices,
## Your eyes become
## The mirror for your
## State of consciousness.

### Eyes

If you observe what
  Your vision notices,
    Your eyes become
      The mirror for your
        State of consciousness.

### Eyes

If you observe what
  Your vision notices,
    Your eyes become
      The mirror for your
        State of consciousness.

### Eyes

If you observe what
  Your vision notices,
    Your eyes become
      The mirror for your
        State of consciousness.

### Eyes

If you observe what
  Your vision notices,
    Your eyes become
      The mirror for your
        State of consciousness.

### Eyes

If you observe what
  Your vision notices,
    Your eyes become
      The mirror for your
        State of conscilusness.

### Eyes

If you observe what
  Your vision notices,
    Your eyes become
      The mirror for your
        State of consciousness.

# Personality

## Humans are both
## Neurotic and Divine.

## Why would you focus on
## The level of personality
## And miss your chance
## To see God?

### Personality

Humans are both
  Neurotic and Divine.

Why would you focus on
  The level of personality
    And miss your chance
      To see God?

### Personality

Humans are both
  Neurotic and Divine.

Why would you focus on
  The level of personality
    And miss your chance
      To see God?

### Personality

Humans are both
  Neurotic and Divine.

Why would you focus on
  The level of personality
    And miss your chance
      To see God?

### Personality

Humans are both
  Neurotic and Divine.

Why would you focus on
  The level of personality
    And miss your chance
      To see God?

# Your Soul Mate

## If you risk looking deeply
## Into the eyes of *any* person,
## You'll find your Soul Mate
## For that moment in time.

### Your Soul Mate

If you risk looking deeply
   Into the eyes of *any* person,
     You'll find your Soul Mate
      For that moment in time.

### Your Soul Mate

If you risk looking deeply
   Into the eyes of *any* person,
     You'll find your Soul Mate
      For that moment in time.

### Your Soul Mate

If you risk looking deeply
   Into the eyes of *any* person,
     You'll find your Soul Mate
      For that moment in time.

### Your Soul Mate

If you risk looking deeply
   Into the eyes of *any* person,
     You'll find your Soul Mate
      For that moment in time.

### Your Soul Mate

If you risk looking deeply
   Into the eyes of *any* person,
     You'll find your Soul Mate
      For that moment in time.

### Your Soul Mate

If you risk looking deeply
   Into the eyes of *any* person,
     You'll find your Soul Mate
      For that moment in time.

# Perceptions

## Arrogance
### Perceives
#### Others as less.

## Humility
### Perceives
#### Others as more.

## Enlightenment
### Perceives
#### No other.

**Perceptions**

**Arrogance**
  Perceives
    Others as less.
**Humility**
  Perceives
    Others as more.
**Enlightenment**
  Perceives
    No other.

**Perceptions**

**Arrogance**
  Perceives
    Others as less.
**Humility**
  Perceives
    Others as more.
**Enlightenment**
  Perceives
    No other.

# Choice

## Your most profound choice
## Each new moment in time
## Is whether you are
## Lost in thoughts
## Or lost in Love.

### Choice

Your most profound choice
Each new moment in time
Is whether you are
Lost in thoughts
Or lost in Love.

### Choice

Your most profound choice
Each new moment in time
Is whether you are
Lost in thoughts
Or lost in Love.

### Choice

Your most profound choice
Each new moment in time
Is whether you are
Lost in thoughts
Or lost in Love.

### Choice

Your most profound choice
Each new moment in time
Is whether you are
Lost in thoughts
Or lost in Love.

### Choice

Your most profound choice
Each new moment in time
Is whether you are
Lost in thoughts
Or lost in Love.

### Choice

Your most profound choice
Each new moment in time
Is whether you are
Lost in thoughts
Or lost in Love.

# Simplicity

## The mind distorts
## Truth's simplicity
## Into mental complexity
## For its self-perpetuation.

### Simplicity

The mind distorts
  Truth's simplicity
    Into mental complexity
      For its self-perpetuation.

### Simplicity

The mind distorts
  Truth's simplicity
    Into mental complexity
      For its self-perpetuation.

### Simplicity

The mind distorts
  Truth's simplicity
    Into mental complexity
      For its self-perpetuation.

### Simplicity

The mind distorts
  Truth's simplicity
    Into mental complexity
      For its self-perpetuation.

### Simplicity

The mind distorts
  Truth's simplicity
    Into mental complexity
      For its self-perpetuation.

### Simplicity

The mind distorts
  Truth's simplicity
    Into mental complexity
      For its self-perpetuation.

# Peace of Mind

## Peace of mind
## Is impossible.

## Where Mind is
## Peace is not.


### Peace of Mind

Peace of mind
Is impossible.
Where Mind is
Peace is not.


### Peace of Mind

Peace of mind
Is impossible.
Where Mind is
Peace is not.


### Peace of Mind

Peace of mind
Is impossible.
Where Mind is
Peace is not.


### Peace of Mind

Peace of mind
Is impossible.
Where Mind is
Peace is not.


### Peace of Mind

Peace of mind
Is impossible.
Where Mind is
Peace is not.


### Peace of Mind

Peace of mind
Is impossible.
Where Mind is
Peace is not.

# The Final Frontier

**The only thing**
**Left to work on**
**Is the concept that**
**You have anything**
**Left to work on.**

### The Final Frontier

The only thing
  Left to work on
    Is the concept that
      You have anything
        Left to work on.

### The Final Frontier

The only thing
  Left to work on
    Is the concept that
      You have anything
        Left to work on.

### The Final Frontier

The only thing
  Left to work on
    Is the concept that
      You have anything
        Left to work on.

### The Final Frontier

The only thing
  Left to work on
    Is the concept that
      You have anything
        Left to work on.

### The Final Frontier

The only thing
  Left to work on
    Is the concept that
      You have anything
        Left to work on.

### The Final Frontier

The only thing
  Left to work on
    Is the concept that
      You have anything
        Left to work on.

# Beyond Beliefs

## When you go beyond beliefs,
## You discover that Truth is
## A state of consciousness,
## Not an idea.

### Beyond Beliefs

When you go beyond beliefs,
You discover that Truth is
A state of consciousness,
Not an idea.

### Beyond Beliefs

When you go beyond beliefs,
You discover that Truth is
A state of consciousness,
Not an idea.

### Beyond Beliefs

When you go beyond beliefs,
You discover that Truth is
A state of consciousness,
Not an idea.

### Beyond Beliefs

When you go beyond beliefs,
You discover that Truth is
A state of consciousness,
Not an idea.

### Beyond Beliefs

When you go beyond beliefs,
You discover that Truth is
A state of consciousness,
Not an idea.

### Beyond Beliefs

When you go beyond beliefs,
You discover that Truth is
A state of consciousness,
Not an idea.

# Conditioning

You are beginning to fathom
The depth of your conditioning
When you question whether
Even beliefs as basic as
'Your body must die'
Were loaned to you
After you arrived
On this Planet.

### Conditioning

You are beginning to fathom
The depth of your conditioning
When you question whether
Even beliefs as basic as
'Your body must die'
Were loaned to you
After you arrived
On this Planet.

### Conditioning

You are beginning to fathom
The depth of your conditioning
When you question whether
Even beliefs as basic as
'Your body must die'
Were loaned to you
After you arrived
On this Planet.

### Conditioning

You are beginning to fathom
The depth of your conditioning
When you question whether
Even beliefs as basic as
'Your body must die'
Were loaned to you
After you arrived
On this Planet.

### Conditioning

You are beginning to fathom
The depth of your conditioning
When you question whether
Even beliefs as basic as
'Your body must die'
Were loaned to you
After you arrived
On this Planet.

# Section Five

# Where Is Happiness Hidden?

## Meditations and Illuminators

### Lost and Found

To think that
   You can find
      The Answer
         Is to be lost.

To embrace
   Life's mystery
      Not knowing
         Is to be found.

## Meditations and Illuminators

# Where Is Happiness Hidden?

**\*Week 18:** Put up copies of the Illuminator **"Listening"** (page 248) in many places, including one above the reflection of your head in the mirror.

Once a day for ten minutes, sit in front of the mirror and look at the Illuminator "Listening" for about thirty seconds, and then close your eyes and listen to the sounds (or the silence) in the room. Repeatedly notice whether you are listening to the sounds around you or to your thoughts. Keep coming back to the external sounds. Then open your eyes and look at the Illuminator again for about thirty seconds, and then close your eyes and listen again. Repeat this process until the ten minutes has passed.

Spend the other ten minute period outside, preferably in Nature away from all mechanical sounds (although this can also be effective sitting beside a freeway – you will just have a very different experience). Get comfortable. Close your eyes for about thirty seconds. Put all your attention on listening to whatever sounds are occurring. Repeatedly notice if you are listening to the sounds around you or to your thoughts. Keep coming back to the external sounds. After about thirty seconds, open your eyes and take in the colors and hues and textures of whatever fills your eyes while you listen to the sounds. Try not to label the visual images or judge them as good or bad. Let your eyes and ears drink in the environment. Then, after about thirty seconds, close your eyes and just listen. After thirty seconds, open them again. Repeat this process until ten minutes has passed.

**\*Week 19:** Put up copies of the Illuminator **"External Reality"** (page 251) in many places, including one above the reflection of your head in the mirror.

This week's opportunity is to let go of the need for external reality to be a certain way for you to be present with yourself and to be happy. When you drive on the freeway, be sure to stay in the right hand lane the whole way. If you have no reason to go on the freeway, spend twenty minutes a day driving nowhere on some four lane road. Once on the freeway, under no circumstances are you to change lanes. As you drive along in the right lane, enjoy what is around you – the trees, sky, buildings, and people in other vehicles (especially the children, who are usually more available to the present than adults, and the person in the vehicle in front of you who may be going very slowly). Celebrate the journey itself instead of hurrying to get to your destination or thinking about the past or future. Experience being in the Here and Now while you drive.

**Week 20:** Put up copies of the Illuminator **"Quantum Leap"** (page 249) in many places, including one above the reflection of your head in the mirror.

For ten minutes, twice a day, sit in front of the mirror, look at the Illuminator "Quantum Leap" for thirty seconds. Then close your eyes, let go of your thoughts, and feel into your Heart for thirty seconds. Open your eyes and absorb the Illuminator again for thirty seconds. Then close your eyes and dive back into your Heart. Repeat this process until ten minutes have passed.

**Week 21:** Put up copies of the Illuminator "**Full Circle**" (page 253) in many places, including one above the reflection of your head in the mirror.

It is time for you to alter your concept of "external" and "internal" so that you can stop being separate. Wherever you are this week, look around and say to yourself, "This is me." When you see another person, say to yourself, "Hello, me." If there is anyone or anything that you perceive as not being you, spend some extra time with that person or object until you can embrace it as an external manifestation of some internal part of you, whether you want to admit it or not. By the end of the week, hopefully you will be seeing only your Self wherever you look.

\* If you are doing only one Meditation per section, both of these are equally recommended.

**NOTE:** You are a little more than halfway through these Meditations. Perhaps you would like to take a few minutes to take an inventory of how this transformational process is affecting you. If so, ask yourself the following questions:

♥ Why do I perceive Life the way I do? Which perspectives serve me and which ones do not?

♥ Is Life easy or difficult?

♥ What are my core beliefs that create the basis of my orientation toward Earth's Reality?

♥ Do I know that I am safe here on this planet?

♥ Am I becoming aware of any previously unconscious assumptions I have had about myself, others, Life, and Reality?

♥ Are my intentions good? Are other people's?

♥ Am I learning the knack of using my will to:
   1. make more conscious choices?
   2. respond to situations and to people in more loving ways?
   3. feel compassion for myself when I am not loving myself?

♥ Am I satisfied with how high of a priority Love is in my life?

What you receive from Life is proportional to the depth of your involvement. The same is true of these Meditations. Take a moment to renew your commitment to awaken your Spirit. May your Heart be touched even more deeply on the second half of this journey. Namaste.

# Lost and Found

To think that
You can find
The Answer
Is to be lost.

To embrace
Life's mystery
Not knowing
Is to be found.

**Lost and Found**

To think that
You can find
The Answer
Is to be lost.

To embrace
Life's mystery
Not knowing
Is to be found.

**Lost and Found**

To think that
You can find
The Answer
Is to be lost.

To embrace
Life's mystery
Not knowing
Is to be found.

**Lost and Found**

To think that
You can find
The Answer
Is to be lost.

To embrace
Life's mystery
Not knowing
Is to be found.

**Lost and Found**

To think that
You can find
The Answer
Is to be lost.

To embrace
Life's mystery
Not knowing
Is to be found.

# Listening

## If your awareness flows
## Down the river of sound,
## All thoughts become still
## And you are Here, Now.


### Listening

If your awareness flows
   Down the river of sound,
      All thoughts become still
         And you are Here, Now.

### Listening

If your awareness flows
   Down the river of sound,
      All thoughts become still
         And you are Here, Now.

### Listening

If your awareness flows
   Down the river of sound,
      All thoughts become still
         And you are Here, Now.

### Listening

If your awareness flows
   Down the river of sound,
      All thoughts become still
         And you are Here, Now.

### Listening

If your awareness flows
   Down the river of sound,
      All thoughts become still
         And you are Here, Now.

### Listening

If your awareness flows
   Down the river of sound,
      All thoughts become still
         And you are Here, Now.

# Quantum Leap

## Empty your mind,
## Fill your Heart.

## Don't settle for less.

**Quantum Leap**

Empty your mind,
 Fill your Heart.

Don't settle for less.

**Quantum Leap**

Empty your mind,
 Fill your Heart.

Don't settle for less.

**Quantum Leap**

Empty your mind,
 Fill your Heart.

Don't settle for less.

**Quantum Leap**

Empty your mind,
 Fill your Heart.

Don't settle for less.

**Quantum Leap**

Empty your mind,
 Fill your Heart.

Don't settle for less.

**Quantum Leap**

Empty your mind,
 Fill your Heart.

Don't settle for less.

# Fascination

**Fascination turned inward
Keeps you forever exploring
The infinite inner blossoming
Of the mystery called 'You.'**

### Fascination

**Fascination turned inward
Keeps you forever exploring
The infinite inner blossoming
Of the mystery called 'You.'**

### Fascination

**Fascination turned inward
Keeps you forever exploring
The infinite inner blossom'ng
Of the mystery called "You.'**

### Fascination

**Fascination turned inward
Keeps you forever exploring
The infinite inner blossoming
Of the mystery called 'You.'**

### Fascination

**Fascination turned inward
Keeps you forever exploring
The infinite inner blossoming
Of the mystery called "You.'**

### Fascination

**Fascination turned inward
Keeps you forever exploring
The infinite inner blossoming
Of the mystery called 'You.'**

### Fascination

**Fascination turned inward
Keeps you forever exploring
The infinite inner blossoming
Of the mystery called "You.'**

# External Reality

**External reality
Can be either
Thick or thin.**

**The thinner
The external,
The more joyful
The internal.**

## External Reality

External reality
Can be either
Thick or thin.

The thinner
The external,
The more joyful
The internal.

## External Reality

External reality
Can be either
Thick or thin.

The thinner
The external,
The more joyful
The internal.

## External Reality

External reality
Can be either
Thick or thin.

The thinner
The external,
The more joyful
The internal.

## External Reality

External reality
Can be either
Thick or thin.

The thinner
The external,
The more joyful
The internal.

# The Tree of Life

## When efforting matures,
## Patience blossoms and
## Drops the fruits
## Of allowing
## Into your lap.

### The Tree of Life

When efforting matures,
Patience blossoms and
Drops the fruits
Of allowing
Into your lap.

### The Tree of Life

When efforting matures,
Patience blossoms and
Drops the fruits
Of allowing
Into your lap.

### The Tree of Life

When efforting matures,
Patience blossoms and
Drops the fruits
Of allowing
Into your lap.

### The Tree of Life

When efforting matures,
Patience blossoms and
Drops the fruits
Of allowing
Into your lap.

### The Tree of Life

When efforting matures,
Patience blossoms and
Drops the fruits
Of allowing
Into your lap.

### The Tree of Life

When efforting matures,
Patience blossoms and
Drops the fruits
Of allowing
Into your lap.

# Full Circle

## As you fall into inner infinity,
## You discover that every atom
## Contains the whole Universe.

### Full Circle

As you fall into inner infinity,
You discover that every atom
Contains the whole Universe.

### Full Circle

As you fall into inner infinity,
You dicsover that every atom
Contains the whole Universe.

### Full Circle

As you fall into inner infinity,
You discover that every atom
Contains the whole Universe.

### Full Circle

As you fall into inner infinity,
You dicsover that every atom
Contains the whole Universe.

### Full Circle

As you fall into inner infinity,
You discover that every atom
Contains the whole Universe.

### Full Circle

As you fall into inner infinity,
You dicsover that every atom
Contains the whole Universe.

# Section Six

# What Is Beyond the Mind?

## Meditations and Illuminators

### The Witness

The witness
Floats in the middle of
The stream of thoughts
Without ever getting wet.

## Section Six
## Meditations and Illuminators

# What Is Beyond the Mind?

**Week 22:** Put up copies of the Illuminator "**Learning**" (page 268) in many places, including one above the reflection of your head in the mirror.

Do the Repeating Question in the mirror for ten minutes twice a day (or if you are with a partner, once a day by yourself and once a day with your partner, asking and answering for five minutes each):

**"What are you unlearning?"**

**Week 23:** Put up copies of the Illuminator "**Who Are You?**" (page 259) in many places, including one above the reflection of your head in the mirror.

Once a day for ten minutes, go outdoors where you have a panoramic view of the sky. Lie on your back on the grass and watch the clouds float by, seeing the clouds as thoughts and the sky as you. If there are no clouds, feel into the infinite nature of the sky. Some days you may want to do this in the daylight and others at night, attempting to take the infinite depth of the stars into your eyes without labeling them by constellations or even as stars.

Also, do the Repeating Question in the mirror for ten minutes once a day:

**"Who are you?"**

Notice both what your responses are and who is the one asking the question. Search within yourself for the place from which the question is arising.

**Week 24:** Put up copies of the Illuminator "**Discovering Love**" (page 261) in many places, including one above the reflection of your head in the mirror.

Do the Repeating Question in the mirror for ten minutes twice a day (or if you are with a partner, once a day by yourself and once a day with your partner, asking and answering for five minutes each):

**"What do you really want?"**

**\*Week 25:** Put up copies of the Illuminator "**Desiring or Enjoying?**" (page 260) in many places, including one above the reflection of your head in the mirror.

**Part One:** Buy a box of 250 round toothpicks at the supermarket. For ten minutes, twice a day, sit on the floor or at a table and dump the toothpicks out of the box. Then, one at a time, pick them up and put them back in the box. If you fill the box before the ten minutes is up, dump the toothpicks back out and once again put them back into the box one at a time until the ten minutes is up. When the timer goes off, no matter where you are in this process, pick up all the rest of the toothpicks together and put them back in the box.

The whole time you are doing this notice whether you are desiring or enjoying each moment. Are you present with and enjoying each toothpick as you pick it up and place it in the box or are you somewhere else?

**Part Two:** As you move through your life this week, notice, moment by moment, are you desiring or enjoying? Let your mantra for the week be, "Desiring or Enjoying?...Desiring or Enjoying?"

**Week 26:** Put up copies of the Illuminator **"Thoughts"** (page 262) in many places, including one above the reflection of your head in the mirror.

Do the Repeating Question in the mirror for ten minutes twice a day (or if you are with a partner, once a day by yourself and once a day with your partner, asking and answering for five minutes each):

### "What are your thoughts?"

Notice that this question can be interpreted at least two ways - "What is the material that your thoughts are made from?" and, more literally, "What thoughts are you having right now or do you have in general?" Let the way that you hear the meaning of this question dance back and forth between these two and any other interpretations you might discover.

**Week 27:** Put up copies of the Illuminator **"The Witnesss"** (page 263) in many places, including one above the reflection of your head in the mirror.

For ten minutes twice a day, sit in front of the mirror and look at the aphorism, "The Witness," for about thirty seconds, and then close your eyes and watch any thoughts that occur for several minutes. Do not try to change your thoughts or diminish their frequency or label them in any way. Observe them with curiosity. One effective way to do this is to consciously sit in your Heart and look up into your head from below to see what thoughts are going on above you.

Another helpful image may be for you to picture yourself sitting beside a river underneath a bridge for cars. As the cars drive across the bridge, you can hear them above you, but you are still sitting by the river. Let your Heart be that river and the cars be the thoughts that pass through your mind.

Another image is that you are standing beside a railroad track and the thoughts are the cars of the train passing by you. You stay standing in one place as you watch your thoughts go whooshing by.

Another possibility is to see "Silence" as being center stage, and thoughts as being mere whispers from offstage, out on the horizon of your consciousness.

After several minutes of observing the thoughts passing above you or in front of you, open your eyes and look at the aphorism again for about thirty seconds and then close your eyes and again observe. Repeat this process until the ten minutes has passed.

\* If you are choosing to do only one Meditation per section, this one is recommended.

# Who Are You?

**Just as the clouds are not the sky,
Your thoughts are not you.**

**You are the empty space in which
Your thoughts are floating.**

### Who Are You?

Just as the clouds are not the sky,
  Your thoughts are not you.

You are the empty space in which
  Your thoughts are floating.

### Who Are You?

Just as the clouds are not the sky,
  Your thoughts are not you.

You are the empty space in which
  Your thoughts are floating.

### Who Are You?

Just as the clouds are not the sky,
  Your thoughts are not you.

You are the empty space in which
  Your thoughts are floating.

### Who Are You?

Just as the clouds are not the sky,
  Your thoughts are not you.

You are the empty space in which
  Your thoughts are floating.

### Who Are You?

Just as the clouds are not the sky,
  Your thoughts are not you.

You are the empty space in which
  Your thoughts are floating.

### Who Are You?

Just as the clouds are not the sky,
  Your thoughts are not you.

You are the empty space in which
  Your thoughts are floating.

# Desiring or Enjoying?

## Desiring creates pursuit.
## Enjoying creates gratitude.
## The one you focus on grows.

### Desiring or Enjoying?

Desiring creates pursuit.
   Enjoying creates gratitude.
      The one you focus on grows.

### Desiring or Enjoying?

Desiring creates pursuit.
   Enjoying creates gratitude.
      The one you focus on grows.

### Desiring or Enjoying?

Desiring creates pursuit.
   Enjoying creates gratitude.
      The one you focus on grows.

### Desiring or Enjoying?

Desiring creates pursuit.
   Enjoying creates gratitude.
      The one you focus on grows.

### Desiring or Enjoying?

Desiring creates pursuit.
   Enjoying creates gratitude.
      The one you focus on grows.

### Desiring or Enjoying?

Desiring creates pursuit.
   Enjoying creates gratitude.
      The one you focus on grows.

# Discovering Love

## Desire's absence
## Creates space for
## Love's presence.

**Discovering Love**

**Desire's absence**
   **Creates space for**
      **Love's presence.**

**Discovering Love**

**Desire's absence**
   **Creates space for**
      **Love's presence.**

**Discovering Love**

**Desire's absence**
   **Creates space for**
      **Love's presence.**

**Discovering Love**

**Desire's absence**
   **Creates space for**
      **Love's presence.**

**Discovering Love**

**Desire's absence**
   **Creates space for**
      **Love's presence.**

**Discovering Love**

**Desire's absence**
   **Creates space for**
      **Love's presence.**

# Thoughts

**Your thoughts
Can't bully you around
If you don't empower them
By believing they are real.**

### Thoughts

Your thoughts
Can't bully you around
If you don't empower them
By believing they are real.

### Thoughts

Your thoughts
Can't bully you around
If you don't empower them
By believing they are real.

### Thoughts

Your thoughts
Can't bully you around
If you don't empower them
By believing they are real.

### Thoughts

Your thoughts
Can't bully you around
If you don't empower them
By believing they are real.

### Thoughts

Your thoughts
Can't bully you around
If you don't empower them
By believing they are real.

### Thoughts

Your thoughts
Can't bully you around
If you don't empower them
By believing they are real.

# The Witness

**The witness**
   **Floats in the middle of**
      **The stream of thoughts**
         **Without ever getting wet.**

### The Witness

The witness
   Floats in the middle of
      The stream of thoughts
         Without ever getting wet.

### The Witness

The witness
   Floats in the middle of
      The stream of thoughts
         Without ever getting wet.

### The Witness

The witness
   Floats in the middle of
      The stream of thoughts
         Without ever getting wet.

### The Witness

The witness
   Floats in the middle of
      The stream of thoughts
         Without ever getting wet.

### The Witness

The witness
   Floats in the middle of
      The stream of thoughts
         Without ever getting wet.

### The Witness

The witness
   Floats in the middle of
      The stream of thoughts
         Without ever getting wet.

# Inner Voices

**Listen very sensitively
To your inner voices and
Choose which to empower:
The shout of doubt...
Or...
The whisper of trust.**

### Inner Voices

Listen very sensitively
To your inner voices and
Choose which to empower:
The shout of doubt...
Or...
The whisper of trust.

### Inner Voices

Listen very sensitively
To your inner voices and
Choose which to empower:
The shout of doubt...
Or...
The whisper of trust.

### Inner Voices

Listen very sensitively
To your inner voices and
Choose which to empower:
The shout of doubt...
Or...
The whisper of trust.

### Inner Voices

Listen very sensitively
To your inner voices and
Choose which to empower:
The shout of doubt...
Or...
The whisper of trust.

# Why?

## *Any* answer to 'Why?'
## Must always be a lie.

## You cannot find
## Truth in your mind.

**Why?**

*Any* answer to 'Why?'
  Must always be a lie.
You cannot find
  Truth in your mind.

**Why?**

*Any* answer to 'Why?'
  Must always be a lie.
You cannot find
  Truth in your mind.

**Why?**

*Any* answer to 'Why?'
  Must always be a lie.
You cannot find
  Truth in your mind.

**Why?**

*Any* answer to 'Why?'
  Must always be a lie.
You cannot find
  Truth in your mind.

**Why?**

*Any* answer to 'Why?'
  Must always be a lie.
You cannot find
  Truth in your mind.

**Why?**

*Any* answer to 'Why?'
  Must always be a lie.
You cannot find
  Truth in your mind.

# In Between

## Truth lives where there is no 'I'...
## In the spaces between thoughts.

## Let your whole effort be
## To fall into this void...
## Forever.

### In Between

Truth lives where there is no 'I'...
In the spaces between thoughts.

Let your whole effort be
To fall into this void...
Forever.

### In Between

Truth lives where there is no 'I'...
In the spaces between thoughts.

Let your whole effort be
To fall into this void...
Forever.

### In Between

Truth lives where there is no 'I'...
In the spaces between thoughts.

Let your whole effort be
To fall into this void...
Forever.

### In Between

Truth lives where there is no 'I'...
In the spaces between thoughts.

Let your whole effort be
To fall into this void...
Forever.

### In Between

Truth lives where there is no 'I'...
In the spaces between thoughts.

Let your whole effort be
To fall into this void...
Forever.

### In Between

Truth lives where there is no 'I'...
In the spaces between thoughts.

Let your whole effort be
To fall into this void...
Forever.

# Emptiness

## The mind fills emptiness
## With *any* thought form
## Instead of stepping aside
## To create the silent void
## From which Love arises.

### Emptiness

The mind fills emptiness
  With *any* thought form
    Instead of stepping aside
      To create the silent void
        From which Love arises.

### Emptiness

The mind fills emptiness
  With *any* thought form
    Instead of stepping aside
      To create the silent void
        From which Love arises.

### Emptiness

The mind fills emptiness
  With *any* thought form
    Instead of stepping aside
      To create the silent void
        From which Love arises.

### Emptiness

The mind fills emptiness
  With *any* thought form
    Instead of stepping aside
      To create the silent void
        From which Love arises.

### Emptiness

The mind fills emptiness
  With *any* thought form
    Instead of stepping aside
      To create the silent void
        From which Love arises.

### Emptiness

The mind fills emptiness
  With *any* thought form
    Instead of stepping aside
      To create the silent void
        From which Love arises.

# Learning

**Learning
Inspires
 Your mind.

Unlearning
Frees
 Your spirit.**

## Learning

**Learning
 Inspires
  Your mind.
Unlearning
 Frees
  Your spirit.**

## Learning

**Learning
 Inspires
  Your mind.
Unlearning
 Frees
  Your spirit.**

## Learning

**Learning
 Inspires
  Your mind.
Unlearning
 Frees
  Your spirit.**

## Learning

**Learning
 Inspires
  Your mind.
Unlearning
 Frees
  Your spirit.**

# Identity

**When you lose your identity as
Father/son, mother/daughter,
Secretary, lawyer, waiter,
Rich, poor, good, bad,
Sad, happy, angry,
You find you.**

### Identity

When you lose your identity as
Father/son, mother/daughter,
Secretary, lawyer, waiter,
Rich, poor, good, bad,
Sad, happy, angry,
You find you.

### Identity

When you lose your identity as
Father/son, mother/daughter,
Secretary, lawyer, waiter,
Rich, poor, good, bad,
Sad, happy, angry,
You find you.

### Identity

When you lose your identity as
Father/son, mother/daughter,
Secretary, lawyer, waiter,
Rich, poor, good, bad,
Sad, happy, angry,
You find you.

### Identity

When you lose your identity as
Father/son, mother/daughter,
Secretary, lawyer, waiter,
Rich, poor, good, bad,
Sad, happy, angry,
You find you.

# Understanding

**The desire to understand
Can imprison your Spirit
At the level of Thinking.**

**Understanding fills the mind,
But cannot awaken the Soul.**

## Understanding

The desire to understand
Can imprison your Spirit
At the level of Thinking.

Understanding fills the mind,
But cannot awaken the Soul.

## Understanding

The desire to understand
Can imprison your Spirit
At the level of Thinking.

Understanding fills the mind,
But cannot awaken the Soul.

## Understanding

The desire to understand
Can imprison your Spirit
At the level of Thinking.

Understanding fills the mind,
But cannot awaken the Soul.

## Understanding

The desire to understand
Can imprison your Spirit
At the level of Thinking.

Understanding fills the mind,
But cannot awaken the Soul.

## Understanding

The desire to understand
Can imprison your Spirit
At the level of Thinking.

Understanding fills the mind,
But cannot awaken the Soul.

## Understanding

The desire to understand
Can imprison your Spirit
At the level of Thinking.

Understanding fills the mind,
But cannot awaken the Soul.

# The Human Race

When the human race
Decides to stop racing,
Love can take the lead
And then *everyone* wins.

### The Human Race

When the human race
Decides to stop racing,
Love can take the lead
And then *everyone* wins.

### The Human Race

When the human race
Decides to stop racing,
Love can take the lead
And then *everyone* wins.

### The Human Race

When the human race
Decides to stop racing,
Love can take the lead
And then *everyone* wins.

### The Human Race

When the human race
Decides to stop racing,
Love can take the lead
And then *everyone* wins.

### The Human Race

When the human race
Decides to stop racing,
Love can take the lead
And then *everyone* wins.

### The Human Race

When the human race
Decides to stop racing,
Love can take the lead
And then *everyone* wins.

# Section Seven

# Strolling Down
# the Spiritual Path

## Meditations and Illuminators

### The Spiritual Path

When you boldly march down
The spiritual path searching,
You can miss the stroll itself
Wherein lies *all* that you seek.

## Meditations and Illuminators

# Strolling Down the Spiritual Path

**Week 28:**   Put up copies of the Illuminator **"Spiritual Pursuits"** (page 277) in many places, including one above the reflection of your head in the mirror.

When you are trying to make a decision between two activities this week, if you perceive that one is "more spiritual" and the other is "less spiritual," consciously choose the "less spiritual" alternative. For instance, if you have time to either meditate or go to a movie, go to the movie if that seems less spiritual to you. Or eat a hamburger instead of brown rice, if the hamburger seems less spiritual to you. Or have a beer instead of going for a walk in Nature. Or watch television instead of going to your group therapy.

Notice whether the activity itself is inherently more spiritual or if it is your belief about the activity that makes it *seem* more spiritual.

**Week 29:**   Put up copies of the Illuminator **"Seeking God"** (page 279) in many places, including one above the reflection of your head in the mirror.

Do the Repeating Question in the mirror for ten minutes twice a day (or if you are with a partner, once a day by yourself and once a day with your partner, asking and answering for five minutes each):

### "Where is God?"

**\*Week 30:**   Put up copies of the Illuminator  **"Nowhere"** (page 282) in many places, including one above the reflection of your head in the mirror.

For this week, when you approach any type of line (in the grocery store, bank, gas station, toll plaza, etc.) always choose the longest one. Then, instead of "waiting" with the feeling that you are wasting time, enjoy the moment.

As you stand in line, be present with whomever is next to you. Open your Heart to another human being instead of spacing out or reading the tabloids.

If you are in your car (at the gas station or toll plaza), either make contact with someone in the car next to you or enjoy your surroundings. Look at the sky or trees, or celebrate the creativity it took to build the structures around you.

The longer the line, the more relaxed you can become. Give up hurrying to get to your next appointment or to finish "running" errands. Meander through your errands, stopping to smell the flowers along the way.

**Week 31:**   Put up copies of the Illuminator "**Jello**" (page 281) in many places, including one above the reflection of your head in the mirror.

**Part One:** For the whole week, brush your teeth with the other hand than you usually do (your "non-dominant" hand).

**Part Two:** Make your favorite color of Jello in a juice glass. After the Jello is set, dip the glass in hot water and turn it upside down to release the Jello onto a plate. Now wiggle the plate and watch the Jello. Finally, eat the Jello, especially if you think that it is unhealthy for you.

**Week 32:**    Put up copies of the Illuminator **"The Awakened Ones"** (page 284) in many places, including one above the reflection of your head in the mirror.

For ten minutes twice a day, make eye contact with yourself in the mirror (or if you are with a partner, once a day by yourself and once a day with one another) and repeat the following sentence. Breathe between each time you say the sentence and then wait to say it again until you are coming from a place in yourself that really means it rather than becoming rote in any way):

**"I am already Enlightened."**

As the week progresses, notice if you are increasingly able to let go of your pictures of what Enlightenment is and of who you are *supposed* to be in order to fit those pictures.

**Week 33:**    Put up copies of the Illuminator **"The Spiritual Path"** (page 278) in many places, including one above the reflection of your head in the mirror.

Take a twenty minute walk each day this week with no goal in mind. Stop as frequently as you want. Say a loving "Hello" to whomever crosses your path. Pay close attention to anything that attracts you. See if the present is more available to you as you enjoy "strolling down the spiritual path."

\* If you are choosing to do only one Meditation per section, this one is recommended.

# Spiritual Pursuits

## If your life purpose is
## To evolve spiritually,
## Then free yourself
## From chasing after
## *All* spiritual goals.

### Spiritual Pursuits

If your life purpose is
To cvolvc spiritually,
Then free yourself
From chasing after
*All* spiritual goals.

### Spiritual Pursuits

If your life purpose is
To evolve spiritually,
Then free yourself
From chasing after
*All* spiritual goals.

### Spiritual Pursuits

If your life purpose is
To evolve spiritually,
Then free yourself
From chasing after
*All* spiritual goals.

### Spiritual Pursuits

If your life purpose is
To evolve spiritually,
Then free yourself
From chasing after
*All* spiritual goals.

### Spiritual Pursuits

If your life purpose is
To evolve spiritually,
Then free yourself
From chasing after
*All* spiritual goals.

### Spiritual Pursuits

If your life purpose is
To evolve spiritually,
Then free yourself
From chasing after
*All* spiritual goals.

# The Spiritual Path

When you boldly march down
The spiritual path searching,
You can miss the stroll itself
Wherein lies *all* that you seek.

### The Spiritual Path

When you boldly march down
The spiritual path searching,
You can miss the stroll itself
Wherein lies *all* that you seek.

### The Spiritual Path

When you boldly march down
The spiritual path searching,
You can miss the stroll itself
Wherein lies *all* that you seek.

### The Spiritual Path

When you boldly march down
The spiritual path searching,
You can miss the stroll itself
Wherein lies *all* that you seek.

### The Spiritual Path

When you boldly march down
The spiritual path searching,
You can miss the stroll itself
Wherein lies *all* that you seek.

### The Spiritual Path

When you boldly march down
The spiritual path searching,
You can miss the stroll itself
Wherein lies *all* that you seek.

### The Spiritual Path

When you boldly march down
The spiritual path searching,
You can miss the stroll itself
Wherein lies *all* that you seek.

# Seeking God

**Seeking God
Keeps you from
Seeing God
Inside Now.**

### Seeking God

Seeking God
Keeps you from
Seeing God
Inside Now.

### Seeking God

Seeking God
Keeps you from
Seeing God
Inside Now.

### Seeking God

Seeking God
Keeps you from
Seeing God
Inside Now.

### Seeking God

Seeking God
Keeps you from
Seeing God
Inside Now.

### Seeking God

Seeking God
Keeps you from
Seeing God
Inside Now.

### Seeking God

Seeking God
Keeps you from
Seeing God
Inside Now.

# Time

**You can worry about
Spending time or
Saving time or
Wasting time.**

**Or you can just relax
And have a good time.**

### Time

You can worry about
Spending time or
Saving time or
Wasting time.

Or you can just relax
And have a good time.

### Time

You can worry about
Spending time or
Saving time or
Wasting time.

Or you can just relax
And have a good time.

### Time

You can worry about
Spending time or
Saving time or
Wasting time.

Or you can just relax
And have a good time.

### Time

You can worry about
Spending time or
Saving time or
Wasting time.

Or you can just relax
And have a good time.

# Jello

## Wiggle.
## Jiggle.
## Squiggle.
## Giggle.

**Jello**

Wiggle.
Jiggle.
Squiggle.
Giggle.

**Jello**

Wiggle .
Jiggle.
Squiggle.
Giggle.

**Jello**

Wiggle.
Jiggle.
Squiggle.
Giggle.

**Jello**

Wiggle .
Jiggle.
Squiggle.
Giggle.

**Jello**

Wiggle.
Jiggle.
Squiggle.
Giggle.

**Jello**

Wiggle .
Jiggle.
Squiggle.
Giggle.

# Nowhere

**Do you realize that**
***Nowhere* is both**
***No where***
**And**
　　　***Now here*?**

**Where was it that**
**You were headed**
**In such a hurry?**

### Nowhere

Do you realize that
*Nowhere* is both
*No where*
And
　*Now here*?
Where was it that
You were headed
　In such a hurry?

### Nowhere

Do you realize that
*Nowhere* is both
*No where*
And
　*Now here*?
Where was it that
You were headed
　In such a hurry?

### Nowhere

Do you realize that
*Nowhere* is both
*No where*
And
　*Now here*?
Where was it that
You were headed
　In such a hurry?

### Nowhere

Do you realize that
*Nowhere* is both
*No where*
And
　*Now here*?
Where was it that
You were headed
　In such a hurry?

# Spiritual Seriousness

**Spiritual seriousness is
A holy-veiled hautiness
That makes you believe
*Your* purpose on Earth
Is greater than a flower's.**

### Spiritual Seriousness

Spiritual seriousness is
A holy-veiled hautiness
That makes you believe
*Your* purpose on Earth
Is greater than a flower's.

### Spiritual Seriousness

Spiritual seriousness is
A holy veiled hautiness
That makes you believe
*Your* purpose on Earth
Is greater than a flower's.

### Spiritual Seriousness

Spiritual seriousness is
A holy-veiled hautiness
That makes you believe
*Your* purpose on Earth
Is greater than a flower's.

### Spiritual Seriousness

Spiritual seriousness is
A holy veiled hautiness
That makes you believe
*Your* purpose on Earth
Is greater than a flower's.

### Spiritual Seriousness

Spiritual seriousness is
A holy-veiled hautiness
That makes you believe
*Your* purpose on Earth
Is greater than a flower's.

### Spiritual Seriousness

Spiritual seriousness is
A holy veiled hautiness
That makes you believe
*Your* purpose on Earth
Is greater than a flower's.

# The Awakened Ones

## The only difference between Enlightened persons and Unenlightened ones is that The enlightened ones Accept themselves Exactly as they are: Unenlightened!

### The Awakened Ones

The only difference between
Enlightened persons and
Unenlightened ones is that
The enlightened ones
Accept themselves
Exactly as they are:
Unenlightened!

### The Awakened Ones

The only difference between
Enlightened persons and
Unenlightened ones is that
The enlightened ones
Accept themselves
Exactly as they are:
Unenlightened!

### The Awakened Ones

The only difference between
Enlightened persons and
Unenlightened ones is that
The enlightened ones
Accept themselves
Exactly as they are:
Unenlightened!

### The Awakened Ones

The only difference between
Enlightened persons and
Unenlightened ones is that
The enlightened ones
Accept themselves
Exactly as they are:
Unenlightened!

# Section Eight

# Loving Others

## Meditations and Illuminators

### Unconditional Love

Love can only be
    'Unconditional.'

If your Love has
    *Any* strings attached,
        Then it is not Love.

## Meditations and Illuminators

# Loving Others

**Week 34:**    Put up copies of the Illuminator **"Deceit"** (page 292) in many places, including one above the reflection of your head in the mirror.

Do the Repeating Question in the mirror for ten minutes twice a day (or if you are with a partner, once a day by yourself and once a day with your partner, asking and answering for five minutes each):

**"How are you fooling yourself?"**

**Week 35:**    Put up copies of the Illuminator **"Strength"** (page 293) in many places, including one above the reflection of your head in the mirror.

Do the Repeating Question in the mirror for ten minutes twice a day (or if you are with a partner, once a day by yourself and once a day with your partner, asking and answering for five minutes each):

**"How are you protecting yourself?"**

**Week 36:**    Put up copies of the Illuminator **"The Greatest Gift"** (page 295) in many places, including one above the reflection of your head in the mirror.

For a total of twenty minutes a day, engage in conversations with different people where your primary focus is to listen without trying to change anyone in any way. Be sure you are in an intimate setting where you can talk freely.

Initiate each conversation by asking an open ended question, such as, "How is your life going?" The phrasing of the words is not nearly as important as your intent behind the words. When the tone of your voice communicates that you are really interested, people are more likely to speak openly.

Let people know that you are empathizing with them by paraphrasing back to them after every few sentences what you understand them to be saying. Then give them room to validate that they feel understood or to say, "No, that's not quite right. What I said was......." (This is Carl Rogers' "active listening.")

The attitude to have while you listen is to put your own values and judgements aside and to become curious what others' experience of Life is. Find a sense of wanting to be inside their skin, seeing the world through their eyes. And bring along your compassion.

Sometimes it is easier to start with people you do not know very well because you are not personally invested in how they lead their life. Then you can try being with close friends or your lover in this way.

Remember, your only job is to receive others without trying to "fix" them in any way because there is nothing wrong with them. The struggles they are going through are exactly what they need right now in order to learn whatever they need to learn. Your gifts are your attentiveness, curiosity, and empathy. As you become an empty vessel, you start to notice how your presence, without your having to "do" anything, makes a difference.

**Week 37:**     Put up copies of the Illuminator **"Commitment"** (page 298) in many places, including one above the reflection of your head in the mirror .

Ask two alternating Repeating Questions in the mirror for ten minutes twice a day (or if you are with a partner, once a day by yourself and once a day with your partner, asking and answering for five minutes each).

First ask the question, "What is Commitment?" Then respond with whatever word or phrase comes forward. Receive that response with a "Thank-you," breathe, and ask, "What is Freedom?" Answer spontaneously, then give a "Thank-you," and go back to the first question, 'What is Commitment?"

Alternate these two questions until the ten minutes has passed (or five minutes each if with a partner):

**"What is Commitment?" alternating with "What is Freedom?"**

**Week 38:**     Put up copies of the Illuminator *"Communication"* (page 302) in many places, including one above the reflection of your head in the mirror.

This week's Meditation is called a "Heart Share." For twenty minutes once a day, place a candle between you and your reflection in the mirror. Take a moment to make eye contact with yourself. Take a deep breath and relax into your body. Then either close your eyes or look at the flame of the candle as you begin to speak from your Heart. Talk vulnerably about what your life is really about:

♥ What is your mission here on Earth?
♥ What you are learning from your life experiences?
♥ What are the most essential elements of your spiritual evolution?
♥ How are your priorities shifting as you become more aware?
♥ What is important to your Heart?
♥ Are there any people in your life (including yourself) that you still
     need to forgive?

Let the teacher in you come forward to impart both the wisdom and the yet-to-be-known in you. Take an inventory of the purpose of your life and speak your deepest intentions while you are on the Earth.

At the end of the twenty minutes, gently look into your eyes in the mirror. Namaste (place your hands in the prayer position and bow to the person in the mirror while staying in eye contact as you send and receive the non-verbal message, "The God/Goddess in me honors the God/Goddess in you." Be sensitive to what feelings arise as you melt into the attitude of revering and respecting the person in the mirror.

If you have a partner, do this process with each other one day and by yourself the next. Sit on pillows facing each other with a candle between you. One person speaks for ten minutes while the other listens, with both of you either closing your eyes or looking at the flame of the candle. After ten minutes, make eye contact and gently Namaste to each other. Then switch, with the second person speaking, not in response to what the first one said, but just allowing his or her individual Truth to unfold. Again, as you begin sharing, both close your eyes or look at the candle. After this person's ten minutes have passed, look into each other's eyes and finish with a Namaste.

You may want each of you to do two rounds of ten minutes for a total of forty minutes on the days you participate in this Heart Share with each other.

**Week 39:** Put up copies of the Illuminator **"Touching Souls"** (page 304) in many places, including one above the reflection of your head in the mirror.

This week's Meditation is a variation of the Eastern meditation, often known as "Tratak." For ten minutes twice a day, sit in front of the mirror and look into your own eyes without any words. Start by looking at the iris of either eye. Become fascinated with the miracle of its patterns, colors, sparkle, and luminescence. Notice how diamond-like it is. After focusing on the iris for several minutes, look directly into the infinite blackness within your pupil. Keep diving into the whole Universe contained within that void. Touch your own Soul inside your pupil.

If you are participating with a partner, do this once a day by yourself for ten minutes and once a day with your partner for ten minutes. Be sure to focus on only one of your partner's eyes (usually the left one) by looking at the iris first and then into the pupil. Touch souls with this god/goddess in a human body.

**\*Week 40:** Put up copies of the Illuminator **"Giving"** (page 296) in many places, including above the reflection of your head in the mirror.

Every day this week, find some way to anonymously give to someone. There are many possibilities if you start to look for them:

- ♥ Secretly put a flower on someone's desk at work.
- ♥ Send an unsigned card of appreciation to a friend.
- ♥ Put money in any expired parking meters as you walk down the street.
- ♥ Pay the highway or bridge toll of the car behind you (be sure to disappear before they can thank you).
- ♥ If a waiter or waitress gives you great service, besides leaving an exorbitant tip, later send an anonymous thank-you note to the restaurant manager, mentioning the person by name.

Once you start looking for ways to give without any expectation of receiving anything in return, a whole new world opens to you. **Give away what you want to receive or you feel you lack.** If you want more money, send an anonymous donation to your favorite charity or to a friend in need. If you feel a lack of Love in your life, offer someone a hug or listen to them with your Heart. Be creative. Your reward is the feeling that arises from your Soul and puts a smile on your face.

\* If you are choosing to do only one Meditation per section, this one is recommended.

# Blaming

## The ego sees faults.
## Love sees Love.

## Which are you
## Looking for?

### Blaming

The ego sees faults.
Love sees Love.

Which are you
Looking for?

### Blaming

The ego sees faults.
Love sees Love.

Which are you
Looking for?

### Blaming

The ego sees faults.
Love sees Love.

Which are you
Looking for?

### Blaming

The ego sees faults.
Love sees Love.

Which are you
Looking for?

### Blaming

The ego sees faults.
Love sees Love.

Which are you
Looking for?

### Blaming

The ego sees faults.
Love sees Love.

Which are you
Looking for?

# Judgement

## Whenever you judge others,
## You give them your power
## By polluting your purity
## With poisonous thoughts.

### Judgement

Whenever you judge others,
You give them your power
By polluting your purity
With poisonous thoughts.

### Judgement

Whenever you judge others,
You give them your power
By polluting your purity
With poisonous thoughts.

### Judgement

Whenever you judge others,
You give them your power
By polluting your purity
With poisonous thoughts.

### Judgement

Whenever you judge others,
You give them your power
By polluting your purity
With poisonous thoughts.

### Judgement

Whenever you judge others,
You give them your power
By polluting your purity
With poisonous thoughts.

### Judgement

Whenever you judge others,
You give them your power
By polluting your purity
With poisonous thoughts.

# Deceit

## A lie's greatest deceit is
## How it fools its creator
## Into believing it is true.

### Deceit

A lie's greatest deceit is
How it fools its creator
Into believing it is true.

### Deceit

A lie's greatest deceit is
How it fools its creator
Into believing it is true.

### Deceit

A lie's greatest deceit is
How it fools its creator
Into believing it is true.

### Deceit

A lie's greatest deceit is
How it fools its creator
Into believing it is true.

### Deceit

A lie's greatest deceit is
How it fools its creator
Into believing it is true.

### Deceit

A lie's greatest deceit is
How it fools its creator
Into believing it is true.

# Strength

## Vulnerability unveils
## The potency of softness
## By disarming battling egos.

### Strength

Vulnerability unveils
  The potency of softness
    By disarming battling egos.

### Strength

Vulnerability unveils
  The potency of softness
    By disarming battling egos.

### Strength

Vulnerability unveils
  The potency of softness
    By disarming battling egos.

### Strength

Vulnerability unveils
  The potency of softness
    By disarming battling egos.

### Strength

Vulnerability unveils
  The potency of softness
    By disarming battling egos.

### Strength

Vulnerability unveils
  The potency of softness
    By disarming battling egos.

# Friendship

## A true friend keeps
## Seeing your Love,
## Especially when
## You do not.

**Friendship**

A true friend keeps
Seeing your Love,
Especially when
You do not.

**Friendship**

A true friend keeps
Seeing your Love,
Especially when
You do not.

**Friendship**

A true friend keeps
Seeing your Love,
Especially when
You do not.

**Friendship**

A true friend keeps
Seeing your Love,
Especially when
You do not.

**Friendship**

A true friend keeps
Seeing your Love,
Especially when
You do not.

**Friendship**

A true friend keeps
Seeing your Love,
Especially when
You do not.

# The Greatest Gift

## The greatest gift
## You can ever give
## Is to truly receive
## Another human being.

### The Greatest Gift

The greatest gift
  You can ever give
    Is to truly receive
      Another human being.

### The Greatest Gift

The greatest gift
  You can ever give
    Is to truly receive
      Another human being.

### The Greatest Gift

The greatest gift
  You can ever give
    Is to truly receive
      Another human being.

### The Greatest Gift

The greatest gift
  You can ever give
    Is to truly receive
      Another human being.

### The Greatest Gift

The greatest gift
  You can ever give
    Is to truly receive
      Another Illuman being.

### The Greatest Gift

The greatest gift
  You can ever give
    Is to truly receive
      Another human being.

# Giving

## True giving occurs when,
## After having given,
## You have more
## Instead of less.

### Giving

True giving occurs when,
After having given,
You have more
Instead of less.

### Giving

True giving occurs when,
After having given,
You have more
Instead of less.

### Giving

True giving occurs when,
After having given,
You have more
Instead of less.

### Giving

True giving occurs when,
After having given,
You have more
Instead of less.

### Giving

True giving occurs when,
After having given,
You have more
Instead of less.

### Giving

True giving occurs when,
After having given,
You have more
Instead of less.

# Unconditional Love

## Love can only be 'Unconditional.'

## If your Love has
## *Any* strings attached,
## Then it is not Love.

---

### Unconditional Love

Love can only be
'Unconditional.'

If your Love has
*Any* strings attached,
Then it is not Love.

### Unconditional Love

Love can only be
'Unconditional.'

If your Love has
*Any* strings attached,
Then it is not Love.

### Unconditional Love

Love can only be
'Unconditional.'

If your Love has
*Any* strings attached,
Then it is not Love.

### Unconditional Love

Love can only be
'Unconditional.'

If your Love has
*Any* strings attached,
Then it is not Love.

### Unconditional Love

Love can only be
'Unconditional.'

If your Love has
*Any* strings attached,
Then it is not Love.

### Unconditional Love

Love can only be
'Unconditional.'

If your Love has
*Any* strings attached,
Then it is not Love.

# Commitment

## Commitment is a quality
## To be felt in the Present,
## Not a promise for the future.

### Commitment

Commitment is a quality
To be felt in the Present,
Not a promise for the future.

### Commitment

Commitment is a quality
To be felt in the Present,
Not a promise for the future.

### Commitment

Commitment is a quality
To be felt in the Present,
Not a promise for the future.

### Commitment

Commitment is a quality
To be felt in the Present,
Not a promise for the future.

### Commitment

Commitment is a quality
To be felt in the Present,
Not a promise for the future.

### Commitment

Commitment is a quality
To be felt in the Present,
Not a promise for the future.

# Lovers' Illusion

## Chasing tomorrow's promises
## Keeps you from being inside
## The true *Forever* within Now.

### Lovers' Illusion

Chasing tomorrow's promises
Keeps you from being inside
The true *Forever* within Now.

### Lovers' Illusion

Chasing tomorrow's promises
Keeps you from being inside
The true *Forever* within Now.

### Lovers' Illusion

Chasing tomorrow's promises
Keeps you from being inside
The true *Forever* within Now.

### Lovers' Illusion

Chasing tomorrow's promises
Keeps you from being inside
The true *Forever* within Now.

### Lovers' Illusion

Chasing tomorrow's promises
Keeps you from being inside
The true *Forever* within Now.

### Lovers' Illusion

Chasing tomorrow's promises
Keeps you from being inside
The true *Forever* within Now.

# On The Same Side

## Being in harmony while
## Exploring differences
## Creates Love that is
## Beyond agreement.

### On The Same Side

Being in harmony while
Exploring differences
Creates Love that is
Beyond agreement.

### On The Same Side

Being in harmony while
Exploring differences
Creates Love that is
Beyond agreement.

### On The Same Side

Being in harmony while
Exploring differences
Creates Love that is
Beyond agreement.

### On The Same Side

Being in harmony while
Exploring differences
Creates Love that is
Beyond agreement.

### On The Same Side

Being in harmony while
Exploring differences
Creates Love that is
Beyond agreement.

### On The Same Side

Being in harmony while
Exploring differences
Creates Love that is
Beyond agreement.

# Useful Words

## The most useful words
## Help launch you into
## The bliss of no words.

### Useful Words

The most useful words
Help launch you into
The bliss of no words.

### Useful Words

The most useful words
Help launch you into
The bliss of no words.

### Useful Words

The most useful words
Help launch you into
The bliss of no words.

### Useful Words

The most useful words
Help launch you into
The bliss of no words.

### Useful Words

The most useful words
Help launch you into
The bliss of no words.

### Useful Words

The most useful words
Help launch you into
The bliss of no words.

# Communication

## Words from the head
## Perpetuate thinking.

## Words from the Heart
## Melt you into intimacy.


### Communication

Words from the head
  Perpetuate thinking.

Words from the Heart
  Melt you into intimacy.

### Communication

Words from the head
  Perpetuate thinking.

Words from the Heart
  Melt you into intimacy.

### Communication

Words from the head
  Perpetuate thinking.

Words from the Heart
  Melt you into intimacy.

### Communication

Words from the head
  Perpetuate thinking.

Words from the Heart
  Melt you into intimacy.

### Communication

Words from the head
  Perpetuate thinking.

Words from the Heart
  Melt you into intimacy.

### Communication

Words from the head
  Perpetuate thinking.

Words from the Heart
  Melt you into intimacy.

# A Sexual Secret

## Sex is renewed
## By risking *all*,
## Each moment.

### A Sexual Secret

Sex is renewed
  By risking *all*,
    Each moment.

### A Sexual Secret

Sex is renewed
  By risking *all*,
    Each moment.

### A Sexual Secret

Sex is renewed
  By risking *all*,
    Each moment.

### A Sexual Secret

Sex is renewed
  By risking *all*,
    Each moment.

### A Sexual Secret

Sex is renewed
  By risking *all*,
    Each moment.

### A Sexual Secret

Sex is renewed
  By risking *all*,
    Each moment.

# Touching Souls

**Touching Souls
In silent union,
Mind becomes empty,
Heart becomes full.**

### Touching Souls

**Touching Souls
In silent union,
Mind becomes empty,
Heart becomes full.**

### Touching Souls

**Touching Souls
In silent union,
Mind becomes empty,
Heart becomes full.**

### Touching Souls

**Touching Souls
In silent union,
Mind becomes empty,
Heart becomes full.**

### Touching Souls

**Touching Souls
In silent union,
Mind becomes empty,
Heart becomes full.**

### Touching Souls

**Touching Souls
In silent union,
Mind becomes empty,
Heart becomes full.**

### Touching Souls

**Touching Souls
In silent union,
Mind becomes empty,
Heart becomes full.**

# Spiritual Sex

## When your sexual roots
## Explode into the Earth,
## Your spiritual wings can
## Fly freely into Heaven.

### Spiritual Sex

When your sexual roots
Explode into the Earth,
Your spiritual wings can
Fly freely into Heaven.

### Spiritual Sex

When your sexual roots
Explode into the Earth,
Your spiritual wings can
Fly freely into Heaven.

### Spiritual Sex

When your sexual roots
Explode into the Earth,
Your spiritual wings can
Fly freely into Heaven.

### Spiritual Sex

When your sexual roots
Explode into the Earth,
Your spiritual wings can
Fly freely into Heaven.

### Spiritual Sex

When your sexual roots
Explode into the Earth,
Your spiritual wings can
Fly freely into Heaven.

### Spiritual Sex

When your sexual roots
Explode into the Earth,
Your spiritual wings can
Fly freely into Heaven.

# Freedom

**Death is freedom
From time and space.**

**Sex is freedom
From time.**

**Love is Freedom.**

### Freedom

Death is freedom
From time and space.

Sex is freedom
From time.

Love is Freedom.

### Freedom

Death is freedom
From time and space.

Sex is freedom
From time.

Love is Freedom.

### Freedom

Death is freedom
From time and space.

Sex is freedom
From time.

Love is Freedom.

### Freedom

Death is freedom
From time and space.

Sex is freedom
From time.

Love is Freedom.

# The Appendix

**The Index of
Aphorisms/Illuminators**

**The Index of Parables**

**Retreats and Workshops**

# The Index of Aphorisms/Illuminators

# The Index of Aphorisms/Illuminators

# The Index of Aphorisms/Illuminators

# The Index of Parables

# Retreats and Workshops

The flyers on the following pages are a sampling of some ways that
Peter Rengel or Peter and his wife, Donna Spitzer,
can bring their Love and wisdom to you and your friends.

If you are interested in sponsoring
a retreat or workshop in your area,
contact Peter or Donna through:

**Imagine Publications**
**P.O. Box 278**
**Fairfax, CA 94978**

**Phone:  415-459-3113**
**Fax:  415-459-5115**

# Awakening Your Soul

## A Day to Open Your Heart

♥ See the value of by-passing psychological processing and going straight to Love ♥

### Love

**Love is not an idea.**

**Love is**
**A vibration**
**To attune to.**

♥ Learn how to empty yourself rather than trying to fill yourself up ♥

### Emptiness

**The mind fills emptiness**
**With *any* thought form**
**Instead of stepping aside**
**To create the silent void**
**From which Love arises.**

♥ Discover how to directly choose to be in Love ♥

### Choice

**Your most profound choice**
**Each new moment in time**
**Is whether you are**
**Lost in thoughts**
**Or lost in Love.**

This one day retreat combines the most powerful transformational tools that Peter Rengel has learned or created over twenty years. Special meditations and partnered exercises create opportunities to touch profound states of consciousness, feel joy arising in your Heart, experience the beauty of your innocence, laugh uninhibitedly, and feel loved, lovable, and loving at new levels. Deepen your inner peace, whether you have ever meditated or not.

**– This space is for specific information on this workshop in your area –**

Peter Rengel is a teacher and a student of his own writings, *Living Life in Love* and *Seeds of Light*. His life is devoted to loving all Beings, especially his wife, Donna. Peter enjoys assisting people to transcend psychology in order to awaken their Love and to live in harmony with their spiritual nature. He lives with his family in Marin County, California, and facilitates retreats and workshops around the world.

314

# Deepening Your Love

## A Workshop for Couples

### with

### Peter Rengel and Donna Spitzer

This one day (or weekend) workshop offers you the opportunity to:

♥ Rekindle romance with your sweetheart

♥ Renew gratitude toward your beloved

♥ Reignite your passion for intimacy with your lover

Adopt useful attitudes for a harmonious relationship:

♥ Learn to stay on "the same side" during difficult discussions

♥ Let go of your stubbornness and reap the rewards of surrender

♥ See the world through your lover's eyes and gain compassion

Master ways to communicate with Love:

♥ Become a more sensitive listener

♥ Speak honestly without hurting one another

♥ Respect each other's boundaries

This group consists of approximately fifteen couples who see relationship as a vehicle for spiritual growth. The level of truth telling and vulnerability shared together creates a sense of safety and sacredness. The trust, tenderness, and appreciation that builds between you and your lover and among the couples as the group unfolds is very beautiful to be part of.

**– This space is for specific information on this workshop in your area –**

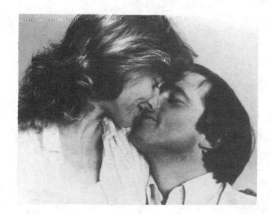

Peter Rengel is a spiritual counselor and the author of *Living Life in Love* and *Seeds of Light*. He is also a facilitator with the Human Awareness Institute and leads workshops and retreats around the world.

Donna Spitzer is a Lomi Bodywork Practitioner, a couples' workshop leader, and a facilitator with the Human Awareness Institute. Donna is a professional singer and has been a Montessori teacher.

315

# Living Life in Love

## A Weekend Retreat to Awaken Your Soul

### with

### Peter Rengel

This in-depth exploration of Love involves various meditations to gently open your Heart and partnered exercises to share your Heart energy with others. If you are seeking a soft, nurturing way to experience profound levels of consciousness, you will find this group to be an inspirational catalyst for transforming your life. You will have the opportunity to directly experience feeling loved, lovable and loving at new levels. You will also find your sense of inner peace tangibly deepened, whether you have ever meditated or not.

The meditations are designed to assist you in stepping outside of your mind so that you are not run by your thoughts. As you begin to develop the knack of witnessing your thoughts rather than being lost in the middle of them, you can free yourself to live in your Heart instead of in your head. You are offered concrete tools to get out of the endlessly looping trap of your thoughts without focusing on psychological processing, which can easily be another trap. If you empty your mind, your Heart can fill with Love.

This is much more than just another workshop. This is an opportunity to change the very core of your relationship to your thinking process. The deeper your commitment is to this internal shift, the more you will get out of this potentially life altering experience.

The following quotes are from people who have participated in past groups:

"I was affected profoundly. It's now easier and more natural to be in my Heart."

"In 17 years of doing all kinds of workshops, this group, far more than any other, opened my Heart to experience Love and gave me tools to be 'in Love' in my life."

"The class was an opportunity to walk into my dreams, to shut off my mind, and have a chance to really be inside my Heart."

"I now know that I can choose to worry or I can choose to be in my Heart."

**– This space is for specific information on this workshop in your area –**

Peter Rengel is a teacher and a student of his own writings, *Living Life in Love* and *Seeds of Light*. His life is devoted to loving all Beings, especially his wife, Donna. Peter enjoys assisting people to transcend psychology in order to awaken their Love and to live in harmony with their spiritual nature. He lives with his family in Marin County, California, and facilitates retreats and workshops around the world.

# The Human Awareness Institute

At the heart of the Human Awareness Institute (HAI) is a team of seven facilitators, including Peter Rengel and his wife, Donna Spitzer, plus Anne Watts, Chip August, Felicia Seaton, Sarah Jo Sand, as well as Stan Dale, HAI's founder. They travel all around the world to lead life changing, experiential workshops that transform people in the areas of Love, intimacy, relationships, and sexuality. Many of the over thirty thousand participants say that their first workshop with HAI was the single most significant turning point in their lives.

These weekends provide an opportunity to unleash your infinite capacity to love and be loved. You are supported to discover and shed fears, judgements, and disempowering beliefs and behaviors that keep you separate from others. You are encouraged to explore new ways to relate and communicate that profoundly deepen your ability to be intimate.

See if our Mission Statement is meaningful to you:

> *The Human Awareness Institute empowers individuals to be potent, loving, contributing human beings. HAI promotes personal growth and social evolution by replacing ignorance and fear with awareness and love. HAI aims to create a world where people live together in dignity, respect, understanding, trust, kindness, compassion, honesty, and love. The Human Awareness Institute is committed to Creating a World Where Everyone Wins.*

HAI offers a wide variety of workshops and events, including six levels of weekend workshops; two levels of Couples' Workshops; one day workshops – Pathways to Intimacy, Heart Meditations, Healing the Inner Child, Opening to Intimacy, Healing Anger, as well as support groups, parties, and much more. HAI is based in the San Francisco Bay Area and offers these activities there, as well as in other parts of the United States and internationally.

For more information about HAI and the U.S. workshops, please call or write to:

**The Human Awareness Institute**

**1730 South Amphlett Boulevard, #225**
**San Mateo, CA 94402**

**415-571-5524 or 1-800-800-4117**

**In Australia, call Human Awareness Australia in Canberra at 616-297-4999.**

# *Living Life in Love* T-Shirts

# Let Your Love Show!

Your Love blossoms when you wear this unique T-shirt with the same exquisite design as the cover of this book with only the words "Living Life in Love" on it.

It is a fun conversation piece and can create opportunities for you to meet people who enjoy seeing you wear your Heart on your chest instead of on your sleeve!

This T-shirt is also a perfect gift for anyone who loves to love and to be loved.

Order this work of art on high quality, white Hanes T-shirts in sizes Medium, Large, or Extra Large. See the "Order Form" on the last page of this book.

## Choice

Your most profound choice
Each new moment in time
Is whether you are
Lost in thoughts
Or lost in Love.

# Imagine ♥ Publications Order Form

☎ Telephone Inquiries: Call 415-459-3113 for more information. To actually order your book(s) or T-Shirt(s), see "Mail Orders" below.

✉ Mail Orders: Please send your personal check or money order (no credit cards accepted) to: "Imagine Publications," P.O. Box 278, Fairfax, CA 94978

---

Please send me the following via the U.S. Postal Book Rate (Allow two weeks for delivery):

☐ ___ Copies of *Living Live in Love* @ **$18.95 each**          **Total** _____

☐ ___ *Living Life in Love* **T-Shirts** @ **$14.95 each** ___M ___L ___XL **Total** _____

☐ ___ Copies of Peter's first book, *Seeds of Light*, @ **$9.95 each**          **Total** _____
(See the ad on the bottom half of this page.)
**SUBTOTAL** _____

**If sent to a California address, add Sales Tax of 7.25% onto the Subtotal** _____

**Add Postage and Handling Fee** _____
($3 for the first book, plus $1.50 for each additional book. T-shirt P&H is $2 each)

**TOTAL AMOUNT DUE** _____

---

Method of Payment: ☐ Check   ☐ Money Order

**Mail order to:**

Name _____          Phone Number _____

Address _____ City _____ State ____ Zip _____

---

## Peter Rengel's First Book:

# *Seeds of Light*

### *Inspirations From My Higher Self*

*Seeds of Light's* spiritual aphorisms explore topics as varied as the human condition. Peter's years of counseling experience are combined with his personal journey of transformation that led him around the world. He gently reminds us that joy and satisfaction are achieved by embracing the "what is" of daily life. This book is the seed for *Living Life in Love*.

> **"Simple is powerful. Peter Rengel has penned universal principles about the core of our lives in clear, often lyrical, prose."**
>
> Dan Millman, Author of *Way of the Peaceful Warrior*

> **"I honor Peter's experience in this book because it expresses me as well."**
>
> Richard Moss, M.D., Author of *The I That Is We*